THE
HOLT
READER

December '83

For Janice & Ed —
whose friendship continues
to mean so much to us.
Happy reading in all your
spare hours!

Sandra

THE
HOLT
READER

JOHN SCARRY
Hostos Community College, City University of New York

SANDRA SCARRY
Ramapo College of New Jersey

HOLT, RINEHART and WINSTON

New York Chicago San Francisco Philadelphia
Montreal Toronto London Sydney
Tokyo Mexico City Rio de Janeiro Madrid

Copyright Acknowledgments begin on page 517.

Publisher: Robert Rainier
Acquisitions Editor: Nedah Abbott
Developmental Editor: Anne Boynton-Trigg
Project Editor: Melanie Miller
Production Manager: Lula Schwartz
Design Supervisor: Robert Kopelman
Text Design: Barbara Bert/North 7 Atelier Ltd.

Library of Congress Cataloging in Publication Data
Main entry under title:

The Holt reader.

Includes index.
1. College readers.   2. English language—Rhetoric.
I. Scarry, John.   II. Scarry, Sandra, 1946-
PE1417.H63   1983   808'.0427   83-8475

ISBN 0-03-061536-4

Copyright © 1984 by CBS College Publishing
Address correspondence to:
383 Madison Avenue
New York, N.Y.   10017

CBS COLLEGE PUBLISHING
Holt, Rinehart and Winston
The Dryden Press
Saunders College Publishing

For Our Parents
John and Delia Scarry
Helge and Astrid Gustafson
and for our daughter
Siobhán Lisa

CONTENTS

UNIT **8: SELF AND SOCIETY**   287

WRITING SKILL: Definition and Analysis   287

UNIT 9: OUR ENDURING VALUES   335

WRITING SKILL: Cause and Effect   335

This is not a cry for women's rights, gentlemen. It is a cry for the companionship for which we married you.

No man should have proprietary rights over land who does not use that land wisely and lovingly.

We can replace the outmoded industrial imperative—the ''standard of living'' concept—by the more human ''quality of life'' concept.

Strangers to the desert cannot believe that a sandy gully, which looks like a good place to camp, may become, without warning, a raging flood . . .

Can anyone believe it is possible to lay down such a barrage of poisons on the surface of the earth without making it unfit for all life?

Ultimately, the use of mass transit exclusively will become inevitable; all signs point to that.

UNIT 12: FURTHER READINGS 479

PREFACE

Good writing always stimulates us and changes the way we look at the world. Novels expand our imagination, poems lead us to a new awareness of the power of language, and horror stories can even make our hair stand on end. The basic assumption of this book is that good expository writing will not only stimulate a student's thinking, but it will also inspire that student to produce successful college essays. *The Holt Reader* is a reading and writing program that combines structured rhetoric and stimulating themes into one integrated whole. This integration helps to reinforce each part of the teaching process, while at the same time carefully chosen examples guide the student from perceptive reading to structured written response. For example, all of the selections in Unit 4 share the same theme, "The World of Work," and all of them teach one rhetorical mode, Process. This combination of rhetoric and theme is to be found in each unit of the book, with the exception of Unit 12, which contains additional readings that may be used as optional assignments.

Our starting point was the choice of readings, many of which are taken from the works of famous writers and all of which have been tested at length in our classrooms. We have included only those selections that our students found provocative. For example, we have used essays by Jane O'Reilly and James Baldwin that are lively discussions of a wide range of relationships, while an essay that Virginia Woolf wrote during the early days of World War II provides a controversial analysis of some of the root causes of human conflict. Our students also enjoyed our blend of traditional and contemporary selections produced by men and women whose writings deal with a variety of modern concerns. E. B. White's autobiographical "Once More to the Lake" shares the same unit with an essay by Maria

L. Muñiz, while in another unit Herodotus and James Thurber join with Katherine Anne Porter and Margaret Mead to examine the relationships between the sexes.

Our classroom experience with these readings led us to devise two aids to reading that we have incorporated into our book. As we discussed each writer with our students, it became clear that they wanted more than a simple recitation of biographical facts or a listing of additional works that could be consulted. We realized that our students needed a *context* that would help them see the writer's life and work in a broader perspective. At the same time, such a context would prepare them for a deeper reading of the selection. We believe that the biographical and critical sketch of each author in *The Holt Reader* does provide this needed context and will give students a broader perspective as they begin to read each selection.

The student is also guided through a more comprehensive reading by a feature we have called "Previewing the Writer." Immediately *before* the student reads the selection, three points or questions direct the student to the most significant concerns of the piece. Again, this aspect of our book came directly out of our own classroom experience, when we saw that our students read with more enjoyment and awareness after they had been alerted to these main points in each selection.

The selections in *The Holt Reader* will provoke discussion of significant and challenging issues, but they will also have another important function, namely, to lead student writers toward successful writing of their own. Here also we have used our classroom experience to show the different steps needed to construct a piece of writing. First, a single paragraph or similar excerpt from the professional model is analyzed in detail ("The Writer's Technique") and the student is guided through an imitation ("Paragraph Practice") of the writer's approach. The aim of these activities, and our aim throughout the book, is to show students that the best way they can support their ideas is through the extensive use of supporting details as they write. "Essay Practice" provides further specific guidance for the writing of a complete essay, using a detailed outline based on the professional model. Finally, "Essay Topics" invites the student to use several ideas and suggestions as the basis for independent essay writing, using both the theme of the selection and his or her own personal experience.

In all of these exercises, and in our introductions to the

various units, our emphasis has been on a realistic, step-by-step approach to writing. Writing theory is discussed, but the major emphasis in *The Holt Reader* is on practical examples and specific aids to writing. For this reason "Focus on Terms" has been placed at the end of each unit to provide information that, in most books, is usually found in a glossary or an appendix. *The Holt Reader* integrates this additional material and uses the context of the selections in the unit to teach this further writing skill.

In the process of gathering materials and writing this book, we found that our students were genuinely interested in essays produced by other students who had read the same selections and had worked on the same exercises. We have chosen eleven student essays produced by our own students, and we have designed writing activities for each of these essays. This feature of the book provides an opportunity for students to enjoy and evaluate the writing of their peers while using that writing as a springboard for essays of their own.

The Holt Reader is an anthology with a difference. It contains examples of traditional prose along with some of our best contemporary writing, but it is more than a collection of readings—it is an entire writing program, designed to actively help students participate in the composing process. By relating the selections and the various parts of this program to the needs of an individual student or a particular class, the instructor will be using our book as we hoped it would be used, as a flexible teaching tool, one that stimulates critical thinking and produces effective student writing.

Acknowledgments

We wish to thank all of our colleagues and friends who have helped us during the preparation of *The Holt Reader*. We are grateful first of all to Henry Salerno of the State University of New York at Fredonia for his invaluable help during the early stages of our work. His active support, encouragement, and thoughtful suggestions gave the project a positive start it might not otherwise have enjoyed. Diana Diaz and Alfredo Villanueva of Hostos Community College, CUNY, and Elsa Nunez-Wormack of Ramapo College were all most supportive and understanding throughout the entire progress of the work.

Very special thanks go to the faculty and staff at Marymount Manhattan College for their genuine interest in the development of our book, especially John Costello, Priscilla Hoagland Costello, Donna Wolf, and Sister Margaret Ann Landry, RSHM. To them, and to the students of Marymount who continue to teach us so much, our thanks.

We owe a real debt to our student essayists, each of whom added so much to our book. Robert Nemiroff was most helpful with background information on Lorraine Hansberry, Michael Buckley patiently supplied us with factual material and insights when it came to theatrical and other figures, and we had the support and encouragement of other friends, including Oscar Collier and Sister Helen Scarry, RJM. Philip Winters was, as always, unfailingly generous with his professional counsel.

We are indebted to the staff at Holt, Rinehart and Winston, including Nedah Abbott, Susan Gowing, Emily Barosse, and particularly Anne Boynton-Trigg, who was always available with helpful answers to our questions and thoughtful guidance. Our special thanks go to Melanie Miller, whose care and commitment during the final stages of the project will remain one of our happiest memories of the book.

Finally, *The Holt Reader* could not have assumed its present form without the active cooperation of a number of professionals who used their knowledge of the teaching of composition to make judgments and suggestions on our manuscript at each stage of its development, from inception to the final revisions. Our thanks to all of the following writing teachers: Jay Balderson, Western Illinois University; Joseph I. Bommarito, Charles Stewart Mott Community College; Raymond Brebach, Drexel University; Linda Dyer Doran, Volunteer State Community College; Josephine Gorgio, Community College of Rhode Island; Dorothy M. Guinn, Arizona State University; Douglas Krienke, Sam Houston State University; Nevin K. Laib, Texas Tech University; Jonathan T. Launt, Central Piedmont Community College; Robert J. Pelinski, University of Illinois at Chicago Circle; Audrey J. Roth, Miami-Dade Community College; Raymond A. St. John, Bob Jones University; Ron Smith, Utah State University; Mark L. Waldo, Ohio State University.

1

A SENSE OF PLACE

WRITING SKILL: *Writer and Audience*

> Some people write by day, others by night. Some people need silence, others turn on the radio. Some write by hand, some by typewriter, some by talking into a tape recorder. Some people write their first draft in one long burst and then revise; others can't write the second paragraph until they have fiddled endlessly with the first.

This is William Zinsser's description of some of the many different conditions under which people write. You may work in one or more of these ways, or you may work under completely different circumstances. In most situations your approach to writing and your actual use of materials will be strictly your own business. The ultimate purpose of your writing, however, will not be so private. Every time you write you must ask yourself your purpose in writing, and even more important, who your audience is.

Every professional writer has both a definite purpose and a defined audience in mind, even before taking pen in hand. This must also be part of your own thinking as a writer. For whom are you writing? What can you assume about your readers' interest in your subject? How much do they already know? These are among the questions you should have in mind as you approach each writing task. You must always begin with this awareness of your audience, and you must maintain this awareness so that your writing will have focus and continuity, in addition to a definite sense of direction and purpose.

This first unit presents a number of writers, each one with a unique personality and each one with a concern for his or her audience. The diary or private journal has always been an important means of personal expression, and the diary of Anne Frank is one of the most famous examples of this form. Anne Frank had a definite purpose in writing. As she put her thoughts on paper during the darkest days of World War II, she helped relieve the great stress she was under, making her anxious years in hiding a little more bearable. Every writer needs an audience, even if it is only an audience of one, and in Anne Frank's case that audience was an imaginary friend named Kitty that she created in her loneliness. The truths and insights expressed by this extraordinary young woman continue to move and influence people she never dreamed would read her words.

Simone de Beauvoir has always been a public figure. Some of her best-known works are her autobiographical volumes, books that have been described as among the most important writings of the women's movement. Autobiography, by definition, represents a writer's decision to describe his or her life for a wide audience. Anne Frank wrote her diary only for herself, but Simone de Beauvoir writes to reach as many people as possible. In the following selection from *The Prime of Life*, the writer is telling her own experience, and we realize that the situation she is describing is a very universal one.

When Simone de Beauvoir writes about her personal life she concentrates on her inner landscape, but Ernesto Galarza's description of his native Mexican village is a clear description of an external reality. In the selection from *Barrio Boy* the writer speaks to a North American audience and serves as our guide on a comprehensive tour of the streets and buildings of his home town, a place that would be unfamiliar to most of his readers. Galarza also gives us carefully chosen glimpses of the life of his people. As a result, we gain an insight into how a community in any culture, including our own, could be described for an audience that is unfamiliar with the subject.

The final selection of the unit is an excerpt from Charles Lindbergh's last book, *Autobiography of Values*. In this selection, the famous aviator gives us a picture of another culture and in the process helps us gain a fresh perspective on our own. Lindbergh's subject is a tribe in Africa, and throughout the description the writer carefully keeps his audience in mind. We are that audience, and Lindbergh's feelings as he records his African experience could well be our own reactions to another culture, even one that we observe from the comfort of our own environment.

Writing is a private act, which often has very public results. As a writer, you must be able to see not only the words that you produce on the page, but also what effect these words will produce in the minds of your readers. Constant awareness of your audience will help you achieve one of the great rewards of writing: the sense of having real control over your material.

🐌 *Anne Frank* 🐌

Anne Frank was born in Frankfurt-am-Main, Germany, in 1929. By 1933 her father, Otto Frank, had become so alarmed by the rise of the Nazi party that he moved his family to Holland. The situation became even worse in 1939 when World War II began in Europe. By 1942 the forces of anti-Semitism in Nazi-occupied Holland were so strong that the Frank family was forced to go into hiding. It was in the concealed third floor of an Amsterdam building, in constant fear of being caught, that Anne Frank wrote the major part of her diary.

In August 1944 the hiding place was discovered by the police. With the single exception of Otto Frank, all perished in concentration camps; Anne died at Bergen-Belsen in March 1945, only two months before the liberation of Holland. After the war Anne's diary was found and published in book form. It was translated into several languages and immediately became an international best-seller. Interest in Anne's story has continued over the years, and her book has inspired adaptations for the theater, movies, and television.

The Diary of a Young Girl is the story of youth struggling for survival in a world torn apart by war. It is also the story of every young person's search for meaning in a world where all values seem to be questioned. In the following selections from the diary, Anne Frank explains her reasons for keeping a journal, tells what writing means to her, and shares her fears and hopes for the future. The quality of her writing and the obvious maturity of her thinking are astonishing in such a young person: Anne Frank was only fifteen in August 1944 when she wrote the final entry in her journal.

One of Anne Frank's biographers has written this analysis of her personality: "She was gracious, capricious at times, and full of ideas. She had a tender, but also a critical spirit; a special gift for feeling deeply and for fear; but also her own special kind of courage . . ."

The following excerpts from Anne Frank's diary more than confirm this judgment.

PREVIEWING THE WRITER

• Note some of Anne Frank's basic concerns about her own life and the lives of those around her.

• Anne Frank is both a realist and an optimist. Note the details in her journal entries that show her realism. Where in her entries does she most clearly reveal her optimism?

- Note Anne Frank's comments about adults. As you read the various entries, what changes do you notice in her thinking about older people?

 from *THE DIARY OF A YOUNG GIRL*

SATURDAY, 20 JUNE, 1942[1]

I haven't written for a few days, because I wanted first of all to think about my diary. It's an odd idea for someone like me to keep a diary; not only because I have never done so before, but because it seems to me that neither I—nor for that matter anyone else—will be interested in the unbosomings of a thirteen-year-old schoolgirl. Still, what does that matter? I want to write, but more than that, I want to bring out all kinds of things that lie buried deep in my heart.

There is a saying that "paper is more patient than man"; it came back to me on one of my slightly melancholy days, while I sat chin in hand, feeling too bored and limp even to make up my mind whether to go out or stay at home. Yes, there is no doubt that paper is patient and as I don't intend to show this cardboard-covered notebook, bearing the proud name of "diary," to anyone, unless I find a real friend, boy or girl, probably nobody cares. And now I come to the root of the matter, the reason for my starting a diary: it is that I have no such real friend.

Let me put it more clearly, since no one will believe that a girl of thirteen feels herself quite alone in the world, nor is it so. I have darling parents and a sister of sixteen. I know about thirty people whom one might call friends—I have strings of boy friends, anxious to catch a glimpse of me and who, failing that, peep at me through mirrors in class. I have relations, aunts and uncles, who are darlings too, a good home, no—I don't seem to lack anything. But it's the same with all my friends, just fun and joking, nothing more. I can never bring myself to talk of anything outside the common round. We don't seem to be able to get any closer, that is the root of the trouble. Perhaps I lack confidence, but anyway, there it is, a stubborn fact and I don't seem to be able to do anything about it.

Hence, this diary. In order to enhance in my mind's eye

---

[1] This entry was written less than a month before Anne Frank and her family went into hiding.

the picture of the friend for whom I have waited so long, I don't
want to set down a series of bald facts in a diary like most people
do, but I want this diary itself to be my friend, and I shall call
my friend Kitty.

Saturday, 1 May, 1943
Dear Kitty,
    If I just think of how we live here, I usually come to the   5
conclusion that it is a paradise compared with how other Jews
who are not in hiding must be living. Even so, later on, when
everything is normal again, I shall be amazed to think that we,
who were so spick and span at home, should have sunk to such
a low level. By this I mean that our manners have declined. For
instance, ever since we have been here, we have had one oil-
cloth on our table which, owing to so much use, is not one of
the cleanest. Admittedly I often try to clean it with a dirty dishcloth, which is more hole than cloth. The table doesn't do us
much credit either, in spite of hard scrubbing. The Van Daans[2]
have been sleeping on the same flannelette sheet the whole
winter; one can't wash it here because the soap powder we get
on the ration isn't sufficient, and besides it's not good enough.
Daddy goes about in frayed trousers and his tie is beginning to
show signs of wear too. Mummy's corsets have split today and
are too old to be repaired, while Margot[3] goes about in a brassiere two sizes too small for her.
    Mummy and Margot have managed the whole winter with   6
three vests[4] between them, and mine are so small that they
don't even reach my tummy.
    Certainly, these are all things which can be overcome.   7

Wednesday, 23 February, 1944
    . . . I looked out of the open window . . . over a large area   8
of Amsterdam, over all the roofs and on to the horizon, which
was such a pale blue that it was hard to see the dividing line.
"As long as this exists," I thought, "and I may live to see it,
this sunshine, the cloudless skies, while this lasts, I cannot be
unhappy."

[2] A married couple who were hiding with the Frank family.

[3] Anne Frank's sister.

[4] Undershirts.

The best remedy for those who are afraid, lonely, or un-   9
happy is to go outside, somewhere where they can be quite
alone with the heavens, nature, and God. Because only then
does one feel that all is as it should be and that God wishes to
see people happy, amidst the simple beauty of nature. As long
as this exists, and it certainly always will, I know that then there
will always be comfort for every sorrow, whatever the circumstances may be. And I firmly believe that nature brings solace
in all troubles.

Oh, who knows, perhaps it won't be long before I can   10
share this overwhelming feeling of bliss with someone who feels
the way I do about it.

Tuesday, 4 April, 1944

I am the best and sharpest critic of my own work. I know   11
myself what is and what is not well written. Anyone who
doesn't write doesn't know how wonderful it is; I used to be-
moan the fact that I couldn't draw at all, but now I am more
than happy that I can at least write. And if I haven't any talent
for writing books or newspaper articles, well, then I can always
write for myself.

I want to get on; I can't imagine that I would have to lead   12
the same sort of life as Mummy and Mrs. Van Daan and all the
women who do their work and are then forgotten. I must have
something besides a husband and children, something that I
can devote myself to!

I want to go on living even after my death! And therefore   13
I am grateful to God for giving me this gift, this possibility of
developing myself and of writing, of expressing all that is in
me.

I can shake off everything if I write; my sorrows disappear,   14
my courage is reborn. But, and that is the great question, will
I ever be able to write anything great, will I ever become a
journalist or a writer? I hope so, oh, I hope so very much, for
I can recapture everything when I write, my thoughts, my ideals
and my fantasies.

Saturday, 15 July, 1944

"For in its innermost depths youth is lonelier than old   15
age." I read this saying in some book and I've always remembered it, and found it to be true. Is it true then that grownups
have a more difficult time here than we do? No. I know it isn't.

Older people have formed their opinions about everything, and don't waver before they act. It's twice as hard for us young ones to hold our ground, and maintain our opinions, in a time when all ideals are being shattered and destroyed, when people are showing their worst side, and do not know whether to believe in truth and right and God.

Anyone who claims that the older ones have a more difficult time here certainly doesn't realize to what extent our problems weigh down on us, problems for which we are probably much too young, but which thrust themselves upon us continually, until, after a long time, we think we've found a solution, but the solution doesn't seem able to resist the facts which reduce it to nothing again. That's the difficulty in these times: ideals, dreams, and cherished hopes rise within us, only to meet the horrible truth and be shattered. 16

It's really a wonder that I haven't dropped all my ideals, because they seem so absurd and impossible to carry out. Yet I keep them, because in spite of everything I still believe that people are really good at heart. I simply can't build up my hopes on a foundation consisting of confusion, misery, and death. I see the world gradually being turned into a wilderness, I hear the ever approaching thunder, which will destroy us too, I can feel the sufferings of millions and yet, if I look up into the heavens, I think that it will all come right, that this cruelty too will end, and that peace and tranquillity will return again. 17

In the meantime, I must uphold my ideals, for perhaps the time will come when I shall be able to carry them out. 18

THE WRITER'S THEMES

1. What are the reasons Anne Frank gives for keeping a journal? Are these the usual reasons a person has for keeping a diary?
2. Anne Frank tells us that she wants "to bring out all kinds of things that lie deep" in her heart. What do you feel are among the deepest thoughts and perceptions Anne Frank expresses in her journal?
3. Throughout these entries, Anne Frank emphasizes her feeling of being alone. What are the passages that most ob-

viously reveal this sense of loneliness? What seems to make her feel so alone?

THE WRITER'S TECHNIQUE

In her diary entry of May 1, 1943, Anne Frank reports that the comfort of the people hiding in the attic has sunk to a "low level." She then explains what she means:

> For instance, ever since we have been here, we have had one oilcloth on our table which, owing to so much use, is not one of the cleanest. Admittedly I often try to clean it with a dirty dishcloth, which is more hole than cloth. The table doesn't do us much credit either, in spite of hard scrubbing. The Van Daans have been sleeping on the same flannelette sheet the whole winter; one can't wash it here because the soap powder we get on the ration isn't sufficient, and besides it's not good enough. Daddy goes about in frayed trousers and his tie is beginning to show signs of wear too. Mummy's corsets have split today and are too old to be repaired, while Margot goes about in a brassiere two sizes too small for her.
>
> Mummy and Margot have managed the whole winter with three vests between them, and mine are so small that they don't even reach my tummy.

Notice that Anne Frank does not simply report that conditions in the hiding place are bad; she proves it by giving details that support her observation. She begins with the table, an important piece of furniture in their tiny attic, and the one place where all the members of the group would gather. The tablecloth, she notes, is old and dirty, and even the dirty dishcloth that is used to clean it is "more hole than cloth."

Next, Anne Frank concentrates on the people in the attic, beginning with the Van Daans, who not only have to use the same "flannelette sheet the whole winter," but cannot even wash it. As the description continues, the writer becomes more personal; she gives brief descriptions of her own family, beginning with her father, who "goes about in frayed trousers," and continuing with her mother and sister Margot, both of whom wear ill-fitting, worn-out clothes. Finally, and most personally, we have Anne herself, whose undershirts are so small "they don't even reach my tummy." All of these supporting details help to prove Anne's statement that conditions in the attic have sunk to "a low level."

PARAGRAPH PRACTICE

Write a paragraph of your own, using Anne Frank's paragraph as your model. Your paragraph could be an explanation of a very personal situation, or it could be a description of a more general social condition. Some possible topic sentences for your paragraph might be:

> I am disgusted that my wardrobe has become so shabby and outdated. For instance . . .

> I am surprised, with all the advertisements for new goods, that more and more people are collecting objects from the past. For instance . . .

Notice that Anne Frank uses a pattern in her description. After indicating the condition of the communal table, she describes the clothing of the people who live with her, beginning with those who are not related to her, proceeding to the members of her own family, and ending with herself.

Your own paragraph will have a greater sense of organization if you choose a pattern for your supporting details. If you choose to describe your wardrobe, you might arrange your description according to the items of clothing that are worn during the different seasons of the year. If you describe the kinds of collectibles people are interested in, you might organize your details by beginning with small objects and ending with very large items, or you may go from inexpensive items to more expensive ones. On the other hand, you may choose the easy-to-find pieces first and then move to the more unusual or strange collectibles. Remember that your reader will be impressed not only by your choice of details, but also by the way in which you arrange those details.

ESSAY PRACTICE

The following outline will help you plan a complete essay of at least five paragraphs. The theme of your essay will be closely related to the selections from *The Diary of a Young Girl*.

The following sentence may serve as your thesis sentence:

¶ 1. We can more easily cope with difficult situations when we find ways of dealing with fear, loneliness, or unhappiness.

This thesis sentence will also be the central idea for your introductory paragraph. One good way to make your introduction interesting for your reader is to tell why the topic you are writing about is important to you. In this way the reader will have a basis for understanding your reasons for writing about your topic. A well-thought-out introduction is also your first opportunity to interest your reader in the subject you are about to develop.

Each of the sentences below is the topic sentence for one of the paragraphs that you will write to develop your thesis. You may use the suggested details to develop each paragraph, or you may supply details of your own.

¶ 2. Most of us have fears that may be real or imaginary.

[DETAILS: How can friends or family help us deal with our fears? How can we educate ourselves about them? Is it better to avoid fearful situations if we can?]

¶ 3. A sense of loneliness can also be difficult to overcome.

[DETAILS: In such situations, is it helpful to join organizations or volunteer groups? To what extent are hobbies useful? Is it useful to initiate relationships and be a friend, rather than always expect others to come to you?]

¶ 4. The best remedy for those who are unhappy is . . .

[DETAILS: When a person feels unhappy, what should that person do? Is it important to look for the cause of the unhappiness, or is it enough to simply get up and *do* something?]

Be certain to use transitions between paragraphs, to make your writing flow smoothly. (For a discussion of transitions, see p. 121.) In addition, be sure that your conclusion is effective. It should give your reader a clear signal that you have come to the end of your essay. (See p. 282 for a discussion of conclusions.)

ESSAY TOPICS

1. a. Anne Frank describes herself as "the best and sharpest critic" of her own work. Write a critical analysis of your own writing. Be as objective as you can about your strengths and weaknesses as a writer.

    b. Anne Frank tells us that she can "shake off everything" if she writes: "my sorrows disappear, my courage is reborn." Describe your own emotional reactions when you write. What happens to you when you begin the act of writing?

2. Imagine you are just beginning to keep a diary. Write the first entry in that diary. Your entry might contain your reflections on why you have decided to start a journal, or you might wish to indicate your present situation by enumerating your problems and counting your blessings.

3. In the darkest period of World War II Anne Frank could write: "In the meantime, I must uphold my ideals . . ." Describe a time you were discouraged by circumstances around you, but you felt strongly that you had to uphold your own ideals. How did you accomplish this?

₃ *Simone de Beauvoir* ₃

Simone de Beauvoir was born in Paris in 1908. She studied mathematics and philosophy and received her university degree in 1929. In 1931 she accepted her first teaching assignment, in the south of France, and during the 1930s she taught in various places throughout the country. It was also during this time that her lifelong friend and associate Jean-Paul Sartre encouraged her to begin writing novels and short stories. Since that time she has achieved worldwide fame as a writer of fiction, plays, travel books, and essays. One of her most famous works is *The Second Sex*, a monumental book that has been described as one of the most important studies written by a woman about women.

Simone de Beauvoir is perhaps best known for her four autobiographical volumes, *Memoirs of a Dutiful Daughter, The Prime of Life, Force of Circumstance,* and *A Very Easy Death.* The following passage, taken from the opening pages of *The Prime of Life,* describes an important moment in the author's life. She has just obtained her degree from the University of Paris and has just furnished her own room. She is about to begin her life as a working adult.

PREVIEWING THE WRITER

• Simone de Beauvoir describes her interest in a schoolgirl's room that was pictured in a magazine. How closely does the writer imitate the design of that room when she is finally able to decorate a room of her own?

• The writer seems to have at least two attitudes toward material things. Where does she indicate an interest in her possessions? Where does she seem to show a disregard for material things?

• Having reached adulthood, Simone de Beauvoir looks back on her childhood and makes judgments on that part of her life. What are these judgments? Does she feel positive or negative about her childhood?

from *THE PRIME OF LIFE*

THE MOST INTOXICATING aspect of my return to Paris   1
in September, 1929, was the freedom I now possessed. I had
dreamed of it since childhood, when I played with my sister at
being a "grown-up" girl. I have recorded elsewhere my pas-

sionate longing for it as a student. Now, suddenly, it was mine.
I was astonished to find an effortless buoyancy in all my movements. From the moment I opened my eyes every morning I
was lost in a transport of delight. When I was about twelve I
had suffered through not having a private retreat of my own at
home. Leafing through *Mon Journal* I had found a story about
an English schoolgirl, and gazed enviously at the colored illustration portraying her room. There was a desk, and a divan,
and shelves filled with books. Here, within these gaily painted
walls, she read and worked and drank tea, with no one watching her—how envious I felt! For the first time ever I had glimpsed
a more fortunate way of life than my own. And now, at long
last, I too had a room to myself. My grandmother had stripped
her drawing room of all its armchairs, occasional tables, and
knickknacks. I had bought some unpainted furniture, and my
sister had helped me to give it a coat of brown varnish. I had a
table, two chairs, a large chest which served both as a seat and
as a hold-all, shelves for my books. I papered the walls orange,
and got a divan to match. From my fifth-floor balcony I looked
out over the Lion of Belfort and the plane trees on the Rue
Denfert-Rochereau. I kept myself warm with an evil-smelling
kerosene stove. Somehow its stink seemed to protect my solitude, and I loved it. It was wonderful to be able to shut my
door and keep my daily life free of other people's inquisitive-
ness. For a long time I remained indifferent to the décor of my
surroundings. Possibly because of that picture in *Mon Journal* I
preferred rooms that offered me a divan and bookshelves, but
I was prepared to put up with any sort of retreat in a pinch. To
have a door that I could shut was still the height of bliss for me.

I paid rent to my grandmother, and she treated me with
the same unobtrusive respect she showed her other lodgers. I
was free to come and go as I pleased. I could get home with
the milk, read in bed all night, sleep till midday, shut myself
up for forty-eight hours at a stretch, or go out on the spur of
the moment. My lunch was a bowl of borsch at Dominique's,
and for supper I took a cup of hot chocolate at La Coupole. I
was fond of hot chocolate, and borsch, and lengthy siestas and
sleepless nights: but my chief delight was in doing as I pleased.
There was practically nothing to stop me. I discovered, to my
great pleasure, that "the serious business of living" on which
grownups had held forth to me so interminably was not, in fact,
quite so oppressive after all. Getting through my examinations,

on the other hand, had been no joke. I had worked desperately hard, always with the fear of possible failure, always tired, and with various stubborn obstacles to overcome. Now I encountered no such resistance anywhere: I felt as though I were on vacation forever. A little private tutoring and a part-time teaching job at the Lycée Victor-Duruy guaranteed me enough to live on. These duties did not even prove a burden to me, since I felt that by performing them I was involved in a new sort of game: I was playing at being a grownup. Hunting for private pupils, having discussions with senior mistresses or parents, working out my budget, borrowing, paying back, adding up figures—all these activities amused me because I was doing them for the first time. I remember how tickled I was when I got my first salary check. I felt I had played a practical joke on someone.

THE WRITER'S THEMES

1. Throughout the passage, Simone de Beauvoir emphasizes her independence from other people. However, there are people who are definitely a part of her life. Make a list of these people, beginning with the least important and ending with the most important. How is the writer dependent on each person you have listed?
2. At more than one point in the passage, Simone de Beauvoir reveals her attitude toward money. List all of the evidence that shows this attitude and then analyze the author's feelings about money.
3. The writer describes in detail her life in Paris in the late 1920s, and she also gives us frequent glimpses of her earlier life. Based on the details she provides in the passage, describe her life as a child and as an adolescent.

THE WRITER'S TECHNIQUE

In paragraph two, Simone de Beauvoir describes in detail the new feeling of freedom she now possessed:

> I paid rent to my grandmother, and she treated me with the same unobtrusive respect she showed her other lodgers. I was free to come and go as I pleased. I could get home with the milk, read

in bed all night, sleep till midday, shut myself up for forty-eight hours at a stretch, or go out on the spur of the moment. My lunch was a bowl of borsch at Dominique's, and for supper I took a cup of hot chocolate at La Coupole. I was fond of hot chocolate, and borsch, and lengthy siestas and sleepless nights: but my chief delight was in doing as I pleased.

The writer first pictures herself as being treated just like her grandmother's "other lodgers" and then describes in detail how she was "free to come and go" as she pleased. These details show her independence of all the usual restraints of time schedules and eating habits that set the pattern of most of our daily lives. Simone de Beauvoir could come home in the early morning ("I could get home with the milk"), or she could turn night into day by reading "in bed all night." This detail also contradicts the usual belief that bed is a place of rest; here the author turns it into a place where she actively reads. The writer also turns around the usual ideas of time by sleeping "till mid-day," shutting herself up "for forty-eight hours at a stretch," or deciding to go out "on the spur of the moment."

The writer's eating habits are also unusual. Lunch is "a bowl of borsch at Dominique's" but supper is merely "a cup of hot chocolate" at another restaurant. The writer sums up this picture of her life of freedom by pointing out that she was fond of doing all of these things, but "my chief delight was in doing as I pleased."

The writer uses specific details of her daily life to show how truly free and independent that life really was. All of her decisions were made only for herself, and they clearly went against the commonly accepted norms of day-to-day behavior.

PARAGRAPH PRACTICE

Write a paragraph of your own, using the above section from the Simone de Beauvoir passage as your model. Your paragraph might be a description of a time you could come and go as you pleased. You may, for example, wish to describe a weekend trip or you might choose to describe a summer day at home, without school, job, or any other responsibility.

Notice how specific Simone de Beauvoir is in her use of supporting details. She realizes that it is not enough for her audience to know that she was "free to come and go" as she pleased. She tells her readers *where* she went and *when* she went there. She also tells us exactly *what* she ate for lunch and dinner, and she even names the restaurants where she ate her meals.

In your own paragraph make your description immediate by giving your reader specific details as to how you spent your time. On that day when you felt so free, *where* did you go? *When* did you go there? *What* exactly did you do?

ESSAY PRACTICE

The following outline will help you plan a complete essay of at least five paragraphs. The theme of your essay will be closely related to the selection from Simone de Beauvoir.

The following sentence may serve as your thesis sentence:

¶ 1. The lives of most adults are filled with obligations; luckily, there are usually some areas of freedom that compensate for this.

This thesis sentence will also be the central idea for your introductory paragraph. One very effective way to write an interesting introduction is to construct it around a brief story or incident. A well-chosen anecdote will perform one of the main tasks of any introduction: to get your reader's attention. The central paragraphs of your essay will serve to maintain this interest.

Each of the sentences below is the topic sentence for one of the paragraphs that you will write to develop your thesis. You may use the suggested details to develop each paragraph, or you may supply details of your own.

¶ 2. I have a number of obligations in my life, some more serious than others.

[DETAILS: What are the obligations you have toward the different members of your family? You may also feel a sense of obligation toward various friends and co-workers. In addition, there may be obligations to local institutions, including a church. In this paragraph, be sure to arrange your details in order of increasing seriousness, so that your most important obligation is given last.]

¶ 3. I also enjoy some areas of freedom in my life.

[DETAILS: Your examples could range from the time you enjoy on weekends, holidays, and summer vacations, to special meetings with friends, or private time alone with a hobby or other means of relaxation.]

¶ 4. If I could get rid of one of my obligations, it would improve my life.

> [DETAILS: Imagine that you could get rid of one of your obligations. Which one would you choose? Why would you want to remove it from your life? What would your life be like once you were able to do this? Specifically, how would your life improve?]

Be certain to use transitions between paragraphs to make your writing flow smoothly. (For a discussion of transitions, see p. 121.) In addition, make sure that your conclusion is effective. It should give your reader a clear signal that you have come to the end of your essay. (See p. 282 for a discussion of conclusions.)

ESSAY TOPICS

1. a. Describe the first time you were able to decorate your own room. Your description is to be read by people who have never had the chance to decorate their own rooms. What style of decoration did you choose? How much money did you have at your disposal? Did you do the work yourself, or did you allow someone to help you?
    b. You are a professional decorator. A client wants to know what, in your opinion, was the most attractive room you ever saw. Describe this room for your client. Was it a bedroom, a living room, or some kind of workroom? What impressed you most about the room? Why do you remember it?
2. You have been asked to speak to a group of people who want to learn how to budget their money. Help them by describing how you handled money when you earned your first paychecks. How did you make up your first budget? How differently do you handle your money now?
3. Simone de Beauvoir describes her erratic schedule and tells us that her "chief delight" was in doing as she pleased. Write an autobiographical sketch in which you describe a favorite period in your life, a time when you could do just what you wanted to do with your time. Be sure to provide specific details so that your reader will have a clear idea of how you spent your time during this period. How long do you feel you could be happy without a specific structure to your daily life?

❧ *Ernesto Galarza* ❧

Ernesto Galarza was born in Jalcocotán, Mexico, in 1905. In the author's own words, during the time of the Mexican Revolution his family was "in continuous flight from the revolutionary wind that swept Mexico after 1910." The Galarza family moved to Sacramento, California, where Ernesto attended school. He did graduate work at Stanford University and received his Ph.D. from Columbia University in 1944.

He has taught at San Jose State University, Notre Dame University, and at the Harvard Graduate School of Education, among other institutions. Dr. Galarza has also worked as a consultant for the National Farmers' Union, the Ford Foundation, the Republic of Bolivia, and the Human Resources Corporation of San Francisco.

Ernesto Galarza is the author of many books and articles, including *Mexican-Americans in the Southwest* and *Farm Workers and Agri-Business in California, 1947–1960. Barrio Boy* began as a series of anecdotes the writer told to his family. He also told his stories at other informal gatherings and before long his recollections were enjoying a limited circulation among various schools and libraries. The writer finally expanded his notes and observations into a book. As Ernesto Galarza has pointed out, "In many ways the experiences of a multitude of boys like myself, migrating from countless villages like Jalcocotán and starting life anew in *barrios* like the one in Sacramento, must have been similar."

In the following selection from *Barrio Boy*, Ernesto Galarza takes us through his native town, showing us the turkey vultures (*zopilotes*) hopping in the streets, pointing out the town's drab little plaza, and telling us that the town even lacked local *Autoridades* (authorities who enforce the law). As we read the selection, however, we are more impressed by what the town *does* have. This is a community where all the people share a common tradition.

PREVIEWING THE WRITER

- Jalcocotán lacks many modern conveniences, but what basic features does it have in common with larger towns and even cities?
- Note the details of life in Jalcocotán that indicate the economic level of the people.
- In Jalcocotán the people live close to nature. Note the different ways the people are controlled by nature. How do the people adapt to nature?

from *BARRIO BOY*

THE ONE AND ONLY street in Jalcocotán was hardly   1
more than an open stretch of the mule trail that disappeared
into the forest north and south of the pueblo. Crosswise, it was
about wide enough to park six automobiles hub to hub. Length-
wise, you could walk from one end to the other in eight minutes, without hurrying, the way people walked in the village.
The dirt surface had been packed hard by hundreds of years of
traffic—people barefooted or wearing the tough leather sandals
called huaraches; mule trains passing through on the way to
the sea or to Tepic; burros carrying firewood and other products
of the forest; *zopilotes* hopping heavily here and there; pigs,
dogs, and chickens foraging along the ditch.

There was a row of cottages on each side of the street,   2
adobe boxes made of the same packed earth on which the houses
stood. At one end of the street wall of every cottage there was
a doorway, another in the wall standing to the back yard corral.
There were no windows. The roofs were made of palm thatch,
with a steep pitch, the ridge pole parallel to the street. Back of
the houses were the *corrales*, fenced with stones piled about
shoulder high to a man. Between the *corrales* there were narrow
alleys that led uphill to the edge of the forest on the upper side
of the village, and to the arroyo on the lower side. The eaves
of the grass roofs hung well over the adobe walls to protect
them from the battering rains. In the summer time the overhang
provided shade at midday, when it seemed as if all the suffo-
cating heat of the heavens was pouring through a funnel with
the small end pointed directly at Jalco.

Since there were no sidewalks, from the front door to the   3
street was only a step. Our pueblo was too high up the mountain, the connecting trails were too steep and narrow to allow
ox carts and wagons to reach it. Like the forest, our only street
belonged to everybody—a place to sort out your friends and
take your bearings if you were going anywhere.

Midway down the street, on the arroyo side, there was a   4
small chapel, also of adobe, the only building in the town that
had a front yard, a patch of sun-baked clay squeezed between
two cottages. Back of the patio stood the squat adobe box of the
chapel, with a red tile roof and a small dome in one corner
topped with a wooden cross. Once upon a time the walls of the

chapel had been plastered and whitewashed, but the rains and the sun had cracked and blistered them. The adobe was exposed in jagged patches with flecks of grey straw showing like wood grain on the ancient mud. The base of the walls, pelted by the rain, was chewed as if beavers had worked on it.

Directly across the street from the chapel, the row of cottages was interrupted by the plaza. In any pueblo of some importance this would have been the *zocalo*, or the *plaza mayor*, or more grandiloquently, the *plaza de armas*. In Jalco it was a square without a name, about forty steps wide along the street and as many deep. Once, so it was said by the oldest people in the village, there had been a fountain in the center of the plaza, and a collection had been taken to buy a bust of Benito Juarez[1] for a centerpiece of the park. When I knew the drab little plaza, there was no fountain and no bust. The surface of the square was, like the street, a sheet of hardpan. Holes had been chopped in it and some trees planted. An acacia shaded one corner of the upper side of the lot. Three smaller trees lined one side of the square; in the spring they flamed with brilliant crimson blossoms like cups of fire, which is why they were called *copas de fuego*.

In a village like Jalcocotán there was little use for either the chapel or the plaza. We had no resident priest; *jalcocotecanos* with serious matters to lay before their patron saints or the Virgin of Guadalupe walked to Tepic, forty kilometers to the north, with its magnificent basilica. If it was a matter in which the whole village was concerned, a pilgrimage was organized to the shrine of Nuestra Señora de Talpa, where couples were married and babies baptized. Even less ever happened in the plaza than in the chapel. There was no police, no fire department, no post office, no public library. No one was ever elected mayor or sheriff or councilman. There was no jail or judge or any other sort of *Autoridades*, which explained why there was no city hall in Jalco. The shrunken, sun-beaten plaza was there nevertheless, solitary except when children played in it or passing mule drivers rested under the shade of its trees. It was a useless spot in our everyday life, but just by being there, the public square, like the chapel, gave our one and only street a touch of dignity, the mark of a proper pueblo.

---

[1] Benito Juarez (1806–1872), Mexican revolutionary and statesman who was twice president of Mexico.

Like the plaza, the street had no name. On a nameless 7
street the houses, naturally, had no numbers. The villager was
indoors and in bed after dark so there was no need for lights,
of which our street had none.

Having a single gutter in the middle of the street instead 8
of one on each side was a piece of simple and practical engineering. The shallow ditch made a slightly crooked dividing line
through the center of the town. On either side of it each family
took care of its frontage on the street, sprinkling it to settle the
dust in the dry season, or sweeping the litter into the ditch.
When it rained the trench collected the runoff, making a small
torrent that scoured the gutter clean. During a downpour people stood in the doorways to watch the stuff that passed bobbing
on the chocolate water—corncobs, banana peelings, twigs, . . .
or a dead rat drowned in the flash flood.

Whatever happened in Jalcocotán had to happen on our 9
street because there was no other place for it to happen. Two
men, drunk with tequila, fought with machetes on the upper
edge of the village until they were separated and led away by
the neighbors. A hundred faces peered around doorways
watching the fight. When someone died people joined the funeral procession as it passed by their doors. If a stranger arrived
on horseback, the clopping of horseshoes on the rocks of the
trail announced his arrival before he could turn into the street.
Arriving in Jalco was like stepping on a stage. The spectators
were already in the doorways, watching.

The narrow lanes between the corrals on the lower side of 10
the street led to the arroyo which ran the length of the village.
The turbulent waters, even in the dry season, twisted and
churned among the boulders, slapping them and breaking into
spray, or dividing around them in serpentines of blue-green
foam. Below the village the arroyo was checked by a natural
dam of rocks and silt, over which it dropped into a quiet pond
before rushing on to the sea.

On both sides the arroyo, here and there, had slammed 11
boulders into the bank or against the trunks of trees. Downstream from these rocks the water formed small ponds over a
floor of white sand and speckled pebbles. In these nooks the
women of the village washed clothes, kneeling waist high in
the water.

On the edge of the pond, at the far side, there was an 12
enormous walnut tree, standing like an open umbrella whose
ribs extended halfway across the still water of the pool. The

scars on the trunk of the mighty bole showed where the arroyo had bashed it during storms of former years. But the nogal had always won these battles. The arroyo, when the storms had passed, gave up and backed away, leaving around the trunk a small beach where the pond lapped gently on the gravel.

The arroyo was as much a part of the pueblo as the street. 13 Like the street, it had no name; it just tumbled into town from the timber stands up the mountain that fed it the year round, and tumbled out from the pond to pick up and carry to the ocean the seepage of the forest below. It could rage dangerously in the summer freshets, called *avenidas,*[2] pounding at the lower side of the village with boulders and ramming it with tree trunks a man could hardly circle with his two arms. Most of the year, it brought driftwood downstream and delivered it to the *jalco-cotecanos* who chopped it into kindling. It supplied the pond with fish, but most important of all, it piped the sweet seepage of the forest to our town, always cold, transparent, and greenish blue. We called it *agua zarca*, good for drinking and washing.

Like the *monte* and the street, the arroyo was common 14 property. Those who lived along the upper side of the street used the lanes between the cottages on the lower side on their way to wash, to fill their red clay *cantaros,*[3] or to water their stock.

....

It was in the evening, when dusk was falling and supper 15 was being prepared, that Jalco shaded itself little by little into the forest, the arroyo, the sky, and the mountain to which it belonged. Westward toward the sea, a rose and purple mist nearly always lingered after sunset.

The eastern slopes of the range became patches of black- 16 blue. From the slant of the shadows and the signs in the sky, everyone knew when this would happen—almost to the minute. The men and the boys of working age came down or up the trail at about the right time to reach the street a few steps ahead of or a few steps behind the dusk. They walked, each man and his sons, to their cottages. On both sides of the street the doors were open. In the kitchens, the coals glowed in the adobe *pretiles* where the cooking was done, illuminated by the tin oil lamps, three inches round and two deep, the *candiles* that swung from the ceiling.

[2] Flash floods, usually following a cloudburst.

[3] Jars.

Through the doors, opened to receive the returning toilers 17 and to freshen the air inside the cottages, came the sounds and sights of the street at sundown. There was the soft clapping of the women patting the ration of tortillas for the evening meal. The smoky light from the wicks of the *candiles* flickering through the doorways cast wobbling shadows on the threshold as people moved about. The air outside was a blend of the familiar smells of supper time—tortillas baking, beans boiling, chile roasting, coffee steaming, and kerosene stenching. The hens were clucking in their roosts in the corrals by the time the street was dark.

After supper, if the weather was warm, the men squatted 18 on the ground, hunched against the wall of the house and smoked. The women and the girls ate supper and put away the kitchen things, the *candiles* turned down to save kerosene. They listened to the tales of the day if the men were in a talking mood. When they pulled on their cigarettes, they made ruby dots in the dark, as if they were putting periods into the low-toned conversation. The talk just faded away, the men went indoors, the doors were shut and barred, and there was nothing on the street but the dark and the rumble of the arroyo.

THE WRITER'S THEMES

1. The people of Jalcocotán are isolated from people elsewhere, but they are dependent on each other. Where does the author emphasize the isolation of the village? Where does he show the people acting cooperatively?
2. Where does the author show nature as a threat to the village and its inhabitants? Where is nature seen as a helpful force?
3. What aspects of the village give the impression of poverty? What details does the writer provide that show the dignity of Jalcocotán?

THE WRITER'S TECHNIQUE

In the last two paragraphs, Ernesto Galarza describes the evening activities of the people of Jalcocotán. Here are those two paragraphs:

Through the doors, opened to receive the returning toilers and to freshen the air inside the cottages, came the sounds and sights of the street at sundown. There was the soft clapping of the women patting the ration of tortillas for the evening meal. The smoky light from the wicks of the *candiles* flickering through the doorways cast wobbling shadows on the threshold as people moved about. The air outside was a blend of the familiar smells of supper time—tortillas baking, beans boiling, chile roasting, coffee steaming, and kerosene stenching. The hens were clucking in their roosts in the corrals by the time the street was dark.

After supper, if the weather was warm, the men squatted on the ground, hunched against the wall of the house and smoked. The women and the girls ate supper and put away the kitchen things, the *candiles* turned down to save kerosene. They listened to the tales of the day if the men were in a talking mood. When they pulled on their cigarettes, they made ruby dots in the dark, as if they were putting periods into the low-toned conversation. The talk just faded away, the men went indoors, the doors were shut and barred, and there was nothing on the street but the dark and the rumble of the arroyo.

Notice that in the opening paragraph the writer first shows us that the doors have been opened to let in some fresh air and to welcome home the returning workers. Next, we are taken inside the cottages where the women prepare the evening meal. We also see the smoky light casting shadows as the people move around inside the houses. The writer then shows us the scene inside and outside the houses; he described "the air outside" as having "a blend of the familiar smells of supper time" although we know that the different actions he now describes— "tortillas baking, beans boiling, chile roasting, coffee steaming . . ."—are all going on inside the houses. The chickens clucking outside the houses "by the time the street was dark" provide an additional outside detail, but we are also told that they make their sounds "in their roosts in the corrals."

This combination of exterior and interior details continues in the next paragraph. After supper the men hunch against the outside wall of the house and smoke. Inside, the women and girls eat their own supper and put away the kitchen things. Then, if the men are in the mood to talk, the women and girls can listen to their conversation as it floats indoors. Finally, the talk stops, the men go inside, the cottages are closed, and there is "nothing on the street but the dark and the rumble of the arroyo."

PARAGRAPH PRACTICE

Write two paragraphs of your own, using the above two paragraphs from *Barrio Boy* as your model. You might wish to describe a typical scene in your home at the end of the day. First, describe the different members of your family as they come through the door. Then describe the preparations for the evening meal and include several details of the general scene as people wait for dinner.

In your second paragraph, describe what people do after supper. If all the action takes place indoors, show the two main scenes of activity in two different places. You might wish to describe the after-dinner activity that takes place in the kitchen and the living room. Or, if you have set your scene in good weather, you might divide your description between the kitchen and the front steps, or the kitchen and the street.

No matter which combination of rooms or areas you choose, you should imitate Galarza's practice of keeping *two* areas or *two* activities before the reader at all times. In this way, the reader will be given a broader picture of the entire scene. This approach also gives more variety to your writing and makes it more interesting to read.

ESSAY PRACTICE

The following outline will help you plan a complete essay of at least five paragraphs. The theme of your essay will be closely related to Ernesto Galarza's *Barrio Boy*.

The following sentence may serve as your thesis sentence:

¶ 1.   For those who have never seen my neighborhood, a description of the various buildings will help them visualize the place.

This thesis sentence will also be the central idea for your introductory paragraph. In your introduction, give some background information that will help your reader understand why you are writing about your topic. For example, relate an event that occurred in your neighborhood that will entice your audience to read further.

Each of the sentences below is the topic sentence for one of the paragraphs that you will write to develop your thesis.

You may use the suggested details to develop each paragraph, or you may supply details of your own.

¶ 2.   There is a special atmosphere in my neighborhood.

[DETAILS: What is the character of the *public* buildings in your neighborhood? What are some of the other factors, such as the age of the buildings or their condition, that contribute to the total impression of your neighborhood?]

¶ 3.   The houses in my neighborhood give the feeling of . . .

[DETAILS: Describe the character of the *houses* in your neighborhood. Can you classify these houses into two or three types?]

¶ 4.   There is one building in my neighborhood that is especially important because . . .

[DETAILS: Choose *one building* in your neighborhood that is important as a social center or that is a favorite place for you or other people. The building does not have to be impressive as a piece of architecture—it simply has to be important to you or to the neighborhood.]

Be certain to use transitions between paragraphs, to make your writing flow smoothly. (For a discussion of transitions, see p. 121.) In addition, be sure that your conclusion is effective. It should give your reader a clear signal that you have come to the end of your essay. (See p. 282 for a discussion of conclusions.)

ESSAY TOPICS

1.   Children often ask their parents what the world was like when they were children. Imagine your child has just asked you what your world was like when you were growing up. Choose the details of your description in such a way that your child would be able to understand your early environment.

2.   a.   Describe a place you have lived where there was a very strong feeling of community. How did this close neighborhood spirit reveal itself? How did this spirit benefit the community?

   b.   Describe a place you have lived that did not have a very good community spirit. Why do you think there was this lack of community spirit?

3. One of the requirements in a social science course you are taking is that you present a plan for an ideal community. Give a detailed analysis of this community. What would be the best location for such a community? How large should it be? What facilities should it have, and what should it *not* have? Make your presentation specific enough so that your audience will be able to visualize the place and have a sense of its atmosphere.

Charles A. Lindbergh

Charles Lindbergh was born in Detroit, Michigan, in 1902. He attended the University of Wisconsin from 1920 to 1922, and then went to flying school in Nebraska. During the early 1920s he was a mechanic and stunt flyer throughout the Midwest, and by 1926 he was an airmail pilot flying routes between Chicago and St. Louis. The following year he made his historic nonstop flight from New York to Paris, a feat that remains one of the great milestones in the history of aviation. After this epic flight, Lindbergh went on a goodwill tour of Central America and the Caribbean.

During the 1930s Lindbergh was a designer, inventor, and consultant for various government agencies and private airlines. He was also very active in military aircraft design in World War II. It was during his later years, until his death in 1974, that Lindbergh became increasingly interested in conservation and the environment. He studied various groups of people throughout the world and devoted considerable attention to saving the humpbacked whale and the blue whale from extinction. He also realized that "the science I worshiped and the aircraft I loved [were] destroying the civilization I expected them to serve." Lindbergh had come to this conclusion in Africa in 1964. "I realized," the aviator recalled, "that if I had to choose, I would rather have birds than airplanes."

The following selection, taken from Lindbergh's last book, describes a part of that 1964–1965 visit to Africa. It shows the man of science and Western technology learning about what is basic in life while he also learns another meaning of the word "civilization."

PREVIEWING THE WRITER

- Lindbergh is concerned with two worlds, the world of civilization as he knows it and the world of another culture. What impression does he give of his own world? What impression does he give of the world of East Africa?
- Lindbergh devotes a good deal of attention to the Masai tribe. What details about the lives of these people does Lindbergh choose to present? Does Lindbergh seem to favor their way of life? Is there an implied criticism of his own way of life?
- The writer believes that we can learn a great deal from another culture such as the Masai. What can Western countries learn from the African people that Lindbergh describes?

from *AUTOBIOGRAPHY OF VALUES*

IT WAS MY THIRD TRIP to East Africa. Just before we left, I had been immersed in briefings and conferences on future jet-powered civil aircraft. Speeds up to two thousand miles an hour had been projected. Costs up to thirty million dollars per plane had been discussed, in New York and later in Paris. During the Paris conferences Anne and I attended a formal dinner, with elaborate foods and wines. Its service and table settings and the gold-walled, tapestried salon were like those of Louis XVI's Versailles.

Then we had flown to Nairobi, in the heart of East African game country, where we rented a four-wheel-drive Land-Rover, bought a small tent, food, water containers, kerosene lantern, and other essential equipment, and set off for Masai lands to the south. We took no guide or servant.

Our first night out we selected a campsite on the right bank of the dry Selengai, about two-thirds of the way between Nairobi and the Tanzania border. Twilight had fallen when we arrived at the river bed and shifted into four-wheel drive to cross it. Animal marks were everywhere—tracks in sand, dung piles, water holes. A quarter of a mile upriver, elephants were standing.

We decided to pitch our tent between spreading acacia trees near the edge of a ten-foot earth cliff, from which the river bed stretched clear both ways. It seemed a perfect location, a few paces downriver from a well-worn game trail, and sheltered by a jut of bank so that we were not likely to be in the way of night-cruising elephants. The remaining minutes of twilight gave us time to bring in firewood—long-dead branches and tree trunks, enough to make embers that would last the night. Two giraffes watched us, their heads rising high above bushes some fifty yards away. Elephants plodded up and down the river bed. Two bulls stopped, faced our camp, and stood watching, like the giraffes inland. Their tusks grew whiter as their gray bodies merged with the night. We pitched tent by the light of our campfire and a rising full moon. Nearby, hyenas yelled, and a herd of zebra galloped upriver as we cooked supper.

The tent's cloth walls let through all the jungle noises— lions roaring, elephants wallowing in a water hole across the river bed, a rhinoceros clumping on the game trail. That night we became a part of the jungle, living as primitive man lived in ages past. I felt as separate from my civilization as I had felt from East African animals at that formal Paris dinner a few days before. My sense of immersion was deepened because the only weapon I carried was a Masai spear, which I used as a post on which to hang our kerosene lantern.

When we woke the next morning, elephant, giraffe, and zebra were gone—replaced by a herd of cattle at the water hole. Several Masai elders, naked except for the dark-red folded blankets slung across their shoulders, stood in an acacia tree's shade. Their spears, stuck upright in the ground around them, were within easy reach. Other Masai were repairing damage done to the water hole by elephants during the night. Spear-carrying boys herded the cattle. Thin clouds of dust marked the approach of other herds of cattle coming for water. 6

Three women, close-shaved bronze heads above wide bead necklaces and long red cotton dresses, came to stare at our tent and Land-Rover. An elder approached, spear shouldered above swinging blanket, unaware of his nakedness. He pointed to his left eye, swollen and bloodshot. I sponged it with a bit of cotton my wife had dipped in saline solution, and he appeared satisfied. Before leaving he pointed upriver, straightened seven fingers, and said: "*Simba.*" Seven lions were nearby. 7

The Masai were ready to protect their cattle from all carnivores. Even herdboys were expected to chase away marauding lions. I remembered listening to a Masai describing how to kill a lion with a spear. "The impact of a charging lion is very great," he said. "You must hold your shield high enough so its claws cannot get above the top." As he took his stance and grasped his spear, the implement became transformed from a harmless pole to a quivering arm of power. It was the same difference as between seeing a rifle in its case and holding one, loaded, at your shoulder. 8

The Masai were spearmen and seldom carried bows and arrows. Elephant, lion, rhinoceros, buffalo—there was no animal of the jungle they had not been known to attack. The spear was their primary weapon, too, for the tribal battles that were fought, usually over stolen cattle. An intra-Masai war had been fought only three days before, and less than a half hour's drive from the road we had followed to our camp. Four thousand warriors were said to have formed one side; twenty-five hundred, the other. Eighteen men were killed. The "weaker" 9 side had won. Europeans in the area were concerned lest fighting break out again after women of the defeated tribe chided their men, as was apparently usual, about losing both cattle and the battle.

Our sense of being part of the environment passed once 10 the Masai arrived. We could not talk to them at the water hole. None of them spoke English, and of their language I knew but a few words. Aside from the visit of the women and the elder, they carried on their work as though my wife and I did not exist. I was reminded of the South Pacific natives whose villages and campsites I visited during the war. I once watched a line of naked spear bearers walk along a Biak coast past our military camp. Three or four miles away, American and Japanese forces were engaged in combat, just as Masai forces had been engaged not far from our camp. In the South Pacific, American troops barely noticed natives walking by. I may have been the only man who stared at those spear bearers. Unless they were struck accidentally by a shell or bomb fragment, Biak natives had been as safe as my wife and I were in the midst of Masai tribal conflicts. A minority, in each instance foreigners, was separate from the immediate issues of life and death.

Among the tribes of East Africa I felt I had moved back- 11 ward thousands of years. There, man lived surrounded by other animals, many stronger than he; he was independent of machinery, even the wheel. Many Masai think "civilization" is not progress. They feel sorry for the white man because he has lost the contact with nature. They question our basic values. "You speak of freedom in your country," a Masai elder told me, "but we have known freedom far greater than yours."

Is civilization progress? Living among the primitive always 12 makes me wonder. On what yardstick does one measure? In the environment of America or Europe, progress usually seemed to me as obvious as civilization itself. It was in the airplanes I flew, in the cities where I landed, in the factories I visited and the motor vehicles that carried me to them, in the machinery inside. There was progress in food processing, childbearing, nursery nipples, diapers, shoelaces, and razor blades. In fact, anything thought to be unprogressive was antisocial. But progress can be conceived, I think, only within an accepted framework.

In Africa I felt surrounded by the framework of living 13 events, rather than of works, and there civilization lost much of its importance. In building a campfire and pitching a tent, I realized how little planning—checking and rechecking—basic life demands. A quarter hour gathering wood, another quarter hour setting up poles and cord-tautening cloth sheets, a few minutes to draw buckets of water from spring or stream, to light a lantern, to spade a hole—simple acts, simply learned, repeated.

Contrast this to the elaborate organization that supports apartment houses, electric appliances, oil furnaces: the pipelines, the dynamos, and the high-tension cables that supply them; the electricians, well drillers, agents, postmen, accountants, executives, and other specialists who make them work; the architects, builders, bankers, masons, carpenters, plumbers, truck drivers, trainmen, miners, lathe operators, insurance salesmen. Camped in its jungles, I feel that Africa's contribution to the progress of mankind will stem from its primitive and sensate qualities, and that through these qualities a wisdom is imparted to the intellect essential to the very existence of human life. [14]

Yet, simple as it seemed to us, our camp became elaborate compared with a Masai's hut of poles and cow dung. The cans of food we opened belied our sense of independence of civilization's ways: meat from Argentina, peas from California, peaches from Japan, English marmalade and biscuits. The Masai could live indefinitely on blood and milk from his cattle, and occasionally a little beef. Ships, warehouses, and canning factories were not life lines to his diet. [15]

Only from the framework of the primitive can one realize what fantastic complication our civilization depends on and imposes, what intricate organization the status of a "modern" requires. Africa brings to the intellect's awareness the sensate qualities of life. These are recognizably simple, found in the dances of the Masai, in the prolificacy of the Kikuyu, in the nakedness of boys and girls. You feel these qualities in the sun on your face and the dust on your feet, in the prick of thorns and from the heat of embers, in the yelling of hyenas and the bark of zebras. [16]

The primitive teaches that life itself, unforced life, is progress, a fact our civilization tends more and more to overlook. [17]

THE WRITER'S THEMES

1. Lindbergh feels close to the world he finds in Africa. Where in the selection does he indicate this closeness to the African

world? Where does he show that he is not totally immersed in this African culture?

2. Lindbergh refers to the "fantastic complication" of our civilization. He also tells us that the Masai feel that civilization "is not progress." Where does Lindbergh suggest that civilization as we know it in the West may not necessarily mean progress?

3. According to Lindbergh what can the Masai, who live far from our civilization, teach us about the real values of civilization?

THE WRITER'S TECHNIQUE

In paragraph four, Charles Lindbergh describes the first night he and his wife spent on the banks of the dry Selengai River near the border between Nairobi and Tanzania. Here is the paragraph:

> We decided to pitch our tent between spreading acacia trees near the edge of a ten-foot earth cliff, from which the river bed stretched clear both ways. It seemed a perfect location, a few paces downriver from a well-worn game trail, and sheltered by a jut of bank so that we were not likely to be in the way of night-cruising elephants. The remaining minutes of twilight gave us time to bring in firewood—long-dead branches and tree trunks, enough to make embers that would last the night. Two giraffes watched us, their heads rising high above bushes some fifty yards away. Elephants plodded up and down the river bed. Two bulls stopped, faced our camp, and stood watching, like the giraffes inland. Their tusks grew whiter as their gray bodies merged with the night. We pitched tent by the light of our campfire and a rising full moon. Nearby, hyenas yelled, and a herd of zebra galloped upriver as we cooked supper.

At the opening of the paragraph, the writer indicates that he and his wife decided to pitch their tent "near the edge of a ten-foot earth cliff" because it was such a good location, being near an established game trail and protected by a bank of the river, "so that we were not likely to be in the way of night-cruising elephants."

Lindbergh then tells how the local animals acted while he and his wife were gathering firewood: two giraffes simply "watched" while elephants "plodded up and down the river bed." Two male elephants stopped and stood watching them.

As the writer and his wife pitch their tent they can hear the yelling of nearby hyenas, and as they cook their supper they notice "a herd of zebra" galloping upriver.

Charles Lindbergh uses specific details of his thinking, his actions, and the reactions of the wildlife around him to give us a detailed picture of a person responding to life in a primitive area. Although he and his wife are in an unusual situation, there is little if any sense of threat; the giraffes and elephants merely watch them, and even the two bull elephants that stop simply "stood watching, like the giraffes inland." The hyenas merely laugh nearby and zebras gallop away. In the passage we see people resting in an area where the abundant animal life is not at all threatening to human outsiders.

PARAGRAPH PRACTICE

Write a paragraph of your own, using Charles Lindbergh's paragraph as your model. You could describe a place where you stopped for an evening (for example, a hotel or motel), you could describe a place where you spent a night or longer with a friend, or you could describe a place where you once camped.

Notice how Lindbergh places his supporting details in a certain order. First, he indicates *where* they decided to stay and he tells *why* it was such a good location. Next, he describes their preparations for the evening (gathering firewood) and gives a detailed description of the nearby wildlife, some of which noticed their human neighbors while others did not. The paragraph ends with Lindbergh and his wife pitching their tent and cooking supper.

In your own paragraph give your reader a detailed picture of your overnight stay. First, indicate *when* you stayed there and *why* you were staying in that particular place. Next, include several supporting details as you describe either the people you were staying with, or your fellow guests at the hotel or motel, or even any wildlife you observed if you camped at a wilderness site.

ESSAY PRACTICE

The following outline will help you plan a complete essay of at least five paragraphs. The theme of your essay will be closely related to the selection from *Autobiography of Values*.

The following sentence may serve as your thesis sentence:

¶ 1. Although great strides have been made in this century, a disturbing lack of progress and even some backward movement may be observed in certain areas of our lives.

This thesis sentence will also be the central idea for your introductory paragraph. One effective technique to use in an introduction is to point out a widely held belief (for example, that industrial civilization equals progress) and then indicate that you intend, in the course of your essay, to take an opposite point of view.

Each of the sentences below is the topic sentence for one of the paragraphs that you will write to develop your thesis. You may use the suggested details to develop each paragraph, or you may supply details of your own.

¶ 2. There are some signs of progress that are very obvious in our society.

[DETAILS: Point out those signs of progress that you feel are most evident today and that signify the greatest advances for our way of life.]

¶ 3. Unfortunately, other areas of our lives have not experienced improvement.

[DETAILS: Point out such social problems as the existence of war, human greed, and other destructive tendencies.]

¶ 4. The most disturbing thought is that we seem to be losing ground in some areas of our lives.

[DETAILS: Have machines and other modern technology had a negative impact on our lives? Have we lost contact with nature?]

Be certain to use transitions between paragraphs to make your writing flow smoothly. (For a discussion of transitions, see p. 121.) In addition, be sure that your conclusion is effective. It should give your reader a clear signal that you have come to the end of your essay. (See p. 282 for a discussion of conclusions.)

ESSAY TOPICS

1. Write a feature article for your local newspaper in which you supply details of an experience you had with a government agency, private business, or some other office that

proved to you how complicated modern life can be. For example, you may have tried to obtain satisfaction from a company over a defective product, or you may have been caught in the red tape of a government agency of some kind. How complicated did the situation become? What did you do?

2. a. Prepare a speech that you will give to a group of engineering majors about the dangers of technology. What should they be especially careful of as they go on to their careers?

   b. Describe a situation in which you suddenly found yourself aware of the disadvantages of our technology. You may have been in a power blackout, or found yourself in an elevator that broke down; or you may have been inconvenienced by a strike that interrupted an important service. How did you react?

3. Write an essay on the home or dormitory in which you live. How could the lives of the people who live there be simplified? What changes would make their lives less complicated? Would the quality of their lives be better, and would they be happier?

Focus on Terms: Thesis and Topic Sentence

Thesis and *topic sentence* report the central idea of a piece of writing. In good writing, every sentence and paragraph supports the central idea the writer is trying to communicate. When we refer to a complete piece of writing we call the central idea a thesis; when we are discussing a single paragraph we call the central idea a topic sentence.

For example, in her diary entry of April 4, 1944, Anne Frank begins a paragraph by announcing: "I am the best and sharpest critic of my own work." This is a topic sentence. Throughout the paragraph, the writer supports this idea by providing an honest assessment of her skills as a writer and as an artist. Her analysis of her own strengths and limitations continues to the final sentence, when she notes that, if all else fails, "I can always write for myself."

At the end of the selection from *Autobiography of Values,* Charles Lindbergh gives us the thesis sentence for the entire piece when he writes that "only from the framework of the primitive can one realize what fantastic complication our civilization depends on and imposes, what intricate organization the status of a 'modern' requires." Throughout the selection the writer has described at length the life of a primitive people, along with his own sense of the complicated nature of our own lives. Here, the thesis statement summarizes the twin concerns the writer has dealt with throughout the piece.

The opening sentence of the excerpt from Simone de Beauvoir's *The Prime of Life* is both a topic sentence for the first paragraph and the thesis sentence for the entire selection: "The most intoxicating aspect of my return to Paris in September, 1929, was the freedom I now possessed." In the paragraph that follows that sentence, and throughout the remainder of the selection, the writer's examples support this central idea of the freedom she enjoyed at this stage of her life.

It is very necessary for your reader, and necessary for your own sense of structure as a writer, that your paragraphs contain clear topic sentences and that your essay contains, at some point, a thesis statement that reports the main idea for your whole essay.

Student Essay 🐦🐦 *Martha Schanel*

In the following essay the student not only describes a place, she
also gives her readers a *feeling* for that place. The writer also
shows us that, even though she shares it with other people, this
private place is truly her own.

• Notice the writer's clear opening statement. It is a thesis
sentence that immediately establishes what she is going to write
about and that also gives the reader a good indication of her
attitude toward her subject.

PRIVACY

PRIVACY IS A wonderful space for me, where I can be   1
with whomever I choose, whenever I choose. My space is a red
house nestled in oak trees, bounded on one side by a lake, on
another by a pond, and on the other two sides by carefully
clipped hedges. The water, which by its nature draws children
and dogs to its bank, is for my house a kind of moat, keeping
all but the most adventurous swimming, fishing, and playing
on the opposite shore. Although the hedges are no real barrier
to anyone who would venture to cross them, they set boundaries, like living fences, for those who have not been invited
within, to a more intimate space. It is at this perimeter that I
begin to choose who may enter my space and share it for a time.

I have a neighbor who often walks down the bumpy road   2
on which we live and stops by the hedges of my front yard to
talk with me. He asks if my tomatoes have set fruit yet or if I
think the drought will hurt the sugar pea crop. I eagerly invite
him into my garden and together we peruse the vegetables and
flowers. We share hints and secrets that only another home
farmer would recognize as the wisdom it is. But my neighbor
has never asked where I will be vacationing this summer or
what I think of the world situation; and I know nothing of his
opinions and daily "goings-on." We are both content in the
garden.

My house sees frequent guests, those who would dine   3
with my family and me, enjoying an evening of light conversation or perhaps discussing business or projects that we share.
These guests may frequently gather in my living room but never
unexpectedly or without invitation. The impromptu visit is reserved for friends.

My close friend is a welcome sight at my back door. She 4
has seldom if ever had dinner in my dining room or drunk
demitasse in front of the living room fireplace. But over the
years she has consumed gallons of coffee at my kitchen table
and feasted on such delicacies as peanut butter and jelly sandwiches on my back porch. I have invited her into my space not
to see the Doulton crystal and the Minton china, but the plastic
cup and the paper plate.

My life in the red house is shared by three men: my hus- 5
band of more than a dozen years and my two sons. I recall that
a few years back I begged for an hour of solitude—free from the
constant demands of toddlers. My life seemed to have no privacy. The laundry room, the kitchen, not even the bathroom
provided space in which I could be alone. That is changing now
as the boys become older and more independent. They insist
on a degree of privacy for themselves and so insure it for me.

But the person who enters my private world most often 6
and to the greatest degree is my husband. He has no interest
in my garden and he rarely gossips over a cup of coffee in the
kitchen, but he alone can follow to my most private room to see
the best and the worst of what I am. Beyond this space there
are only the unspoken thoughts and dreams which are known
only to me and my Creator.

Strategies for Writing

1. Write a thesis sentence of your own for this student essay.
   How different would the essay be if the writer had used
   your thesis sentence?
2. Examine the topic sentence at the beginning of each paragraph in the essay and select those topic sentences you believe are the strongest. Why did you choose the topic sentences you did?
3. Write an essay on the subject of privacy. Choose as your
   audience either a group of students who live in a dormitory
   or a group of people who intend to share a vacation home
   together. Keep in mind that your choice of details and your
   emphasis will depend on the audience you have selected.
4. Write an essay in which you give advice to a young person
   who is about to live away from home for the first time. How
   should this person deal with this new freedom? In how
   many areas of life will this person be able to do as he or she
   pleases?

2

 **OBSERVING OUR WORLD**

WRITING SKILL: Description

Good description is basic to good writing. When we describe, our choice of words will determine whether or not we succeed in helping our reader see an abstract idea, a state of mind, a familiar object, or even something that has never been seen. Every time we describe an idea, a person, or an object, we make our description real by using specific details in a certain order. For example, if you are trying to describe the concept of justice, you could relate the details of a particular case where you believe justice was done. If you were to describe a person you know, you would be sure to tell what kind of clothes that person wears, how he or she talks, and any number of other details you feel would make that individual an immediate presence for your reader. If you had to describe an object such as a stereo system or a motorcycle, you would be careful to include in your description specific indications of the size, color, and special features of the object. No matter what you are describing, your writing will be more real and more memorable for your reader if you are careful to build your description around a series of specific, appropriate details.

Some writers choose to describe the external landscape,

the world of our sense impressions. Other writers prefer to observe our inner world; they deal with the landscapes of our psychology. Still other writers, usually the most interesting, deal with both worlds as they try to show us how the two landscapes merge and become one in our minds.

Each of the selections in this unit contains a description of the external world and each leads us to consider important aspects of our inner world. For example, in *Dreamy*, Sherry Sonnett provides us with a description of an actual environment that is so detailed we feel we could almost reconstruct it after we have read the story. We also feel that we could construct a detailed psychological profile of the woman who is described in the story. Here, the description of a person's physical world leads us to an understanding of that person's inner world.

In "On Feline Play," Konrad Lorenz is also concerned with psychology, in this case the psychology of young cats at play. The writer's description of feline behavior not only tells us how and why cats play the way they do, it also treats of a larger issue, that of the whole value of play. The writer's description of cats at play invites us to apply these findings to an important area of our own lives. As he describes the actions of animals, Lorenz invites us to apply these physical facts to the interior world of human psychology.

George Orwell's newspaper essay, " 'The Moon under Water,' " is not only a room-by-room description of a British bar and restaurant (or "pub," as it is known), but it is also a description of a way of life. As Orwell takes us through the different parts of the pub, we are shown the ways in which "The Moon under Water" provides a comfortable place for people of all ages to come together and relax. Orwell's description of his favorite pub could be a model for a description of almost any popular gathering place.

When you describe an object or a place, your first task is to select the right details for your reader. The selection of these details will help your reader form a dominant impression of that object or place. If you leave out important details, your description will lack depth and your reader will be left with only a sketchy impression. Here, for example, is a description of the rooms of a house:

> My room is at one end of the house. There is a hallway that leads to the dining room and the kitchen, and there are bedrooms upstairs.

The description is clear, but it is far from complete. We can form a picture in our minds, but the writer has not helped us with a detailed description of the arrangement of the rooms or what is in them.

Here is an example of description from one of the selections in this unit, an excerpt from J. M. Synge's *The Aran Islands*. Selected details have been placed in italics.

> My room is at one end of the cottage, *with a boarded floor and ceiling, and two windows opposite each other.* Then there is the kitchen *with earth floor and open rafters, and two doors opposite each other* opening into the open air, *but no windows.* Beyond it there are *two small rooms of half the width of the kitchen with one window apiece.*

Note how much more detail there is in Synge's description. The writer does not simply point out where his room is; he notes that it has a "boarded floor and ceiling, and two windows opposite each other." He does not simply tell us that there is a kitchen, he tells us that it is a kitchen "with earth floor and open rafters." Notice that in describing these rooms, the writer is careful to show us floors, ceilings, and windows, details that help give us a sense of an entire room in each case. We are also given details that help correct an impression we *might* have: Synge points out that the kitchen has no windows; it is the one room in the house where we would expect to find them.

All of the details chosen by Synge lead us to a dominant impression of the house where he is staying: this is a primitive place. Having established this impression by his use of earth floor, open rafters, and no windows where we would expect them, the writer goes on to give a similar impression of the last two rooms of the house. He does this when he points out that they are half the width of the kitchen. By his careful use of selected details, the writer strengthens the impression he wishes to emphasize. Each part of the description supports the whole.

Because he supplies such a number and variety of details, Synge's description is clear, and we have a very good idea of his surroundings. If he had wished to, the writer could have added details of color, noise, texture, movement, and smell to make his description even more vivid. Here, for example, is part of the same excerpt from *The Aran Islands*, but with some additional details. These added details have been placed in italics.

My room is at one end of the cottage, with a *red* boarded floor and *grey* ceiling, and two *rattling* windows opposite each other. Then there is the kitchen, *usually filled with people preparing meals and talking, while the smells of cooking food fill the room,* with earth floor and open rafters, *smooth to the touch,* and two doors opposite each other . . .

With these added details we can see the colors of the floor and ceiling, and we can hear the windows rattling. We can also see the movement of people working and talking in the kitchen, while we smell the food that is being prepared there. We can also feel the texture of the open rafters. For his own artistic purposes, J. M. Synge chose not to include such details because he wanted a stark setting.

When you describe an idea, or an object, or a person, be sure that you use significant, memorable details to help your reader see each part of what you are describing. The more specific you are, the more your reader will be convinced by your description.

◀ *Sherry Sonnett* ▶

Sherry Sonnett is an American writer who has written several movies and TV shows, in addition to children's books and short stories. She has also written articles for such publications as *Glamour* and the *New York Times*. She is currently writing a novel.

"Dreamy" is a portrait of a woman who, in the words of one critic, "sets out to embrace total freedom." It is the story of a woman who seeks relief in the orderliness of a new life in which there is no pressure and where everything has its place. This is a world that may be flat and uneventful, but it is also a world where there is safety and security. In "Dreamy" fantasy becomes reality.

PREVIEWING THE WRITER

- Note the quality of the woman's relationship with each person she encounters or each person she describes.
- Note the details that show the woman's desire to control her environment. Which details show this personality trait the most?
- Note how the writer uses time to divide the different parts of the story.

DREAMY

ONE MORNING, quite early and without the aid of an alarm clock, I will rise up cleanly from the dreary, dirty sheets of my unmade bed. Slipping my feet into warm soft slippers, drawing a crisp pressed robe around my smooth rounded shoulders, I will enter my orderly kitchen and brew a cup of strong aromatic coffee, which I will sip as I read the morning newspaper, each section and the ads. I will do the crossword puzzle straight through with the exception of two unknown letters. I will dress, washing my face in sparkling water, combing my shiny, lustrous hair, doing each task calmly, quietly, precisely. I will pack a small neat suitcase, mostly sweet-smelling, even folded underwear and safely packaged toilet essentials. Dressed and ready to depart, I will pause before my large, spotless mirror and I will be content with the self-contained image reflected there. Then, silently slipping my key in the lock, I will softly close the door absolutely, and I will take pleasure in this, knowing that such perfect union must be esteemed. I will go to my car, a small blue roadster, and I will place the suitcase securely on the rear seat. I will slip another well-made key into its one perfect opposite, and when the smoothly tuned engine springs into life, I will drive off and disappear forever.

I will drive until nightfall, the only car on miles of unblemished concrete stretching rhythmically through silent green valleys and across rolling molded hills. I will come to a medium-size city, discreet in its boundaries, in a region I have never been in. I will drive through the heart of this city, permanently noting the location of various places of interest, but I will stop a bit removed from the center, somewhere on its perimeter, distanced from the clutter and noise of the heart. I will find and rent at a reasonable sum a furnished room with kitchen in a boardinghouse once grand but now declined genteel. I will sleep that night between clean sheets, although not of the best quality. Long into the night, I shall lie in the darkness on my back. My head will rest comfortably on the supporting pillow beneath it and the covers will be pulled neatly and evenly across my chest, my arms on top of them stationary at my sides. Imprecise sounds will filter through the heavy, old but newly laundered curtains, and I will hear each one separately and trace its source and understand it. I will listen to those sounds and know them.

In the morning, I will dress quickly and go out into the street. Around the corner from my new home, I will find a diner, painted gray, with green plastic on the seats and counter. As I eat bacon and eggs, toast, and coffee, I will search through the job ads listed in the local newspaper. By lunchtime I will be employed as ticket taker at the local movie theater or saleswoman at the five-and-ten. My employer will show me what exactly my job consists of, and at each step I will nod my head and firmly fix it in my brain until I need only do it once or twice for it to be automatic. I will begin that very day and at its end my employer and I will express our mutual satisfaction.

I will stop on my return to my new home at a small neighborhood grocery to purchase the few things I will want—the usual staples, a flavorful tea, imported biscuits, a particularly thin slice of veal. As I enter the boarding house, its proprietor and I will nod to each other, smiling circumspectly, respecting the other's privacy. In my room I will slip off my coat and hang it on a wide wooden hanger made especially for coats such as mine. I will arrange the kitchen in the manner most convenient for me and then I will prepare my dinner. The cooking odors will permeate the room, adding to its warmth.

I will eat this meal on a mahogany table set before the window and, as I slice and swallow precise bite after precise bite, I will view the street below. Two or three old men are quietly talking and enjoying the evening air. Occasionally, they look off down the street at a group of children playing with a ball. By their posture and the movements of their hands as they talk, I can tell they are good men who have lived good lives and I can see that they watch the children with pleasure and not regret. A young man and woman, their arms around each other, come out of a house opposite and amble slowly out of sight, leaving behind the sound of a laugh. A woman appears and calls out to one of the children, a boy of eight, and when he runs to her she offers him a slice of freshly baked chocolate cake.

As I finish my meal and the evening shadows lengthen and seep out into night, I will smoke a cigarette, each inhalation smooth and cool, and I will watch the delicate smoke trail up and out my window, joining the fresh night air which cools my face. I will wash my few dishes, clean the sink, and wipe the counter space. I will neatly fold the dishcloth with which I have dried the dishes and drape it over a rack suitably placed over the sink.

Drawing from my purse a newly purchased book, the characters of which are old familiar friends, I will draw my feet up under me on my easy chair, so comfortable it seems made for the curve of my back and the line of my bottom. For an hour or two, while the night spends itself in comings and goings, I will read this book, turning each page silently and watching it fall flat against its companions. Then I will stretch luxuriously, close the book and place it on a small polished table. I will undress. Again between clean sheets, I will lie on my back in the darkness, although not for so long this night as the last, and I will hear the imprecise sounds and I will understand them.

Each day and each night will be like this. My life will have shape and form. My needs and expectations and desires will coincide perfectly with what my life provides. I will have everything.

THE WRITER'S THEMES

1. How does the woman in the story plan to gain control of her life? Are her aims realistic or unrealistic?
2. What are the details in the story that most clearly reveal the woman's personality?
3. What is the woman's attitude toward the people with whom she comes in contact? What is her attitude toward those people she merely observes?

THE WRITER'S TECHNIQUE

In the first paragraph of her story, Sherry Sonnett describes, in great detail, the woman waking up and preparing to leave her house:

> One morning, quite early and without the aid of an alarm clock, I will rise up cleanly from the dreary, dirty sheets of my unmade bed. Slipping my feet into warm soft slippers, drawing a crisp pressed robe around my smooth rounded shoulders, I will enter my orderly kitchen and brew a cup of strong aromatic coffee, which I will sip as I read the morning newspaper, each section and the ads. I will do the crossword puzzle straight through with the exception of two unknown letters. I will dress, washing my face in sparkling water, combing my shiny, lustrous hair, doing each task calmly, quietly, precisely. I will pack a small neat suitcase, mostly sweet-smelling, even folded underwear and safely packaged toilet essentials. Dressed and ready to depart, I will pause before my large, spotless mirror and I will be content with the self-contained image reflected there. Then, silently slipping my key in the lock, I will softly close the door absolutely, and I will take pleasure in this, knowing that such perfect union must be esteemed. I will go to my car, a small blue roadster, and I will place the suitcase securely on the rear seat. I will slip another well-made key into its one perfect opposite, and when the smoothly tuned engine springs into life, I will drive off and disappear forever.

The writer first shows the woman waking up "without the aid of an alarm clock" and then shows her slipping her feet into "warm soft slippers" and "drawing a crisp pressed robe" around her shoulders. She then goes into her kitchen, brews a cup of "strong aromatic coffee," and reads the morning newspaper. Next, she gets dressed and packs "a small neat suitcase." Just before she leaves the woman gives a final look in the mirror and leaves the house. She places her suitcase in her car, starts the motor, and drives off, to "disappear forever."

Notice that the writer not only takes us through the various steps that most of us take as we begin the day, but she also provides us with a number of adjectives and adverbs that help us form an even more precise picture of the woman's morning. The sheets of her "unmade" bed are "dreary" and "dirty"; her slippers are "warm" and "soft," and the robe she puts around her "smooth rounded" shoulders is "crisp" and "pressed." The kitchen where she brews "strong aromatic" coffee is an "orderly" place. The water she uses for washing is "sparkling," and her hair is "shiny" and "lustrous." So far the writer has used only adjectives to expand her descriptions, but now she uses adverbs to sum up how the woman has done each task: "calmly, quietly, precisely."

The remainder of the paragraph continues this use of adjectives and adverbs as we watch the woman prepare to leave. She "silently" slips the key in the lock, "softly" closes the door, goes to her "small blue" car and places her suitcase "securely" on the seat. After she turns the key, the "smoothly tuned" engine starts and she disappears. She has left her home forever.

PARAGRAPH PRACTICE

Write a paragraph of your own, using as your model the structure of this first paragraph from "Dreamy." Your paragraph could be a description of yourself as you get ready to go out for an evening.

Notice that Sherry Sonnett gives a structure to her paragraph by clearly indicating the different actions of the woman in the story. The writer makes those actions more real by her consistent use of adjectives and adverbs. When you write your own paragraph be sure that you place each action in the proper sequence. Then, either at the same time or when you review your paragraph, add at least three adjectives and three adverbs to help make your description more vivid and direct. For example, if you are looking forward to going somewhere for an evening, you might use such adverbs as "eagerly" or "excitedly" to describe your actions as you get ready. If you are not especially looking forward to the evening, you might describe yourself as choosing your clothes "carelessly" or "reluctantly."

ESSAY PRACTICE

The following outline will help you plan a complete essay of at least five paragraphs. The theme of your essay will be closely related to Sherry Sonnett's "Dreamy."

The following sentence may serve as your thesis sentence, and will also be the main idea of your introductory paragraph:

¶ 1.   One of the best ways to understand a person's life is to see an entire day in that life, from morning to night.

Each of the sentences below is the topic sentence for one of the paragraphs that you will write to develop your thesis. You may use the suggested details to develop each paragraph, or you may supply details of your own.

¶ 2.   Getting up and getting out of the house in the morning is a difficult job in itself.

[DETAILS: Describe a typical morning as you get ready for the day. What do you try to do in advance that will make your morning easier? What *must* be done before you can leave the house?]

¶ 3.   My typical day includes . . .

[DETAILS: Describe a typical morning or afternoon at school or at work. If you go to school and you work, divide your paragraph into two parts. End your paragraph with your coming home at the end of the day.]

¶ 4.   In the evening . . .

[DETAILS: Describe what you have to do in the evening or what you enjoy doing, when all of your responsibilities for the day are over.]

Be certain that you use transitions between paragraphs to make your writing flow smoothly. In addition, be sure that your conclusion gives your reader a clear signal that you have come to the end of your essay.

ESSAY TOPICS

1.   Sometimes we would like to run away from the responsibilities and unending concerns of our daily life. Where would you go if you could take a leave of absence from all of your

responsibilities? Using "Dreamy" as your model, describe your first day of total freedom.

2. Describe a typical day in the life of someone you actually know. This person's attitude toward life may be one of struggle and determination, or the person might see a spirit of humor and good will in all areas of his or her daily life. In writing your description of this person, make sure that all of the details you choose support the main impression of that person.

3. a. At what point should a person not be blamed for wanting to leave a difficult situation? Give at least two examples of people who should be able to escape to a better life, despite the fact that society might not approve of their decision. In each case, describe the person's life and tell how the person found himself or herself in this difficult situation. To what extent can the people you describe really make a change in their lives?

   b. Often we feel that events in our lives happen *to* us, and we are powerless to control them. For example, to what extent are we powerless in terms of health, relationships, or money? Give at least three or four examples of people's lack of control in these areas of their lives, and indicate how people could enjoy more control in these areas.

🍋 *J. M. Synge* 🍋

J. M. Synge (pronounced *sing*) was born in a suburb of Dublin in 1871. At the age of seventeen he entered Trinity College; he received his B.A. in 1892. By this time Synge was seriously considering a musical career, and he went to Germany with the idea of becoming a violinist. Instead, he turned to literature and moved to Paris where he began an intense study of French writers.

The great event in Synge's life as a writer came in 1898, when he met with the Irish poet W. B. Yeats in Paris. Yeats told the younger man that he was wasting his time in France and urged him to visit the Aran Islands off the west coast of Ireland, and find inspiration there. Synge followed this advice, making his first visit to the Aran Islands that same year. He returned again and again, in addition to traveling extensively throughout other parts of Ireland. He became a close observer of the stories, speech, and customs of the peasants; stories told in the folk idiom soon became a central part of his own work. In the words of one critic, Synge "had his fingers upon the life-pulse of Ireland."

Synge is primarily remembered as a playwright and while his plays have a distinctly Irish setting, such works as *The Playboy of the Western World, The Tinker's Wedding,* and *Riders to the Sea* have become standard plays of the international repertory.

The following selection is from *The Aran Islands,* one of Synge's best-known prose works. The writer is making his first visit to the Aran Islands, and has just left the northernmost island, Aranmor, to stay on the middle island of Inishmaan.

PREVIEWING THE WRITER

• Note how the writer describes the life of the people. What parts of the people's lives does the writer concentrate on and what parts does he not include in his description?

• Note the writer's relationship with the people he is observing. To what extent does the writer attempt to be a part of the life of the people?

• Note the writer's observations on the use of language in the Aran Islands. How closely does Synge observe the language of the people? To what extent is language a subject of interest to the people?

from *THE ARAN ISLANDS*

I AM SETTLED AT LAST on Inishmaan in a small cottage with a continual drone of Gaelic coming from the kitchen that opens into my room.

Early this morning the man of the house came over for me   2
with a four-oared curagh[1]—that is, a curagh with four rowers
and four oars on either side, as each man uses two—and we set
off a little before noon.

It gave me a moment of exquisite satisfaction to find myself   3
moving away from civilisation in this rude canvas canoe of a
model that has served primitive races since men first went on
the sea.

We had to stop for a moment at a hulk that is anchored   4
in the bay, to make some arrangements for the fish-curing of
the middle island, and my crew called out as soon as we were
within earshot that they had a man with them who had been
in France a month from this day.

When we started again, a small sail was run up in the   5
bow, and we set off across the sound with a leaping oscillation
that had no resemblance to the heavy movement of a boat.

The sail is only used as an aid, so the men continued to   6
row after it had gone up, and as they occupied the four cross-
seats I lay on the canvas at the stern and the frame of slender
laths, which bent and quivered as the waves passed under them.

When we set off it was a brilliant morning of April, and   7
the green, glittering waves seemed to toss the canoe among
themselves, yet as we drew nearer this island a sudden thunderstorm broke out behind the rocks we were approaching, and
lent a momentary tumult to this still vein of the Atlantic.

We landed at a small pier, from which a rude track leads   8
up to the village between small fields and bare sheets of rock
like those in Aranmor. The youngest son of my boatman, a boy
of about seventeen, who is to be my teacher and guide, was
waiting for me at the pier and guided me to his house, while
the men settled the curagh and followed slowly with my baggage.

My room is at one end of the cottage, with a boarded floor   9
and ceiling, and two windows opposite each other. Then there
is the kitchen with earth floor and open rafters, and two doors
opposite each other opening into the open air, but no windows.
Beyond it there are two small rooms of half the width of the
kitchen with one window apiece.

The kitchen itself, where I will spend most of my time, is   10
full of beauty and distinction. The red dresses of the women
who cluster round the fire on their stools give a glow of almost

---

[1] A small boat made of tarred canvas that has been stretched over a
wooden frame.

Eastern richness, and the walls have been toned by the turf-smoke to a soft brown that blends with the grey earth-colour of the floor. Many sorts of fishing-tackle, and the nets and oil-skins of the men, are hung upon the walls or among the open rafters; and right overhead, under the thatch, there is a whole cowskin from which they make pampooties.[2]

Every article on these islands has an almost personal char-   11
acter, which gives this simple life, where all art is unknown, something of the artistic beauty of mediæval life. The curaghs and spinning-wheels, the tiny wooden barrels that are still much used in the place of earthenware, the home-made cradles, churns, and baskets, are all full of individuality, and being made from materials that are common here, yet to some extent pe-culiar to the island, they seem to exist as a natural link between the people and the world that is about them.

The simplicity and unity of the dress increases in another   12
way the local air of beauty. The women wear red petticoats and jackets of the island wool stained with madder,[3] to which they usually add a plaid shawl twisted round their chests and tied at their backs. When it rains they throw another petticoat over their heads with the waistband round their faces, or, if they are young, they use a heavy shawl like those worn in Galway. Occasionally other wraps are worn, and during the thunder-storm I arrived in I saw several girls with men's waistcoats but-toned round their bodies. Their skirts do not come much below the knee, and show their powerful legs in the heavy indigo stockings with which they are all provided.

The men wear three colours: the natural wool, indigo, and   13
a grey flannel that is woven of alternate threads of indigo and the natural wool. In Aranmor many of the younger men have adopted the usual fisherman's jersey, but I have only seen one on this island.

As flannel is cheap—the women spin the yarn from the   14
wool of their own sheep, and it is then woven by a weaver in Kilronan for fourpence a yard—the men seem to wear an in-definite number of waistcoats and woollen drawers one over the other. They are usually surprised at the lightness of my own dress, and one old man I spoke to for a minute on the pier, when I came ashore, asked me if I was not cold with 'my little clothes.'

[2] Moccasins made from cowhide.

[3] A red dye.

As I sat in the kitchen to dry the spray from my coat, several men who had seen me walking up came in to me to talk to me, usually murmuring on the threshold, 'The blessing of God on this place,' or some similar words.

The courtesy of the old woman of the house is singularly attractive, and though I could not understand much of what she said—she has no English—I could see with how much grace she motioned each visitor to a chair, or stool, according to his age, and said a few words to him till he drifted into our English conversation.

For the moment my own arrival is the chief subject of interest, and the men who come in are eager to talk to me.

Some of them express themselves more correctly than the ordinary peasant, others use the Gaelic idioms continually and substitute 'he' or 'she' for 'it,' as the neuter pronoun is not found in modern Irish.

A few of the men have a curiously full vocabulary, others know only the commonest words in English, and are driven to ingenious devices to express their meaning. Of all the subjects we can talk of war seems their favourite, and the conflict between America and Spain is causing a great deal of excitement.[4] Nearly all the families have relations who have had to cross the Atlantic, and all eat of the flour and bacon that is brought from the United States, so they have a vague fear that 'if anything happened to America,' their own island would cease to be habitable.

Foreign languages are another favourite topic, and as these men are bilingual they have a fair notion of what it means to speak and think in many different idioms. Most of the strangers they see on the islands are philological students, and the people have been led to conclude that linguistic studies, particularly Gaelic studies, are the chief occupation of the outside world.

'I have seen Frenchmen, and Danes, and Germans,' said one man, 'and there does be a power of Irish books along with them, and they reading them better than ourselves. Believe me there are few rich men now in the world who are not studying the Gaelic.'

They sometimes ask me the French for simple phrases, and when they have listened to the intonation for a moment, most of them are able to reproduce it with admirable precision.

---

[4] The Spanish-American War was fought in 1898.

THE WRITER'S THEMES

1. The writer is not only observing the culture of the Aran Islands, he is also making judgments and comparisons with other cultures. Where in the selection does the writer observe, where does he make judgments, and where does he seem to make comparisons?
2. J. M. Synge describes several aspects of life in the Aran Islands. Review these different aspects and note the degree of attention the author devotes to each one. To which aspect of life on the islands does the writer devote most of his attention? What does this tell us about the writer's own values and interests?
3. J. M. Synge describes a people who must cooperate with nature, as part of their daily lives. How do the people of the Aran Islands adapt to their natural environment?

THE WRITER'S TECHNIQUE

In paragraph eleven of this selection from *The Aran Islands*, J. M. Synge describes some of the items on the island of Inishmaan that seem to reflect the life of the people. Here is the paragraph:

> Every article on these islands has an almost personal character, which gives this simple life, where all art is unknown, something of the artistic beauty of mediæval life. The curaghs and spinning-wheels, the tiny wooden barrels that are still much used in the place of earthenware, the home-made cradles, churns, and baskets, are all full of individuality, and being made from materials that are common here, yet to some extent peculiar to the island, they seem to exist as a natural link between the people and the world that is about them.

Notice that Synge begins the paragraph by indicating that every "article" on the island "has an almost personal character." He then gives a list of these articles, which includes the curaghs, the spinning wheels, the tiny barrels used in place of earthenware dishes, the cradles, the churns (for making butter), and the baskets. In the course of making this list, the writer deals directly with the lives of the islanders by touching upon a wide range of their daily activities. The curaghs are used by the men for fishing and for transportation; the spinning wheels, the churns, the tiny barrels, and the baskets remind us of the women and their domestic duties; and the cradles remind us of the next generation of islanders. Having identified the various items and shown the life of the people to be reflected in them, the writer then suggests that the items "seem to exist as a natural link between the people and the world that is about them." These items reflect the personalities of their owners.

PARAGRAPH PRACTICE

Write a paragraph of your own, using J. M. Synge's paragraph as your model. Your paragraph could be a description of a person or a family that you know. How do the possessions of that person or that family reflect the personality of that individual or that family? If you choose to describe one person, you might wish to concentrate on the contents of that person's room. If you choose to describe the personality of a whole family, you might wish to describe the items in their living room. You also could take items from various rooms to describe either a person or a family. If you choose a family, be sure that the range of your examples reflects the different generations of that family. If you describe an individual, be sure you include a range of details so that your reader has a clear idea of the person's interests or activities.

When you have finished your paragraph, review what you have written. Have you used effective details—is each one a physical object that your reader can interpret? Is there a true range of examples so that your reader has a broad view of the individual or group you are describing?

ESSAY PRACTICE

The following outline will help you plan a complete essay of at least five paragraphs. The theme of your essay will be closely related to the selection from J. M. Synge's *The Aran Islands*.

The following sentence may serve as your thesis sentence, and will also be the main idea of your introductory paragraph:

¶ 1. I will never forget the time I found myself in a strange environment.

Each of the sentences below is the topic sentence for one of the paragraphs that you will write to develop your thesis.

You may use the suggested details to develop each paragraph, or you may supply details of your own.

¶ 2. My surroundings could best be described as . . .

[DETAILS: Describe the area, including any open land, the streets, the buildings, and any other outstanding physical features that you remember.]

¶ 3. The people around me were . . .

[DETAILS: Describe two or three typical residents or visitors you saw in this place. How did they differ from you in appearance and actions?]

¶ 4. My reaction to these new experiences was . . .

[DETAILS: Describe your immediate reactions; include any later thoughts you may have had about your experience.]

Be certain that you use transitions between paragraphs to make your writing flow smoothly. In addition, be sure that your conclusion gives your reader a clear signal that you have come to the end of your essay.

ESSAY TOPICS

1. Describe a situation in which you encountered a person from another culture, or a person who had values that were very different from your own. How did you respond to this other person? What did you learn from the encounter?
2. a. Imagine that you are in a very remote place. Describe this place as completely as you can.
   b. If you had the opportunity to spend some time on the Aran Islands and live as J. M. Synge lived, would you go? Why or why not?
3. When J. M. Synge describes the people who live on the island, he is careful to choose a central room (the kitchen) that not only reveals the atmosphere of the place, but also provides him with an opportunity to describe the local people who visit and talk in that central place.

   Choose a place that you know well and write a three-part description of it. You could, for example, choose a cafeteria, a library, or a public train or bus station. First, give sufficient physical details so that your reader will be able to see the place. Then add to your description by indicating the atmosphere of the place; this will help your reader *feel* what you are describing. Finally, describe the people who may be regularly seen in this place. Your essay will achieve greater interest if you are careful to include a variety of details and show a variety of people in the place you have chosen to describe.

🍂 George Orwell 🍂

George Orwell (1903–1950) was born in Bengal, India. After being educated in England, he returned to the Far East where he served on the Burmese police force until 1927. He then came back to Europe, lived for a year and a half in Paris, and in his own words was "writing novels and short stories which no one would publish." When Orwell's work did begin to appear, the books he was able to publish were based on his own experience. *Down and Out in Paris and London* appeared in 1933, and *Burmese Days* followed a year later.

In 1936 Orwell went to Spain to observe the Civil War that was raging there and this experience resulted in one of his most famous books, *Homage to Catalonia* (1938). Medically unfit for service in the British army when World War II began, Orwell turned to journalism for a living, and in 1943 he became the literary editor of the weekly *Tribune*. This provided him with a sense of freedom and security and he was able to spend more of his time writing novels. *Animal Farm* was published in 1945 and four years later his most famous novel, *1984*, appeared.

George Orwell was very socially conscious, and several of his books deal with social and political trends in modern society. Perhaps this is why the writer V. S. Pritchett called Orwell "the conscience of his generation."

There is yet another aspect to George Orwell's work, and this is illustrated by " 'The Moon under Water,' " an essay that originally appeared in the London *Evening Standard* on February 9, 1945. In the essay, Orwell gives us a picture of an ideal place where people can relax and enjoy each other's company. In this detailed description of a pub (derived from "public house," the British term for a bar and restaurant), Orwell draws a picture of society as we would like to see it, a society where people are at their ease. One critic has said that in his writings George Orwell "sought for the roots of the dying decencies." In " 'The Moon under Water' " Orwell gives us a detailed description of those decencies.

PREVIEWING THE WRITER

• Note all of the different qualities Orwell looks for in the perfect pub.

• Note that Orwell uses a certain sequence to take us through the different rooms of "The Moon under Water." What impression do we get of the pub because of the order the writer uses?

• Orwell is describing his ideal pub, but there are probably many other pubs that he would consider less than ideal.
Note at least five criticisms Orwell could make of those pubs
that would not meet his standards.

THE MOON UNDER WATER

MY FAVOURITE PUBLIC HOUSE, "The Moon under   1
Water", is only two minutes from a bus stop, but it is on a side-
street, and drunks and rowdies never seem to find their way
there, even on Saturday nights.

Its clientèle, though fairly large, consists mostly of "reg-   2
ulars" who occupy the same chair every evening and go there
for conversation as much as for the beer.

If you are asked why you favour a particular public house,   3
it would seem natural to put the beer first, but the thing that
most appeals to me about "The Moon under Water" is what
people call its "atmosphere".

To begin with, its whole architecture and fittings are un-   4
compromisingly Victorian. It has no glass-topped tables or other
modern miseries, and, on the other hand, no sham roof-beams,
ingle-nooks or plastic panels masquerading as oak. The grained
woodwork, the ornamental mirrors behind the bar, the cast-iron
fireplaces, the florid ceiling stained dark yellow by tobacco-
smoke, the stuffed bull's head over the mantelpiece—everything has the solid comfortable ugliness of the nineteenth century.

In winter there is generally a good fire burning in at least   5
two of the bars, and the Victorian lay-out of the place gives one
plenty of elbow-room. There are a public bar, a saloon bar, a
ladies' bar, a bottle-and-jug for those who are too bashful to
buy their supper beer publicly, and upstairs, a dining-room.

Games are only played in the public, so that in the other   6
bars you can walk about without constantly ducking to avoid
flying darts.

In "The Moon under Water" it is always quiet enough to   7
talk. The house possesses neither a radio nor a piano, and even
on Christmas Eve and such occasions the singing that happens
is of a decorous kind.

The barmaids know most of their customers by name, and   8

take a personal interest in everyone. They are all middle-aged women—two of them have their hair dyed in quite surprising shades—and they call everyone "dear", irrespective of age or sex. ("Dear", not "Ducky": pubs where the barmaid calls you "Ducky" always have a disagreeable raffish atmosphere.)

Unlike most pubs, "The Moon under Water" sells tobacco 9 as well as cigarettes, and it also sells aspirins and stamps, and is obliging about letting you use the telephone.

You cannot get dinner at "The Moon under Water", but 10 there is always the snack counter where you can get liver-sausage sandwiches, mussels (a speciality of the house), cheese, pickles and those large biscuits with caraway seeds in them which only seem to exist in public houses.

Upstairs, six days a week, you can get a good, solid lunch— 11 for example, a cut off the joint, two vegetables and boiled jam roll—for about three shillings.[1]

The special pleasure of this lunch is that you can have 12 draught stout with it. I doubt whether as many as ten per cent of London pubs serve draught stout, but "The Moon under Water" is one of them. It is a soft, creamy sort of stout, and it goes better in a pewter pot.

They are particular about their drinking vessels at "The 13 Moon under Water" and never, for example, make the mistake of serving a pint of beer in a handleless glass. Apart from glass and pewter mugs, they have some of those pleasant strawberry-pink china ones which are now seldom seen in London. China mugs went out about thirty years ago, because most people like their drink to be transparent, but in my opinion beer tastes better out of china.

The great surprise of "The Moon under Water" is its gar- 14 den. You go through a narrow passage leading out of the sa-loon, and find yourself in a fairly large garden with plane trees under which there are little green tables with iron chairs round them. Up at one end of the garden there are swings and a chute for the children.

On summer evenings there are family parties, and you sit 15 under the plane trees having beer or draught cider to the tune of delighted squeals from children going down the chute. The prams with the younger children are parked near the gate.

Many as are the virtues of "The Moon under Water" I 16 think that the garden is its best feature, because it allows whole

[1] About seventy-five cents.

families to go there instead of Mum having to stay at home and mind the baby while Dad goes out alone.

And though, strictly speaking, they are only allowed in the garden, the children tend to seep into the pub and even to fetch drinks for their parents. This, I believe, is against the law, but it is a law that deserves to be broken, for it is the puritanical nonsense of excluding children—and therefore to some extent, women—from pubs that has turned these places into mere boozing-shops instead of the family gathering-places that they ought to be. 17

"The Moon under Water" is my ideal of what a pub should be—at any rate, in the London area. (The qualities one expects of a country pub are slightly different.) 18

But now is the time to reveal something which the discerning and disillusioned reader will probably have guessed already. There is no such place as "The Moon under Water". 19

That is to say, there may well be a pub of that name, but I don't know of it, nor do I know of any pub with just that combination of qualities. 20

I know of pubs where the beer is good but you can't get meals, others where you can get meals but which are noisy and crowded, and others which are quiet but where the beer is generally sour. As for gardens, offhand I can only think of three London pubs that possess them. 21

But, to be fair, I do know of a few pubs that almost come up to "The Moon under Water". I have mentioned above ten qualities that the perfect pub should have, and I know one pub that has eight of them. Even there, however, there is no draught stout and no china mugs. 22

And if anyone knows of a pub that has draught stout, open fires, cheap meals, a garden, motherly barmaids and no radio, I should be glad to hear of it, even though its name were something as prosaic as "The Red Lion" or "The Railway Arms". 23

THE WRITER'S THEMES

1. In the first half of paragraph four, Orwell describes the features that "The Moon under Water" does not have, and in the rest of that paragraph he describes some of the features the pub does have.

List each negative feature that the writer mentions. Next to each of these features, supply the word or words Orwell uses to make that feature negative. List all of the positive points the writer makes. Next to each point give the word or words Orwell uses to make that feature positive.

2. Orwell describes the qualities of "The Moon under Water" in a certain order, ending with the garden, which the writer calls the pub's "best feature."
   a. To which feature or features does the writer devote most of his attention?
   b. Based on the order in which the pub's features have been presented, what conclusions can you come to about the personality of the writer?
3. At the conclusion of his essay, Orwell tells us that he has mentioned "ten qualities that the perfect pub should have . . ." Review the essay and list these ten qualities. Write a sentence of your own to describe each item on your list.

THE WRITER'S TECHNIQUE

In the fourth paragraph of "The Moon under Water", George Orwell gives us our first view of his ideal pub. Here is our introduction to "The Moon under Water":

> To begin with, its whole architecture and fittings are uncompromisingly Victorian. It has no glass-topped tables or other modern miseries, and, on the other hand, no sham roof-beams, inglenooks or plastic panels masquerading as oak. The grained woodwork, the ornamental mirrors behind the bar, the cast-iron fireplaces, the florid ceiling stained dark yellow by tobacco-smoke, the stuffed bull's head over the mantelpiece—everything has the solid comfortable ugliness of the nineteenth century.

Notice that in his first sentence, the writer provides us with a general impression of the pub by giving us an indication of the pub's quality: its "whole architecture and fittings are uncompromisingly Victorian." He then emphasizes this nineteenth-century Victorian quality by pointing out what the pub does *not* have; it has "no glass-topped tables," "no imitation roof-beams," and no "plastic panels" that pretend to be oak. Orwell then provides us with the details that do give "The Moon under

Water'' its old Victorian charm: the woodwork, the mirrors, the fireplaces, the fancy ceiling that is yellow with smoke, and the stuffed animal head over the mantel. All of these details give the pub ''the solid comfortable ugliness of the nineteenth century.''

PARAGRAPH PRACTICE

Write a paragraph of your own, describing the general impression of a place you know well. Use the above excerpt from the Orwell essay as your model. Your opening sentence should convey the ''whole'' impression of the place you are describing. Next, become more specific. Write one or two sentences describing what the place does not have. Then write at least three or four sentences that will show your reader what the place *does* have. Keep in mind that Orwell concluded his paragraph by telling us that all of the furnishings and other details in the pub made it ''solid'' and ''comfortable.'' Write a one-sentence conclusion to your own paragraph. Your sentence should summarize all of the qualities that make this place special for you.

For example, you might wish to describe a favorite restaurant or a sports area. You could also describe a classroom or a library that you found was an especially comfortable place for you to learn. If you choose a classroom, begin by helping the reader form an impression of the room. Is it completely modern, or is there an old-fashioned feeling about it? What does it *not* have that helps to give it this feeling? Specifically, what gives it its atmosphere? If your classroom is totally modern you could say that it is ''bright'' and ''efficient''; if it is not quite so up-to-date but you enjoy being in the room, you might wish to conclude that the atmosphere is ''quiet'' and ''restful.''

ESSAY PRACTICE

The following outline will help you plan a complete essay of at least five paragraphs. The theme of your essay will be closely related to George Orwell's ''The Moon under Water.''

The following sentence may serve as your thesis sentence, and will also be the main idea of your introductory paragraph:

¶ 1.   Each of us would like to have a place where we could enjoy a special atmosphere and interesting people.

Each of the sentences below is the topic sentence for one of the paragraphs that you will write to develop your thesis. You may use the suggested details to develop each paragraph, or you may supply details of your own.

¶ 2. My favorite place gives the general impression of . . .

[DETAILS: Begin by describing where this place is located; then describe its atmosphere, being careful that all of the details you use contribute to the overall impression of the place. *The place you are describing could be real or you could imitate Orwell's essay by creating an ideal place that exists only in your imagination.*]

¶ 3. Every part of this place is special to me.

[DETAILS: Take your reader through each part of your place. By the middle of your paragraph you should be describing the best feature of the place. Write at least three sentences to describe this best feature.]

¶ 4. The people who come here are . . .

[DETAILS: What kind of people are generally seen in this place? Is there a kind of person who especially enjoys coming here? Is there a type of person who would feel uncomfortable here?]

Be certain that you use transitions between paragraphs to make your writing flow smoothly. In addition, be sure that your conclusion gives your reader a clear signal that you have come to the end of your essay.

ESSAY TOPICS

1. Orwell describes his ideal pub as having "solid comfortable ugliness." Describe something you have enjoyed (it could be anything from an old coat to a broken-down chair) that everyone else thought was ugly, but which you found enjoyable and comfortable.
2. Describe at least two very different gathering places in your neighborhood, or in an area you know well. In each case describe the place and then describe the different types of people who are usually seen there.
3. Write a detailed description of your ideal gathering place. Plan your description by first making a list of at least five qualities you think are most important for this ideal place. Then put your list in order, ending with the most important item.

❧ *Konrad Lorenz* ❧

Konrad Lorenz is famous for his study of animals in their natural environment. His research has led to a greater understanding of human behavioral patterns. Lorenz was born in Vienna, Austria, in 1903 and received his M.D. degree from the University of Vienna in 1928; five years later he obtained his Ph.D. in zoology.

At the University of Vienna, Lorenz lectured in comparative anatomy and animal psychology; and during the 1940s and 1950s he taught psychology throughout Germany and Austria. Some scientists have criticized Lorenz as being too speculative, but he has firmly defended not only his findings but also his method.

Some of his published writings include *Man Meets Dog* and *King Solomon's Ring*. Perhaps his best-known work is *On Aggression*, in which Lorenz makes connections between animal and human aggression.

One critic has pointed out that Lorenz "integrates poetry and science by describing animal behavior with accuracy and beauty." The following essay shows the scientist Lorenz at his poetic best, as he brings us the results of his observations of a cat at play.

PREVIEWING THE WRITER

• Where does Lorenz emphasize that play is related to the serious business of living, including survival?

• According to the author, play can also be a learning process. What is the connection between playing and learning?

• At what points in the essay does the writer seem to make the closest connections between animal behavior and human behavior?

ON FELINE PLAY

THERE ARE CERTAIN things in nature in which beauty and utility, artistic and technical perfection, combine in some incomprehensible way: the web of a spider, the wing of a dragonfly, the superbly streamlined body of the porpoise and the movements of a cat. These last could not be lovelier even had they been designed by a preternaturally gifted dancer striving for choreographic grace, nor could they be more practical even under the tuition of that best of all coaches—the struggle for existence. And it is almost as though the animal were aware of the beauty of its movements, for it appears to delight in them and to perform them for the sake of their own perfection. This game, the game of movements, occupies a very special place in the life of this most elegant of all animals.

What "play" really is is one of the most difficult questions 2 in animal and human psychology. We know exactly what we mean when we say that a kitten, a puppy or a child is playing, but it is very difficult to give a real definition of this highly significant activity. All forms of play have the common quality that they are fundamentally different from "earnest"; at the same time, however, they show an unmistakable resemblance, indeed an imitation of a definite, earnest situation. This even holds good for the abstract games of grown men, certain definite, intellectual capacities and abilities finding expression in their poker or chess matches. In spite of these basic similarities, however, "play" is an enormously wide conception. It embraces activities as different as the stiff, hard-and-fast ceremonial of a baroque quadrille, and the carpentering efforts of a growing boy. It is play when a young rabbit runs and doubles back from sheer ebullience, although no predatory beast is after him, and it is play when a little boy pretends to be an engine-driver. The reader is probably beginning to fear that I am lapsing into an abstract lecture on the common properties of these human and animal activities, which entitle us to give them the same name. But I will return to the theme of the chapter heading: feline play. Perhaps some observations of a real case will give us some helpful clues for the elucidation of the problems of play.

A kitten is playing with its classical plaything, a ball of 3 wool. Unfailingly, it begins to paw at the object, first gently and enquiringly with outstretched forearm and inwardly flexed paw. Now with extended claws, it draws the ball toward itself, pushes it away again or jumps a few steps backward, crouching. It lies low, raises its head with tense expression, glaring at the plaything. Then its head drops so suddenly that you expect its chin to bump the floor. The hind feet perform peculiar, alternately treading and clawing movements as though the kitten were seeking a firm hold from which to spring. Suddenly it bounds in a great semicircle and lands on its toy with stiff forepaws pressed closely together. It will even bite it, if the game has reached a pitch of some intensity. Again it pushes the ball and this time it rolls under a cupboard which stands too close to the floor for the kitten to get underneath. With an elegant "prac-

tised" movement, it reaches with one arm into the space and
fishes its plaything out again. It is at once clear to anyone who
has ever watched a cat catching a mouse, that our kitten, which
we have reared apart from its mother, is performing all those
highly specialized movements which aid the cat in the hunting
of its most important prey—the mouse. In the wild state, this
constitutes its "daily bread."

If we now improve on our plaything by attaching a thread   4
to it and letting it dangle from above, the kitten will exhibit
entirely different prey-catching movements. Jumping high, it
grabs the prey with both paws at once, bringing them together
in a wide, sweeping movement from the sides. During this
movement, the paws appear abnormally large, for all the digits
with their extended claws are widely spread, and the dewclaws
are bent at right angles to the paw. This grasping movement,
which many kittens delightedly perform in play, is identical to
the last detail with the movement used by cats to grab a bird
just leaving the ground.

Another movement, often observed in the play of young   5
cats, is less easy to explain in its biological meaning, since its
practical application is soon seen. In a lightning movement of
upturned pads and claws the kitten reaches under the plaything
and throws it in a high arc over its own shoulder, to follow it
immediately with a jump. Or, particularly with larger play-
things, the kitten sits before the object, rears itself stiffly erect,
reaches underneath it with a paw from each side and throws it
back over its head in a steeper and higher semicircle. Frequently
the animal follows the flying object with its eyes and pursues it
with a high leap, landing where it fell. The practical purpose of
these two series of movements is the catching of fishes, the first
series for smaller, the second for larger ones.

Still more interesting and aesthetically beautiful are the   6
movements of kittens playing either together or with their
mother. Their biological meaning is less easily explained than
that of the prey-catching movements, since, when cats play together, instinctive movements, whose practical application ex-
tends to many different things, are performed in colorful confusion on one and the same object.

Behind the coalbox, a kitten sits watching her brother who   7
is seated in the middle of the kitchen floor unaware of this
scrutiny. Like a bloodthirsty tiger the watcher quivers with anticipation, whips his tail to and fro, and describes the move-

ments of head and tail which are performed also by adult cats. Its sudden spring belongs to the realm of an entirely different set of movements, designed not for preying but for the fight. Instead of leaping on its brother as on a prey—an action which may alternatively, of course, be performed—it assumes a threatening position while still galloping, arching its back and advancing broadside on. The assaulted kitten likewise humps its back and the two stand thus for some time, with ruffled hair and sideways bent tails. As far as I know, this never takes place between adult cats. Each of the two kittens behaves rather as though the other were a dog, but nevertheless their game goes on like a genuine tomcat fight. Clasping each other firmly with their forepaws, they turn wild somersaults over and over each other, at the same time moving their hind feet in a way that, in play with a human being, can prove extremely painful. Hugging its playmate in the iron grip of its forepaws, the kitten vigorously pushes both hind feet with unsheathed claws against it, repulsing it with a quick succession of kicks. In a genuine fight, these slitting, tearing blows are directed at the unprotected belly of an adversary where their action must be devastating. After their short boxing match the kittens release their hold on one another and now an exciting chase usually follows, in which another uncommonly graceful set of movements is seen. When the fleeing kitten sees the other getting very close, he suddenly turns a somersault that lands him, with a soft and absolutely silent movement, immediately underneath his pursuer. He digs his forepaws into its soft parts, scrabbling its face, at the same time, with his hind feet.

How do these movements of play differ from those of real earnest? In their form, even the most practised eye may fail to detect a difference, but nevertheless there is one. In these games, composed as they are of the movements of catching a prey, fighting a fellow cat and repelling a foe, serious injury is never done to the playmate acting one of these parts. The social inhibition against real biting or deep scratching is fully enforced during play, while, in a case of real earnestness, it is obliterated by the emotion evoking the particular series of movements. In serious situations, the animal is in a particular psychological state which brings with it the readiness for a particular way of behaving—and for this way only. It is typical of play that during it highly specific behavior is incited without the corresponding emotional state. The relationship of all play to play-acting lies in the fact that the player pretends to be obsessed with an emotion which he does not really feel. In play, many separate sets of movements, serving many different biological ends, can be performed in irregular sequence because the particular emotional state which would elicit any one of them in a real emergency is lacking. The movements of fighting are enacted without anger, those of flight without fear and those of preying without hunger or greed. It is not true that the emotions pertaining to the earnest situation are present in an attenuated form. In play they are altogether missing, and the game is broken off immediately should any one of them suddenly swell up in either of the animals concerned. The urge to play arises from a different source, more general in nature than the individual drives which, in an emergency, supply every one of the described movements with specific energy.

But this general urge to play, the desire to indulge in vigorous action, for the mere joy of the thing, is a remarkable phenomenon only occurring in the mentally highest of all living creatures. Bridges has described it aptly from the poet's point of view:

> *I too will something make*
> *And joy in the making;*
> *Although tomorrow it seem*
> *Like empty words of a dream*
> *Remembered on waking.*

Not without reason does the sight of young animals at play touch our hearts, not without reason does play seem to us an activity to be more highly rated mentally than the corresponding actions performed in earnest, with their serious and species-preserving functions. Play differs from serious action not only in a negative sense, but in another positive respect. Play, especially in young animals, always has in it something of discovery. Play is typical of the developing organism; it regresses in the finished animal. I have called play *Vorahmung* (pre-imitation), an expression invented by Karl Groos, to indicate that the playful equivalents of certain innate inherited movements occur in the life of an individual animal before their earnest application has begun. Groos attributes great educational value to play and contends that the different movements are perfected by frequent, playful repetition. We have good grounds for doubting this assertion in its general implication. Instinctive, inherited movements mature like a bodily organ—they require no practice for their consummation as many observers can prove, and, in fact, we are shown by the perfect grace of movement exhibited by a kitten playing at mousing or other games that the movements as such neither require nor are capable of improvement.

Nevertheless, the kitten does learn from his play. He learns, not how to catch the mouse, but what a mouse is. In the first tentative advancement of a paw, in the first modest, hesitating angling movements after the ball of wool, lies a question: Is this the object for which my dark senses long? Which I can stalk, hunt, catch and finally devour? The inherited "pattern" of prey, that is, the inherent mechanisms which elicit "instinctive" prey-concerning movements, are fairly simple and not very comprehensive. Everything that is small, rounded and soft, everything that moves quickly by gliding or rolling, and, above all, everything that flees, evokes in the cat automatically and without previous experience the beautiful, elegant and "cultivated" movements of mouse-catching. 10

THE WRITER'S THEMES

1. What is the writer's definition of play? To what extent may that definition be applied to human behavior?
2. To what extent do humans have the same need for play that animals so clearly exhibit?
3. How can play be a learning experience? What can both humans and animals learn from play?

THE WRITER'S TECHNIQUE

In paragraph three of his essay, Konrad Lorenz shows us a particular example of feline play, a kitten with a ball of wool. Here is a major section from that paragraph:

> A kitten is playing with its classical plaything, a ball of wool. Unfailingly, it begins to paw at the object, first gently and enquiringly with outstretched forearm and inwardly flexed paw. Now with extended claws, it draws the ball toward itself, pushes it away again or jumps a few steps backward, crouching. It lies

low, raises its head with tense expression, glaring at the play-thing. Then its head drops so suddenly that you expect its chin to bump the floor. The hind feet perform peculiar, alternately treading and clawing movements as though the kitten were seeking a firm hold from which to spring. Suddenly it bounds in a great semicircle and lands on its toy with stiff forepaws pressed closely together. It will even bite it, if the game has reached a pitch of some intensity. Again it pushes the ball and this time it rolls under a cupboard which stands too close to the floor for the kitten to get underneath. With an elegant "practised" movement, it reaches with one arm into the space and fishes its plaything out again.

In the first sentence the writer establishes his subject, the kitten, and what the kitten is doing; it is playing with a ball of wool. In the first part of the description Lorenz shows us what the animal does to the ball of wool: it paws it, then it draws the ball toward itself, and then it pushes it away again. After the writer shows the kitten crouching and lying low, he concentrates on the kitten's head, which it raises "with tense expression" as it now glares at the ball of wool. Next, the head drops and the hind feet "perform peculiar . . . movements" as the animal suddenly "bounds in a great semicircle and lands on its toy with stiff forepaws pressed closely together." Lorenz notes that if the kitten is excited, it will even bite the wool. Finally, the kitten is seen pushing the ball of wool under a cupboard. It then "reaches with one arm into the space" and retrieves its plaything once again.

PARAGRAPH PRACTICE

Write a paragraph of your own, using the section from the Konrad Lorenz paragraph as your model. You could describe a person playing a game, either alone or with someone else. Your description could also be of a person who is completely absorbed in some other activity. Your first sentence should announce who the person is, and what the game or activity is; then describe the person beginning the activity. Describe the attitude of the person's head and body and what the person is doing with his or her arms and legs. Then concentrate on the person's face and describe the emotion (or changing emotions) that are registered there. Finally, describe one particular movement or set of movements that seems particularly graceful or that seems to sum up the personality of this individual at this moment.

ESSAY PRACTICE

The following outline will help you plan a complete essay of at least five paragraphs. The theme of your essay will be closely related to the Konrad Lorenz essay.

The following sentence may serve as your thesis sentence, and will also be the main idea of your introductory paragraph:

¶ 1. I know a game I not only enjoy, but find so rewarding that I would recommend it to anyone.

Each of the sentences below is the topic sentence for one of the paragraphs that you will write to develop your thesis. You may use the suggested details to develop each paragraph, or you may supply details of your own.

¶ 2. I have a game that occupies a very special place in my life.

[DETAILS: Describe a game that you enjoy playing. How did you discover the game? How long have you played it?]

¶ 3. Whenever I play this game, I find I discover something very important.

[DETAILS: Describe what you discover about the game and describe what you discover about yourself as you play the game. Also describe what you learn about the strengths and weaknesses of others as you play the game.]

¶ 4. I would recommend this game to anyone because . . .

[DETAILS: Why do you think other people would enjoy this game? Is there a type of person who would not enjoy this game?]

Be certain that you use transitions between paragraphs to make your writing flow smoothly. In addition, be sure that your conclusion gives your reader a clear signal that you have come to the end of your essay.

ESSAY TOPICS

1. Lorenz states that adult games are related to ''definite, earnest'' situations. Choose one or more games adults like to

play. Describe how the game is played and the object of the game. How is the object of the game related to a serious objective in life?

2. Describe the game you enjoyed playing most when you were a child. What do you think your choice of game says about your personality?

3. What are some of the most important lessons about life that children can learn when they play?

Focus on Terms: Objective and Subjective

*O*bjective and *subjective* writing refers to the extent to which a writer's feelings enter into a piece of writing. If a writer is objective, his or her personality will not be obvious in the piece of writing. If the piece is a very subjective one, the subject will tend to be overwhelmed by the writer's own opinions. Business writing and other factual presentations such as instructional books and pamphlets should be objective, while personal essays and newspaper editorials are expected to be subjective. Most writing, however, is a combination of the objective and the subjective, an approach that helps the writer gain the reader's faith while the piece of writing itself becomes more interesting because of this combination.

For example, in the fourth paragraph of his essay, when George Orwell describes the decoration of his favorite pub, his writing is both objective and subjective. The writer provides us with the objective fact that "The Moon under Water" has no glass-topped tables, but when he adds that it does not have any "other modern miseries," we have a clear example of the writer's personal, subjective attitude toward the furnishings he is describing.

In his essay describing cats at play, Konrad Lorenz also combines the objective and subjective approaches to a subject. Much of his essay is made up of a series of objective descriptions of his observations, but the writer does become subjective at times, when, for example, he writes: "Still more interesting and aesthetically beautiful are the movements of kittens playing either together or with their mother." Here the writer is not strictly a scientist, objectively looking at animals; he also makes the very personal judgment that these animal movements are "interesting" and "beautiful."

In a similar way, J. M. Synge is an objective and subjective observer of life on the Aran Islands. For example, when the writer is describing the kitchen where he will spend most of his time, he points out that the room is "full of beauty and distinction." This is a very subjective judgment, but many of the details that follow are factual items. The dresses that the women wear are red (an objective fact), and they give "a glow of almost Eastern richness" (a subjective judgment). The writer is combining objective description with subjective judgment.

Because of the tone the writer uses, Sherry Sonnett's "Dreamy" gives the impression of an objective description of a woman's actions. But if we look closely at the writer's use of individual words, we see a subjective quality to the story: the sheets of her unmade bed (objective fact) are "dreary" and "dirty" (subjective judgment); the boarding house where she decides to stay has a furnished room with a kitchen (objective fact), but the narrator thinks that the boarding house itself is "declined genteel" (subjective judgment).

When you are careful to use well-chosen details, your writing will benefit from the sense of objectivity your writing will convey. When you add your own feelings or attitudes at appropriate points in your writing, you will not only avoid dullness but your facts will also become more colorful for your reader. An essay that shows a good combination of objective detail and subjective feeling is an interesting essay, one that the reader tends to remember with pleasure.

Student Essay ✺ ✺ *Benita Lehmann*

In the following essay, the writer observes the actions and emotions of a woman in the course of a single afternoon and evening. The woman looks for love and security, only to find that someone has violated the basic security of her world.

The essay is very reminiscent of Sherry Sonnett's "Dreamy" in that many of the details used to describe the external world also reveal an inner landscape.

• In this essay the writer is both objective and subjective, and at times seems to combine the two approaches. For example, at many points in her first paragraph the writer is primarily subjective, while in the third paragraph she is largely objective. As you read the essay, judge other sections as either primarily objective or subjective. At what points in the essay does the writer seem to combine the two approaches?

SOME ARE ALONE

SHE IS BACK EARLIER than she had planned. She bolts the door to her apartment and immediately turns on the television. She does not like to cook only for herself, so after work she had stopped at Danny's for pizza. When she had entered the pizzeria she found that her usual table was taken by a group of teenage toughs, tall skinny boys with bad skin, and their thin, sharp girlfriends. She had ordered two slices, plain, and a Nocal orange soda to go. There was a heavy drizzle and she could not stay outside so she had walked the five blocks to her apartment. She had hoped to be out for another two hours before having to return to her studio, only to shower, change, and leave again. Right now, though, there is nowhere else to go, so she stands in her modern, well-decorated, locked apartment and feels the chocolate colored walls press in on her. The television will help. She does not watch it, does not care to which station it is tuned, but she keeps it on. Its constant droning helps to keep the dreams away.

When she is alone she sits at the small round dining table 2 on a straight-back chair. She sits there now and peels the greasy brown bag from her pizza and unscrews the cap from her soda. She does not like to sit on the armchairs or on the sofa. She does not feel comfortable on the thick beige upholstery, nor does she feel comfortable walking on the equally light-colored rug. The bag her dinner came in had torn from the effect of oil and rain, and she feels lucky that the contents of the bag had not dropped onto that rug. The room is perfect and she feels uneasy destroying any of that perfection.

Night is coming, and soon she can go out again. She eats 3 the pizza without heating it. She drinks the Nocal from the bottle. The television throws liquid light on the walls. She brushes the crumbs of her meal onto the torn brown bag and gathers the bag and the empty bottle. She crosses the rug to the door, takes the keys from her purse, and leaves the apartment to throw her trash into the incinerator. When she comes back, it is dark enough to turn on a light.

She stands freshly showered, her hair and makeup per- 4 fect, in front of her open closet. Her business suits hang on one side of the closet with her tailored shirts. This is not important. On the other side of the closet hang her disco dresses and other sexy clothes. She is trying to choose something to wear from this side of the closet. These things are not important either. The bedclothes which sit in a small pile on the floor are not important, nor are the pairs of shoes that stand in lines in front of the closet like soldiers. But, if one were to search carefully behind the rows of shoes, one might find her heart. In the back

of the closet, behind the shoes, are two very ordinary quilts she
had made, by hand, when she was in high school, a pile of well
read *Alfred Hitchcock Mystery Magazines*, and a shoebox kept
closed with a rubber band in which she keeps five letters, a
frilly Valentine written by a beau she had had in college (these
are tied with a blue ribbon), a picture of her mother as a young
girl, a pressed rose which was the first she was ever given, a
lopsided picture of her father taken at a country fair, laughing,
and a button, once white but now faded to yellow, with a dove
and olive branch and the word "peace" written on it in blue.

5 She finally chooses a black wrap-dress from the many
things she owns. From below she picks a pair of strappy high
heeled sandals in silver. She dresses as quickly as possible and
goes into the night to look for someone, some man, never forgetting to lock the door.

6 She is going to the party of a rich client. When she reaches
the street she finds the drizzle has stopped. She hails a cab and
gives the driver the address. As they drive through the silent,
well lit streets her stomach aches and begins to growl. She feels
famished. She looks out the car window at the closed shops.
She dreams of meeting a man tonight. The taxi halts at her
destination. She pays her fare and gets out. It is raining.

7 She enters the townhouse. She gives her coat to a young
man at the door. She enters a room which is decorated with
heaps of roses. The sweet smell is overpowering and she feels
weak. The host comes to her, takes her hands in his, and kissing
her lightly on the cheek says, "So glad you could come, my
dear."

8 She moves through crowds making small talk. She feels
uncomfortably warm. There is an abstract painting on the wall.
She tells a man the painting reminds her of a Wheel of Chance.
She wants to talk on but she sees a fat gold band on his finger.
She drifts away.

9 She moves to the buffet. She is desperately hungry. Heat
waves, rising from the chafing dishes, distort the image in the
mirror over the table. She looks in that mirror at the painting
on the other wall. Beside that painting is a man, smiling. She
thinks he is watching her, looking at her more carefully than
anyone has ever looked at her before, as if he knows all the
days of her life she has waited for him and only him, that although she has known men before, she had never known anyone but him, and all her thoughts and all her imaginings are of

him. She feels he sees her more clearly than she has ever been seen. But she may be dreaming, for when she turns, no one is there.

She searches for him in the crowd. The room suddenly 10 seems smaller and she cannot escape the musky scent of roses. She sees the host and tells him she must leave. He takes her hands in his and kissing her lightly on the cheek says, "So glad you could come, my dear." She gets her coat and leaves.

The rain comes down so heavily the raindrops form but- 11 terflies when they hit the pavement. She goes to the corner to hail a cab, but there are none. A wind whips her coat open and soaks her dress. She finds shelter in an alcove outside a jewelry store. She looks in the window at empty, red shelves. She thinks that, in the morning, someone will fill this window with rows of matched sets of rings, and someone will buy them. She sees the reflection of an older woman in the window and is startled when she realizes it is her own face she sees.

She goes, once again, into the street. A bus is coming and 12 she takes it. She sits huddled in the seat near the driver, who does not speak to her. There is an old man sleeping in the back. Two women, raincoats over their brown uniforms, speak in loud and rapid Spanish. She reaches her stop and gets off. The storm has almost passed. As she walks, her shoes splatter mud against the backs of her legs. For a moment, she thinks she is being followed, but it is only the echo of her own footfall through the deserted streets.

She arrives at her apartment and takes the key from her 13 bag, but when she goes to unlock the door, it swings open by itself. She looks in. The blinds are down but not closed and a fierce blue light from the streetlamps below infiltrates the room. A sign across the street flashes red and hot and headlights from passing cars throw violent stripes on the walls and ceilings. A sudden wind rattles the blind and knocks another piece of glass to the sill where it shatters. Rain has been coming through the broken window. The naked floor is drenched. She turns on the overhead light. Her closet has been flung open. The contents of her shoebox are scattered about the room. She steps over a litter of magazines, into her apartment. Lovingly, she picks up each letter and picture. The pressed rose has been crushed, but she gathers each piece and puts it back in its place. The peace button is there. It has rolled over by the window. The quilts have been cast aside. They lie tangled on the floor.

Nothing important is missing. Everything else, her furni- 14
ture, her television, even the clothes, is gone. She goes outside
to call the police, never forgetting to lock the door.

Strategies for Writing

1. Is the writer's approach in this essay primarily objective or
    subjective? Support your choice by pointing out specific
    words, phrases, and sentences that prove your point.
2. Rewrite paragraph eleven of the essay, being as *subjective* as
    you can. Before you begin to write, carefully review the
    paragraph and choose those objective elements that you will
    either change or eliminate entirely from your rewrite.
3. At times, even the most objective report contains subjective
    elements. Look in your local newspaper for an objective
    account of a recent event. (Do not choose an editorial or
    personal opinion column.) Rewrite the story, making it a
    very subjective report.
4. At the end of the essay, the writer shows the woman having
    been robbed of her material goods, but still able to report
    that "nothing important" is missing. What is it that the
    woman has really lost in the course of the evening? The
    writer tells us that material things are not important to the
    woman, but what are the really important things to her?
    Why are these things important to her?

3

THE SEARCH FOR IDENTITY

WRITING SKILL: Narration

"You won't believe what happened to me . . ." How often have people said this to you, or how often have you found yourself saying this to others? The incident that followed might have been long or short, funny or sad, true or made up, but it was a story that was intended for an audience. That story was a narration.

Narration is one of the oldest and most universal forms of rhetoric because it is, basically, the telling of a story. Every culture uses narration to pass on its values and traditions, and there are a number of societies in the world today that still use the telling of stories to teach and preserve a whole body of information and tradition. All stories, from the story of Moses in the Bible to *Gone With the Wind*, are narratives, and it is a universal fact that everyone likes a good story. This is why a minister emphasizes the point of a sermon by telling an appropriate anecdote, and this is also why a comedian's classic opening has always been, "A funny thing happened to me . . ." Every audience pays attention to a person who tells a story.

We usually think of narration in terms of fiction—novels and short stories that are often meant to entertain us. For example, James Joyce's short story "Eveline" in this unit is a fictional narration[1] in which a sequence of events builds toward a definite climax. However, a narration can also be a part of a nonfiction writer's technique, and the following unit contains three examples of narration used in the writing of an essay. Maria L. Muñiz narrates the story of her life in an autobiographical newspaper essay; in a selection from *The Girl I Left Behind*, Jane O'Reilly looks to the future and uses narrative techniques to persuade us about her position on the role of women in society; and in "Once More to the Lake," E. B. White combines narration, description, and an analysis of the depths to which human awareness can take us.

When you write a narrative, one of the first questions you will have to face is that of point of view. Will you tell your narrative in the first person ("I"), or would it be better to describe the events through the eyes of one of the other people in the story? This is important, because the person you choose will be the "voice" that your reader will hear. The more appropriate your choice of person, the more convincing your narrative will sound. For example, in Joyce's "Eveline" the story is told from the point of view of an all-knowing (omniscient) narrator. Here is the opening paragraph of the story, as Joyce wrote it:

> She sat at the window watching the evening invade the avenue. Her head was leaned against the window curtains and in her nostrils was the odour of dusty cretonne. She was tired.

Joyce could have chosen to write his story in the first person. In that case, the opening paragraph might have read as follows:

> I sat at the window watching the afternoon shadows lengthen in the street outside. When I leaned my head against the curtains I could smell the dusty fabric. I was tired.

Read the following paragraph. After you have finished reading the complete story, ask yourself how your impressions would change if Joyce had chosen the father as narrator.

> I could see Eveline sitting at the window, looking out into the street. I wondered what she was thinking, as she leaned against the curtains. As the afternoon light struck her face, I could see she was tired.

---

[1] Another example of fictional narration is Hugh Garner's story, "A Trip For Mrs. Taylor," in Unit 12.

As Joyce writes the story, his use of an omniscient narrator allows us to overhear Eveline's thoughts, even though we never hear her voice directly. This approach allows the writer to enter into his character's thoughts, while at the same time he is able to give a seemingly objective account of her actions. The writer's use of this objective voice also contributes to the meaning of the story: because Eveline is not able to speak in her own words, we have an even greater feeling for her situation as a victim of circumstances.

Another important factor in the writing of a narrative is the choice of a time sequence. Writers often choose a chronological order, in which every incident is given in the order it actually happened. However, a writer can often make a narrative more intriguing by rearranging the order of events. For example, the narrative could begin with an incident that actually takes place later in the sequence of events. Having gained the reader's attention, the writer can then describe the events in the order in which they occurred.

One variation in the use of time sequence is the flashback technique, which gives a dramatic quality to the narrative. Joyce uses this in "Eveline." At one point in the story, Eveline thinks about her father and what his reaction will be when she leaves home:

> Her father was becoming old lately, she noticed; he would miss her. Sometimes he could be very nice. Not long before, when she had been laid up for a day, he had read her out a ghost story and made toast for her at the fire. Another day, when their mother was alive, they had all gone for a picnic to the Hill of Howth. She remembered her father putting on her mother's bonnet to make the children laugh.

Joyce begins the passage by having Eveline think about the present and then think of a time "not long before" when her father was kind to her. Finally, Eveline thinks of the more distant past when her mother was alive, and we realize that was the best time of all because the family had gone on a picnic together and her father had even made the children laugh. Each incident in the narrative emphasizes Eveline's present loneliness and desperation, as the writer uses the flashback technique to comment on his character's situation.

A narrative can also use the flash-forward technique, as Jane O'Reilly does in the selection from *The Girl I Left Behind*.

In the essay, the writer tries to imagine what her life might be like some twenty years in the future. She even constructs an imaginary conversation with an as yet unborn teenage granddaughter:

> She will begin, as we all do, with the personal. ''There is a boy I like,'' she will say, ''but he doesn't like me. How can I make him like me?''
> ''Why should you make him like you?'' I will answer. ''You are a wonderful person. Wouldn't it be more sensible to like a boy who knows that?''

This conversation has not yet taken place, but it is given an air of reality partly because the question and its answer are so universal, and partly because it relates so directly to one of the writer's main concerns in the essay, the relationship between men and women.

Narration is often used to report on reality. For example, in her autobiographical essay ''Back, But Not Home,'' Maria L. Muñiz tells the story of her separated family and shows us the pain of that separation by giving us a detailed picture from her own childhood:

> I remembered my mother's trembling voice and the sad look on her face whenever she spoke to her mother over the phone. I thought of the many letters and photographs that somehow were always lost in transit.

Telephones, letters, and photographs are all means of communication among people. Here, these details emphasize the communication that never took place among the members of her family: the telephone conversation must serve in place of a visit, the letters that are sent are never received, and the photographs are never seen by the people for whom they are intended. The writer has carefully chosen the details of her narrative in order to make the story of this part of her childhood more vivid and immediate for her readers.

In ''Once More to the Lake,'' E. B. White's narrative is combined with elements of description and comparison and contrast, along with an ongoing analysis of his own feelings as a human being coming to terms with the fact of his own aging. The various elements of the essay are expressed in the framework of a narrative that tells the universal story of a family on vacation. As in all narratives, the events in ''Once More to the

Lake'' grow out of each other and build to a definite climax. After we have finished the essay, we realize that E. B. White's narrative has a significance far beyond the story of a family's vacation.

A writer who tells a story must be conscious of the different elements of narration and how to use them. As you review your narrative, you should judge your choice of point of view and the quantity and quality of the details you have chosen. Have you provided enough incidents for a well-developed narrative, or will you have to include more? Do your details really support the points you wish to make in your narrative? Have you placed your incidents in an effective order?

Narration can be written simply to illustrate an idea or to lead us to a particular way of thinking. It can also provide us with new information on a subject. No matter what form it takes or what the writer's purpose was in writing it, a narrative is always a story with an effective and ordered structure.

❧ *James Joyce* ❧

James Joyce (1882–1941) was born and educated in Ireland, but left there in 1904 to work as a teacher and writer on the Continent. Ten years after he left Ireland his book of short stories, *Dubliners,* was published, to be followed in 1916 by his first novel, *A Portrait of the Artist as a Young Man.* In 1920 Joyce and his family moved from Zürich, Switzerland, to Paris, where his most famous book, *Ulysses,* was published. A few years after *Ulysses* appeared (in 1922), Joyce began work on his last project, a book that would be published in 1939 under the title of *Finnegans Wake.*

Because of his daring experiments in prose, Joyce is considered one of the most important writers of our century. His skillful use of significant detail to create a picture in depth is evident in the following selection from *Dubliners.* ''Eveline'' is the story of a young woman who has an important choice to make. As we watch her arrive at her decision, we realize that Joyce is giving us an unforgettable psychological portrait.

PREVIEWING THE WRITER

• What does the writer reveal about Eveline's past? Is her present situation any different?

• Note the different relationships Eveline has with the people around her. What do all of these relationships have in common? How do they affect Eveline's relationship with Frank?

• Note the different stages Eveline goes through as she tries to make her decision. Where in the story does her sense of determination seem strong? Where do we see that her resolve is weakening?

EVELINE

SHE SAT at the window watching the evening invade 1
the avenue. Her head was leaned against the window curtains and in her nostrils was the odour of dusty cretonne. She was tired.

Few people passed. The man out of the last house passed 2
on his way home; she heard his footsteps clacking along the concrete pavement and afterwards crunching on the cinder path before the new red houses. One time there used to be a field there in which they used to play every evening with other peo-

ple's children. Then a man from Belfast bought the field and built houses in it—not like their little brown houses but bright brick houses with shining roofs. The children of the avenue used to play together in that field—the Devines, the Waters, the Dunns, little Keogh the cripple, she and her brothers and sisters. Ernest, however, never played: he was too grown up. Her father used often to hunt them in out of the field with his blackthorn stick; but usually little Keogh used to keep *nix*[1] and call out when he saw her father coming. Still they seemed to have been rather happy then. Her father was not so bad then; and besides, her mother was alive. That was a long time ago; she and her brothers and sisters were all grown up; her mother was dead. Tizzie Dunn was dead, too, and the Waters had gone back to England. Everything changes. Now she was going to go away like the others, to leave her home.

Home! She looked round the room, reviewing all its familiar objects which she had dusted once a week for so many years, wondering where on earth all the dust came from. Perhaps she would never see again those familiar objects from which she had never dreamed of being divided. And yet during all those years she had never found out the name of the priest whose yellowing photograph hung on the wall above the broken harmonium beside the coloured print of the promises made to Blessed Margaret Mary Alacoque.[2] He had been a school friend of her father. Whenever he showed the photograph to a visitor her father used to pass it with a casual word: 3

—He is in Melbourne now. 4

She had consented to go away, to leave her home. Was that wise? She tried to weigh each side of the question. In her home anyway she had shelter and food; she had those whom she had known all her life about her. Of course she had to work hard both in the house and at business. What would they say of her in the Stores when they found out that she had run away with a fellow? Say she was a fool, perhaps; and her place would be filled up by advertisement. Miss Gavan would be glad. She had always had an edge on her, especially whenever there were people listening. 5

—Miss Hill, don't you see these ladies are waiting? 6

[1] To serve as a lookout.

[2] Margaret Mary Alacoque (1647–1690), a French nun who said that Christ had revealed to her a number of "promises" intended for people who practiced certain religious devotions.

—Look lively, Miss Hill, please.

She would not cry many tears at leaving the Stores.

But in her new home, in a distant unknown country, it would not be like that. Then she would be married—she, Eveline. People would treat her with respect then. She would not be treated as her mother had been. Even now, though she was over nineteen, she sometimes felt herself in danger of her father's violence. She knew it was that that had given her the palpitations. When they were growing up he had never gone for her, like he used to go for Harry and Ernest, because she was a girl; but latterly he had begun to threaten her and say what he would do to her only for her dead mother's sake. And now she had nobody to protect her. Ernest was dead and Harry, who was in the church decorating business, was nearly always down somewhere in the country. Besides, the invariable squabble for money on Saturday nights had begun to weary her unspeakably. She always gave her entire wages—seven shillings[3]— and Harry always sent up what he could but the trouble was to get any money from her father. He said she used to squander the money, that she had no head, that he wasn't going to give her his hard-earned money to throw about the streets, and much more, for he was usually fairly bad of a Saturday night. In the end he would give her the money and ask her had she any intention of buying Sunday's dinner. Then she had to rush out as quickly as she could and do her marketing, holding her black leather purse tightly in her hand as she elbowed her way through the crowds and returning home late under her load of provisions. She had hard work to keep the house together and to see that the two young children who had been left to her charge went to school regularly and got their meals regularly. It was hard work—a hard life—but now that she was about to leave it she did not find it a wholly undesirable life.

She was about to explore another life with Frank. Frank   10
was very kind, manly, open-hearted. She was to go away with him by the night-boat to be his wife and to live with him in Buenos Ayres where he had a home waiting for her. How well she remembered the first time she had seen him; he was lodging in a house on the main road where she used to visit. It seemed a few weeks ago. He was standing at the gate, his peaked cap pushed back on his head and his hair tumbled forward over a

[3] A rather low salary, equivalent in terms of today's buying power to around thirty-five or forty dollars a week.

face of bronze. Then they had come to know each other. He used to meet her outside the Stores every evening and see her home. He took her to see *The Bohemian Girl*[4] and she felt elated as she sat in an unaccustomed part of the theatre with him. He was awfully fond of music and sang a little. People knew that they were courting and, when he sang about the lass that loves a sailor, she always felt pleasantly confused. He used to call her Poppens out of fun. First of all it had been an excitement for her to have a fellow and then she had begun to like him. He had tales of distant countries. He had started as a deck boy at a pound a month on a ship of the Allan Line going out to Canada. He told her the names of the ships he had been on and the names of the different services. He had sailed through the Straits of Magellan and he told her stories of the terrible Patagonians. He had fallen on his feet in Buenos Ayres, he said, and had come over to the old country just for a holiday. Of course, her father had found out the affair and had forbidden her to have anything to say to him.

—I know these sailor chaps, he said.   11

One day he had quarrelled with Frank and after that she   12
had to meet her lover secretly.

The evening deepened in the avenue. The white of two   13
letters in her lap grew indistinct. One was to Harry; the other
was to her father. Ernest had been her favourite but she liked
Harry too. Her father was becoming old lately, she noticed; he
would miss her. Sometimes he could be very nice. Not long
before, when she had been laid up for a day, he had read her
out a ghost story and made toast for her at the fire. Another
day, when their mother was alive, they had all gone for a picnic
to the Hill of Howth. She remembered her father putting on
her mother's bonnet to make the children laugh.

Her time was running out but she continued to sit by the   14
window, leaning her head against the window curtain, inhaling
the odour of dusty cretonne. Down far in the avenue she could
hear a street organ playing. She knew the air. Strange that it
should come that very night to remind her of the promise to
her mother, her promise to keep the home together as long as
she could. She remembered the last night of her mother's illness; she was again in the close dark room at the other side of

[4] *The Bohemian Girl* was a very popular romantic Irish opera, first produced in 1843, that tells the story of a young girl, Arline, who is born into a
noble family but who is kidnapped and raised by wandering gypsies.

the hall and outside she heard a melancholy air of Italy. The organ-player had been ordered to go away and given sixpence. She remembered her father strutting back into the sickroom saying:

—Damned Italians! coming over here! 15

As she mused the pitiful vision of her mother's life laid its 16 spell on the very quick of her being—that life of commonplace sacrifices closing in final craziness. She trembled as she heard again her mother's voice saying constantly with foolish insistence:

—Derevaun Seraun! Derevaun Seraun![5] 17

She stood up in a sudden impulse of terror. Escape! She 18 must escape! Frank would save her. He would give her life, perhaps love, too. But she wanted to live. Why should she be unhappy? She had a right to happiness. Frank would take her in his arms, fold her in his arms. He would save her.

....

She stood among the swaying crowd in the station at the 19 North Wall. He held her hand and she knew that he was speaking to her, saying something about the passage over and over again. The station was full of soldiers with brown baggages. Through the wide doors of the sheds she caught a glimpse of the black mass of the boat, lying in beside the quay wall, with illumined portholes. She answered nothing. She felt her cheek pale and cold and, out of a maze of distress, she prayed to God to direct her, to show her what was her duty. The boat blew a long mournful whistle into the mist. If she went, to-morrow she would be on the sea with Frank, steaming towards Buenos Ayres. Their passage had been booked. Could she still draw back after all he had done for her? Her distress awoke a nausea in her body and she kept moving her lips in silent fervent prayer.

A bell clanged upon her heart. She felt him seize her hand: 20
—Come! 21

All the seas of the world tumbled about her heart. He was 22 drawing her into them: he would drown her. She gripped with both hands at the iron railing.

—Come! 23

No! No! No! It was impossible. Her hands clutched the 24 iron in frenzy. Amid the seas she sent a cry of anguish!

[5] These words are thought to be a confused version of Irish Gaelic words that mean ''The end of pleasure is pain.''

—Eveline! Evvy!   25

He rushed beyond the barrier and called to her to follow.   26
He was shouted at to go on but he still called to her. She set
her white face to him, passive, like a helpless animal. Her eyes
gave him no sign of love or farewell or recognition.

THE WRITER'S THEMES

1. In the course of the story, we obtain a fairly detailed portrait
   of Frank. What impression do you have of him? In what
   way(s) is Frank the opposite of Eveline'e father?
2. What are the most obvious traits of Eveline's personality?
   What are some of the more subtle revelations of that personality? In each case, what evidence does Joyce provide
   that allows us to make our judgment?
3. What impression do we have of the society in which Eveline
   lives? What kinds of details does Joyce give us that help us
   form a picture of this society?

THE WRITER'S TECHNIQUE

In the fifth paragraph of his story, James Joyce shows Eveline
thinking about her decision to leave her home, and the implications of that decision. Here is that paragraph:

> She had consented to go away, to leave her home. Was that wise?
> She tried to weigh each side of the question. In her home anyway
> she had shelter and food; she had those whom she had known
> all her life about her. Of course she had to work hard both in the
> house and at business. What would they say of her in the Stores
> when they found out that she had run away with a fellow? Say
> she was a fool, perhaps; and her place would be filled up by
> advertisement. Miss Gavan would be glad. She had always had
> an edge on her, especially whenever there were people listening.

Notice that Joyce begins the paragraph by restating Eveline's decision: she had "consented to go away, to leave her
home." He then introduces a note of doubt when he has her
think, "Was that wise?" The remainder of the paragraph consists of Eveline's thinking as she tries "to weigh each side of
the question." She begins by thinking of her home life and
reflects that there she at least had "shelter and food . . . [and]
those whom she had known all her life about her."

The next sentence ("Of course she had to work hard . . .") provides a transition from her home to her job, where she had to work just as hard. Eveline then wonders what they would "say of her in the Stores" when they discovered she had run away with Frank. She imagines that they would simply call her a fool and hire someone else to take her place. Eveline's fantasy concludes with her mention of Miss Gavan, a supervisor who had always enjoyed bossing her around, "especially whenever there were people listening."

In the paragraph, Joyce has Eveline ponder her decision to go away with Frank, and allows us to share her thinking about the two worlds she is leaving. While her home may have some positive aspects to it, Eveline's job at the Stores has co-workers who will call her a fool, an impersonal organization that will fill her place with an advertisement, and a supervisor who obviously enjoyed embarrassing her in front of customers. The facts of Eveline's situation seem clear enough, but at this point in the story her difficulty in making a decision remains.

PARAGRAPH PRACTICE

An important part of any decision is making an honest and thorough review of the disadvantages as well as the advantages of any solution to a problem. Write a paragraph in which you describe how you arrived at a decision you once made. In your paragraph, clearly indicate that there were two sides to the problem you faced, and describe at least two advantages and one disadvantage to your solution.

You could begin in the same way that Joyce began his paragraph. Some possible openings might be:

I wanted to switch majors. Was that wise? I tried to weigh both sides of the question.

I wanted to change my career plans. Was that wise? . . .

I wanted to share an apartment with someone else. Was that wise? . . .

Notice that Joyce's paragraph succeeds because he so clearly divides it into two sections, and because he uses a transitional sentence ("Of course she had to work hard both in the house and at business") to show this division. In addition, Joyce is careful to use very specific details to support each part of his paragraph. When he describes Eveline's home life, he indicates food, shelter, and "those whom she had known all her life." When he describes her life at the Stores, Joyce makes us see the quality of her life by including the probable reactions of her co-workers, the impersonal advertisement, and the equally cold Miss Gavan. Your own paragraph will succeed when you are careful to show the two parts of your thinking as you went about making your decision. The more specific your details are as you show these two sides of your thinking, the more convincing your paragraph will be.

ESSAY PRACTICE

The following outline will help you plan a complete essay of at least five paragraphs. The theme of your essay will be closely related to James Joyce's "Eveline."

The following sentence may serve as your thesis sentence, and will also be the main idea of your introductory paragraph:

¶ 1.   Not all children can live up to the expectations their families have for them.

Each of the sentences below is the topic sentence for one of the paragraphs that you will write to develop your thesis. You may use the suggested details to develop each paragraph, or you may supply details of your own.

¶ 2.   A family often makes demands on its different members.

[DETAILS: Describe some of the usual demands made by a family on each member of that family. You could develop this paragraph by providing specific examples of demands parents make on their children, the kinds of demands children make on their parents, and the kinds of demands brothers and sisters make on each other. You might also want to include demands made by grandparents or relatives on the different members of a family.]

¶ 3.   Sometimes these demands are unjust or put too much pressure on the individual.

[DETAILS: How can family members demand too much of each other? What are some of the unfair demands that a family can make on an individual? How can a person respond if too much pressure is placed on him or her?]

¶ 4.   The results of this kind of pressure can often be unfortunate, or even tragic.

[DETAILS: In this paragraph you should tell the story of a person you know who could not or would not live up to the demands made by his or her family. What happened to this person? What is the lesson of your story for all of us?]

Be certain that you use transitions between paragraphs to make your writing flow smoothly. In addition, be sure that your conclusion gives your reader a clear signal that you have come to the end of your essay.

ESSAY TOPICS

1. What was the most difficult decision you ever had to make? Write a description of how you handled this decision. Narrate the events that led up to the problem, how you approached the problem, and how you finally formulated your solution to the problem.

2. a. Eveline had made a promise to her mother "to keep the house together as long as she could." By the time the story opens and we find Eveline preparing to leave her home, has she already fulfilled her promise? Is she now truly free to go away with Frank and start a new life in another country?

   b. Describe a time you felt under a moral obligation, or an occasion when you made a promise that you felt you had to keep. Was it difficult for you to keep the promise? Were you ever tempted to break your promise?

3. a. Before she went to the dock to go on the boat with Frank, Eveline left two letters behind. One was to her brother Harry, and the other was to her father. Choose one of these letters and write what you believe were the contents of that letter. If you choose the letter to Harry, keep in mind the kinds of subjects Eveline would cover and the kinds of comments she would make to her brother. If you choose to write the letter she left for her father, keep in mind her relationship with him, as it is described in the story. In either case, use details from the story to provide details for your letter.

   b. All of us have written, or have wanted to write, letters to people, but often we cannot bring ourselves to mail those letters. In many cases we have not even written them. Write a letter to someone you have always wanted to write to, but never did. After you have finished your letter, ask yourself if you want to send it.

🌢 *Maria L. Muñiz* 🌢

Maria L. Muñiz was born in Cuba in 1958. She came to the United States with her family when she was five years old, and began her schooling in New York. In 1978 she graduated from New York University, receiving her B.A. degree in Journalism and English Literature *cum laude*.

Since 1978, Maria L. Muñiz has been an editor for Catalyst, a national nonprofit organization that works to expand family and career options for women in business and the professions. She has researched, edited, and written books published through Catalyst, among them *What to Do with the Rest of Your Life: The Catalyst Career Guide for Women in the '80s*, and *Marketing Yourself: The Catalyst Women's Guide to Successful Résumés and Interviews*. Maria Muñiz has also contributed to *Family Circle* and *Seventeen* magazines. She is currently manager of Special Projects for the Career and Family Center at Catalyst in New York City.

The following essay originally appeared in the *New York Times* on July 13, 1979.

PREVIEWING THE WRITER

• Note how the writer connects the world of international politics and her personal world. How are these worlds connected? To what extent does the writer not want those worlds to be connected?

• Note the difficulties the writer experienced as she grew up. Which of these experiences do you feel hurt her the most?

• Note what the writer feels she now understands about herself. What does she feel she has yet to understand in order for the picture of her life to be complete?

BACK, BUT NOT HOME

WITH ALL THE TALK about resuming diplomatic rela-   1
tions with Cuba, and with the increasing number of Cuban ex-
iles returning to visit friends and relatives, I am constantly being
asked, "Would you ever go back?" In turn, I have asked myself,
"Is there any reason for me to go?" I have had to think long
and hard before finding my answer. Yes.

I came to the United States with my parents when I was   2
almost five years old. We left behind grandparents, aunts, un-

cles and several cousins. I grew up in a very middle-class neighborhood in Brooklyn. With one exception, all my friends were Americans. Outside of my family, I do not know many Cubans. I often feel awkward visiting relatives in Miami because it is such a different world. The way of life in Cuban Miami seems very strange to me and I am accused of being too "Americanized." Yet, although I am now an American citizen, whenever anyone has asked me my nationality, I have always and unhesitatingly replied, "Cuban."

Outside American, inside Cuban. 3

I recently had a conversation with a man who generally 4
sympathizes with the Castro regime. We talked of Cuban politics and although the discussion was very casual, I felt an old anger welling inside. After 16 years of living an "American" life, I am still unable to view the revolution with detachment or objectivity. I cannot interpret its results in social, political or economic terms. Too many memories stand in my way.

And as I listened to this man talk of the Cuban situation, 5
I began to remember how as a little girl I would wake up crying because I had dreamed of my aunts and grandmothers and I missed them. I remembered my mother's trembling voice and the sad look on her face whenever she spoke to her mother over the phone. I thought of the many letters and photographs that somehow were always lost in transit. And as the conversation continued, I began to remember how difficult it often was to grow up Latina in an American world.

It meant going to kindergarten knowing little English. I'd 6
been in this country only a few months and although I understood a good deal of what was said to me, I could not express myself very well. On the first day of school I remember one little girl's saying to the teacher: "But how can we play with her? She's so stupid she can't even talk!" I felt so helpless because inside I was crying, "Don't you know I can understand everything you're saying?" But I did not have words for my thoughts and my inability to communicate terrified me.

As I grew a little older, Latina meant being automatically 7
relegated to the slowest reading classes in school. By now my English was fluent, but the teachers would always assume I was somewhat illiterate or slow. I recall one teacher's amazement at discovering I could read and write just as well as her American pupils. Her incredulity astounded me. As a child, I began to realize that Latina would always mean proving I was as good

as the others. As I grew older, it became a matter of pride to prove I was better than the others.

As an adult I have come to terms with these memories and they don't hurt as much. I don't look or sound very Cuban. I don't speak with an accent and my English is far better than my Spanish. I am beginning my career and look forward to the many possibilities ahead of me. 8

But a persistent little voice is constantly saying, "There's something missing. It's not enough." And this is why when I am now asked, "Do you want to go back?" I say "yes" with conviction. 9

I do not say to Cubans, "It is time to lay aside the hurt and forgive and forget." It is impossible to forget an event that has altered and scarred all our lives so profoundly. But I find I am beginning to care less and less about politics. And I am beginning to remember and care more about the child (and how many others like her) who left her grandma behind. I have to return to Cuba one day because I want to know that little girl better. 10

When I try to review my life during the past 16 years, I almost feel as if I've walked into a theater right in the middle of a movie. And I'm afraid I won't fully understand or enjoy the rest of the movie unless I can see and understand the beginning. And for me, the beginning is Cuba. I don't want to go "home" again; the life and home we all left behind are long gone. My home is here and I am happy. But I need to talk to my family still in Cuba. 11

Like all immigrants, my family and I have had to build a new life from almost nothing. It was often difficult, but I believe the struggle made us strong. Most of my memories are good ones. 12

But I want to preserve and renew my cultural heritage. I want to keep "la Cubana" within me alive. I want to return because the journey back will also mean a journey within. Only then will I see the missing piece. 13

THE WRITER'S THEMES

1. Trace the writer's growing awareness of the Cuban situation as it relates to herself. How is her awareness as an adult different from her awareness as a child?

2. Trace the writer's ability to communicate with other people. With whom does she have misunderstandings? With whom does she not even try to communicate? When does her inability to communicate with others teach her important lessons?
3. What does the writer hope to gain by returning to Cuba? What do you think she means when she says that ''the journey back will also mean a journey within''?

THE WRITER'S TECHNIQUE

In paragraph five of her essay, Maria L. Muñiz indicates ''how difficult it often was to grow up Latina in an American world.'' In paragraph six she explains what she means:

> It meant going to kindergarten knowing little English. I'd been in this country only a few months and although I understood a good deal of what was said to me, I could not express myself very well. On the first day of school I remember one little girl's saying to the teacher: ''But how can we play with her? She's so stupid she can't even talk!'' I felt so helpless because inside I was crying, ''Don't you know I can understand everything you're saying?'' But I did not have words for my thoughts and my inability to communicate terrified me.

Notice that in her opening sentence the writer indicates the period of her life that she is writing about (she was in kindergarten), and she indicates a major problem she had at that time—she knew ''little English.'' She then explains this problem a little further: she had been in America ''only a few months'' and even though her comprehension was good, she could not express herself very well. The writer now gives us a specific example of her difficulty by quoting a cruel remark made by one of her schoolmates. The writer felt ''helpless'' when she heard the remark because she understood what was being said but could not react to it openly. She concludes by observing that, at the time, she ''did not have words'' for her thoughts, and her ''inability to communciate'' terrified her. She emphasizes this isolation by letting us hear the classmate's cruel remark while she had to remain silent. The fact that Maria Muñiz cannot express her thoughts serves to increase her sense of helplessness.

PARAGRAPH PRACTICE

Write a paragraph of your own, using the Maria L. Muñiz paragraph as your model. You could write about either a pleasant or an unpleasant experience that you once had. Begin your paragraph by identifying this particular point in your life. If you were in school, note the grade or semester you were in; if you were at work, point out how long you had been at that job. Next, describe your experience. Be sure to provide at least one specific example of an action or a remark that you feel illustrates the positive or negative quality of the experience. What did someone else say or do that makes the incident especially memorable for you? Then describe your reaction to this incident or remark. Finally, come to a one-sentence conclusion about your experience.

Your paragraph will have added strength and a good sense of variety if you carefully combine, as Maria L. Muñiz does, the external events of the incident and your own internal reactions to those events.

ESSAY PRACTICE

The following outline will help you plan a complete essay of at least five paragraphs. The theme of your essay will be closely related to the Maria L. Muñiz essay.

The following sentence may serve as your thesis sentence, and will also be the main idea of your introductory paragraph:

¶ 1.   Our perceptions of people, even those closest to us, often change as we grow up.

Each of the sentences below is the topic sentence for one of the paragraphs that you will write to develop your thesis. You may use the suggested details to develop each paragraph, or you may supply details of your own.

¶ 2.   When I was a child, there was one person close to me who I thought was . . .

[DETAILS: Narrate your earliest memories of this person. Be sure to establish how you perceived him or her. For example, was this person an overwhelming figure to you, one who perhaps inspired a mixture of fear and fascination?]

¶ 3.   As I grew older, I began to see that my perceptions were
not accurate.

[DETAILS: When did your perception of this person change? Narrate the details of the moment or incident which you remember
as the turning point in your attitude toward this person.]

¶ 4.   Now that I am grown up, I have a much better understanding of this person.

[DETAILS: What is your mature judgment of this person? What is
your present relationship with this person? Have you ever told
him or her about your different attitudes?]

Be certain that you use transitions between paragraphs to
make your writing flow smoothly. In addition, be sure that your
conclusion gives your reader a clear signal that you have come
to the end of your essay.

ESSAY TOPICS

1. a.   There is a great deal of current interest in tracing one's
own family roots. What benefits are there for a person
who researches his or her family history? Do you believe
people do this kind of research primarily to find out
about their ancestors or to find out about themselves?
    b.   Write a narrative in which you describe someone in your
own family. The person could be a popular or a notorious member of the family, or the person could be
special only to you. What is it about this family member's personality that makes you want to describe him
or her?

2.   Writing of the struggles she and her family had to go through
as immigrants to this country, Maria L. Muñiz points out
that she believes "the struggle made us strong."
    a.   To what extent does struggle make a person strong? Is
there a point at which struggle has no further value for
a person?
    b.   Narrate the story of someone you know who endured
a great deal of struggle. Did the struggle make the person stronger, or did it have the opposite effect?

3. a.   Narrate, as fully as you can, the story of your family's
arrival in this country. Why did those members of your

family decide to come to America? What difficulties did they face when they came here?

b. Tell the story of your family's move to where you now live. Why did your family decide to move? What difficulties did the family encounter in the process of making this move?

◂፮ E. B. White ፮◂

E. B. White has been described as the finest essayist in the United States. He was born in Mount Vernon, New York, in 1899 and received his B.A. from Cornell University in 1921. For the next two years he was a reporter for the Seattle *Times.* Later, back in New York, he worked in an advertising agency.

E. B. White began his long association with the *New Yorker* magazine in 1926 and for many years wrote the editorials in the "Talk of the Town" section. During the late 1930s and early 1940s he also contributed to *Harper's* magazine.

In addition to his numerous essays, E. B. White is well known for his children's books, including *Charlotte's Web* and *Stuart Little.* He has also revised and arranged for publication *The Elements of Style,* a guide for writers written by William Strunk, one of E. B. White's professors at Cornell. Today in its revised form it is widely used by college students as a useful guide for their own writing.

One critic has commented on E. B. White's writing in this way: "He says wise things gracefully . . . His style is crisp and tender, and incomparably his own." "Once More to the Lake" is E. B. White at his best. The essay is autobiographical and was written in August 1941.

PREVIEWING THE WRITER

• Note the writer's desire, throughout the essay, to control change of all kinds.

• Note the writer's comparisons of the past with the present. Which time period does the writer seem to prefer?

• Note how the writer connects himself with the different generations of his family. When is he reminded of his father? When does he make connections between himself and his own son?

ONCE MORE TO THE LAKE

ONE SUMMER, along about 1904, my father rented a   1
camp on a lake in Maine and took us all there for the month of August. We all got ringworm from some kittens and had to rub Pond's Extract on our arms and legs night and morning, and my father rolled over in a canoe with all his clothes on; but

outside of that the vacation was a success and from then on none of us ever thought there was any place in the world like that lake in Maine. We returned summer after summer—always on August 1 for one month. I have since become a salt-water man, but sometimes in summer there are days when the restlessness of the tides and the fearful cold of the sea water and the incessant wind that blows across the afternoon and into the evening make me wish for the placidity of a lake in the woods. A few weeks ago this feeling got so strong I bought myself a couple of bass hooks and a spinner and returned to the lake where we used to go, for a week's fishing and to revisit old haunts.

I took along my son, who had never had any fresh water   2 up his nose and who had seen lily pads only from train windows. On the journey over to the lake I began to wonder what it would be like. I wondered how time would have marred this unique, this holy spot—the coves and streams, the hills that the sun set behind, the camps and the paths behind the camps. I was sure that the tarred road would have found it out, and I wondered in what other ways it would be desolated. It is strange how much you can remember about places like that once you allow your mind to return into the grooves that lead back. You remember one thing, and that suddenly reminds you of another thing. I guess I remembered clearest of all the early mornings, when the lake was cool and motionless, remembered how the bedroom smelled of the lumber it was made of and of the wet woods whose scent entered through the screen. The partitions in the camp were thin and did not extend clear to the top of the rooms, and as I was always the first up I would dress softly so as not to wake the others, and sneak out into the sweet outdoors and start out in the canoe, keeping close along the shore in the long shadows of the pines. I remembered being very careful never to rub my paddle against the gunwale for fear of disturbing the stillness of the cathedral.

The lake had never been what you would call a wild lake.   3 There were cottages sprinkled around the shores, and it was in farming country although the shores of the lake were quite heavily wooded. Some of the cottages were owned by nearby farmers, and you would live at the shore and eat your meals at the farmhouse. That's what our family did. But although it wasn't wild, it was a fairly large and undisturbed lake and there were places in it that, to a child at least, seemed infinitely remote and primeval.

I was right about the tar: it led to within half a mile of the 4
shore. But when I got back there, with my boy, and we settled
into a camp near a farmhouse and into the kind of summertime
I had known, I could tell that it was going to be pretty much
the same as it had been before—I knew it, lying in bed the first
morning, smelling the bedroom and hearing the boy sneak quietly out and go off along the shore in a boat. I began to sustain
the illusion that he was I, and therefore, by simple transposi-
tion, that I was my father. This sensation persisted, kept crop-
ping up all the time we were there. It was not an entirely new
feeling, but in this setting it grew much stronger. I seemed to
be living a dual existence. I would be in the middle of some
simple act, I would be picking up a bait box or laying down a
table fork, or I would be saying something, and suddenly it
would be not I but my father who was saying the words or
making the gesture. It gave me a creepy sensation.

We went fishing the first morning. I felt the same damp 5
moss covering the worms in the bait can, and saw the dragonfly
alight on the tip of my rod as it hovered a few inches from the
surface of the water. It was the arrival of this fly that convinced
me beyond any doubt that everything was as it always had
been, that the years were a mirage and that there had been no
years. The small waves were the same, chucking the rowboat
under the chin as we fished at anchor, and the boat was the
same boat, the same color green and the ribs broken in the same
places, and under the floorboards the same fresh-water leavings
and débris—the dead helgramite, the wisps of moss, the rusty
discarded fishhook, the dried blood from yesterday's catch. We
stared silently at the tips of our rods, at the dragonflies that
came and went. I lowered the tip of mine into the water, ten-
tatively, pensively dislodging the fly, which darted two feet
away, poised, darted two feet back, and came to rest again a
little farther up the rod. There had been no years between the
ducking of this dragonfly and the other one—the one that was
part of memory. I looked at the boy, who was silently watching
his fly, and it was my hands that held his rod, my eyes watching. I felt dizzy and didn't know which rod I was at the end of.

We caught two bass, hauling them in briskly as though 6
they were mackerel, pulling them over the side of the boat in a
businesslike manner without any landing net, and stunning
them with a blow on the back of the head. When we got back
for a swim before lunch, the lake was exactly where we had left
it, the same number of inches from the dock, and there was

only the merest suggestion of a breeze. This seemed an utterly enchanted sea, this lake you could leave to its own devices for a few hours and come back to, and find that it had not stirred, this constant and trustworthy body of water. In the shallows, the dark, water-soaked sticks and twigs, smooth and old, were undulating in clusters on the bottom against the clean ribbed sand, and the track of the mussel was plain. A school of minnows swam by, each minnow with its small individual shadow, doubling the attendance, so clear and sharp in the sunlight. Some of the other campers were in swimming, along the shore, one of them with a cake of soap, and the water felt thin and clear and unsubstantial. Over the years there had been this person with the cake of soap, this cultist, and here he was. There had been no years.

Up to the farmhouse to dinner through the teeming, dusty   7 field, the road under our sneakers was only a two-track road. The middle track was missing, the one with the marks of the hooves and the splotches of dried, flaky manure. There had always been three tracks to choose from in choosing which track to walk in; now the choice was narrowed down to two. For a moment I missed terribly the middle alternative. But the way led past the tennis court, and something about the way it lay there in the sun reassured me; the tape had loosened along the backline, the alleys were green with plantains and other weeds, and the net (installed in June and removed in September) sagged in the dry noon, and the whole place steamed with midday heat and hunger and emptiness. There was a choice of pie for dessert, and one was blueberry and one was apple, and the waitresses were the same country girls, there having been no passage of time, only the illusion of it as in a dropped curtain—the waitresses were still fifteen; their hair had been washed, that was the only difference—they had been to the movies and seen the pretty girls with the clean hair.

Summertime, oh, summertime, pattern of life indelible,   8 the fade-proof lake, the woods unshatterable, the pasture with the sweetfern and the juniper forever and ever, summer without end; this was the background, and the life along the shore was the design, the cottages with their innocent and tranquil design, their tiny docks with the flagpole and the American flag floating against the white clouds in the blue sky, the little paths over the roots of the trees leading from camp to camp and the paths leading back to the outhouses and the can of lime for sprinkling, and at the souvenir counters at the store the miniature birch-bark canoes and the postcards that showed things looking a little better than they looked. This was the American family at play, escaping the city heat, wondering whether the newcomers in the camp at the head of the cove were "common" or "nice," wondering whether it was true that the people who drove up for Sunday dinner at the farmhouse were turned away because there wasn't enough chicken.

It seemed to me, as I kept remembering all this, that those times and those summers had been infinitely precious and worth saving. There had been jollity and peace and goodness. The arriving (at the beginning of August) had been so big a business in itself, at the railway station the farm wagon drawn up, the first smell of the pine-laden air, the first glimpse of the smiling farmer, and the great importance of the trunks and your father's enormous authority in such matters, and the feel of the wagon under you for the long ten-mile haul, and at the top of the last long hill catching the first view of the lake after eleven months of not seeing this cherished body of water. The shouts and cries of the other campers when they saw you, and the trunks to be unpacked, to give up their rich burden. (Arriving was less exciting nowadays, when you sneaked up in your car and parked it under a tree near the camp and took out the bags and in five minutes it was all over, no fuss, no loud wonderful fuss about trunks.)

Peace and goodness and jollity. The only thing that was wrong now, really, was the sound of the place, an unfamiliar nervous sound of the outboard motors. This was the note that jarred, the one thing that would sometimes break the illusion and set the years moving. In those other summertimes all motors were inboard; and when they were at a little distance, the noise they made was a sedative, an ingredient of summer sleep. They were one-cylinder and two-cylinder engines, and some were make-and-break and some were jump-spark, but they all made a sleepy sound across the lake. The one-lungers throbbed and fluttered, and the twin-cylinder ones purred and purred, and that was a quiet sound, too. But now the campers all had outboards. In the daytime, in the hot mornings, these motors made a petulant, irritable sound; at night, in the still evening when the afterglow lit the water, they whined about one's ears like mosquitoes. My boy loved our rented outboard, and his great desire was to achieve single-handed mastery over it, and authority, and he soon learned the trick of choking it a little (but not too much), and the adjustment of the needle valve.

Watching him I would remember the things you could do with the old one-cylinder engine with the heavy flywheel, how you could have it eating out of your hand if you got really close to it spiritually. Motorboats in those days didn't have clutches, and you would make a landing by shutting off the motor at the proper time and coasting in with a dead rudder. But there was a way of reversing them, if you learned the trick, by cutting the switch and putting it on again exactly on the final dying revolution of the flywheel, so that it would kick back against compression and begin reversing. Approaching a dock in a strong following breeze, it was difficult to slow up sufficiently by the ordinary coasting method, and if a boy felt he had complete mastery over his motor, he was tempted to keep it running beyond its time and then reverse it a few feet from the dock. It took a cool nerve, because if you threw the switch a twentieth of a second too soon you would catch the flywheel when it still had speed enough to go up past center, and the boat would leap ahead, charging bull-fashion at the dock.

We had a good week at the camp. The bass were biting 11 well and the sun shone endlessly, day after day. We would be tired at night and lie down in the accumulated heat of the little bedrooms after the long hot day and the breeze would stir almost imperceptibly outside and the smell of the swamp drift in through the rusty screens. Sleep would come easily and in the morning the red squirrel would be on the roof, tapping out his gay routine. I kept remembering everything, lying in bed in the mornings—the small steamboat that had a long rounded stern like the lip of a Ubangi, and how quietly she ran on the moonlight sails, when the older boys played their mandolins and the girls sang and we ate doughnuts dipped in sugar, and how sweet the music was on the water in the shining night, and what it had felt like to think about girls then. After breakfast we would go up to the store and the things were in the same place—the minnows in a bottle, the plugs and spinners disarranged and pawed over by the youngsters from the boys' camp, the Fig Newtons and the Beeman's gum. Outside, the road was tarred and cars stood in front of the store. Inside, all was just as it had always been, except there was more Coca-Cola and not so much Moxie and root beer and birch beer and sarsaparilla. We would walk out with the bottle of pop apiece and sometimes the pop would backfire up our noses and hurt. We explored the streams, quietly, where the turtles slid off the sunny logs and dug their way into the soft bottom; and we lay on the town wharf and fed worms to the tame bass. Everywhere we went I had trouble making out which was I, the one walking at my side, the one walking in my pants.

One afternoon while we were there at that lake a thunderstorm came up. It was like the revival of an old melodrama that I had seen long ago with childish awe. The second-act climax of the drama of the electrical disturbance over a lake in America had not changed in any important respect. This was the big scene, still the big scene. The whole thing was so familiar, the first feeling of oppression and heat and a general air around camp of not wanting to go very far away. In mid-afternoon (it was all the same) a curious darkening of the sky, and a lull in everything that had made life tick; and then the way the boats suddenly swung the other way at their moorings with the coming of a breeze out of the new quarter, and the premonitory rumble. Then the kettle drum, then the snare, then the bass drum and cymbals, then crackling light against the dark, and the gods grinning and licking their chops in the hills. Afterward the calm, the rain steadily rustling in the calm lake, the return of light and hope and spirits, and the campers running out in joy and relief to go swimming in the rain, their bright cries perpetuating the deathless joke about how they were getting simply drenched, and the children screaming with delight at the new sensation of bathing in the rain, and the joke about getting drenched linking the generations in a strong indestructible chain. And the comedian who waded in carrying an umbrella. 12

When the others went swimming, my son said he was going in, too. He pulled his dripping trunks from the line where they had hung all through the shower and wrung them out. Languidly, and with no thought of going in, I watched him, his hard little body, skinny and bare, saw him wince slightly as he pulled up around his vitals the small, soggy, icy garment. As he buckled the swollen belt, suddenly my groin felt the chill of death. 13

THE WRITER'S THEMES

1. Throughout the essay, E. B. White tries to deny the changes that have taken place at his favorite lake. Where do we first see a weakening in this denial of change? Specify the other

sections in the essay where this denial of change is also evident.

2. What seems to be the nature of the writer's relationship with his son? What is the writer's attitude toward the other people at the lake?

3. Discuss the presence of nature in the essay. Is nature seen as a positive or negative force? Trace the different faces of nature that are seen throughout the essay.

THE WRITER'S TECHNIQUE

In paragraph eight of his essay, E. B. White gives us a detailed picture of a typical American vacation. Here is the paragraph:

> Summertime, oh, summertime, pattern of life indelible, the fade-proof lake, the woods unshatterable, the pasture with the sweet-fern and the juniper forever and ever, summer without end; this was the background, and the life along the shore was the design, the cottages with their innocent and tranquil design, their tiny docks with the flagpole and the American flag floating against the white clouds in the blue sky, the little paths over the roots of the trees leading from camp to camp and the paths leading back to the outhouses and the can of lime for sprinkling, and at the souvenir counters at the store the miniature birch-bark canoes and the postcards that showed things looking a little better than they looked. This was the American family at play, escaping the city heat, wondering whether the newcomers in the camp at the head of the cove were ''common'' or ''nice,'' wondering whether it was true that the people who drove up for Sunday dinner at the farmhouse were turned away because there wasn't enough chicken.

Notice that the writer first establishes the time of year (''Summertime, oh, summertime'') and then, every example he gives of that season denies the passage of time. The lake cannot fade, the silence of the woods cannot be shattered, and the pasture has its sweetfern and juniper ''forever and ever.'' It is ''summer without end.'' Having dealt with time, White now gives examples of ''life along the shore,'' with its tranquil cottages, the docks, the American flag, the different paths, and the souvenir counter. The final part of the picture is the people, ''the American family at play.'' They are from the city; they wonder about their vacation neighbors, and they are concerned with such things as their daily meals.

Notice that, in a single paragraph, the writer establishes the time of year, gives his examples to prove that time really stands still at this lake in Maine, and sketches in details of the physical location. He also indicates the kinds of people who are vacationing there.

PARAGRAPH PRACTICE

Write a paragraph of your own, using the E. B. White paragraph as your model. Follow the writer's example by first establishing the time and then supply details that will help the reader see the place you are describing. Next, describe the people who are in that place. You could describe a summer vacation, or you could choose another time of year and a very different setting. For example, if you wanted to describe Christmas in the city, the three parts of your paragraph could be organized as follows:

It was December, the month when . . .

The city seems charming at this time because . . .

Everywhere I look, the people are . . .

At each stage in the development of your paragraph, be sure to give specific examples of time, place, and action. Write at least two sentences that will establish the time of year; write at least four sentences in which you describe the place; and write at least three sentences in which you show specific examples of what the people are doing in this place at this time of year. The more details and examples you provide, the more complete your paragraph will be and the more you will help your reader visualize the scene you are describing.

ESSAY PRACTICE

The following outline will help you plan a complete essay of at least five paragraphs. The theme of your essay will be closely related to E. B. White's "Once More to the Lake."

The following sentence may serve as your thesis sentence, and will also be the main idea of your introductory paragraph:

¶ 1. Often, when we return to a place we used to know, not only has the place changed but our perception of it has also changed.

Each of the sentences below is the topic sentence for one of the paragraphs that you will write to develop your thesis. You may use the suggested details to develop each paragraph, or you may supply details of your own.

¶ 2. I decided to visit a place I used to know.

[DETAILS: Why did you want to revisit this place? What meaning did the place once have for you?]

¶ 3. Now the place seemed to be . . .

[DETAILS: Describe in detail what the place actually looked like when you returned to it.]

¶ 4. After my visit, I realized that . . .

[DETAILS: What were your thoughts after your visit? How had time changed your perception of the place?]

Be certain that you use transitions between paragraphs to make your writing flow smoothly. In addition, be sure that your conclusion gives your reader a clear signal that you have come to the end of your essay.

ESSAY TOPICS

1. A parent and child often share special times together. Sometimes this can be a single, unique experience or it can be a series of events that remain in the memory. Use examples from your own experience to describe periods in your life when you shared important experiences with one or both of your parents. If you are a parent, use your experience(s) with your own child to provide examples for your answer. What did you do together that was so special? Why does the experience remain in your mind?

2. When you have known a place for some time, you begin to have a sense of nostalgia about it. Describe a place you knew well as a child. Why does it have a special meaning for you? Provide as many details as you can, so that your reader can share some of your special feelings.

3. E. B. White regrets the paved roads and outboard motors that mar the peace of his lake in Maine. Describe a place you know that once had a good atmosphere for you but which, with time and so-called "improvements," has changed. When did you first notice the changes? What is your feeling about the place now?

◄§ *Jane O'Reilly* §►

Jane O'Reilly is a journalist, essayist, and social critic. She was born and raised in St. Louis and graduated from Radcliffe College. Since 1960 she has regularly published articles in such periodicals as the *New Republic*, *Time*, and *New York* magazine. In 1975 Jane O'Reilly worked in Washington, D.C., as a guest columnist for the *Washington Star*. Her articles have also appeared in the *New York Times Book Review* and *Viva* magazine.

Twice married and divorced, Jane O'Reilly has been a single parent since 1967. She now lives with her son in New York City and in Vermont.

In the following selection, taken from her book *The Girl I Left Behind*, the writer imagines what her life and the lives of her child and grandchild might be like twenty years from now.

PREVIEWING THE WRITER

• According to the writer, what are the benefits of growing older? What does the writer see as the eventual fate of most women?

• Note the writer's analysis of women's current problems in society. What difficulties remain, despite the changes brought about by the women's movement?

• Note how the writer imagines her grandchild's attitudes and opinions. Are these attitudes and opinions typical of every generation of young people?

from *THE GIRL I LEFT BEHIND*

TWENTY-ONE YEARS AGO I was a bride. In another   1
twenty-one years I will be sixty-five.

Which makes me forty-four. I like being forty-four. The   2
actresses in television ads who play young housewives scrubbing their floors are younger than I am, and I don't care. Good luck, young housewives. There is a sweet pleasure all its own in being told, ''Gee, you don't look forty-four,'' although, as Gloria Steinem says, this is the way forty-four looks. Gloria, being two years older, is my leader in inspirational aging.

I had always hoped to wither gracefully, like a prune, or   3
like Georgia O'Keeffe.[1] Alas, I appear to be settling, but until

---

[1] The American painter (b. 1887).

it turns into sagging, I am not going to worry. By the time I have jowls I intend to be wise, and I consider that a fair trade. For the moment, I will settle for the completely unexpected benefit of middle age: I know my own mind. I know who I am and what I can do. I know what I want to do and what I won't do. I will learn to tap dance, I will not learn to ski. I might still be angry, but I will not be depressed.

By the time I am sixty-five I won't be so sure of myself. 4 Life, I have observed, has a way of undoing yesterday's certainties. I have an extremely good chance—if I last and the world lasts—of ending up my life alone and poor. That is the final destiny of more than half of American women over sixty-five today and I would like to change it—for them and for me.

Perhaps my son will help me out. Perhaps his future wife, 5 a rich lawyer, will help him help me out. Maybe they will have a baby. I hope it's a girl. Or a boy. I guess I won't get to choose, and I certainly hope they don't. The prospect of a world filled with deliberately anointed first-born sons is more than I can contemplate. Maybe they will want to choose a girl, and be able to give her a nice start in life by having her grown in an artificial womb. In theory this technological advance would mean a great saving of physical stress for the rich lawyer, but in practice I am afraid that twenty-five years also will not be a long enough time for the idea of feminism to safeguard us against the possibilities of parthenogenesis. If men don't need us to have babies, there is always the chance that they will decide they don't need us at all. What will we do then? Wage the ultimate war between the sexes?

Well, as I was saying, if I last and the world lasts, maybe 6 I will have a grandchild. I don't really feel it is important if my son and the grandchild's mother are married, but I hope they stay together. I would wish for them the kind of family that is a "still point of the turning world." They will promise each other love, courtesy, and equality. But, when the baby comes, it will all fall apart.

Until the first midnight nursing my grandchild's mother 7 will have been unfailingly, prematurely certain. She will have been kind to the old dingbat (me) but she will have been secretly positive that the problems I worried about are, for her, solved. Maybe she will be right. Maybe she will live in a world of excellent day care, where maternity leave is paired with paternity leave and neither parent will lose seniority. Maybe her law firm will see her need to go home at three o'clock in the afternoon as a positive plus in her efforts to achieve partnership. But I doubt it.

I think she will be another in a long generation of sorrow- 8 ful young women who think they have changed the system by becoming part of it, until they discover that caring for a baby is not considered part of the system. She will discover that mothers cannot, after all, have it all, *not even* if they change the system. Neither can fathers, if they want to raise their children too. I will be interested to see how the mother of my grandchild works it out. I will be absolutely fascinated to see how my son works it out. I'm sure he doesn't expect to have to take care of anyone, but I'm not absolutely certain he doesn't expect to be taken care of, either.

While they are working it out, I will get to see a lot of my 9 granddaughter. Okay, I did care. I had a son. Now I want a girl. I know, I know, she's not mine. But, still, I plan to give her chicken soup and Junket with chocolate bits in the bottom and I will read her *Mary Poppins* on the couch under the window with the blooming narcissus. Just like my mother, and my grandmother, did for me.

I know, I know. My son and his family will actually be 10 living in Alaska, and they will never remember to write. Just like me. But the only way I can imagine getting to sixty-five is to plan a perfect day twenty-one years from now, and the plan requires a granddaughter and narcissus.

A few more details: I will be living in Vermont in a house 11 with a porch, fifteen bib-front aprons, and three rocking chairs. And a typewriter. The first peas will be ripe, and the pond almost warm enough for swimming. My granddaughter will have come to visit because she wanted to. She will be small and quick, with snapping black eyes and a ferocious curiosity. She will, as yet, suspect neither her possibilities nor her limitations. Obviously she takes after her mother's side of the family, although when she smiles there is a trace of her father, and when she scowls there is a trace of me. We will sit on the porch, shelling peas and rocking, and we will talk about history.

She will begin, as we all do, with the personal. "There is 12 a boy I like," she will say, "but he doesn't like me. How can I make him like me?"

"Why should you make him like you?" I will answer. 13 "You are a wonderful person. Wouldn't it be more sensible to like a boy who knows that?"

She will ignore me. "Why do I feel so funny when I am   14
around him? I don't feel like myself. I feel . . . *little.*"

I will put down the peas, and gaze across the meadow,   15
and say: "I know. It is like a disease we pass on, from mother
to daughter. It's called being a woman in a man's world."

She will be irritated (being, after all, only fifteen). "What   16
do you know about it?" she will demand. "Nobody loves you."
And then she will add, with painful contrition, "Except me, of
course. And your friends. And Daddy. And Mom."

After twenty-one years, this point will still pain me. "I   17
tried," I will explain, more to myself than to her. "I tried very
hard. But there was some fatal lack of coincidence between men
and women of my generation. The men seemed to suffer some
dreadful lack of imagination, a tragic failure of generosity. And
meanwhile, the women learned things that could never be un-
learned. We knew, when we lost our innocence, that we risked
the loss of love. But our certainty that enlightenment is always
worth the pain was cold comfort when we discovered, more
often than not, that we could not apply what we had learned
to our private lives without destroying love."

"But," I will then say briskly, "your generation will be   18
different. It is possible, you will see, for love to be defined as
an attachment between equals instead of as a power struggle."

Naturally, she will be more interested in the drama than   19
in my unproven optimism. "But then what happened? Weren't
you very sad? What did you *do?*"

"Oh, yes," I will remember, "many of us were very sad.   20
And angry. And frightened. One part of our society seemed to
be learning to get in touch with their feelings while the women
had to learn to control ours. We had to practice self-confidence
the way you practice French."

"What was the hardest thing?" she will ask.   21

"Not giving up," I will answer at once. "I was not   22
especially brave myself. I could hide behind words. I did
not have to stay with a mean husband or face every day an
office or a factory where I was not wanted." She will nod at
this, remembering her third-grade year, when she was very
unpopular.

"For me, and most of my friends, the hardest thing was   23
to keep going. When we were about your mother's age, in our
forties, many of us had managed to change our lives. We had
become people we never expected to be. Doctors, politicians,

foreign correspondents. And then we found that we had become only ordinary extraordinary women. We were not so special after all, but only doing what men had done all along. We had changed ourselves, but we had not yet changed anything else, except perhaps the expectations of our children. And we no longer had the time to do the things we had done so well— to comfort and nurse and make Junket. It was awful. We felt like failures and we blamed ourselves and denied that our successes were worth having." I will hesitate here, remembering a summer when every woman I knew went limp, declared her job boring or insupportable, decided she did not *feel* like a doctor or a politician or whatever. That was the summer—one of many—when we no longer knew who we were.

"Then what?" my granddaughter will ask, her attention wandering.   24

I am not sure I will be able to answer: "We kept going, and we changed things. We learned how to combine the responsibilities of masculinity with the tenderness of femininity. We invented a new way to live, and we taught men."   25

She will jump up, scattering peas, and run down to the pond, saying: "Anyway, everything's solved now." But talking is not a solution. It isn't now, and it won't be in twenty-one years. Talking is only a start.   26

That night at dinner the girl I will leave behind me, the girl we have given a start, will look at me and say: "But, Granny, were you happy being a feminist?"   27

Of course I was happy being a feminist. After all, consider the alternatives.   28

THE WRITER'S THEMES

1. Jane O'Reilly places her imaginary conversation more than twenty years in the future and looks back on the aims and methods of today's women's movement. How accurate is the writer's report on the goals and methods of the women's liberation movement as we observe them today?
2. Why does the writer choose to have the conversation with her granddaughter rather than, for example, her son's wife? How different would the conversation have been if she had chosen to share her thoughts with her daughter-in-law?

3. Throughout the essay the writer makes several different predictions about life in the future: babies may be grown in
artificial wombs, we may have excellent daycare for children, and we will be able to choose the sex of our children.
What is the writer's attitude toward these changes (some of
which already seem to be coming true)?

THE WRITER'S TECHNIQUE

In paragraph eleven of her essay, Jane O'Reilly gives us a picture of her life as she imagines it might be when she is sixty-
five. Here is that paragraph:

> A few more details: I will be living in Vermont in a house with
> a porch, fifteen bib-front aprons, and three rocking chairs. And
> a typewriter. The first peas will be ripe, and the pond almost
> warm enough for swimming. My granddaughter will have come
> to visit because she wanted to. She will be small and quick, with
> snapping black eyes and a ferocious curiosity. She will, as yet,
> suspect neither her possibilities nor her limitations. Obviously
> she takes after her mother's side of the family, although when
> she smiles there is a trace of her father, and when she scowls
> there is a trace of me. We will sit on the porch, shelling peas
> and rocking, and we will talk about history.

The writer begins by indicating where she will be living
and how her home will look. Notice that the writer is careful to
include a typewriter in her short list of furnishings.

Next, the writer shows us the area around the house with
the pond and the ripe peas, and then introduces another person, her granddaughter, who has come to visit. We are given
some idea of the young girl's physical appearance, but more
attention is devoted to her personality. The writer also shows
how the granddaughter shares characteristics with different
members of the family. Finally, the writer shows herself and
her granddaughter together "on the porch, shelling peas and
rocking," as they talk.

PARAGRAPH PRACTICE

Write a paragraph of your own, using Jane O'Reilly's paragraph
as your model. Your paragraph could be a description of yourself with another person; the other person could be a relative

or simply a friend. First, describe for your reader where you are and then give some indications of the furnishings of the place. You might wish to include at least one item that reflects your own interests or personality. Next, provide a brief description of the atmosphere of the surrounding area. What details can you provide that would help your reader visualize your surroundings?

At this point in your paragraph, introduce the person who is with you. Give a brief description of this person's physical appearance, but devote most of your description to his or her personality. Finally, show yourself engaged in some activity with this other person. The activity could be as simple as a quiet conversation.

ESSAY PRACTICE

The following outline will help you plan a complete essay of at least five paragraphs. The theme of your essay will be closely related to Jane O'Reilly's *The Girl I Left Behind*.

The following sentence may serve as your thesis sentence, and will also be the main idea of your introductory paragraph:

¶ 1.   As children we think we can do almost anything, but as we get older we begin to realize our limitations.

Each of the sentences below is the topic sentence for one of the paragraphs that you will write to develop your thesis. You may use the suggested details to develop each paragraph, or you may supply details of your own.

¶ 2.   All of us reach a point in our lives when we realize both our possibilities and our limitations.

[DETAILS: When did you decide what your possibilities were? Indicate how you explored those possibilities. Did you discover them on your own, or did someone else help you? When did you first begin to realize your limitations? When you discuss these limitations, you might include such areas as time, energy, talent, money, and health.]

¶ 3.   Later, we reach a point when we decide that there are certain things we will no longer do.

[DETAILS: What are the things you have decided you will no longer do? In each case, how and when did you come to your decision?]

¶ 4. There comes a time in life when we can decide what we really want to do.

[DETAILS: What are some of the really important experiences you have decided you want to have in your life? In each case, why do you want to have the experience?]

Be certain that you use transitions between paragraphs to make your writing flow smoothly. In addition, be sure that your conclusion gives your reader a clear signal that you have come to the end of your essay.

ESSAY TOPICS

1. a. Although many women today have joined the work force, do men still expect women to take care of them?
   b. Tell the story of what you consider to be the best relationship you ever observed between a man and a woman. How did these two people divide their responsibilities?
2. a. Jane O'Reilly states that "mothers cannot, after all, have it all, *not even* if they change the system. Neither can fathers, if they want to raise their children too." What realizations do a man and a woman have to have if both of them want careers and want to raise children? What concessions will society have to make if there is to be a change in our approaches to the related problems of careers and child care?
   b. Although many social attitudes and customs have changed in recent years, for many people it is not enough to say that men and women are equal. What real changes have there been in such areas as education, day care, and the world of work? To what extent have our laws and our changing attitudes affected our ways of thinking and acting in these areas of our lives?
3. When Jane O'Reilly speaks of young married people, she notes that they "will promise each other love, courtesy, and equality. But, when the baby comes, it will all fall apart."
   How does the arrival of a baby change people's lives? Tell the story of a young couple you know whose lives changed with the arrival of a child (or children).

Focus on Terms: Transitions

When you use a *transition* in your writing, you are giving a signal to your reader that a change of some kind is about to take place. This signal may be a word, a phrase, or a sentence; or it could be one or more paragraphs that relate one part of your piece of writing to another part. Transitional devices are significant because they show how details in a piece of writing are related to each other. They also help a reader connect different ideas found in different parts of the same piece of writing.

A frequently used method to show transition is the repetition of important words or phrases. For example, at the end of the fourth paragraph of "Back, But Not Home" Maria L. Muñiz notes that she cannot interpret the Cuban revolution objectively because "too many memories stand in my way." At the beginning of her next paragraph the writer makes a transition from the word "memories" by using the word "remember": she observes that she "began to remember how as a little girl I would wake up crying. . . ." The same idea of *remembering* continues to the end of the paragraph, as Muñiz tells us that she "began to remember how difficult it often was to grow up Latina in an American world." At this point the writer uses another well-known transitional device when she uses a pronoun to refer to a noun previously used. The idea of *Latina* that has concluded the paragraph becomes a transition to the beginning of the next paragraph with the use of "it": "It meant going to kindergarten knowing little English." The writer continues the same transition into the next paragraph, which she begins by stating, "As I grew a little older, Latina meant . . ." The writer has deliberately used the noun *Latina* and the pronoun *it* to provide transitions among central sections of her essay. An additional example of this type of transition is seen at the end of the second paragraph of *The Girl I Left Behind,* when Jane O'Reilly tells us that Gloria Steinem is her "leader in inspirational aging." The key word that she uses to conclude this paragraph is "aging," and the writer echoes it with the word "wither" as she begins paragraph three: "I had always hoped to wither gracefully . . ."

In addition, transitions can be used to remind the reader of previous ideas in previous paragraphs, or even to summarize whole sections of material. For example, in her essay Jane O'Reilly refers back to previous paragraphs to provide transitions for her readers. In the beginning paragraphs of her essay, the writer echoes an entire phrase to provide a transition. In paragraph four the writer predicts that the final years of her life will be lonely and poor "if I last and the world lasts." We come across the same phrase in paragraph six when the writer again refers to that part of her life, the time when she will most likely have a grandchild: "Well, as I was saying, if I last and the world lasts, maybe I will have a grandchild."

Sometimes a transition can be a word or phrase such as "later," "after a while," or "as a result." Other transitions that are often used include "however," "furthermore," "on the other hand," and "finally." The following list is intended to provide you with a number of frequently used transitions that you may use in your own writing:

> *to introduce:* to begin with, first of all
> *to show time:* meanwhile, previously, several days later
> *to show sequence:* next, then, second
> *to show special relationships:* nearby, beyond, below
> *to make an addition:* furthermore, in addition
> *to highlight a point:* most important, my main argument is . . .
> *to compare:* likewise, also
> *to contrast:* however, on the contrary
> *to show cause:* because, an important factor is . . .
> *to show effect:* therefore, as a result
> *to emphasize:* indeed, in particular
> *to conclude:* finally, in conclusion

When you use transitions in your writing you help your reader see how each succeeding idea relates to the other ideas you are expressing. These signposts are important to your reader because each serves as a guide through the various parts of your piece of writing.

Student Essay ❧ ❧ *David Castaldo*

The following essay is a narrative, but it also contains a detailed character description along with several other rhetorical features that help to make it an interesting and effective piece of writing.

Notice especially the effective opening of the essay. The writer engages our interest by describing a photograph that represents a scene from his past, and then proceeds to relate events from that past. In effect, most of the essay is a single detailed flashback.

The essay is also a striking piece of writing when we realize that the author has used a wartime situation to frame his portrait of a very peaceful person.

• The writer's technique in the following essay includes a careful use of transitions. For example, the repetition of the can of Coke in paragraph two provides a clear transition from the first paragraph. What is the transition from paragraph two to paragraph three? Identify the other transitions the writer uses to guide his readers from one part of his essay to another.

MEMORY OF A STRANGER

RECENTLY, my wife and I were looking through some old photographs. At one point she stopped sorting and gazed intently at a particular photograph. Handing it to me she asked, "Who's drinking the Coke?" I took it in my hands. The picture had been taken in a Saigon bar sometime toward the end of my tour of duty in Vietnam. There were several soldiers, including myself, sitting around a table that was literally covered with beer cans. In their midst was one lonely Coke can.

I had to laugh. To my left was Larry Proctor. He was not only the owner of the Coke can, he was also my roommate for several months that year. Like many Army decisions, there seemed to be no rhyme or reason for putting Larry and me together, for, by any standard, we were strange companions.

Together, he and I were a Mutt and Jeff combination. He was Mutt, tall and lean, while I was Jeff, short and stocky. He was, in fact, almost a foot taller than I was. The comparison didn't end there, though. He was fair, blue-eyed, and blonde, with the fresh look of an Iowan farm boy. (Not surprisingly, he was.) I was somewhat fair, with the dark eyes and hair of my Italian background. Although I was from a rural area of New Jersey, I had never been on a real farm, much less milked a cow before breakfast.

The differences between us were more than physical. Larry was from what was known as the Bible Belt and, much to my surprise, on our first night together he read his Bible and knelt to say his prayers. I had not been religious since I heard my first God and Country sermon from an Army chaplain. It was a bit of culture shock, but I would get used to it. There were other strange habits. One of the prime activities in our unit was drinking. When we were not in the field, drinking was a nightly occurrence. Often it was a time to gather socially and unwind, but it still revolved around disposing of a case or two of beer. It quickly became noticeable that, although present and participating, Larry did not drink. At first, this marked him as an outsider. The fact that I was quite a drinker myself and the fact that I was the owner of a large stereo system made our room a center for some of our bull sessions. These smaller groups helped others, as well as myself, to learn that Larry wasn't all that much different from us. He enjoyed life, liked to joke and kid around and had many interests similar to ours. We quickly learned that he was just a good guy, unusually good, but nevertheless still one of us.

Larry probably found me even stranger than I found him, and I think that the differences, and our mutual respect for those differences, enhanced our friendship. Larry was the gentle giant, never seeming to become upset. I, on the other hand, was the terrible Turk, outraged at the slightest provocation, cursing the fates whenever possible. Soon I discovered myself becoming embarrassed at these outbursts, particularly when they were directed at Larry or if they happened in his presence. The embarrassment was greater in the former instance, as he refused to become upset or reply in anger, even at my most inspired performances. Eventually I discovered that Larry had a calming effect.

I often remember Larry's dragging me back after a trip to one of the local bars, and I have often suspected that he put me to bed once or twice. (An example of his Christian charity, I suppose.) I can't imagine how I got there otherwise.

Larry felt the need to help or share. This extended to his girlfriend's soon to become famous chocolate chip cookies. In a particularly ungrateful moment I complained that her cookies didn't contain enough chocolate chips. The next shipment found him somewhat reluctant to share. He ate practically the whole can without offering me any, until finally I was forced to ask for some. Hearing my request, he sorted out the cookies while informing me that he was looking for one with sufficient chips. At last he stopped, announced that he had found one, and handed me the can. There was one cookie left, the largest I had ever seen. It took up the entire bottom of the can and was practically all chocolate chip. I was forced to take my ration card out of hibernation and buy him a Coke.

Larry and I lost touch after the Army, but sometimes after watching the news I think of him and feel comfortable, knowing that there are still people like him around.   9

Strategies for Writing

1. How many rhetorical elements beyond pure narration does the writer use in his essay? For example, where do we find the writer employing description and comparison and contrast as part of his narration?

2. Review the essay, examining the writer's use of time sequence. Beginning with the second paragraph, how does the writer deal with the element of time? Trace the writer's time sequence in the main paragraphs of the essay, where he presents the story of his friendship.

3. Narrate the story of the most unusual friendship you ever observed. Why did this friendship strike you as unusual? In your opinion, what were the main reasons this friendship was successful?

4. Write the story of a friendship you had with someone for a limited period of time. What first brought you together with this person? How did your friendship change over the period of time you were together? How and why did your relationship end?

4

THE WORLD OF WORK

WRITING SKILL: Process

We see process described every day. Friends want to tell us how they lost ten pounds or how they refinished a piece of furniture; "how to" books teach us any number of skills, from how to study for the GRE to how to cook Chinese; pamphlets and brochures show us how to pass a driving test or how to apply for a bank loan; booklets come with some of our purchases to help us understand how to operate and maintain everything from a digital watch to a washing machine. Learning itself is a process, and no matter what skill we are trying to acquire, we learn by following a process.

The explanation of a process may take one of two forms, the *directional* or the *informational*. The directional method is intended to show a person in a step-by-step manner how he or she could actually accomplish a process. For example, the instructions that come with a bicycle that needs to be assembled are intended to be used, and so fall under the category of directional process. The informational approach to process does not intend to teach you how to accomplish something but describes a process purely for information or entertainment. The excerpt in this unit from Camara Laye's book *The Dark Child* is an example of this approach. The writer describes the process of making a piece of gold jewelry simply for our information.

The other selections in this unit are also examples of the informational approach to process, and each process is usually presented in a straightforward, step-by-step fashion. At times, however, a writer will choose to interrupt this direct approach by giving the definition of a term or by providing a description that the writer feels will add depth and color to the writing. For example, in the selection from *A Mortal Flower,* Han Suyin describes the process of looking for a job. This description is part of a detailed picture that includes a portrait of her family and more than a glimpse of political and social conditions in the China of the 1930s. Throughout these descriptions, however, the search for a job dominates and we are constantly aware of this young woman's quest, from her first letter of application to the final interview.

When Agnes De Mille writes about her personal experience as a ballet student, she shows us the process by which a ballerina learns the art of the dance. Here, in the writer's own words, is a part of that process:

> The lungs may be bursting, the heart pounding in the throat, sweat springing from every pore, but hands must float in repose, the head stir gently as though swooning in delight. The diaphragm must be lifted to expand the chest fully, proudly; the abdomen pulled in flat. The knees must be taut and flat to give the extended leg every inch of length. The leg must be turned outward forty-five degrees in the hip socket so that the side of the knee and the long unbroken line of the leg are presented to view and never the lax, droopy line of a bent knee. The leg must look like a sword. The foot arches to prolong the line of extension. The supporting foot turns out forty-five degrees to enhance the line of the supporting leg, to keep the hips even, and to ensure the broadest possible base for the support and balancing of the body.

Notice how the writer deals with each part of the body as she describes the process of dancing. She begins with what happens internally (''the lungs may be bursting . . .''), and then proceeds to the visible parts of the body. Each part—the chest, the abdomen, the knees, the leg, and the foot—is shown as a part of the total process that is a dancer in action.

When you approach the writing of a process essay, you must ask yourself how much your reader already knows about the subject. When writing such an essay, it is very easy to assume either too little or too much knowledge on the part of your reader. For example, if you are describing the process of baking a cake, you may safely assume that your reader knows that an oven is involved, but you should not assume that the same reader knows how hot the oven should be for the baking process. If you are providing instructions for a person who is assembling a bicycle or a toy, you may assume it will be understood that tools will be needed. However, if a special tool is required for a particular part of the process, that tool should be clearly identified.

The writing of a process may be a very practical assignment, or it may be an exercise in pure enjoyment. Such an exercise may increase your awareness of something you are familiar with by describing it in a new way, or it may introduce you to something you have not encountered before. If you are reading a piece of writing that shows a process, note the steps that are given and decide whether or not that information is useful. If you include process in your own writing, always keep your reader in mind by making sure that you are clear and complete at all times, and that you have anticipated as many of your reader's needs and possible problems as you can.

•§ *Agnes De Mille* ż•

Agnes De Mille is one of America's most famous dancers and choreographers. She was born in New York and graduated *cum laude* from the University of California at Los Angeles. During the 1920s she studied dancing in the United States and in England.

She first appeared in New York in 1927, and throughout the 1930s she toured America and Europe as a dance recitalist and choreographer. During the 1950s Agnes De Mille headed a dance troupe that toured over one hundred American cities. She is perhaps most famous for her choreography of such shows as *Oklahoma!*, *Brigadoon*, *Paint Your Wagon*, and *Carousel*.

Agnes De Mille is also the author of several books, many of them autobiographical. Some of her books include *To a Young Dancer* and *The Book of the Dance*. Her most recent book, *Reprieve*, is the story of her recovery from a crippling stroke that she suffered in 1976.

The following selection is from her first volume of autobiography, *Dance to the Piper*, published in 1951.

PREVIEWING THE WRITER

• Note the process that is a part of every dance lesson. Note also how the writer takes us through each stage in the process of learning how to dance.

• Note the attention the author pays to the history of ballet. How much of the tradition of ballet does she describe?

• What does the author learn about herself as she goes through the process of learning ballet technique?

from *DANCE TO THE PIPER*

WE WENT DOWN for our audition on a summer morning. The studio was an enormous bare room with folding chairs pushed against the white walls for the mothers to sit on while they watched their daughters sweat. Across one end of the hall hung a large mirror. Around the other three sides stretched the traditional barre. I gave my audition in a bathing suit. Kosloff himself put me through the test. He did not say how talented I was or how naturally graceful. He said my knees were weak, my spine curved, that I was heavy for my age and had "no juice." By this he meant, I came to learn, that my muscles were dry, stubborn and unresilient. He said I was a bit old to start training; I was at the time thirteen. I looked at him in mild surprise. I hardly knew what emotion to give way to, the astonishment of hurt vanity or gratitude for professional help. I was sent off (I keep saying "I"—my sister of course was with me but from the start I took for granted that these lessons were mine. She just came along). We were sent off to buy blocked toe slippers, fitted right to the very ends of our toes, and to prepare proper practice dresses.

The first lesson was a private one conducted by Miss Fredova. Miss Fredova was born Winifred Edwards and had received her training in London from Anna Pavlova. She was as slim as a sapling and always wore white like a trained nurse. She parted her dark hair in the center and drew it to the nape of her neck in glossy wings, Russian style. She was shod in low-heeled sandals. She taught standing erect as a guardsman, and beat time with a long pole. First she picked up a watering can and sprinkled water on the floor in a sunny corner by the barre. This she explained was so that we should not slip. Then she placed our hands on the barre and showed us how to turn out our feet ninety degrees from their normal walking stance into first position. Then she told us to *plier* or bend our knees deeply, keeping our heels as long as possible on the floor. I naturally stuck out behind. I found the pole placed rigidly against my spine. I naturally pressed forward on my insteps. Her leg and knee planted against my foot curbed this tendency. "I can't move," I said, laughing with winning helplessness.

"Don't talk," she said. "Down-ee, two-ee, three-ee, four-ee. Down the heels, don't rock on your feet."

At the end of ten minutes the sweat stuck in beads on my forehead. "May I sit down?" I asked.

"You must never sit during practice. It ruins the thigh muscles. If you sit down you may not continue with class." I of course would have submitted to a beating with whips rather than stop. I was taking the first steps into the promised land. The path might be thorny but it led straight to Paradise. "Down-ee, two-ee, three-ee, four-ee. *Nuca.* Give me this fourth position. Repeat the exercise."

So she began every lesson. So I have begun every practice period since. It is part of the inviolable ritual of ballet dancing. Every ballet student that has ever trained in the classic technique in any part of the world begins just this way, never any other. They were dreary exercises and I was very bad at them but these were the exercises that built Taglioni's leg. These repeated stretches and pulls gave Pavlova her magic foot and Legnani hers and Kchessinska hers. This was the very secret of how to dance, the tradition handed down from teacher to pupil for three hundred years. A king had patterned the style and named the steps, the king who built Versailles. Here was an ancient and enduring art whose technique stood like the rules of harmony. All other kinds of performance in our Western theater had faded or changed. What were movies to this? Or Broadway plays?

I, a complacent child, who had been flattered into believing I could do without what had gone before, now inherited the labor of centuries. I had come into my birthright. I was fourteen, and I had found my life's work. I felt superior to other adolescents as I stood beside the adults serene and strong, reassured by my vision.

I bent to the discipline. I learned to relax with my head between my knees when I felt sick or faint. I learned how to rest my insteps by lying on my back with my feet vertically up against the wall. I learned how to bind up my toes so that they would not bleed through the satin shoes. But I never sat down. I learned the first and all-important dictate of ballet dancing— never to miss the daily practice, hell or high water, sickness or health, never to miss the barre practice; to miss meals, sleep, rehearsals even but not the practice, not for one day ever under any circumstances, except on Sundays and during childbirth.

I seemed, however, to have little aptitude for the business. What had all this talk about God-given talent amounted to? It was like trying to wiggle my ears. I strained and strained. Nothing perceptible happened. A terrible sense of frustration drove me to striving with masochistic frenzy. Twice I fainted in class. My calves used to ache until tears stuck in my eyes. I learned every possible manipulation of the shoe to ease the aching tendons of my insteps. I used to get abominable stitches in my sides from attempting continuous jumps. But I never sat down. I learned to cool my forehead against the plaster of the walls. I licked the perspiration off from around my mouth. I breathed through my nose though my eyes bugged. But I did not sit and I did not stop.

Ballet technique is arbitrary and very difficult. It never becomes easy; it becomes possible. The effort involved in making a dancer's body is so long and relentless, in many instances so painful, the effort to maintain the technique so grueling that unless a certain satisfaction is derived from the disciplining and punishing, the pace could not be maintained. Most dancers are to an extent masochists. "What a good pain! What a profitable pain!" said Miss Fredova as she stretched her insteps in her two strong hands. "I have practiced for three hours. I am exhausted, and I feel wonderful."

My strongest impression of the Kosloff studio was, beside the sunlight on the floor and the white walls, the smell of sweat, the salty smell of clean sweat, the musty smell of old sweat on unwashed dresses, the smell of kitchen soap and sweat on the fresh dresses. Every dance studio smells of this—moist flesh, moist hair, hot glue in the shoes, hot socks and feet, and soap. 11

Paradoxically enough ballet dancing is designed to give the impression of lightness and ease. Nothing in classic dancing should be convulsive or tormented. Derived from the seventeenth- and eighteenth-century court dances the style is kingly, a series of harmonious and balanced postures linked by serene movement. The style involves a total defiance of gravity, and because this must perforce be an illusion, the effect is achieved first by an enormous strengthening of the legs and feet to produce great resilient jumps and second by a co-ordination of arms and head in a rhythm slower than the rhythm of the legs which have no choice but to take the weight of the body when the body falls. But the slow relaxed movement of head and arms gives the illusion of sustained flight, gives the sense of effortless ease. The lungs may be bursting, the heart pounding in the throat, sweat springing from every pore, but hands must float in repose, the head stir gently as though swooning in delight. The diaphragm must be lifted to expand the chest fully, proudly; the abdomen pulled in flat. The knees must be taut and flat to give the extended leg every inch of length. The leg must be turned outward forty-five degrees in the hip socket so that the side of the knee and the long unbroken line of the leg are presented to view and never the lax, droopy line of a bent knee. The leg must look like a sword. The foot arches to prolong the line of extension. The supporting foot turns out forty-five degrees to enhance the line of the supporting leg, to keep the hips even, and to ensure the broadest possible base for the support and balancing of the body. 12

It should always be remembered that the court, and therefore the first, ballet dances were performed by expert swords- 13 men and derive much of their style from fencing positions. The discipline embraces the whole deportment. The lifted foot springs to attention the minute it leaves the floor. The supporting foot endures all; the instep must never give way even when the whole weight of the body drops and grinds on the single slim arch. The legs can be held in their turned position by the great muscles across the buttocks only by pulling the buttocks in flat. The spine should be steady, the expression of the face noble, the face of a king to whom all things are possible. The eyebrows may not go up, the shoulders may not lift, the neck may not stiffen, nor the mouth open like a hooked fish.

The five classic positions and the basic arm postures and steps were named at the request of Louis XIV by his great ballet master, Pécourt, Lully's collaborator, codified, described and fixed in the regimen of daily exercise which has become almost ceremonial with time. Since then the technique has expanded and diversified but the fundamental steps and nomenclature remain unchanged. The "Royale" is still the faked beaten jump it was when Louis XIV, not as nimble in the legs as he would have liked to appear, failed to achieve a proper *entrechat quatre*.

The ideal ballet body is long limbed with a small compact torso. This makes for beauty of line; the longer the arms and legs the more exciting the body line. The ideal ballet foot has a high taut instep and a wide stretch in the Achilles' tendon. This tendon is the spring on which a dancer pushes for his jump, the hinge on which he takes the shock of landing. If there is one tendon in a dancer's body more important than any other, it is this tendon. It is, I should say, the prerequisite for all great technique. When the heel does not stretch easily and softly like a cat's, as mine did not, almost to the point of malformation, the shock of running or jumping must be taken somewhere in the spine by sticking out behind, for instance, in a sitting posture after every jump. I seemed to be all rusty wire and safety pins. My torso was long with unusually broad hips, my legs and arms abnormally short, my hands and feet broad and short. I was besides fat. What I did not know was that I was constructed for endurance and that I developed through effort alone a capacity for outperforming far, far better technicians. Because I was built like a mustang, stocky, mettlesome and sturdy, I became a good jumper, growing special compensating muscles up the front of my shins for the lack of a helpful heel. But the long, cool, serene classic line was forever denied me.

THE WRITER'S THEMES

1. What are the various steps Agnes De Mille goes through in the process of becoming a dancer? Trace her learning experience, from her first interview, through her first lessons, to her awareness of the long historical tradition of ballet.
2. Many people begin to learn a skill, but do not stay with it. Where does Agnes De Mille show her determination to become a ballet dancer? Where does she begin to show a deeper awareness of all that ballet represents?
3. Agnes De Mille had certain physical limitations as a dancer. What were her limitations? How well did she accept those limitations? How did she deal with them?

THE WRITER'S TECHNIQUE

In paragraph eight, Agnes De Mille describes how she began her study of ballet and how she responded to the discipline needed for the study of the dance:

> I bent to the discipline. I learned to relax with my head between my knees when I felt sick or faint. I learned how to rest my insteps by lying on my back with my feet vertically up against the wall. I learned how to bind up my toes so that they would not bleed through the satin shoes. But I never sat down. I learned the first and all-important dictate of ballet dancing—never to miss the daily practice, hell or high water, sickness or health, never to miss the barre practice; to miss meals, sleep, rehearsals even but not the practice, not for one day ever under any circumstances, except on Sundays and during childbirth.

Notice that the writer tells us in detail how she "bent to the discipline." For example, she learned "how to relax" when she felt sick or faint, and she learned how to rest her insteps and how to bind up her toes "so that they would not bleed through the satin shoes." Agnes De Mille then points out what she never did: she "never sat down" and then she states "the first and all-important dictate of ballet dancing—never to miss the daily practice . . ." She concludes the paragraph by giving examples of what a ballet dancer may miss (meals and sleep are included), "but not the practice, not for one day ever under any circumstances . . ."

Note that at the beginning of the paragraph the writer

provides a series of specific details relating to the discipline that is needed to learn ballet. Then she makes the most important point of all, that a ballet student is not to miss the daily practice. Notice how she emphasizes this point by repeating the idea that a student is ''never to miss the daily practice,'' ''never to miss the barre practice,'' not even for a day. She also emphasizes her point by stating what a student *can* miss, and we are left with the basic, unbreakable rule of the dance.

PARAGRAPH PRACTICE

Write a paragraph of your own, using Agnes De Mille's paragraph as your model. The paragraph could show how you engaged in the process of learning something, either inside or outside of school. You could, for example, describe a particular course you took that demanded your complete concentration, or you could tell about something you learned from a friend or by yourself. As you write your paragraph, imitate Agnes De Mille's technique by showing your reader at least three or four steps in that process. Follow this by stating the most important principle of the skill that you learned.

Conclude your paragraph by describing the things you could *not* do while you were learning this skill. What things had to be eliminated while you were involved in the actual learning process? These could include such activities as going to the movies, watching television, or even dating.

ESSAY PRACTICE

The following outline will help you plan a complete essay of at least five paragraphs. The theme of your essay will be closely related to the selection by Agnes De Mille.

The following sentence may serve as your thesis sentence, and will also be the main idea of your introductory paragraph:

¶ 1. The learning process is a combination of our having the right attitude, the right teachers, and the right degree of determination to succeed.

Each of the sentences below is the topic sentence for one of the paragraphs that you will write to develop your thesis. You may use the suggested details to develop each paragraph, or you may supply details of your own.

¶ 2. When we set out to learn something, the attitudes of our parents or friends are always important.

[DETAILS: Describe a time you learned something and you were encouraged by parents, friends, or both. Who gave you the most encouragement or the most useful advice?]

¶ 3. Another important part of the learning process is the presence of an encouraging teacher.

[DETAILS: Describe the teacher who guided you in your learning experience. How was this teacher an important and positive influence on you?]

¶ 4. Often, another important part of the learning process is our own determination to succeed.

[DETAILS: How strong was your own desire to learn this new subject or new skill? How did your own sense of determination help you overcome moments of doubt and uncertainty?]

Be certain that you use transitions between paragraphs to make your writing flow smoothly. In addition, be sure that your conclusion gives your reader a clear signal that you have come to the end of your essay.

ESSAY TOPICS

1. Select a profession that requires extensive preparation in order to rise to the top of that profession. Explain each of the several steps in this process, in their proper sequence. What exactly does a person have to do to get to the top of the profession you have chosen to describe?

2. All of us are anxious when we begin something new. We may be attending a new school, or we may be starting to learn something we have not studied before. Write a process essay in which you give the stages you went through in order to learn something new. How did you begin the process? You may want to include your emotional reactions as you began to learn, or you might want to indicate the biggest obstacle that you had to overcome.

3. Some people, like Agnes De Mille, seem to know at an early age what they want to do with their lives. When is the best time in life to choose a career? How can a person be sure that the choice is a realistic one?

❧ Han Suyin ❧

Han Suyin, whose real name is Rosalie Chou, was born and raised in Peking. Later she went to medical school in China and Belgium; when her studies were interrupted by World War II, she returned to China. There she met and married her first husband, a general with the Nationalist Chinese Army. He was killed in 1945. After the death of her husband, Han Suyin resumed her medical studies and became a doctor. In 1952 she married an Englishman, Leonard Comber, and for some years lived with her husband and daughter in Singapore.

Han Suyin is the author of several novels, including *A Many Splendored Thing,* the story of a love affair between an Oriental woman and a British journalist in Hong Kong during World War II. The novel was later made into a well-known Hollywood film and also inspired the popular song, ''Love is a Many Splendored Thing.'' Her most recent work of fiction is *Till Morning Comes,* a story of modern China that begins in the closing days of World War II and includes the years of that country's Cultural Revolution.

Han Suyin has also written a series of autobiographical books that describe her childhood and adolescence in China during the 1920s and 1930s. The following selection is from one of those volumes, *A Mortal Flower,* and describes an incident when the writer was a teenager looking for her first job.

PREVIEWING THE WRITER

- How many people help Han Suyin look for her first job?
- The author's search for a job involves a process. What are the different steps the writer goes through in her search for a job?
- Note the different parts of the job interview. How many different events happen in the course of that interview?

from *A MORTAL FLOWER*

EVERY DAY I walked from home to the American nuns' temporary college, behind the North Sea Park, and back again. It was the mule track I trudged, the one in front of our house, and the white dust came up to my ankles, filling my tennis shoes. Passing over the great marble bridge in front of the park I would linger to see the white thirteenth-century pagoda, crowned with gold, commanding the mirror lake. The willows become green-swathed and supple in the patchy spring, and my parents debated where I could apply for a job: to the Belgian bank? or the French bank? But my job was decided, not by them, nor me, but by my friend Hilda Kuo.

Hilda takes an enormous amount of space, though so little   2
time, in my adolescence. Even today, her memory stirs me; I long to see her again. She was three years older than I, and for a short while all I wanted to look like, sound like, dress like. She was the only girl I knew who told me I wrote excellent letters. She made a plaster cast of my face. She had opinions on everything. She took a picture of me, at sixteen, which I have still. She and I were nearly killed, falling off a hillside road in her small car. Hilda was so full of life, I cannot believe her dead.

I met her in the street, I walking, she riding a Mongolian   3
pony on the pavement, and that was Hilda all over. She stopped the pony and we talked. I told her I needed a job. 'Why don't you apply where I work, at the P.U.M.C.?'

I said: 'What is that?'   4

'It's that big hospital there, you goof.' She pointed with   5
her riding-whip to the green-tiled roofs that rose high above the low grey houses and shops. 'The Yu Wang Fu,' I said, giving it the Chinese name. 'Rockefeller Foundation.' I was awed.

The massive marble and pillared palace had been the res-   6
idence of the Emperor's uncle, now acquired by the Rockefeller Foundation, and turned into a hospital and a teaching school called the Peking Union Medical College. When anyone said 'Rockefeller Foundation' there was even more reverence in their voice than when they said 'Generalissimo Chiang Kaishek'.

The day after meeting Hilda I wrote a letter to the Rocke-   7
feller Foundation, applying for a job.

Neither Father nor Mother thought I would get in. 'You   8
have to have pull. It's an American thing, Rockefeller Foundation. You must have pull.'

Mother said: 'That's where they do all those experiments   9
on dogs and people.' All the Big Shots of the Nanking government also came here to have medical treatment, and sometimes took away a nurse to become 'a new wife'.

It made sense to me, typing in a hospital; I would learn   10 about medicine, since I wanted to study medicine. And as there was no money at home for me to study, I would earn money, and prepare myself to enter medical school. I had already discovered that a convent-school education was not at all adequate, and that it would take me at least three more years of hard study before being able to enter any college at all. Science, mathematics, Chinese literature and the classics . . . with the poor schooling given to me, it would take me years to get ready for a university.

'I will do it.' But clenched teeth, decision tearing my bowels, were not enough; there was no money, no money, my mother said it, said it until I felt as if every morsel of food I ate was wrenched off my father's body.

'No one is going to feed you doing nothing at home.' Of course, one who does not work must not eat unless one can get married, which is called: 'being settled at last.' But with my looks I would never get married, I was too thin, too sharp, too ugly. Mother said it, Elder Brother had said it. Everyone agreed that I should work, because marriage would be difficult for me.

Within a week a reply came. The morning postman brought it, and I choked over my milk and coffee. 'I'm to go for an interview. At the Peking Union Medical College. To the Comptroller's office.'

Father and Mother were pleased. Mother put the coffeepot down and took the letter. 'What good paper, so thick.' But how could we disguise the fact that I was not fifteen years old? I had claimed to be sixteen in the letter. In fact, said Papa, it was not a lie since Chinese are a year old when born, and if one added the New Year as an extra year, as do the Cantonese and the Hakkas, who become two years old when they reach their first New Year (so that a baby born on December 31st would be reckoned two years old on the following January 2nd), I could claim to being sixteen.

'You *look* sixteen,' said Mama, 'all you have to do is to stop hopping and picking your pimples. And lengthen your skirt.'

What dress should I wear? I had two school uniforms, a green dress, a brown dress, and one dress with three rows of frills for Sunday, too dressy for an interview. I had no shoes except flat-heeled school shoes, and tennis shoes. There was no time to make a dress and in those years no ready-made clothes existed. Mother lengthened the green dress, and added her voile

scarf. I squeezed two pimples on my forehead, then went to the
East market and bought some face powder, Butterfly brand,
pink, made in Shanghai by a Japanese firm.

The next morning, straw-hatted, with powder on my nose,   17
I went with my father to the gates of the hospital.

'It's not this gate, this is for the sick. It's the other gate,   18
round the corner,' said the porter.

The Yu Wang Fu Palace occupied a whole city block. We   19
walked along its high grey outer wall, hearing the dogs scream
in the kennels, and came to its other gate which was the Administration building gate. It had two large stone lions, one male,
one female. We crossed the marble courtyard, walked up the
steps with their carved dragons coiling in the middle, into an
entrance hall, with painted beams and intricate painted ceiling,
red lacquered pillars, huge lamps. There was cork matting on
the stone floor.

'I'll leave you,' said Papa. 'Try to make a good impres-   20
sion.' And he was gone.

I found the Comptroller's office easily, there was a mes-   21
senger in the hall directing visitors. An open door, a room, two
typewriters clattering and two women making them clatter.

I stood at the door and one of the women came to me.   22
She had the new style of hair, all upstanding curls, which I
admired, a dress with a print round the hem; she was very
pregnant, so that her belly seemed to be coming at me first. She
smiled. 'Hello, what can I do for you?'

'I have an interview.'   23

She took the letter from my hand. 'Glad you could come.   24
Now, just sit you down. No, sit down *there.* I'll tell Mr. Harned
you've come.'

The office had two other doors besides the one to the cor-   25
ridor, on one was 'Comptroller', on the other 'Assistant Comptroller'. That was the one she went through and returned from.

'Mr. Harned will see you now.'   26

Mr. Harned was very tall, thin, a small bald head, a long   27
chin, enormous glasses. I immediately began to quiver with
fright. His head was like a temple on top of a mountain, like
the white dagoba on the hill in the North Sea Park. I could not
hear a word of what he said. A paper and a pencil were in my
hand, however, and Mr. Harned was dictating to me, giving
me a speed test in shorthand.

I went out of his office and the pregnant secretary sat me   28

in front of her own typewriter. I turned a stricken face to her.
'I couldn't hear. I couldn't hear what he said . . .'

'Wait, I'll tell him.' She bustled off. At the other desk was   29
a blonde, thin girl, who had thrown one look at me and then
gone back to clattering. The pregnant one reappeared, a pink
sheet in hand: 'Now just copy this on the typewriter, best you
can.'

I hit the keys, swiftly; the typewriter was the same make   30
as mine, a Royal.

'My, you are fast. I'll tell Mr. Harned.'   31

And Mr. Harned came out, benign behind those enormous   32
goggle glasses. 'Well, Miss Chou, we've decided to take you
on as a typist, at thirty-five local dollars a month. To start Monday. Is that all right?'

I nodded, unable to speak. Had he said ten dollars I would   33
have accepted.

The kind secretary said: 'Now take your time, and wipe   34
your face. How old are you, by the way?'

'Sixteen, nearly.'   35

'Is that all? Why my eldest is bigger than you, and she   36
isn't through school yet. I told Mr. Harned you were shy and
upset, and that's why you couldn't take dictation. He's all right,
just takes getting used to, that's all.'

'I couldn't understand his English.'   37

'Oh, you'll get used to it. Now, I won't be around on   38
Monday, I'm going to have a baby. It's your letter that got them
interested in you, you wrote such good English, better than all
the other letters we've had. Mr. Harned will give you a try.'
She whispered. 'I put in a good word for you.'

'Thanks, thanks a lot . . . I need the money, I . . .'   39

'Yes, dear, we know.' Obviously she wanted her type-   40
writer back, and her chair. I was still sitting on it. 'Well, toodle-
doo for now, hope you enjoy yourself in this job. I've been here
six months and I've enjoyed *every minute*. Don't let Mr. Harned
worry you, he's really great, once you get used to him.'

I had a job, had a job, had a job . . . I walked home tread-   41
ing on air, I could not have sat in a rickshaw. Outside our house
was the mule track, and opposite the house was the well, a well
which nestled under a tree. All the creaky squeaky water-carts
of the quarter come here to fill their barrels from this well. The
well winch was turning, clear water, the beautiful clear spring
underground water of Peking gushed out, one by one the water-

carts lined up, the men naked to the waist, wiping their sweat, and spitting. While her husband drew the well water the well woman sat as usual by the stone margin, breasts exposed, feeding her last baby.

Oh, how wonderful life, happy like this water, gushing 42 out so clean and so cold, ice-cold in the June heat! I smiled at the well woman, who had wonderful teeth, and though she was so filthy her skin was always clear and smooth; she never combed her hair, she was a real northern woman, slovenly, unkempt, though she and her husband owned that beautiful well. Mother hated her, and the well woman laughed at Mother, laughed deliberately, standing well back on her planted hips and legs, carrying her large baby across her stomach, breasts hanging like two melons on either side of her open jacket; rippled with well-water laughter.

The more Mama shouted at the well woman, the more she 43 laughed, and her husband who turned the handle of the well-beam and made the water gush stared at Mama, and in his drawling Peking blurr said: 'Now what is she angry about on this beautiful day?' And the water-carriers chuckled. I smiled at them now. I had a job, a job, gushing money like water from a well . . .

THE WRITER'S THEMES

1. Han Suyin shows herself surrounded by members of her family, a close friend, and people at the hospital where she goes for her interview. Who, of all these people, is the most helpful to her? How does this person help her?
2. Throughout the selection, the author gives indications of the various foreign influences that were present in China at that time. Review the selection and note each indication of the presence of foreigners in China. Using all of these details, what impression do you get of the country's economic and social structure?
3. At the beginning of the selection we see the author trudging through white dust; at the end, the promised money from her new job is gushing "like water from a well . . ." How has success changed her view of the world?

THE WRITER'S TECHNIQUE

In paragraph ten of the selection from *A Mortal Flower*, Han Suyin analyzes her reasons for wanting to be a typist in a hospital. Here is the paragraph:

> It made sense to me, typing in a hospital; I would learn about medicine, since I wanted to study medicine. And as there was no money at home for me to study, I would earn money, and prepare myself to enter medical school. I had already discovered that a convent-school education was not at all adequate, and that it would take me at least three more years of hard study before being able to enter any college at all. Science, mathematics, Chinese literature and the classics . . . with the poor schooling given to me, it would take me years to get ready for a university.

The writer begins by noting that her decision to work in a hospital ''made sense'' to her. She then explains why it made sense. First, she would ''learn about medicine''; she would also ''earn money'' and prepare herself ''to enter medical school.'' She then looks backward and ahead and concludes that a convent-school education was ''not at all adequate'' and that she would not be able to enter college for another three years. Next, she lists the subjects she would need for university study, and she concludes that with her ''poor schooling'' it would take her years ''to get ready for a university.''

Notice that, in the paragraph, Han Suyin combines financial and educational considerations; she will work now so that she will be able to go to school later. However, the greater part of the paragraph is devoted to an honest appraisal of her academic strengths and weaknesses, and her future needs. The writer is making a frank assessment of her present position and her long-range goals.

PARAGRAPH PRACTICE

Write a paragraph of your own, using Han Suyin's paragraph as your model. You could describe any plan that you made at a critical point in your life. You could, for example, describe the factors that went into your decision to go to college. Pattern your writing after that of Han Suyin:

> It made sense to me, going to college.

Then describe why it made sense, both in terms of what you would learn and the money you would eventually earn. Next, review your earlier education and judge it as adequate or inadequate as a basis for your higher education. Finally, reach a conclusion as to how much time it will take you to finish your degree.

Your paragraph could also be a description of some other activity which included a mixture of motives and results. Here are some other possible opening sentences for your paragraph:

> It made sense to me, going on vacation alone that year.

> It made sense to me, learning how to change the oil in my car.

> It made sense to me, taking a year off from school.

Be sure to follow Han Suyin's pattern of first telling what it was that made sense, then dealing with the financial aspects, and finally describing what was known and what was still unknown. Also, be sure to give a short, one-sentence conclusion to your paragraph.

ESSAY PRACTICE

The following outline will help you plan a complete essay of at least five paragraphs. The theme of your essay will be closely related to the selection from *A Mortal Flower.*

The following sentence may serve as your thesis sentence, and will also be the main idea of your introductory paragraph:

¶ 1.   Looking for a job is part of a larger process that includes establishing yourself in a position and then deciding how much of a commitment you should make to that job.

Each of the sentences below is the topic sentence for one of the paragraphs that you will write to develop your thesis. You may use the suggested details to develop each paragraph, or you may supply details of your own.

¶ 2.   Looking for a job can be very difficult.

> [DETAILS: What are the different approaches one has to take in order to find a job? What is the most difficult part of the search for a job?]

¶ 3. When you get a job and that job is important to you, it is crucial that you make a good first impression.

   [DETAILS: What do you do in order to make a good impression in a new job? How do you let the people around you know that you want to be where you are, and that you want to stay there?]

¶ 4. It often happens that after you have been in a job for a period of time, you know that you should either make a real commitment to the job or go on to something different.

   [DETAILS: How do you know when a job has given you all that it is going to give? What are the signs—in yourself as well as in those around you—that tell you it is time to move on to something different?]

Be certain that you use transitions between paragraphs to make your writing flow smoothly. In addition, be sure that your conclusion gives your reader a clear signal that you have come to the end of your essay.

ESSAY TOPICS

1. What should a person concentrate on when looking for a job? In your essay you should include every step in the process, from writing a résumé to how you should dress on the day of the interview.
2. Describe the process of writing a résumé. Take your reader through each stage of writing a résumé, commenting on what should be included and what should be avoided in each section of the résumé.
3. Describe your most memorable job interview. As you write your description, be sure you describe the setting for the interview, the appearance and personality of the interviewer, and your own actions and reactions during the interview.

❧ *Camara Laye* ❧

Camara Laye (1928–1980) was born into a Moslem family in Kouroussa, French Guinea. *The Dark Child*, written while the author was still in his twenties, is the story of his childhood and adolescence in West Africa. The book is not only a personal story, but also an account of his family and his village. We are given a portrait of his father, who was a goldsmith and metal worker. We also see his mother, in addition to other people of his village who were important influences on him during his youth.

Camara Laye left his village and went to Paris to study engineering, and it was in the French capital that he wrote his autobiography, a work that one critic has noted was written "to relieve his exile at a time when he was far from his people." The book was published in 1954 and was immediately well received. As the Haitian novelist Philippe Thoby-Marcelin has observed, the book has "the aura of dignity with which he surrounded his family and his people as he paints them with candid sincerity . . ."

The writer later returned to his country and worked there as a civil servant. His second book, *The Radiance of the King*, appeared in English in 1956. It is a heavily symbolic story of a white man wandering in Africa. Another novel, *Dramouss*, was published ten years later.

In the following selection from *The Dark Child*, Camara Laye shows his father producing a piece of jewelry for a woman of the village. In the process, the writer also shows us how the people of his village live and work together.

PREVIEWING THE WRITER

• Note the portrait of the writer's father that emerges in the selection. What are the details that reveal the most about his personality?

• Note the attitude of the village people toward the writer's father. What do all of these attitudes have in common?

• What are the various steps in the process of making a piece of gold jewelry, as described by the writer?

from *THE DARK CHILD*

OF ALL THE DIFFERENT kinds of work my father engaged in, none fascinated me so much as his skill with gold. No other occupation was so noble, no other needed such a delicate touch. And then, every time he worked in gold it was like a festival—indeed it *was* a festival—that broke the monotony of ordinary working days.

So, if a woman, accompanied by a go-between, crossed the threshold of the workshop, I followed her in at once. I knew what she wanted: she had brought some gold, and had come to ask my father to transform it into a trinket. She had collected it in the placers of Siguiri where, crouching over the river for months on end, she had patiently extracted grains of gold from the mud. 2

These women never came alone. They knew my father had other things to do than make trinkets. And even when he had the time, they knew they were not the first to ask a favor of him, and that, consequently, they would not be served before others. 3

Generally they required the trinket for a certain date, for the festival of Ramadan or the Tabaski or some other family ceremony or dance. 4

Therefore, to enhance their chances of being served quickly and to more easily persuade my father to interrupt the work before him, they used to request the services of an official praise-singer, a go-between, arranging in advance the fee they were to pay him for his good offices. 5

The go-between installed himself in the workshop, tuned up his *cora*, which is our harp, and began to sing my father's praises. This was always a great event for me. I heard recalled the lofty deeds of my father's ancestors and their names from the earliest times. As the couplets were reeled off it was like watching the growth of a great genealogical tree that spread its branches far and wide and flourished its boughs and twigs before my mind's eye. The harp played an accompaniment to this vast utterance of names, expanding it with notes that were now soft, now shrill. 6

I could sense my father's vanity being inflamed, and I already knew that after having sipped this milk-and-honey he would lend a favorable ear to the woman's request. But I was not alone in my knowledge. The woman also had seen my father's eyes gleaming with contented pride. She held out her grains of gold as if the whole matter were settled. My father took up his scales and weighed the gold. 7

"What sort of trinket do you want?" he would ask. 8
"I want. . . ." 9
And then the woman would not know any longer exactly 10

what she wanted because desire kept making her change her mind, and because she would have liked all the trinkets at once. But it would have taken a pile of gold much larger than she had brought to satisfy her whim, and from then on her chief purpose in life was to get hold of it as soon as she could.

"When do you want it?" 11

Always the answer was that the trinket was needed for an 12
occasion in the near future.

"So! You are in that much of a hurry? Where do you think 13
I shall find the time?"

"I am in a great hurry, I assure you." 14

"I have never seen a woman eager to deck herself out who 15
wasn't in a great hurry! Good! I shall arrange my time to suit you. Are you satisfied?"

He would take the clay pot that was kept specially for 16
smelting gold, and would pour the grains into it. He would then cover the gold with powdered charcoal, a charcoal he prepared by using plant juices of exceptional purity. Finally, he would place a large lump of the same kind of charcoal over the pot.

As soon as she saw that the work had been duly under- 17
taken, the woman, now quite satisfied, would return to her household tasks, leaving her go-between to carry on with the praise-singing which had already proven so advantageous.

At a sign from my father the apprentices began working 18
two sheepskin bellows. The skins were on the floor, on opposite sides of the forge, connected to it by earthen pipes. While the work was in progress the apprentices sat in front of the bellows with crossed legs. That is, the younger of the two sat, for the elder was sometimes allowed to assist. But the younger—this time it was Sidafa—was only permitted to work the bellows and watch while waiting his turn for promotion to less rudimentary tasks. First one and then the other worked hard at the bellows: the flame in the forge rose higher and became a living thing, a genie implacable and full of life.

Then my father lifted the clay pot with his long tongs and 19
placed it on the flame.

Immediately all activity in the workshop almost came to a 20
halt. During the whole time that the gold was being smelted, neither copper nor aluminum could be worked nearby, lest some particle of these base metals fall into the container which held the gold. Only steel could be worked on such occasions, but the

men, whose task that was, hurried to finish what they were doing, or left it abruptly to join the apprentices gathered around the forge. There were so many, and they crowded so around my father, that I, the smallest person present, had to come near the forge in order not to lose track of what was going on.

If he felt he had inadequate working space, my father had 21 the apprentices stand well away from him. He merely raised his hand in a simple gesture: at that particular moment he never uttered a word, and no one else would: no one was allowed to utter a word. Even the go-between's voice was no longer raised in song. The silence was broken only by the panting of the bellows and the faint hissing of the gold. But if my father never actually spoke, I know that he was forming words in his mind. I could tell from his lips, which kept moving, while, bending over the pot, he stirred the gold and charcoal with a bit of wood that kept bursting into flame and had constantly to be replaced by a fresh one.

What words did my father utter? I do not know. At least 22 I am not certain what they were. No one ever told me. But could they have been anything but incantations? On these occasions was he not invoking the genies of fire and gold, of fire and wind, of wind blown by the blast-pipes of the forge, of fire born of wind, of gold married to fire? Was it not their assistance, their friendship, their espousal that he besought? Yes. Almost certainly he was invoking these genies, all of whom are equally indispensable for smelting gold.

The operation going on before my eyes was certainly the 23 smelting of gold, yet something more than that: a magical operation that the guiding spirits could regard with favor or disfavor. That is why, all around my father, there was absolute silence and anxious expectancy. Though only a child, I knew there could be no craft greater than the goldsmith's. I expected a ceremony; I had come to be present at a ceremony; and it actually was one, though very protracted. I was still too young to understand why, but I had an inkling as I watched the almost religious concentration of those who followed the mixing process in the clay pot.

When finally the gold began to melt I could have shouted 24 aloud—and perhaps we all would have if we had not been forbidden to make a sound. I trembled, and so did everyone else watching my father stir the mixture—it was still a heavy paste—in which the charcoal was gradually consumed. The next stage

followed swiftly. The gold now had the fluidity of water. The
genies had smiled on the operation!

"Bring me the brick!" my father would order, thus lifting   25
the ban that until then had silenced us.

The brick, which an apprentice would place beside the fire,   26
was hollowed out, generously greased with Galam butter. My
father would take the pot off the fire and tilt it carefully, while
I would watch the gold flow into the brick, flow like liquid
fire. True, it was only a very sparse trickle of fire, but how
vivid, how brilliant! As the gold flowed into the brick, the grease
sputtered and flamed and emitted a thick smoke that caught
in the throat and stung the eyes, leaving us all weeping and
coughing.

But there were times when it seemed to me that my father   27
ought to turn this task over to one of his assistants. They were
experienced, had assisted him hundreds of times, and could
certainly have performed the work well. But my father's lips
moved and those inaudible, secret words, those incantations he
addressed to one we could not see or hear, was the essential
part. Calling on the genies of fire, of wind, of gold and exorcis-
ing the evil spirits—this was a knowledge he alone possessed.

By now the gold had been cooled in the hollow of the   28
brick, and my father began to hammer and stretch it. This was
the moment when his work as a goldsmith really began. I noticed that before embarking on it he never failed to stroke the
little snake stealthily as it lay coiled up under the sheepskin. I
can only assume that this was his way of gathering strength for
what remained to be done, the most trying part of his task.

But was it not extraordinary and miraculous that on these   29
occasions the little black snake was always coiled under the
sheepskin? He was not always there. He did not visit my father
every day. But he was always present whenever there was gold
to be worked. His presence was no surprise to *me*. After that
evening when my father had spoken of the guiding spirit of his
race I was no longer astonished. The snake was there inten-
tionally. He knew what the future held. Did he tell my father?
I think that he most certainly did. Did he tell him everything?
I have another reason for believing firmly that he did.

The craftsman who works in gold must first of all purify   30
himself. That is, he must wash himself all over and, of course,
abstain from all sexual commerce during the whole time. Great
respecter of ceremony as he was, it would have been impossible

for my father to ignore these rules. Now, I never saw him make these preparations. I saw him address himself to his work without any apparent preliminaries. From that moment it was obvious that, forewarned in a dream by his black guiding spirit of the task which awaited him in the morning, my father must have prepared for it as soon as he arose, entering his workshop in a state of purity, his body smeared with the secret potions hidden in his numerous pots of magical substances; or perhaps he always came into his workshop in a state of ritual purity. I am not trying to make him out a better man than he was—he was a man and had his share of human frailties—but he was always uncompromising in his respect for ritual observance.

The woman for whom the trinket was being made, and who had come often to see how the work was progressing, would arrive for the final time, not wanting to miss a moment of this spectacle—as marvelous to her as to us—when the gold wire, which my father had succeeded in drawing out from the mass of molten gold and charcoal, was transformed into a trinket.

There she would be. Her eyes would devour the fragile gold wire, following it in its tranquil and regular spiral around the little slab of metal which supported it. My father would catch a glimpse of her and I would see him slowly beginning to smile. Her avid attention delighted him.

"Are you trembling?" he would ask.

"Am I trembling?"

And we would all burst out laughing at her. For she would be trembling! She would be trembling with covetousness for the spiral pyramid in which my father would be inserting, among the convolutions, tiny grains of gold. When he had finally finished by crowning the pyramid with a heavier grain, she would dance in delight.

No one—no one at all—would be more enchanted than she as my father slowly turned the trinket back and forth between his fingers to display its perfection. Not even the praise-singer whose business it was to register excitement would be more excited than she. Throughout this metamorphosis he did not stop speaking faster and ever faster, increasing his tempo, accelerating his praises and flatteries as the trinket took shape, shouting to the skies my father's skill.

For the praise-singer took a curious part—I should say rather that it was direct and effective—in the work. He was drunk with the joy of creation. He shouted aloud in joy. He plucked his *cora* like a man inspired. He sweated as if he were the trinket-maker, as if he were my father, as if the trinket were his creation. He was no longer a hired censer-bearer, a man whose services anyone could rent. He was a man who created his song out of some deep inner necessity. And when my father, after having soldered the large grain of gold that crowned the summit, held out his work to be admired, the praise-singer would no longer be able to contain himself. He would begin to intone the *douga*, the great chant which is sung only for celebrated men and which is danced for them alone.

But the *douga* is a formidable chant, a provocative chant, 38 a chant which the praise-singer dared not sing, and which the man for whom it is sung dared not dance before certain precautions had been taken. My father had taken them as soon as he woke, since he had been warned in a dream. The praise-singer had taken them when he concluded his arrangements with the woman. Like my father he had smeared his body with magic substances and had made himself invulnerable to the evil genies whom the *douga* inevitably set free; these potions made him invulnerable also to rival praise-singers, perhaps jealous of him, who awaited only this song and the exaltation and loss of control which attended it, in order to begin casting their spells.

At the first notes of the *douga* my father would arise and 39 emit a cry in which happiness and triumph were equally mingled; and brandishing in his right hand the hammer that was the symbol of his profession and in his left a ram's horn filled with magic substances, he would dance the glorious dance.

No sooner had he finished, than workmen and appren- 40 tices, friends and customers in their turn, not forgetting the woman for whom the trinket had been created, would flock around him, congratulating him, showering praises on him and complimenting the praise-singer at the same time. The latter found himself laden with gifts—almost his only means of support, for the praise-singer leads a wandering life after the fashion of the troubadours of old. Aglow with dancing and the praises he had received, my father would offer everyone cola nuts, that small change of Guinean courtesy.

Now all that remained to be done was to redden the trinket 41 in a little water to which chlorine and sea salt had been added. I was at liberty to leave. The festival was over!

THE WRITER'S THEMES

1. What is the process, described in this essay, for making a piece of gold jewelry? As you describe the process, separate the mystical from the physical elements.
2. In addition to the process of making a gold trinket, another process is described in the essay: the process of getting the writer's father to agree to make the piece of jewelry. How do the villagers convince the goldsmith to do the work?
3. What are the attitudes toward the goldsmith that are shared by all of the villagers, including the goldsmith's own son? To what extent do the attitudes differ from person to person?

THE WRITER'S TECHNIQUE

The following sections from *The Dark Child* show the goldsmith during the early stages of his work on the piece of jewelry:

> He would take the clay pot that was kept specially for smelting gold, and would pour the grains into it. He would then cover the gold with powdered charcoal, a charcoal he prepared by using plant juices of exceptional purity. Finally, he would place a large lump of the same kind of charcoal over the pot.
>
> ....
>
> At a sign from my father the apprentices began working two sheepskin bellows. The skins were on the floor, on opposite sides of the forge, connected to it by earthen pipes.
>
> ....
>
> Then my father lifted the clay pot with his long tongs and placed it on the flame.
>
> ....
>
> If he felt he had inadequate working space, my father had the apprentices stand well away from him. He merely raised his hand in a simple gesture: at that particular moment he never uttered a word, and no one else would: no one was allowed to utter a word.

Notice how the writer takes us through the basic steps of the goldsmith's craft. We first see the materials he will use—the clay pot, the charcoal, and the grains of gold—and we see what the goldsmith does with these materials. We see the next part of the goldsmith's method when he orders his apprentices to help with another piece of necessary equipment, the bellows. Then the goldsmith places the clay pot on the flame. Finally, the author points out two other important factors for the success of the operation. If he felt he did not have enough space in which to work, the goldsmith would have his apprentices stand away from him. He would also insist on silence; "no one was allowed to utter a word."

PARAGRAPH PRACTICE

Write a paragraph of your own, using the above sections from *The Dark Child* as your model. Your paragraph could be a description of yourself or someone else in a work situation. If you choose to write about yourself, for example, you might wish to describe yourself writing or doing some other work at home. You could first describe the *materials* you use and how you use them. Next, describe the *conditions* you must have in order to do your work well. Finally, describe the *one condition* (the most important one) that you must have in order to work well.

If you describe someone else, use the same procedure. Some possible examples of people at work are:

—a mechanic repairing a car

—a dentist at work

—a person preparing a meal

Notice that Camara Laye combines the goldsmith's materials, methods, and the conditions necessary for the work. In your description, make sure that you combine the materials, the method, and the conditions under which the work was done. Finally, keep in mind that if you describe a process you have observed many times, your writing is more likely to make a strong impression.

ESSAY PRACTICE

The following outline will help you plan a complete essay of at least five paragraphs. The theme of your essay will be closely related to the selection by Camara Laye.

The following sentence may serve as your thesis sentence, and will also be the main idea of your introductory paragraph:

¶ 1. Careful shopping involves gathering as much information as you can, making an informed judgment about a purchase, and always learning from past shopping experiences.

Each of the sentences below is the topic sentence for one of the paragraphs that you will write to develop your thesis. You may use the suggested details to develop each paragraph, or you may supply details of your own.

¶ 2. When I am about to buy something important, I try to get as much information about the product as I can.

> [DETAILS: How do you obtain the information you need? Do you ask your friends for their advice or recommendations? Do you consult *Consumer Reports* or other magazines?]

¶ 3. When I actually make the purchase, I know that the final decision is really up to me.

> [DETAILS: When you shop, do you compare prices or do you go to the nearest store for the sake of convenience? Do you go alone or do you bring someone with you? What part does the salesperson play in your decision? Do you think it over, or do you buy right away?]

¶ 4. There are several things I have learned about being a careful shopper.

> [DETAILS: What advice can you give someone who is about to make an important purchase? What should that person be sure to do? What should that person be most careful about?]

Be certain that you use transitions between paragraphs to make your writing flow smoothly. In addition, be sure that your conclusion gives your reader a clear signal that you have come to the end of your essay.

ESSAY TOPICS

1. Describe a time you saw a trades- or craftsperson at work and you really appreciated his or her skills. What were the circumstances under which you observed this person? What did the person do or make? Describe the process you observed, as nearly as you can remember it.

    If there were other people present, what were their reactions? After observing this person, what new appreciation did you have for this kind of work?

2. Describe a process you observed one or both of your parents engaged in when you were a child. You might have ob-

served one of your parents baking bread, or you might have seen both of them painting or wallpapering a room.

Based on your recollection of your parents, are you now able to do the same things you saw them do? Did their work inspire you to try different things on your own?

3. What is the most satisfying piece of work you ever did? Describe the steps you went through in the process of doing this work. If you were working for money, did your satisfaction come from the pay you received or was there another reason for your sense of satisfaction with the job?

Focus on Terms: Symbol

A *symbol* is an object we can see that leads us to a further meaning beyond that of the object itself. We are surrounded by symbols in our daily lives, many of them very external and visible: the American flag symbolizes our country, the cross stands for Christianity, and the image of a dove symbolizes peace. Symbols such as these are so universal and accepted that an explanation for any one of them is seldom needed.

Other symbols may be more internal, or personal. For example, a person may regard a particular cottage or farmhouse as symbolic of the idea of home, or someone else could see an old hat as symbolic of freedom or casualness. Private symbols such as these require explanation if their intention is to be understood by other people.

In the selection from Han Suyin's *A Mortal Flower*, the writer begins by describing herself trudging a "mule track" with her tennis shoes filled with "white dust." Near the end of the selection we see her returning home, and again we are shown the mule track. This time, however, the writer points out that "opposite the house was the well" which is seen to gush clear, beautiful water. The writer adds: "Oh, how wonderful life, happy like this water," and she concludes by pointing to the well as a symbol of her new status as a person with a job: "I had a job, a job, gushing money like water from a well . . ." The well is symbolic of her new job, and at this point we are reminded of the dust that had filled her tennis shoes—dust that was symbolic of her lack of money, along with her lack of a sense of direction. By using these symbols of dust, water, and the well, the writer has indicated a dramatic change in her situation.

In the excerpt from *The Dark Child*, Camara Laye also uses symbol to reinforce his meaning. In this case, the writer is dealing with a very universal symbol, but he uses it in a personal way. Gold is universally recognized as a symbol of wealth, but in the selection from *The Dark Child* it takes on the more private symbolic meaning of a celebration. This is the association the author makes as he tells us that every time his father worked with gold, "it was like a festival—indeed it *was* a festival—that broke the monotony of ordinary working days." Camara Laye's description of his father at work leads us to a further symbolic meaning for gold, namely, the value of relationships in a community at a time when ordinary tasks are put aside and people celebrate together. Here, gold becomes symbolic of the festival of life.

If you find yourself using some very well known public symbols in your writing, you may assume that your reader will understand what you mean by using that symbol. However, if you intend to use a symbol that is less well known as a means of explanation, you must be especially careful that your symbolic meaning is made clear to your reader.

Student Essay ✌ ✿ Martha Schanel

The following essay could also have been entitled "How to Succeed in Gardening." In the process of taking us through her description of starting and maintaining a garden, the writer shows us some of the larger implications of her private actions. As you read the essay, notice how the writer divides her essay into three parts, using three successive years to describe her work on this garden.

• The writer's description of her garden can have a larger significance if we keep in mind the fact that, since the Garden of Eden, gardens have often been used to signify harmony and growth, and a place where we can be at peace with nature.

THE PESTS HAVE PESTS

THREE YEARS AGO LAST APRIL, I took a pitchfork and a   1
spade out into my yard and turned over a patch of sod. The soil beneath was dry and hard, a red clay color loaded with rock and not a sign of life. A neighbor who witnessed this event soon suggested that the lawn was in need of fertilizers and weed killers which would restore life and health to the area. A chemical shot in the arm would green up the grass and keep it producing all summer. But I was about to turn this patch of lawn into a vegetable garden and my neighbor was as unaware as I was myself that my hobby not only would change what I did to my piece of land, but would change my whole attitude toward the earth.

That first summer I struggled with mites and aphids and   2
squash borers and hornworms, not to mention the humiliation
of having the smallest tomatoes on the block. I searched through
books and articles looking for natural ways to ward off the pests
and, more importantly, to fortify the soil. The first year was a
complete success—for the insects. They were fed far better than
my family from that early endeavor.

At the onset of my garden's second season, the trees   3
around our neighborhood were infested with gypsy moths, as
were numerous other areas of the Eastern seaboard. Almost as
quickly as the insects invaded, the defending army of chemical
trucks was called on the scene by the neighbors. As the Sevin
and Malathion dripped off the trees, I ran to cover the vegetables. I had become convinced that my job was not to conquer
the land we owned, but to cooperate with it. I had unwittingly
adopted a cause. With determination to participate in Nature's
own balancing act, I resisted the neighbors' subtle suggestions
that we spray our property to insure protection for their trees.
One evening, as I worked on my hands and knees weeding,
my countenance camouflaged by a row of corn stalks, my next-
door neighbor was caught with his hand in the proverbial cookie
jar as he drenched the hedge separating our lots with pesticide.
Red-faced yet still determined, he left quietly, realizing that more
than a privet hedge separated us now. I wondered that night if
he hadn't somehow abdicated his right to own a single tree, if
his purpose was to eradicate the life forms which it supported.

That season our produce yield was moderate. A new phe-   4
nomenon had occurred. My sons were ushering the neighborhood children into the carrot patch to hunt bait for their fishing
expeditions. They had discovered that each time they were sent
to pull carrots for the evening meal, the soil they disturbed was
teeming with worms. It did not take long for the news to travel
to the end of the block. Each youngster would fill a soup can
with worms—quite a tempting meal for the bass in the backyard
pond—and then help himself to a carrot or two, a suitable snack
to take along on a fishing trip. It was also noticed that around
that time the sugar peas had particular difficulty remaining on
the vine till ripe. Baby corn on the cob had special appeal, as
did crispy cucumbers on hot afternoons. Our measure of yield
was indeed distorted by this new yet welcome pest.

Our first two seasons of gardening were not inexpensive.   5
Seeds, potting soil, and plant lighting to start the seeds repre-

sented a significant outlay of money each spring, as did the few supplies needed as the summer wore on. However, the expense was justified as a small one in proportion to what had previously been spent on hobbies or amusements for the family. But in our third season we hit "pay dirt." It began as the others did, starting seeds in February and setting them out in the garden in May. Our only addition was a small birdbath to attract songbirds. But Mother Nature had a new challenge for us. A drought that would force the town to limit the use of water threatened to destroy the neighborhood flower and vegetable gardens. Still convinced that we must cooperate with, not conquer Mother Nature's whims, we began to gather garden refuse. Leaves and grass clippings were collected and placed around the young plants, covering their roots and the surrounding soil so that it would not lose the slightest bit of moisture in the hot summer sun. We gathered our "insurance" from neighbors who were eager to dispose of their garden garbage and to poke fun at our odd collections. By August, when one neighbor's tomato plants were brown and lifeless and another neighbor was seen nightly carrying buckets of bath water into the yard, our plants were thriving—leaves green and new growth plentiful. The mulch had not only conserved moisture but also fed the soil as it decomposed naturally. While across the street lawns were burning and gardens wilting from thirst, Nature herself cared for my plants, holding in moisture with a natural mulch and using insects and worms to carry the freshly made fertilizer to the plant roots. It seemed as though Mother Nature, having tasted our faith in her ways, began to smile on our efforts. The final affirmation came in a rather awful disguise, a grotesque green hornworm about three inches in length and as thick as a dime, and covered with white bumps. Although accustomed to handpicking the destructive insects from the plants, even I was squeamish when this one appeared. In hope of finding some concoction which would save me from this chore, I searched the organic garden pest book and found therein news that the natural balance we sought for our garden was beginning to happen. Our hornworm, now taking on an almost affectionate look, was infected with the larvae of a beneficial parasite, one which would feed on gypsy moth larvae and control its infestation for a radius of one block.

When the harvest began, I sent the children to each of the neighbors with fresh ripe tomatoes and crispy snapbeans—there 6 seemed enough for a dozen families. The garden had changed dramatically in those three seasons, as had I. The humiliation of my first effort had turned to smugness and finally to awe, as I watched and learned to trust a force greater than any I had witnessed before.

Strategies for Writing

1. In this essay, the writer's garden could be seen as symbolic of the harmony between people, and harmony with nature. How does the final sentence of the essay support this idea?
2. In the essay, how does the appearance of the hornworm symbolize the wisdom of nature?
3. The writer observes that, by her garden's second season, she had "adopted a cause" when she realized that she should cooperate with the land. Write an essay in which you discuss your involvement in a cause. Be sure to include the step-by-step process by which you became more and more involved.
4. Write an essay in which you describe the process needed to start a hobby, or any other kind of leisure activity. In your essay, be sure to include each step in the process so that your reader will have a clear idea of what is involved.

5

PERSONAL DISCOVERY

WRITING SKILL: Example

I remember an old Arab in North Africa, a man whose hands had never felt water. He gave me mint tea in a glass so coated with use that it was opaque, but he handed me companionship, and the tea was wonderful because of it. And without any protection my teeth didn't fall out, nor did running sores develop. I began to formulate a new law describing the relationship of protection to despondency. A sad soul can kill you quicker, far quicker, than a germ.

In this excerpt from John Steinbeck's book *Travels with Charley*, the writer provides an example of the idea of companionship. Rather than try to give a formal description of the concept, Steinbeck decided to illustrate what he meant by using an example. It worked. A dull writer would have given only vague generalities and would have neglected to provide specific, memorable details to make the example real for the reader. We remember Steinbeck's old Arab, who never bathed, and we can almost see the unwashed glass in which he offered tea to the writer. Because of these details, this example of friendly companionship becomes a memorable description.

All of us have concepts or ideas in our minds, but they will not become real for our listeners, our readers, or even ourselves unless we use examples to make these concepts more concrete. As writers, when we bring ideas down to earth we not only gain and hold the attention of our readers, we make the presentation of our ideas all the more convincing. If we do not provide the examples that are needed in our writing, we leave it to our readers to supply their own, and this in turn leads to a loss of control over our own writing. With the proper examples, our writing will express our thinking with clarity, concreteness, and conviction.

The use of good examples has a very important advantage for you as a writer. Very simply, it makes your work more interesting to read. The better your examples, the more difficult it is for a reader to put down what you have written. For example, if you were to write about fashionable clothes, no general ideas would have the impact of a single example such as, "A pair of jeans by Gloria Vanderbilt." Similarly, if you want to write about "craftsmanship" in terms of jewelry, your discussion will remain vague and general until you use a specific example such as "an American Indian silver and turquoise ring." Examples *clarify* your writing, and good examples go a long way toward supporting what you want to say.

Each essay in this unit contains examples that help us understand the ideas behind the essay. For example, in Joan Didion's "On Going Home," when the writer thinks of a young girl dancing in a San Francisco bar, she wonders what sense that girl could "make of, say, *Long Day's Journey into Night* . . ." Here, Joan Didion is careful to give us a specific example of a play that relates directly to the meaning of her own essay: Eugene O'Neil's *Long Day's Journey into Night* deals with the same theme of family relationships that we find in the Joan Didion essay. The writer's example not only makes her point more specific, it also relates directly to the theme of her essay.

In Loren Eiseley's essay "The Hidden Teacher," the writer

is concerned with some nontraditional ways of learning, and he begins by using a famous example from the Bible, the story of Job. Job had to suffer in order to learn, and this philosophical approach to the learning process leads Eiseley to the main example of his essay: "For example, I once received an unexpected lesson from a spider." Much of the remainder of the essay is a development of this specific example, as Eiseley relates it to our own position in the universe, both physically and philosophically.

In "The Soul of a Tree," Tom Brown, Jr., and William Owen use examples to help us more easily share their perceptions of life in the wilderness, and how it relates to our own lives. At one point in the essay, the writers describe some hunters who were so concerned with being on schedule that they did not notice "the raccoon who had sat on a rock and watched them ride by . . ." Nor did they notice "the owl at the base of a pine or the screech owl . . ." They also missed the trout and the red squirrel that Tom Brown could plainly see. The authors could have indicated that the hunters were not aware of the wildlife around them, but by providing specific examples of that wildlife they show us exactly what those hunters were missing. At the same time, they are giving us examples of the variety of forest animals.

In James Baldwin's memoir of the playwright Lorraine Hansberry, the writer uses examples to help us form a picture of his friend's personality. At one point in the essay, Baldwin remembers that Lorraine Hansberry accepted criticism, as well as fame, with good humor. Baldwin writes: "She took it all with a kind of astringent good humor, refusing, for example, even to consider defending herself when she was accused of being a 'slum-lord' . . ." He then supports his point with a quotation from the playwright herself, who good-naturedly referred to her sudden drop in popularity with her friends by observing, "'My God, Jimmy, do you realize you're only the second person who's called me today?' . . ." Both of these examples allow Baldwin to come to an important conclusion about his friend: "She was devoted to the human race, but she was not romantic about it."

Good examples that are clear and appropriate give depth and meaning to a writer's work. Carefully chosen examples can also give an extra dimension to that work—the dimension of personality.

❧ *Joan Didion* ❧

Joan Didion was born in Sacramento, California, in 1934. She
went to high school in Sacramento and then attended the University of California at Berkeley. In 1956, the year she received
her B.A., Joan Didion went to New York City as the winner of
a *Vogue* magazine college writing prize. The following year she
met the writer John Gregory Dunne, who was then working for
Time magazine. In 1964 they married and went to California to
work as freelance writers.

Joan Didion's published fiction includes *Run River, Play It
as It Lays,* and *A Book of Common Prayer.* Some observers feel that
she is an even better nonfiction writer than she is a novelist; one
critic has called her "the finest woman prose stylist writing in
English today."

The writer reports that she "had more worries as a child
than I've ever had since. I've gradually been shedding them as
I go through life." For example, she remembers that when she
was a child her mother told her to "stop whining" and try to
write some stories. She did, and found that writing helped her
a great deal. When you write, Didion has noted, "you put the
worries down. You assign . . . problems to different people."

Joan Didion has published three major books of nonfiction,
The White Album, Slouching towards Bethlehem, and *Salvador.* In the
following essay, taken from *Slouching towards Bethlehem,* Didion
looks at her own past and tries to define her relationship with
other members of her family, both present and past.

PREVIEWING THE WRITER

• How many different generations of her family does Joan
Didion include in her essay? What is her attitude toward each
of these generations?

• Note the author's attitude toward her childhood. What
is her strongest emotion as she recalls the various people and
events of that childhood?

• Based on the details provided in the essay, what
impression do we have of the writer's absent husband?

ON GOING HOME

I AM HOME for my daughter's first birthday. By
"home" I do not mean the house in Los Angeles where my
husband and I and the baby live, but the place where my family

is, in the Central Valley of California. It is a vital although troublesome distinction. My husband likes my family but is uneasy in their house, because once there I fall into their ways, which are difficult, oblique, deliberately inarticulate, not my husband's ways. We live in dusty houses (''D-U-S-T,'' he once wrote with his finger on surfaces all over the house, but no one noticed it) filled with mementos quite without value to him (what could the Canton dessert plates mean to him? how could he have known about the assay scales, why should he care if he did know?), and we appear to talk exclusively about people we know who have been committed to mental hospitals, about people we know who have been booked on drunk-driving charges, and about property, particularly about property, land, price per acre and C-2 zoning and assessments and freeway access. My brother does not understand my husband's inability to perceive the advantage in the rather common real-estate transaction known as ''sale-leaseback,'' and my husband in turn does not understand why so many of the people he hears about in my father's house have recently been committed to mental hospitals or booked on drunk-driving charges. Nor does he understand that when we talk about sale-leasebacks and right-of-way condemnations we are talking in code about the things we like best, the yellow fields and the cottonwoods and the rivers rising and falling and the mountain roads closing when the heavy snow comes in. We miss each other's points, have another drink and regard the fire. My brother refers to my husband, in his presence, as ''Joan's husband.'' Marriage is the classic betrayal.

Or perhaps it is not any more. Sometimes I think that those of us who are now in our thirties were born into the last generation to carry the burden of ''home,'' to find in family life the source of all tension and drama. I had by all objective accounts a ''normal'' and a ''happy'' family situation, and yet I was almost thirty years old before I could talk to my family on the telephone without crying after I had hung up. We did not fight. Nothing was wrong. And yet some nameless anxiety colored the emotional charges between me and the place that I came from. The question of whether or not you could go home again was a very real part of the sentimental and largely literary baggage with which we left home in the fifties; I suspect that it is irrelevant to the children born of the fragmentation after World War II. A few weeks ago in a San Francisco bar I saw a pretty young girl on crystal take off her clothes and dance for the cash prize in an "amateur-topless" contest. There was no particular sense of moment about this, none of the effect of romantic degradation, of "dark journey," for which my generation strived so assiduously. What sense could that girl possibly make of, say, *Long Day's Journey into Night?* Who is beside the point?

That I am trapped in this particular irrelevancy is never more apparent to me than when I am home. Paralyzed by the neurotic lassitude engendered by meeting one's past at every turn, around every corner, inside every cupboard, I go aimlessly from room to room. I decide to meet it head-on and clean out a drawer, and I spread the contents on the bed. A bathing suit I wore the summer I was seventeen. A letter of rejection from *The Nation,* an aerial photograph of the site for a shopping center my father did not build in 1954. Three teacups hand-painted with cabbage roses and signed "E.M.," my grandmother's initials. There is no final solution for letters of rejection from *The Nation* and teacups hand-painted in 1900. Nor is there any answer to snapshots of one's grandfather as a young man on skis, surveying around Donner Pass in the year 1910. I smooth out the snapshot and look into his face, and do and do not see my own. I close the drawer, and have another cup of coffee with my mother. We get along very well, veterans of a guerrilla war we never understood. 3

Days pass. I see no one. I come to dread my husband's evening call, not only because he is full of news of what by now seems to me our remote life in Los Angeles, people he has seen, letters which require attention, but because he asks what I have been doing, suggests uneasily that I get out, drive to San Francisco or Berkeley. Instead I drive across the river to a family graveyard. It has been vandalized since my last visit and the monuments are broken, overturned in the dry grass. Because I once saw a rattlesnake in the grass I stay in the car and listen to a country-and-Western station. Later I drive with my father to a ranch he has in the foothills. The man who runs his cattle on it asks us to the roundup, a week from Sunday, and although I know that I will be in Los Angeles I say, in the oblique way my family talks, that I will come. Once home I mention the broken monuments in the graveyard. My mother shrugs. 4

I go to visit my great-aunts. A few of them think now that I am my cousin, or their daughter who died young. We recall an anecdote about a relative last seen in 1948, and they ask if I still like living in New York City. I have lived in Los Angeles 5

for three years, but I say that I do. The baby is offered a hore-
hound drop, and I am slipped a dollar bill "to buy a treat."
Questions trail off, answers are abandoned, the baby plays with
the dust motes in a shaft of afternoon sun.

It is time for the baby's birthday party: a white cake, straw- 6
berry-marshmallow ice cream, a bottle of champagne saved from
another party. In the evening, after she has gone to sleep, I
kneel beside the crib and touch her face, where it is pressed
against the slats, with mine. She is an open and trusting child,
unprepared for and unaccustomed to the ambushes of family
life, and perhaps it is just as well that I can offer her little of
that life. I would like to give her more. I would like to promise
her that she will grow up with a sense of her cousins and of
rivers and of her great-grandmother's teacups, would like to
pledge her a picnic on a river with fried chicken and her hair
uncombed, would like to give her *home* for her birthday, but we
live differently now and I can promise her nothing like that. I
give her a xylophone and a sundress from Madeira, and promise
to tell her a funny story.

THE WRITER'S THEMES

1. In the essay, Joan Didion notes that she finds it difficult to
communicate with the different generations of her family.
Trace the difficulties she has with each generation. How
does she try to communicate with the people around her?
Where do we most clearly see her difficulties in communi-
cating with her own husband and daughter?
2. What is the writer's attitude toward her past? Where in the
essay do we see her thoughts about the future?
3. To what extent does Joan Didion try to relate her own feelings and experiences to the feelings and experiences of others of her generation? To what extent does she convince you
that she might be typical of many of the people of her generation?

THE WRITER'S TECHNIQUE

In the third paragraph of her essay, Joan Didion describes herself as going "aimlessly from room to room" until she finally

decides to meet her own past "head-on." Here is that section from paragraph three:

> I decide to meet it head-on and clean out a drawer, and I spread the contents on the bed. A bathing suit I wore the summer I was seventeen. A letter of rejection from *The Nation*, an aerial photograph of the site for a shopping center my father did not build in 1954. Three teacups hand-painted with cabbage roses and signed "E.M.," my grandmother's initials. There is no final solution for letters of rejection from *The Nation* and teacups hand-painted in 1900. Nor is there any answer to snapshots of one's grandfather as a young man on skis, surveying around Donner Pass in the year 1910. I smooth out the snapshot and look into his face, and do and do not see my own. I close the drawer, and have another cup of coffee with my mother.

Notice that the writer uses for her example a very universal act, that of cleaning out a drawer. She empties the contents of the drawer onto the bed and examines them. There is a personal article of clothing (a bathing suit) and a slightly less personal item (the letter of rejection from a magazine). The writer then moves further back in the history of her family and as she does so, she goes further back in time. The drawer contains a photograph of a planned shopping mall that was going to be built by her father; it also contains teacups hand-painted by her grandmother in 1900. Finally, there is a picture of her grandfather, taken in 1910. When the writer examines this last item, she tells us that she does and does not see her own face.

Joan Didion uses specific examples to show us the contents of this bureau drawer, and it is through these items that we have a glimpse into her own past and that of her family.

PARAGRAPH PRACTICE

Write a paragraph of your own, using Joan Didion's writing as your model. In your paragraph describe a time you decided to clean out a dresser, a closet, a room, or even a garage. What did you find? What people or events were you reminded of as you came across various items? As you begin your paragraph, you could adapt the opening sentence of the Joan Didion section, quoted above:

> I decided to meet it head-on. My room was such a mess . . .

> Since I could no longer get my car into the garage, I decided to meet the problem head-on.

Notice that Joan Didion uses a method in writing her description. She begins with the most personal items and then relates other objects to other members of her family. She also goes from the more recent past to the more distant past. In your own paragraph decide on an order for the items you have chosen to describe. If you are describing a time you cleaned out a closet, you might wish to begin with the shoes and proceed to the clothing that is on hangers—literally, from the ground up. If you are describing something even larger, such as a room or a garage, you could write your description in the order in which you came across the items; that is, you could describe them in the same order in which you found them. Remember that your reader will have a greater sense of what you are describing if you use very specific details and if you put those details in a certain order.

ESSAY PRACTICE

The following outline will help you plan a complete essay of at least five paragraphs. The theme of your essay will be closely related to the Joan Didion essay.

The following sentence may serve as your thesis sentence, and will also be the main idea of your introductory paragraph:

¶ 1.   When a family gets together for a special occasion, every age group benefits from the experience.

Each of the sentences below is the topic sentence for one of the paragraphs that you will write to develop your thesis. You may use the suggested details to develop each paragraph, or you may supply details of your own.

¶ 2.   At family gatherings that include aunts and uncles, grandparents, and cousins, the children's enjoyment is most evident.

[DETAILS: What is learned at these gatherings? What do children gain from such contact with the extended family?]

¶ 3.   At these gatherings, young adults may have both positive and negative experiences.

[DETAILS: What can make a family gathering both a positive and a negative experience? How should a person react if such a meeting turns out badly?]

¶4.   For the old people of the family, gatherings such as these may be the high points of their lives.

[DETAILS: What do older members of a family gain from contact with the younger generations? What can the younger people learn from the older people?]

Be certain that you use transitions between paragraphs to make your writing flow smoothly. In addition, be sure that your conclusion gives your reader a clear signal that you have come to the end of your essay.

ESSAY TOPICS

1. Discuss the values you received from your parents. Are they the same values you hope to give your own children? Give specific examples of what you received from your parents and what you intend to pass on to your children.
2. After we have grown up, or after we have moved away from where we grew up, we often have a different perception about our upbringing. Provide several examples of some of the major perceptions you now have about your family and yourself. How do your perceptions differ from those you had when you were growing up?
3. Many of us find ourselves in two worlds, the world of our childhood and our present world. Perhaps our friends have different values than those of our family, or perhaps we are married to someone of a very different background. Write an essay in which you give several examples of the differences that you find between your two worlds. What are some of the problems created by these differences?

🍂 *James Baldwin* 🍂

James Baldwin was born in New York City in 1924 and was raised in Harlem. A practicing minister while still a teenager, Baldwin also became deeply interested in books and the craft of writing. He soon decided to devote himself completely to a literary career.

Dissatisfied with the intellectual climate of this country, especially where the black artist was concerned, Baldwin moved to Paris, where he lived for ten years. In France and later in America, he wrote a number of novels that earned him a wide reputation. These books included *Giovanni's Room, Another Country,* and *Go Tell It on the Mountain.* Baldwin is also known as an essayist and a social commentator. Among his best-known collections of essays are *Notes of a Native Son* and *The Fire Next Time.* His most recent works include a novel, *If Beale Street Could Talk,* and *The Devil Finds Work,* a book in which Baldwin examines the world of Hollywood movies and how that world affected his own life.

The following essay is the introduction for *To Be Young, Gifted, and Black.* The book is devoted to the life and writings of Lorraine Hansberry, the author of *A Raisin in the Sun,* who died of cancer in 1965 at the age of thirty-five. In the essay Baldwin gives us a portrait of his friend while he also makes a number of important statements about the position of the black artist in our society.

PREVIEWING THE WRITER

• Note Baldwin's description of Lorraine Hansberry's personality. What are the most significant details Baldwin chooses that help us reconstruct her personality?

• Note Baldwin's judgments of Lorraine Hansberry's work. What is his view of her as a writer? What does he believe are her greatest strengths as a literary artist?

• Note Baldwin's comments on the position of the artist, particularly the black artist, in our society. According to Baldwin, what special difficulties does the black artist face in our society?

SWEET LORRAINE

THAT'S THE WAY I always felt about her, and so I won't apologize for calling her that now. *She* understood it: in that far too brief a time when we walked and talked and laughed and drank together, sometimes in the streets and bars and restaurants of the Village, sometimes at her house, sometimes at my house, sometimes gracelessly fleeing the houses of others; and sometimes seeming, for anyone who didn't know us, to be having a knockdown, drag-out battle. We spent a lot of time arguing about history and tremendously related subjects in her Bleecker Street and, later, Waverly Place flat. And often, just when I was certain that she was about to throw me out, as being altogether too rowdy a type, she would stand up, her hands on her hips (for these down-home sessions she always wore slacks) and pick up my empty glass as though she intended to throw it at me. Then she would walk into the kitchen, saying, with a haughty toss of her head, "Really, Jimmy. You ain't *right*, child!" With which stern put-down she would hand me another drink and launch into a brilliant analysis of just why I wasn't "right." I would often stagger down her stairs as the sun came up, usually in the middle of a paragraph and always in the middle of a laugh. That marvelous laugh. That marvelous face. I loved her, she was my sister and my comrade. Her going did not so much make me lonely as make me realize how lonely we were. We had that respect for each other which perhaps is only felt by people on the same side of the barricades, listening to the accumulating thunder of the hooves of horses and the treads of tanks.

The first time I ever saw Lorraine was at the Actors' Studio, in the winter of '57–58. She was there as an observer of the Workshop Production of *Giovanni's Room*.[1] She sat way up in the bleachers, taking on some of the biggest names in the American theater because she had liked the play and they, in the main, hadn't. I was enormously grateful to her, she seemed to speak for me; and afterwards she talked to me with a gentleness and generosity never to be forgotten. A small, shy, determined person, with that strength dictated by absolutely impersonal ambition: she was not trying to "make it"—she was trying to keep the faith.

We really met, however, in Philadelphia, in 1959, when *A Raisin in the Sun* was at the beginning of its amazing career. Much has been written about this play; I personally feel that it will demand a far less guilty and constricted people than the present-day Americans to be able to assess it at all; as an historical achievement, anyway, no one can gainsay its impor-

[1] The dramatic version of James Baldwin's novel *Giovanni's Room*, which had been published in 1956.

tance. What is relevant here is that I had never in my life seen so many black people in the theater. And the reason was that never before, in the entire history of the American theater, had so much of the truth of black people's lives been seen on the stage. Black people ignored the theater because the theater had always ignored them.

But, in *Raisin*, black people recognized that house and all   4
the people in it—the mother, the son, the daughter and the daughter-in-law, and supplied the play with an interpretative element which could not be present in the minds of white people: a kind of claustrophobic terror, created not only by their knowledge of the house but by their knowledge of the streets. And when the curtain came down, Lorraine and I found ourselves in the backstage alley, where she was immediately mobbed. I produced a pen and Lorraine handed me her handbag and began signing autographs. ''It only happens once,'' she said. I stood there and watched. I watched the people, who loved Lorraine for what she had brought to them; and watched Lorraine, who loved the people for what they brought to *her*. It was not, for her, a matter of being admired. She was being corroborated and confirmed. She was wise enough and honest enough to recognize that black American artists are a very special case. One is not merely an artist and one is not judged merely as an artist: the black people crowding around Lorraine, whether or not they considered her an artist, assuredly considered her a witness. This country's concept of art and artists has the effect, scarcely worth mentioning by now, of isolating the artist from the people. One can see the effect of this in the irrelevance of so much of the work produced by celebrated white artists; but the effect of this isolation on a black artist is absolutely fatal. He *is*, already, as a black American citizen, isolated from most of his white countrymen. At the crucial hour, he can hardly look to his artistic peers for help, for they do not know enough about him to be able to correct him. To continue to grow, to remain in touch with himself, he needs the support of that community from which, however, all of the pressures of American life incessantly conspire to remove him. And when he is effectively removed, he falls silent—and the people have lost another hope.

Much of the strain under which Lorraine worked was pro-   5
duced by her knowledge of this reality, and her determined refusal to be destroyed by it. She was a very young woman,

with an overpowering vision, and fame had come to her early—
she must certainly have wished, often enough, that fame had
seen fit to drag its feet a little. For fame and recognition are not
synonyms, especially not here, and her fame was to cause her
to be criticized very harshly, very loudly, and very often by both
black and white people who were unable to believe, apparently,
that a really serious intention could be contained in so glam-
orous a frame. She took it all with a kind of astringent good
humor, refusing, for example, even to consider defending herself when she was being accused of being a "slum-lord" because of her family's real-estate holdings in Chicago. I called
her during that time, and all she said—with a wry laugh—was,
"My God, Jimmy, do you realize you're only the second person
who's called me today? And you know how my phone kept
ringing *before!*" She was not surprised. She was devoted to the
human race, but she was not romantic about it.

When so bright a light goes out so early, when so gifted 6
an artist goes so soon, we are left with a sorrow and wonder
which speculation cannot assuage. One is filled for a long time
with a sense of injustice as futile as it is powerful. And the
vanished person fills the mind, in this or that attitude, doing
this or that. Sometimes, very briefly, one hears the exact inflec-
tion of the voice, the exact timbre of the laugh—as I have, when
watching the dramatic presentation, *To Be Young, Gifted and
Black,* and in reading through these pages. But I do not have
the heart to presume to assess her work, for all of it, for me,
was suffused with the light which was Lorraine. It is possible,
for example, that *The Sign in Sidney Brustein's Window*[2] attempts
to say too much; but it is also exceedingly probable that it makes
so loud and uncomfortable a sound because of the surrounding
silence; not many plays, presently, risk being accused of attempting to say too much! Again, Brustein is certainly a very
willed play, unabashedly didactic; but it cannot, finally, be dismissed or categorized in this way because of the astonishing
life of its people. It positively courts being dismissed as old-
fashioned and banal and yet has the unmistakable power of
turning the viewer's judgment in on himself. *Is all this true or
not true?* the play rudely demands; and, unforgivably, leaves us
squirming before this question. One cannot quite answer the
question negatively, one risks being caught in a lie. But an af-

[2] A play by Lorraine Hansberry, first produced in 1964.

firmative answer imposes a new level of responsibility, both for one's conduct and for the fortunes of the American state, and one risks, therefore, the disagreeable necessity of becoming "an insurgent again." For Lorraine made no bones about asserting that art has a purpose, and that its purpose was action: that it contained the "energy which could change things."

It would be good, selfishly, to have her around now, that small, dark girl, with her wit, her wonder, and her eloquent compassion. I've only met one person Lorraine couldn't get through to, and that was the late Bobby Kennedy. And, as the years have passed since that stormy meeting (Lorraine talks about it in these pages, so I won't go into it here) I've very often pondered what she then tried to convey—that a holocaust is no respector of persons; that what, today, seems merely humiliation and injustice for a few, can, unchecked, become Terror for the many, snuffing out white lives just as though they were black lives; that if the American state could not protect the lives of black citizens, then, presently, the entire State would find itself engulfed. And the horses and tanks are indeed upon us, and the end is not in sight. Perhaps it is just as well, after all, that she did not live to see with the outward eye what she saw so clearly with the inward one. And it is not at all farfetched to suspect that what she saw contributed to the strain which killed her, for the effort to which Lorraine was dedicated is more than enough to kill a man.

I saw Lorraine in her hospital bed, as she was dying. She tried to speak, she couldn't. She did not seem frightened or sad, only exasperated that her body no longer obeyed her; she smiled and waved. But I prefer to remember her as she was the last time I saw her on her feet. We were at, of all places, the PEN Club,[3] she was seated, talking, dressed all in black, wearing a very handsome wide, black hat, thin, and radiant. I knew she had been ill, but I didn't know, then, how seriously. I said, "Lorraine, baby, you look beautiful, how in the world do you do it?" She was leaving, I have the impression she was on a staircase, and she turned and smiled that smile and said, "It helps to develop a serious illness, Jimmy!" and waved and disappeared.

---

[3] PEN is an international association of writers.

THE WRITER'S THEMES

1. In each scene where James Baldwin describes himself with Lorraine Hansberry, he manages to place himself in the background while he emphasizes his friend's presence. In each instance, how does Baldwin write his description so that Lorraine Hansberry always dominates the scene?
2. Although Lorraine Hansberry was dead when Baldwin wrote this tribute, her lively presence is one of the most noticeable features of the piece. How does Baldwin achieve this sense of aliveness as he describes Lorraine Hansberry?
3. Baldwin notes that Lorraine Hansberry was a ''small, shy, determined person.'' Review the essay and, using Baldwin's reports of what she said and what she did, find other adjectives that could also be used to describe her. Do not limit yourself to the adjectives Baldwin uses.

THE WRITER'S TECHNIQUE

In the second paragraph of his essay, James Baldwin describes the first time he met Lorraine Hansberry. Here is that paragraph:

> The first time I ever saw Lorraine was at the Actors' Studio, in the winter of '57–58. She was there as an observer of the Workshop Production of *Giovanni's Room*. She sat way up in the bleachers, taking on some of the biggest names in the American theater because she had liked the play and they, in the main, hadn't. I was enormously grateful to her, she seemed to speak for me; and afterwards she talked to me with a gentleness and generosity never to be forgotten. A small, shy, determined person, with that strength dictated by absolutely impersonal ambition: she was not trying to ''make it''—she was trying to keep the faith.

Notice that the writer begins the paragraph by indicating ''the first time'' he ever saw Lorraine Hansberry was ''at the Actors' Studio, in the winter of '57–58.'' Having established the time and the place of this first meeting, Baldwin tells us why Lorraine Hansberry was there: she was observing a theatrical production of one of Baldwin's own works, *Giovanni's Room*. Next, he points out a friendly act of hers (she defended his work in the face of some negative critical reaction), and he tells us of his feeling of gratitude toward her. He concludes the paragraph with a description that includes a physical detail (Lorraine Hansberry was "small") but this description quickly becomes a sketch of her personality. She was a "shy, determined person" who had a "strength" that was directed by a sense of "ambition," but this ambition was not of a personal nature.

Baldwin's paragraph is a report on his own personal experience, and it is also a description of Lorraine Hansberry's personality. After we have read the paragraph, we realize that she was gentle, generous, small, shy, determined, and strong. Baldwin's description combines facts from his own life along with his perceptions of his friend's personality. The writer has added depth and detail to this portrait by placing his friend in a situation in which he was also very much involved.

PARAGRAPH PRACTICE

Write a paragraph of your own, using James Baldwin's paragraph as your model. For example, your paragraph could be a description of the first time you met a person who later became a good friend. Begin your paragraph by telling *when* and *where* you met this person. Then, indicate why both of you were in this place together. Next, describe one of the other person's actions or reactions that you especially noticed. What did that person do that particularly impressed you? What was your reaction at the time?

After you have finished your paragraph, review what you have written. Have you placed yourself and your friend in a particular place at a specific time? Have you chosen an effective example of one of your friend's actions that impressed you at the time? Finally, is your paragraph a portrait that combines physical details with a description of your friend's personality?

ESSAY PRACTICE

The following outline will help you plan a complete essay of at least five paragraphs. The theme of your essay will be closely related to the James Baldwin essay.

The following sentence may serve as your thesis sentence, and will also be the main idea of your introductory paragraph:

¶ 1. Friendships begin for many different reasons, always lead to revelations of character, and sometimes come to unexpected ends.

Each of the sentences below is the topic sentence for one of the paragraphs that you will write to develop your thesis. You may use the suggested details to develop each paragraph, or you may supply details of your own.

¶ 2. Often, we want to get to know another person for a particular reason; at other times we do not know exactly why we want to begin a particular friendship.

[DETAILS: Describe a friendship you made. How did that friendship begin? Why did you want to begin that particular relationship?]

¶ 3. There comes a point in a relationship when the other person does something or says something you find very revealing.

[DETAILS: At what point in the relationship you are describing did you have a real insight into the personality of your friend? How did this person reveal himself or herself? What effect did this revelation have on your relationship?]

¶ 4. Friendships diminish or end for a variety of reasons.

[DETAILS: How and why did this particular friendship become less important in your life, or even come to an end? What are your feelings about your experience with this person now that you can look back on the beginning of the relationship, and its development?]

Be certain that you use transitions between paragraphs to make your writing flow smoothly. In addition, be sure that your conclusion gives your reader a clear signal that you have come to the end of your essay.

ESSAY TOPICS

1. It often happens that an individual is successful in life because of personality rather than sheer ability. Give examples of people you have known who succeeded or failed in school or career largely as a result of personality. What was there in these individuals' personalities that contributed to their success or failure?

2. James Baldwin notes that, as black artists in our society, he and Lorraine Hansberry were "on the same side of the barricades." Often there is a feeling of friendship between people who share the same problems. Give examples of friendships or associations you have had that began largely because you and the other person shared a common concern, or were working for a common cause. In each case, how long did the relationship last? What did you learn from each relationship?

3. Write a memoir of a person you once knew. Give several examples of experiences you shared with this person, experiences that you believe reveal important aspects of his or her personality. Choose your examples carefully, so that by the end of your essay your reader will have an in-depth portrait of this person.

✿ *Loren Eiseley* ✿

Loren Eiseley (1907–1977) was born in Lincoln, Nebraska, and graduated from the University of Nebraska in 1933. He began his academic career at the University of Kansas in 1937. From 1944 to 1947 he was at Oberlin College in Ohio, and from 1947 to 1959 he was chairman of the Department of Anthropology at the University of Pennsylvania.

Eiseley was also a frequent lecturer, and in 1964–1965 he was a member of the Presidential Task Force on Preservation of National Beauty. He often contributed to such journals as *Science, American Anthropologist, Scientific American,* and *Horizon.* His most famous books include *The Immense Journey, The Firmament of Time,* and *The Mind As Nature.*

Eiseley's constant call is for people to have imagination and reason; reason alone, the scientist argues, will destroy us. The following essay, taken from *The Unexpected Universe,* shows the writer at his most observant and at his most imaginative.

PREVIEWING THE WRITER

• Note those places in the essay where the writer connects the spider's experience of her universe with our human experience of our universe. Note also the two different kinds of human universe alluded to by the writer.

• In the essay, Eiseley reviews human progress through the ages. According to the writer, what has helped us the most in obtaining this progress?

• Note Eiseley's warning as we face the future. What is the greatest danger to us as we go forward in time?

THE HIDDEN TEACHER

THE PUTTING OF formidable riddles did not arise with   1
today's philosophers. In fact, there is a sense in which the experimental method of science might be said merely to have widened the area of man's homelessness. Over two thousand years ago, a man named Job, crouching in the Judean desert, was moved to challenge what he felt to be the injustice of his God. The voice in the whirlwind, in turn, volleyed pitiless questions upon the supplicant—questions that have, in truth, precisely

the ring of modern science. For the Lord asked of Job by whose wisdom the hawk soars, and who had fathered the rain, or entered the storehouses of the snow.

A youth standing by, one Elihu, also played a role in this   2 drama, for he ventured diffidently to his protesting elder that it was not true that God failed to manifest Himself. He may speak in one way or another, though men do not perceive it. In consequence of this remark perhaps it would be well, whatever our individual beliefs, to consider what may be called the hidden teacher, lest we become too much concerned with the formalities of only one aspect of the education by which we learn.

We think we learn from teachers, and we sometimes do.   3 But the teachers are not always to be found in school or in great laboratories. Sometimes what we learn depends upon our own powers of insight. Moreover, our teachers may be hidden, even the greatest teacher. And it was the young man Elihu who observed that if the old are not always wise, neither can the teacher's way be ordered by the young whom he would teach.

For example, I once received an unexpected lesson from a   4 spider.

It happened far away on a rainy morning in the West. I   5 had come up a long gulch looking for fossils, and there, just at eye level, lurked a huge yellow-and-black orb spider, whose web was moored to the tall spears of buffalo grass at the edge of the arroyo. It was her universe, and her senses did not extend beyond the lines and spokes of the great wheel she inhabited. Her extended claws could feel every vibration throughout that delicate structure. She knew the tug of wind, the fall of a raindrop, the flutter of a trapped moth's wing. Down one spoke of the web ran a stout ribbon of gossamer on which she could hurry out to investigate her prey.

Curious, I took a pencil from my pocket and touched a   6 strand of the web. Immediately there was a response. The web, plucked by its menacing occupant, began to vibrate until it was a blur. Anything that had brushed claw or wing against that amazing snare would be thoroughly entrapped. As the vibrations slowed, I could see the owner fingering her guidelines for signs of struggle. A pencil point was an intrusion into this universe for which no precedent existed. Spider was circumscribed by spider ideas; its universe was spider universe. All outside was irrational, extraneous, at best, raw material for spider. As

I proceeded on my way along the gully, like a vast impossible shadow, I realized that in the world of spider I did not exist.

Moreover, I considered, as I tramped along, that to the phagocytes, the white blood cells, clambering even now with some kind of elementary intelligence amid the thin pipes and tubing of my body—creatures without whose ministrations I could not exist—the conscious "I" of which I was aware had no significance to these amoeboid beings. I was, instead, a kind of chemical web that brought meaningful messages to them, a natural environment seemingly immortal if they could have thought about it, since generations of them had lived and perished, and would continue to so live and die, in that odd fabric which contained my intelligence—a misty light that was beginning to seem floating and tenuous even to me.

I began to see that among the many universes in which the world of living creatures existed, some were large, some small, but that all, including man's, were in some way limited or finite. We were creatures of many different dimensions passing through each other's lives like ghosts through doors.

In the years since, my mind has many times returned to that far moment of encounter with the orb spider. A message has arisen only now from the misty shreds of that webbed universe. What was it that had so troubled me about the incident? Was it that spidery indifference to the human triumph?

If so, that triumph was very real and could not be denied. I saw, had many times seen, both mentally and in the seams of exposed strata, the long backward stretch of time whose recovery is one of the great feats of modern science. I saw the drifting cells of the early seas from which all life, including our own, has arisen. The salt of those ancient seas is in our blood, its lime is in our bones. Every time we walk along a beach some ancient urge disturbs us so that we find ourselves shedding shoes and garments, or scavenging among seaweed and whitened timbers like the homesick refugees of a long war.

And war it has been indeed—the long war of life against its inhospitable environment, a war that has lasted for perhaps three billion years. It began with strange chemicals seething under a sky lacking in oxygen; it was waged through long ages until the first green plants learned to harness the light of the nearest star, our sun. The human brain, so frail, so perishable, so full of inexhaustible dreams and hungers, burns by the power of the leaf.

184 🌢 PERSONAL DISCOVERY

The hurrying blood cells charged with oxygen carry more   12
of that element to the human brain than to any other part of
the body. A few moments' loss of vital air and the phenomenon
we know as consciousness goes down into the black night of
inorganic things. The human body is a magical vessel, but its
life is linked with an element it cannot produce. Only the green
plant knows the secret of transforming the light that comes to
us across the far reaches of space. There is no better illustration
of the intricacy of man's relationship with other living things.

The student of fossil life would be forced to tell us that if   13
we take the past into consideration the vast majority of earth's
creatures—perhaps over ninety per cent—have vanished. Forms
that flourished for a far longer time than man has existed upon
earth have become either extinct or so transformed that their
descendants are scarcely recognizable. The specialized perish
with the environment that created them, the tooth of the tiger
fails at last, the lances of men strike down the last mammoth.

In three billion years of slow change and groping effort   14
only one living creature has succeeded in escaping the trap of
specialization that has led in time to so much death and wasted
endeavor. It is man, but the word should be uttered softly, for
his story is not yet done.

With the rise of the human brain, with the appearance of   15
a creature whose upright body enabled two limbs to be freed
for the exploration and manipulation of his environment, there
had at last emerged a creature with a specialization—the brain—
that, paradoxically, offered escape from specialization. Many
animals driven into the nooks and crannies of nature have
achieved momentary survival only at the cost of later extinction.

Was it this that troubled me and brought my mind back   16
to a tiny universe among the grass-blades, a spider's universe
concerned with spider thought?

Perhaps.   17

The mind that once visualized animals on a cave wall is   18
now engaged in a vast ramification of itself through time and
space. Man has broken through the boundaries that control all
other life. I saw, at last, the reason for my recollection of that
great spider on the arroyo's rim, fingering its universe against
the sky.

The spider was a symbol of man in miniature. The wheel   19
of the web brought the analogy home clearly. Man, too, lies at
the heart of a web, a web extending through the starry reaches

of sidereal space, as well as backward into the dark realm of pre-history. His great eye upon Mount Palomar looks into a distance of millions of light-years, his radio ear hears the whisper of even more remote galaxies, he peers through the electron microscope upon the minute particles of his own being. It is a web no creature of earth has ever spun before. Like the orb spider, man lies at the heart of it, listening. Knowledge has given him the memory of earth's history beyond the time of his emergence. Like the spider's claw, a part of him touches a world he will never enter in the flesh. Even now, one can see him reaching forward into time with new machines, computing, analyzing, until elements of the shadowy future will also compose part of the invisible web he fingers.

Yet still my spider lingers in memory against the sunset sky. Spider thoughts in a spider universe—sensitive to raindrop and moth flutter, nothing beyond, nothing allowed for the unexpected, the inserted pencil from the world outside.   20

Is man at heart any different from the spider, I wonder: 21
man thoughts, as limited as spider thoughts, contemplating now the nearest star with the threat of bringing with him the fungus rot from earth, wars, violence, the burden of a population he refuses to control, cherishing again his dream of the Adamic Eden he had pursued and lost in the green forests of America. Now it beckons again like a mirage from beyond the moon. Let man spin his web, I thought further; it is his nature. But I considered also the work of the phagocytes swarming in the rivers of my body, the unresting cells in their mortal universe. What is it we are a part of that we do not see, as the spider was not gifted to discern my face, or my little probe into her world?

We are too content with our sensory extensions, with the   22
fulfillment of that ice age mind that began its journey amidst the cold of vast tundras and that pauses only briefly before its leap into space. It is no longer enough to see as a man sees— even to the ends of the universe. It is not enough to hold nuclear energy in one's hand like a spear, as a man would hold it, or to see the lightning, or times past, or time to come, as a man would see it. If we continue to do this, the great brain—the human brain—will be only a new version of the old trap, and nature is full of traps for the beast that cannot learn.

It is not sufficient any longer to listen at the end of a wire   23
to the rustlings of galaxies; it is not enough even to examine the great coil of DNA in which is coded the very alphabet of

life. These are our extended perceptions. But beyond lies the great darkness of the ultimate Dreamer, who dreamed the light and the galaxies. Before act was, or substance existed, imagination grew in the dark. Man partakes of that ultimate wonder and creativeness. As we turn from the galaxies to the swarming cells of our own being, which toil for something, some entity beyond their grasp, let us remember man, the self-fabricator who came across an ice age to look into the mirrors and the magic of science. Surely he did not come to see himself or his wild visage only. He came because he is at heart a listener and a searcher for some transcendent realm beyond himself. This he has worshiped by many names, even in the dismal caves of his beginning. Man, the self-fabricator, is so by reason of gifts he had no part in devising—and so he searches as the single living cell in the beginning must have sought the ghostly creature it was to serve.

THE WRITER'S THEMES

1. Loren Eiseley tells us that he received "an unexpected lesson" from the spider he observed. What exactly did Eiseley learn from the spider?
2. Eiseley tells us that "man has broken through the boundaries that control all other life." What are the "boundaries" Eiseley refers to?
3. Eiseley refers to "the intricacy of man's relationship with other living things." Using details from the essay, and your own ideas, discuss this intricate relationship. What are some of our present-day actions that are endangering this relationship?

THE WRITER'S TECHNIQUE

In paragraph five, Loren Eiseley describes his encounter with the spider. Here is that paragraph:

> It happened far away on a rainy morning in the West. I had come up a long gulch looking for fossils, and there, just at eye level, lurked a huge yellow-and-black orb spider, whose web

was moored to the tall spears of buffalo grass at the edge of the arroyo. It was her universe, and her senses did not extend beyond the lines and spokes of the great wheel she inhabited. Her extended claws could feel every vibration throughout that delicate structure. She knew the tug of wind, the fall of a raindrop, the flutter of a trapped moth's wing. Down one spoke of the web ran a stout ribbon of gossamer on which she could hurry out to investigate her prey.

Notice that the writer begins by telling us the time and place of the encounter; it was in the West, and the time was morning. Next, he describes the moment he saw the creature, which was "a huge yellow-and-black orb spider," and then tells us where the spider lived, in a web "moored to the tall spears of buffalo grass . . ." We are told that even though the spider's senses "did not extend" beyond her web, her claws "could feel every vibration throughout that delicate structure." She could also feel "the tug of wind, the fall of a raindrop" and when a moth was trapped in the web. Finally, there was "a stout ribbon of gossamer" the spider could use to investigate anything that had been caught in the web.

Eiseley first describes the spider's outward appearance and the location of her web. He then concentrates on how the spider receives information and then shows us how the spider could act on this information; she could "hurry out" on the ribbon of gossamer "to investigate her prey."

PARAGRAPH PRACTICE

Write a paragraph of your own, using Loren Eiseley's paragraph as your model. Your paragraph could be a description of an insect or a wild or domestic animal you have observed. After you have chosen a specific animal, begin by describing it at a particular moment and in a particular place. Then concentrate on the animal's senses and what it can do with those senses. For example, if you have chosen a dog, you could emphasize the dog's excellent sense of smell. Finally, show the animal in action, doing something that is typical of its ordinary behavior.

Notice how Eiseley brings us into the world of the spider; he gives us details of the creature's appearance, senses, environment, and at least one major activity. If your own paragraph follows this plan, and if you are careful to supply specific details, your description will have a sense of order and an immediacy that will help your reader form a clear impression of what you are describing.

ESSAY PRACTICE

The following outline will help you plan a complete essay of at least five paragraphs. The theme of your essay will be closely related to Loren Eiseley's "The Hidden Teacher."

The following sentence may serve as your thesis sentence, and will also be the main idea of your introductory paragraph:

¶ 1. Some of our best learning experiences come from nontraditional sources.

Each of the sentences below is the topic sentence for one of the paragraphs that you will write to develop your thesis. You may use the suggested details to develop each paragraph, or you may supply details of your own.

¶ 2. I once received an unexpected lesson from . . .

[DETAILS: What was your unusual source of knowledge? It might have been a person, or even an object. Describe in detail the circumstances under which you encountered the person or used the object.]

¶ 3. What I learned was . . .

[DETAILS: Explain exactly what you learned and how you learned it.]

¶ 4. I believe that such an approach to learning . . .

[DETAILS: Explain what the experience meant to you. You might also wish to advise your reader how to be more receptive to all sources of knowledge, including the most nontraditional sources.]

Be certain that you use transitions between paragraphs to make your writing flow smoothly. In addition, be sure that your conclusion gives your reader a clear signal that you have come to the end of your essay.

ESSAY TOPICS

1. Eiseley notes that we "think we learn from teachers, and we sometimes do." Give examples of at least two or three

people in your life who have been your most important teachers. Explain what each one of them taught you.

2. Eiseley mentions wars, violence, and population control as examples of the problems people are about to bring with them as they prepare to go to other planets.

   a. What do you consider to be our most serious problems here on earth? Give specific examples and carefully support your choice in each case.

   b. Imagine that we have just begun to colonize other planets. What do you believe would be the major problems we would take with us to these planets? Give specific examples of these problems, placing them in order of increasing importance. The last problem you describe should be the one you consider the most important.

3. Describe in detail a great lesson you once learned by using your own powers of insight. What experience did you have that led you to this insight?

🍋 *Tom Brown, Jr., with William Owen* 🍋

Tom Brown, Jr., has been described as perhaps the most skilled tracker in America today. He has tracked more than six hundred people, from missing children to wanted criminals, who have been lost in the wilds. He is also a naturalist who teaches outdoor survival to small groups at his New Jersey school, The Tracker, and in various other places throughout the country.

When Tom Brown was eight years old he made friends with a young boy named Rick, whose grandfather, Stalking Wolf, was an Apache Indian. Stalking Wolf taught the youngsters how to track, hunt, and fish as the Indians had done for thousands of years. For ten years Tom Brown continued to learn from his Indian teacher, and for nearly twenty years he tested and sharpened his skills in such challenging places as the South Dakota Badlands, the Grand Canyon, and the Grand Teton in Wyoming. Late in 1978 he decided to share what he had learned by teaching wilderness survival to others.

Along with his co-author, Tom Brown has written *The Tracker* and *The Search*, books that describe his early training and experiences as well as his philosophy of nature. Tom Brown emphasizes that in order to survive in the wilderness it is necessary to treat nature as an ally, not an enemy. He points out that when people make concrete sidewalks and confine themselves to cars, they have separated themselves from the earth. They have removed themselves from living, growing things and they have lost touch with humanity. Tom Brown is very aware of the larger meaning of survival—our very survival on this planet.

The following selection is taken from *The Search* and shows the range of Tom Brown's concerns. In "The Soul of a Tree" he gives us a picture of life in the wilderness and takes us with him on a journey of self-discovery. As he describes the world of nature, he searches for a definition of his own nature.

PREVIEWING THE WRITERS

• Note the places in the essay where the author reveals his training and background as a tracker and a naturalist.

• Note the places in the essay where Tom Brown describes animals in human terms.

• Note the places in the essay where Tom Brown makes judgments on the actions and attitudes of other people.

THE SOUL OF A TREE

I WAS ALONE, and there was no emergency. I just 1
wanted to warm myself before I crawled into my leaf hut for
the night. This had been a peaceful time for me, and I was
reminiscing about my childhood and the many evenings I spent
with Rick and Stalking Wolf around the campfire at our good-
medicine cabin. This helped me remember.

It had been a cool day but sunny. I had come across the 2
tracks of about fifteen pack horses and their riders. They were
heading north along a ridge I had explored two days earlier.
They were hunters searching for elk. They would find none up
the valley they were headed toward. The elk had pastured there
a week before, but had moved west over the mountain to a
tender aspen grove. I doubt if these hunters would climb the
mountain to look for them. Most of these pack-animal hunters
just scan the opposite ridges, looking for browsing elk, and then
try to stalk close enough through some very rugged terrain to
get a shot. Theirs is no easy task, because the elk have excellent
senses, and most of these hunters make a devil of a racket climbing down through thick underbrush and up over rocks in order
to get a clear shot. I can't say I'm unhappy about that, and as
I studied the hoofprints, I wondered if they had enough provisions to keep them going until they found some elk. I hoped
not, and I think I was right, because I didn't hear any shots that
day, and that night the storm struck.

In the middle of my dream I became aware of the absence 3
of sound. It is unusual to have no sound in the woods. The
screech owl that worked this part of the mountain was silent.
The mice weren't scurrying with the chipmunks, and the wind
wasn't soughing through the dried leaves. It was quiet and
warm. There was little moon, and the weather had been generally cloudy, and so the blackness of the night wasn't unusual,
but the stillness and the warmth were. "It's a storm." I knew
it instinctively before I said it aloud to myself.

There was a giant oak beside my leaf hut. The reason I 4
had constructed the hut at its base was because the Indians had
always considered the oak a sacred tree and often had tribal
ceremonies beneath it. To me the oak with its deep root system,
reaching far into Mother Earth, and its hardness was good med-

icine. It gave me a sense of security to be near it and a sense of timelessness. This night it seemed to beckon me into its outspread branches.

I climbed high into its branches and secured my right arm   5
to the trunk with my belt. I was going to ride the oak through the storm and hopefully discover its soul in the process. What happened to me that night was a miracle of no less proportions than Constantine's vision of the cross in the sky.[1]

The storm that hit the mountains that night had winds of   6
hurricane force, and the rain at times was driven parallel to the mountain. In the blue light of almost constant bursts of lightning, I saw trees pulled up by the roots and blown across the ravine. One small tree broken in half by the wind was driven into a pine like some spear thrown by a giant. The lightning struck all around me, and the wind howled like a pack of wolves and went on through the night till just before dawn.

All during the storm I clung to the tree with all my strength   7
and felt it twist and sway in my grip. It spoke as it fought against the swirling winds and held on tight to its mother with its miles of roots. "I have met you before, mighty wind. When I was a sapling, you raced over this mountain and tore at my father's trunk and almost toppled him. His mighty weight shielded me. Again when I was young, you came without warning when my branches were heavy with leaves and green fruit and the squirrels were playing at my feet; and then you took a limb from me and with it my youth. You returned many times and broke my branches and gave me a gnarled look, but you have never taken me from my mother or stopped my groping for the sky by taking my upper body. I have been bent and twisted but never broken or uprooted, and I won't give in this time either." The tree creaked and groaned and lost a limb, but it never gave in.

Grasping the trunk with my face pressed into the gray   8
bark, I could see the water as it ran in rushing rivers down the tree's side, following the contours of the bark. The texture changed as did the color when the tree was wet. The gray became an almost determined black, and it softened to the touch and became more pliable. It didn't bruise as easily when hit by flying debris. Instead it would dent.

[1] According to a famous legend, the Roman emperor Constantine, the night before an important battle in the year 312 A.D., had a vision of a cross in the sky. The cross was accompanied by the words, "In this sign you will conquer."

Its leaves, brown and ready to fall, took flight that night, 9 and filled the air around me like a swarm of gnats. The wind seemed to swirl around the tree as if it had a personal vendetta against this oak, causing the leaves to be whipped about like a small tornado. They lashed at my body and head and cut at my arms and ankles. In the morning, when the winds had died down and there was enough light to see, the oak stood naked save for one trembling leaf in jeans and plaid wool clinging to its upper trunk.

When I looked down, what I saw brought gooseflesh alive 10 up and down my back. The large branch that had been broken from the oak had fallen butt end, straight through the leaf hut I had slept in the past two nights. If I had stayed there, I would surely have been killed.

The Indians tell a story about a great battle between the 11 Good Spirit and the Evil Spirit. The Good Spirit wins, but the Evil Spirit, who must live in a cave and never see the sun, continues to send demons to the surface of the earth to harm man and disrupt nature. This wind seemed to be attacking this very oak to which I clung, and there was a moment, when the rain was driving hard into my face and the lightning was striking close, that I felt as if it were attacking me. But the oak twisted and spoke to me at that moment, and I smiled in the knowledge that this oak that was sacred to the Indian was also my friend.

That night in the tree made me understand the oak more 12 than any book. I didn't know her exact age, but I knew she was old. I learned the sounds she makes when a wind of over a hundred knots whips at her branches. I know what her wood sounds like when it is broken green from her ancient body. I know the color she turns as she soaks the rain into her thick skin, and the odor she emits from her wet bark. I know her fully clothed, changing, and naked, and I have seen her bleed. That night in the tree I realized how our ancestors could worship her in their anthropomorphic way, because that night I discovered that she had a soul.

The soul of a tree is not like the soul of a human being. It 13 is its personality. The willow has a soul that cries for man. The ash has a soul that laughs. The birch has a pure soul, the pine is gentle, the dogwood innocent, the aspen fickle, the sweet gum sultry, the beech enchanting, the redwood majestic.

The oak has a sacred soul. It is strong and protective. The 14 oak is a friend to man. The gallant way it stands against the elements is an inspiration, and I honestly feel that she spoke to me that night and beckoned me to come into her branches for protection against the forces. I believe she saved my life. Call it instinct if you care to, or call it intuition, or a sixth sense that registered in my subconscious the fact that there was a weak limb fifty feet over my hut, or call it luck. I call it a miracle.

The night of the storm, I learned all about a tree. The following day I learned about myself. 15

I asked myself a lot of questions that were not easy to answer. Why had I climbed the tree? Why wasn't I killed? What am I supposed to do now—now that I have realized I had been spared? Would this experience change my life? What was there left for me to do or experience for which I had been saved? To me there is no coincidence in this life. Everything has a purpose, and therefore every action or lack of it has a purpose. Most people would squash a tiny insect without realizing that it is a vital link in the food chain that allows them to live. We are learning more and more the interdependency of all life. We see how an insecticide in the fields of Iowa affects the fish in the Gulf of Mexico. We are all related, and nothing is complete without the other. We are all essentially one huge organism like the cells of a large body, each doing our job to keep the whole alive and well. 16

I climbed down out of the tree and pulled what remained of the leaf hut apart in order to get my blanket. The limb of the oak had pierced it through. Again I thanked the Great Spirit for my safety, for my escape. Again I was reassured that my life-style of following instinct, my sixth sense, was valid. 17

The trail north was the one I followed that day. I was curious as to what might have happened to the pack train. I didn't try to follow their trail. It would have been difficult at best after the storm of the previous night, but not impossible. Instead I figured that they would have traveled straight up the valley to a pass that ran between the giant mountains to the east and out of the park. After that storm, I was sure that they would be anxious to get out of these mountains. 18

It was a clear cool day with a breeze out of the west that came down from the mountain carrying my scent before it into the valley. The trail was littered with leaves and branches, but every so often I spotted a print of an animal that had been caught away from its burrow by the storm and was hurrying 19 home before it was discovered—like some husband who lost track of the time at a poker game and is trying to sneak in before his wife discovers what time it is.

The prints of a striped skunk were headed north with me along this trail. He would stop momentarily to look around and sniff the air, but he was quite intent on getting to his hole. I guessed it would be down the mountain toward the stream. Once he stopped to dig by the trail for some insects. I suppose he didn't have much time last night to hunt. I was right. When he left the trail, he headed on an elk run down into the valley and, I hope, safety. A skunk abroad during the day is easy prey for fox, cougar, or even a hungry bear. 20

Suddenly there was a sound similar to an explosive alarm clock coming from the pines above me. It was a red squirrel. Something must be coming. I looked up the elk run and saw a group of cows being led by an antlered bull down the mountain to graze in some of the lowland pasture. If only the hunting party had been here, they would have had a chance at a kill. I wonder how anyone could kill such a magnificent animal. This male was at least 700 pounds and proud with his dark maned neck stretching to catch the scent and lead his herd to a safe feeding ground. He looked back up the mountain for a moment, and at that instant I moved back. First out of his line of vision, and then to a spot where I might conceal myself and watch them pass closely. I knew that as soon as they got downwind, my scent would alert them and send them in a mad dash into the valley. 21

The spot I chose was right on the run and concealed by some boulders and small pine trees. I flattened out behind the rocks and listened as their hooves scraped the rocks in their descent. They passed me on the run, not ten inches from where I lay. They are huge animals, especially if you're looking up at them, so I remained very still and careful not to spook them. One kick from their sharp hoofs could disable a cougar and, I'm sure, crush my skull. Three females passed me with their young bull. About ten yards down the run, one of them caught my scent, gave the alarm, and the race was on. 22

I was tempted to jump up and run after them down the mountain, but knew that their great speed would make me look completely ridiculous. Instead, I looked up to the pine where the red squirrel was chewing on a cone and nodded in gratitude. 23

The trail was a treasure-trove of tracks. Every animal on 24 the mountain must be out repairing or exploring what damage had been caused by the storm. It was exciting to see the prints of porcupine and fox and deer mice crossing each other. I laughed, thinking of the Keystone Kops running in and out of hotel doors, chasing themselves and some criminal. The fox was like that, crisscrossing the trail numerous times in pursuit of some prey—a mouse or red squirrel. I don't believe he was very successful.

At one point on the trail, I saw the prints of a black bear. 25 It must have been five feet long and, judging by the depth of his paw prints, 320 pounds. He was the only animal heading up the mountain. Must have passed the storm in the valley and was heading over the mountain where it might be safer. Why didn't he stay where he was? There was plenty of food here.

I had almost forgotten. The hunting party! They must have 26 gone off the trail and into the valley to camp. I decided to backtrack the bear and see if my assumption was correct.

What I found was interesting indeed. The bear and the 27 hunters had spent the night not twenty yards from each other. I'm glad that most hunters are inept at finding game. It gives the animals better-than-average chance in the woods. On the plains, or in an open area, it is another story. There, all a hunter needs is a good pair of field glasses and a steady hand. The rifles that are used today can fell an elk at five hundred yards. That's almost too far for the animal to be able to scent.

This bear woke up early and headed in the opposite way 28 the hunters were moving. He followed their trail up the mountain. I wished I had been here to see the show. Hunters rustling around, trying to clean up their camp from the storm, not noticing a 300-pound bear sneaking off up the mountain. One thing did impress me. They were making good time. Too good to notice the raccoon who had sat on a rock and watched them ride by. Too good to notice the owl at the base of a pine or the screech owl which sat high up in the branches and slept the day away. Too good to stop and watch the trout feed or notice the way the red squirrel placed mushrooms on tree branches to dry for its winter feasts.

These hunters were good woodsmen. They were clean and 29 careful, but because they had come to kill, they were alien. They missed the essential beauty of this great wilderness area. I'm sure they noticed the mountains and valleys, and could experience the sunsets the same as anyone, but they missed the majority of the abundant animal life that surrounded them constantly.

I came to this wilderness to experience all that it had to offer. I wanted to observe its wildlife and taste its wild grasses. I wanted to sleep under her stars and feel her rain and snow on my face. I wanted to track her game and watch her birds of prey hunt the mountainsides. I came to this wilderness to learn, not to kill. All I would take from her was the knowledge of her heartbeat not the rack of a mature bull elk.

I know that in years to come, I will have no trophies hanging on my den wall. No visual remembrance of my trip to this wilderness. What I will have, instead, is the knowledge of what makes this wilderness different from all the others. That is what I'll be able to relate to my children. I won't be able to tell them how I sighted through the scope of my 357 magnum Winchester and felled a mighty elk with one shot at four hundred yards. I can only tell them that a herd passed ten inches from my nose, and they smelled wet and sour. I can only tell of the grunts they made to each other as they made their way down the mountain, like the grunts of acknowledgement I make when my son points out something interesting to me.

Life in this wilderness area was abundant beyond belief. I have never seen such a variety of life and so much of it. There were raccoons, woodchuck, red bats, and white-tailed rabbit. My time there was meaningful. Up to this time I had discovered a natural cathedral and experienced the soul of an oak. I had come so close to an elk that I could have touched it and had avoided death by choosing a night of danger in a tree. It was, you might say, satisfying.

The group of hunters traveled on. I gave up my pursuit. The area was too interesting to let it pass without a more thorough investigation. I stayed in this area by the stream for three days until the first snowfall, before I decided it was time to be heading on.

THE WRITERS' THEMES

1. Which parts of the essay best demonstrate Tom Brown's skill as a tracker and a naturalist?
2. What is Tom Brown's relationship with nature? Where is nature seen as both hostile and helpful?

3. The narrator closely observes both men and animals in the woods. Compare his treatment of each group. To which group is he more sympathetic?

THE WRITERS' TECHNIQUE

In the third paragraph of the essay, Tom Brown gives us a description of the approaching storm. He has been resting in his leaf hut when he senses a dramatic change in the weather. Here is the paragraph:

> In the middle of my dream I became aware of the absence of sound. It is unusual to have no sound in the woods. The screech owl that worked this part of the mountain was silent. The mice weren't scurrying with the chipmunks, and the wind wasn't soughing through the dried leaves. It was quiet and warm. There was little moon, and the weather had been generally cloudy, and so the blackness of the night wasn't unusual, but the stillness and the warmth were. "It's a storm." I knew it instinctively before I said it aloud to myself.

In order to succeed in this paragraph, the writer must overcome a basic problem: how to interest the reader in a description of silence. He does this in part by making sure that he preserves that silence at all times. This is done by emphasizing the usual sounds that are *not* heard. The writer emphasizes the silence by using the words "quiet" and "stillness" and by providing examples that support the idea of quietude. The screech owl (the very name of the bird gives the impression of noise) is "silent"; the mice and the chipmunks are not to be heard, and even the wind is not making its usual rustling noise. We are therefore all the more surprised when the silence is broken at the very end of the paragraph by the narrator himself: he says, out loud, "It's a storm."

The writer uses another structural device in the paragraph when he follows a particular sequence to direct our attention to the coming storm. Our first indication of this sequence is when the writer mentions the "woods." Next, we are reminded of the "mountain," and we soon become aware that our attention is being directed to the "wind," the "moon," and the "weather" in general. Toward the end of the paragraph we are led to the "blackness of the night," which prepares us for the announcement that the "storm" is coming. It is of course out of the "blackness of the night" (which emphasizes the unknown) that the storm will come.

PARAGRAPH PRACTICE

Write a paragraph of your own, using the paragraph from "The Soul of a Tree" as your model. In your paragraph you could lead your reader through a series of details to the identification of a single source or reason for those details. For example, a roar that disturbs the silence, a metallic squeal that pierces that roar, and a rush of wind could be a train coming into a station.

Some other possibilities for a paragraph of this kind could be:

—Students going from a library to a classroom for a final exam.

—Trying to get to your bedroom door late at night without waking the rest of the family.

—A supervisor walking through a work area in order to speak to a particular employee.

In each case, begin by making a list of the different stages you want your reader to see. Then add details to fill out the description of each of these stages.

ESSAY PRACTICE

The following outline will help you plan a complete essay of at least five paragraphs. The theme of your essay will be closely related to "The Soul of a Tree."

The following sentence may serve as your thesis sentence, and will also be the main idea of your introductory paragraph:

¶ 1.   We can often be more productive during periods of relaxation and solitude than we can in times of intense effort.

Each of the sentences below is the topic sentence for one of the paragraphs that you will write to develop your thesis. You may use the suggested details to develop each paragraph, or you may supply details of your own.

¶ 2.   It is easy to find examples of activities we do under pressure.

[DETAILS: Are tense and demanding situations productive? Consider such examples as competitive sports, public performances or speeches, taking final examinations, or meeting deadlines for term papers.]

¶ 3. We should not overlook the benefits that can come from more relaxed moments or even solitude.

[DETAILS: Are the results of more relaxed moments more creative and inventive? Can daydreaming be productive?]

¶ 4. As for myself, I produce better when . . .

[DETAILS: Under what circumstances do you do your best work? Do you think most people produce better when they have to work under a deadline?]

Be certain that you use transitions between paragraphs to make your writing flow smoothly. In addition, be sure that your conclusion gives your reader a clear signal that you have come to the end of your essay.

ESSAY TOPICS

1. There are certain experiences in life that help us understand ourselves better. Some of these experiences could be going away to school, losing a family member, or starting a family of one's own.

    Write an essay in which you discuss at least three common experiences people have in life which lead them toward a greater degree of self-awareness. As you write about each of these three experiences, be sure to include at least one specific example from your own experience or the experience of people you know.

2. After Tom Brown, Jr., has experienced the storm, he feels he has learned about nature in an unusual way. Describe a time you had a fresh insight into the world of nature. You may have camped out for a summer, or you may have simply walked for an hour through a local park. What made the experience unusual for you? What did you learn?

3. Speaking of the wilderness he experienced, Tom Brown, Jr., notes that he wants to relate all of this to his children. Regardless of whether your experience is urban, suburban, or rural, what do you want to be able to tell your children in the future so that they will have a good idea of what your environment was like?

Focus on Terms: Analogy

Analogy is the comparison of two essentially unlike things. Used to develop a topic, analogy can simplify the complex, make the unfamiliar more understandable, or give the mundane a fresh and delightful perspective.

For example, at one point in "The Soul of a Tree," Tom Brown, Jr., describes the forest animals that were out "repairing or exploring what damage had been caused by the storm." He then observes that it was "exciting to see the prints of porcupine and fox and deer mice crossing each other." It is at this point that we are given an analogy: "I laughed, thinking of the Keystone Kops running in and out of hotel doors, chasing themselves and some criminal. The fox was like that, crisscrossing the trail numerous times in pursuit of some prey—a mouse or red squirrel." Here, we are presented with two very dissimilar creatures—forest animals and comic policemen from old silent movies—and we are asked to think of them as acting in a similar way. As the writer describes them, they are similar: the frantic, erratic movements of the animals are reminiscent of the actions of old Hollywood comedians. At first thought, there is no connection between them, but as their similarities are pointed out, the analogy gives us a comic and endearing view of what would otherwise be a few animal tracks on the forest floor.

Technical writers often use analogy to make complex topics more understandable to people not familiar with the field. Loren Eiseley does this in "The Hidden Teacher" when he compares our immense universe to the spider's small universe of a web in a clump of grass. As Eiseley notes: "The spider was a symbol of man in miniature. The wheel of the web brought the analogy home clearly. Man, too, lies at the heart of a web, a web extending through the starry reaches of sidereal space, as well as backward into the dark realm of prehistory." The earlier parts of the essay were constructed to prepare us for this connection between human universe and spider universe, and much of the remainder of the piece uses the analogy to make the writer's points clear. In terms of the writer's structure and meaning, the analogy is central to our understanding of the essay.

Although we may use analogy infrequently, putting an abstract idea into concrete terms is one of the most effective ways to give the reader an instant grasp of the topic. For example, we sometimes hear people use the worn-out analogy of "ships passing in the night" to describe strangers whose paths cross only briefly, or we may have heard someone explain the process of modern justice by comparing it to a turnstile in a subway.

Discovering how analogy works will expand our appreciation and understanding of what we read, and encourage the use of analogy in our own writing.

Student Essay 🙞 🙝 *David Kasmire*

Going home again after a long time away always results in mixed emotions. We have changed, and we realize that our past can never be recaptured.

In the following student essay, the writer describes himself on a journey that pulls him toward his own past. He soon realizes, however, that his life really belongs in the present and in a place very far from his old home. As we see the writer becoming aware that such a journey brings with it not only recollections but also some very basic questions of identity, we are reminded of Joan Didion's reflections in "On Going Home."

• In his opening paragraph, the writer uses a well-known analogy to help establish his theme. By using the idea of a clock, the writer is able to indicate the changes that take place in the human body over a period of time.

FOR THE FAMILY ALBUM

EVERY SEVEN YEARS, science tells us, each cell in our bodies completely changes. We are not the same persons we were seven years ago. After some dozen of these changes, some internal biological clock signals we have had enough. Before that happens, however, the same clock sends off a few warning bells. Man looks back at his life and asks, "Who am I? Where did I come from? Where am I going?"

In most cases answering such questions is not easy; in fact, it is downright awkward. The answers are usually under our nose.

Recently, when my own biological clock was ticking away   3
as I was ruminating on the big three, I had the opportunity to
come up with a few answers.

My older brother Bill offered me the use of his summer   4
cabin for my vacation. At first I declined because it would mean
going all the way out to the West Coast, a trip I had not made
in many years. Then that old inner directional device started
pulling like gravity, and I accepted. The cabin was situated in
the coastal redwoods near the town where I was born. Our
family had only lived there one year, and I could recall nothing
about it. Everything I knew about it came from the memories
of my brothers and sisters.

When I got off the plane in Oakland, Bill was in the waiting   5
room reading a magazine. His voice seemed much the same as
I remembered it although he was now thin, greyish, and bifo-
caled. As we talked, his voice jerked in nervous little laughs
between intermittent stares. We were two strangers trying to
get to know each other all over again. We put my bags in the
back of his old Ford pick-up and set off through the night down
along the bay to the coast. He was going to stay around for a
few days and show me how the cabin worked and then take
off back up to the valley to do a few chores.

The morning stillness was like a vacuum. The sun shone   6
dimly through the drawn curtains, and as I lay in bed I glanced
around the room at once-familiar objects—a chair, a painting, a
lamp—all pieces of a past I had misplaced long ago. The sound
of a fire crackling in the living room fireplace aroused me out
of a second sleep. Later, we stood in front the fire sipping coffee,
standing on one of Dad's old handmade braided rugs, digging
our toes into the fabric of our lives. An emerald hummingbird
stopped at the window and then darted off, disappearing in the
spray of a neighbor's early morning hose. Later that morning
we took the truck into town so I could find out where to shop.

The town sprawled its funny stucco bungalows over the   7
low hills around the river's mouth down to the sea. There were
one or two shopping centers, a few old churches, and a Spanish
style bank, all interspersed with a few palm trees. There were
even one or two outdoor cafes.

I could feel the old gravitational pull when he seemed to   8
head the truck in the direction of "the house." He talked of
what he remembered of his adventures of being twelve at the
time of the Depression in this town. He wanted to take a picture

of me in front of the house. On the seat between us was his Kodak, that man-invented time machine that defies the *camera obscura*[1] of our minds. We finally stopped on a wide street and there it was. The lawn had recently been turned over, and the brown earth contrasted with the pink stucco. The wide over-hanging eaves gave the little house a very squat look. My stomach tightened slowly into a little ball of old-fashioned anxiety. So this was the place where a clumsy midwife almost prevented my entrance into the world. Again, the idea of the photograph was brought up. I was glued to the seat of the truck. I mumbled something about, "Perhaps some other time." He said, "Sure." I felt his empathy as we drove away in silence.

In the days that followed, I tried to discover what it was 9 like to be a Californian all over again. I rode his bike up and down the coast, stopping for lunch and shopping in small villages nearby, exploring cliffs and beaches and an occasional back road.

My sister drove down for a few days. We walked in the 10 sun on the pier and watched the surfers splashing in the distance. We talked of the various directions our lives had taken over the years, and as I listened to her go on about grandchildren and shopping, I knew that it was now time to go home, the place where I lived. There had been too many years away, with all those cells changing and that inner clock going on and on. It was time to return to New York.

Strategies for Writing

1. Identify the analogy that the writer uses in paragraph eight of his essay.
2. Devise an analogy for the "various directions" the writer refers to in paragraph ten. What would be an appropriate analogy to show the different directions of his own life and the lives of other members of his family?
3. Write an essay in which you provide several examples that will show your reader the basic lifestyle of the area in which you live. You could show the kinds of jobs that most people

[1] Box-like ancestor of the modern camera. The device received reflected images that could later be permanently drawn on paper.

in the area have, what kind of entertainment is available, and even how the land and the climate affect this local life-style.

4. When the writer notes, in his first paragraph, that we ''are not the same persons we were seven years ago,'' he is referring to a scientific fact, but as we read the essay we realize that his meaning is much larger than that.

Write an essay in which you discuss the various kinds of changes that a person can go through that can lead to changes in his or her attitudes and even personality.

6

MATURITY

WRITING SKILL: Classification

We classify ideas, objects, and people in order to give ourselves a degree of control over the world around us. For example, we might classify people's political ideas as liberal, conservative, or radical; a bookstore might classify its books into categories such as biography, history, travel, and sports; or we might classify workers into blue collar, white collar, and professional. When we place items in different categories we understand them better; this helps us think more clearly and make more informed decisions. For example, if we are looking for a new car, there is more than one way to classify all the different cars that are on the market: there are luxury cars, medium comfort cars, and economy cars; there are eight-cylinder cars, six-cyclinder cars, and four-cylinder cars; and if we are looking for a used car, there are cars in excellent condition, cars in need of extensive repairs, and cars that can only be described as clunkers.

There are two useful rules to keep in mind as we approach classification. First, when we classify items we should divide those items into distinct categories, placing each item in only one category. For example, if we divide cars into luxury cars, economy cars, and used cars, we are not making good use of classification because a luxury car may also be a used car. Second, in addition to providing distinct categories, good classification is *complete*, with all the members of a class or type being included. For example, if you divided cars into new or used, any car would fit into one or the other of these categories. A good classification is also *useful;* you have decided to classify the different types of cars, for example, because you are trying to decide what car will be the best value for your money.

Our use of classification not only helps us gain control over the events and circumstances around us, it also controls the way other people receive information from us. For this reason, classification can be an important method of persuasion. For example, you might classify present-day lifestyles in order to persuade someone that one particular way of life is superior to all the others. Classification is persuasive when it is complete and consistent and when the different items being classified are placed in an effective order.

Each of the essays in the following unit uses classification to persuade us about something. In the excerpt from *Passages,* for example, Gail Sheehy is clearly presenting information that is useful; all of us are interested in learning about the different stages of life and how we can be more aware of ourselves at each stage. "During each of these passages," Gail Sheehy writes, "how we feel about our way of living will undergo subtle changes in four areas of perception." She then briefly describes each of these areas and proceeds to classify six different passages of life, using chronological order to show us how each stage of life is related to the others. Gail Sheehy also clearly explains the differences between one period of life and another. For example, when she is describing the passage she calls "The Trying Twenties," the writer points out that our focus "shifts from the interior turmoils of late adolescence . . . and we become almost totally preoccupied with working out the externals."

Finally, by describing each stage as she does, and by placing these stages in the order she does, the writer helps us better understand a complex subject. By the time we have finished reading her essay we see that the writer has shown us the full cycle of human life—at least the cycle that covers our most productive years.

In her essay on various types of friends, Judith Viorst sets out to fulfil one of the other prerequisites for a good classification essay: she aims for completeness. Her essay describes eight types of friends. Toward the end of her essay, the writer takes pains to point out that one of these types was included at the insistence of some women who were aware of her essay while it was still in progress:

> I wanted to write just of women friends, but the women I've talked to won't let me—they say I must mention man–woman friendships too.

In addition, the writer provides us with convenient labels with which to classify our own friends, and as we read the essay we may find ourselves actively using her method of classification.

Three memorable boys from John Updike's childhood are given the headings "A," "B," and "C," instead of the kinds of headings we find in the Judith Viorst essay. The fact that Updike labels the boys in this way suggests that they are types of friends, and he is classifying them. The first boy, "A," is emotionally the furthest from John Updike; in fact, he is the most negative presence as he "*loomed* next door" to the future writer. We move from the "*power* of stupidity" represented by "A," to "B," who made it possible for Updike to experience what he calls "the pattern of friendship," to "C," who is still the writer's friend. As you go through this essay, you may get the feeling a reader often has when presented with an effective classification essay: the feeling that we all share certain universal experiences, whether they be the kinds of people we have known or the different stages we experience in our lives. Each writer in this unit has placed important aspects of human life into categories that are both personal for the writer and meaningful for virtually every reader.

•&• *Gail Sheehy* •&•

Gail Sheehy was educated at the University of Vermont and at Columbia University. She began her writing career with the Rochester *Democrat and Chronicle* in 1961, and from 1963 to 1966 she worked as a feature writer for the *New York Herald Tribune*. She has also written for such periodicals as *McCall's*, the *London Sunday Telegraph,* and *Paris Match.*

Gail Sheehy has also written book-length studies of contemporary social issues, but her most famous single work is her 1976 book, *Passages,* from which the following selection has been chosen. One reviewer of the book noted that the writer's theme deals with the fact that "not only are there crises in every life, not only do they occur with reasonable predictability, but they are . . . entirely natural—comparable . . . to the seasons of the year or to the germination of a seed."

The following selection from *Passages* outlines and illustrates Gail Sheehy's belief that there are four main "passages" in life, and that we must confront each of these milestones in order to go on to the next stage.

PREVIEWING THE WRITER

• Note the writer's emphasis on the choices people have at each stage in life. According to the writer, do these choices become wider or narrower as we get older?

• Note how the writer emphasizes the changes that take place in people's external and internal lives.

• Note how the writer makes distinctions between the attitudes of men and of women toward the various stages of life.

from *PASSAGES*

A PERSON'S LIFE at any given time incorporates both external and internal aspects. The external system is composed of our memberships in the culture; our job, social class, family and social roles, how we present ourselves to and participate in the world. The interior realm concerns the meanings this participation has for each of us. In what ways are our values, goals, and aspirations being invigorated or violated by our present life system? How many parts of our personality can we live out, and what parts are we suppressing? How do we *feel* about our way of living in the world at any given time?

The inner realm is where the crucial shifts in bedrock begin   2
to throw a person off balance, signaling the necessity to change and move on to a new footing in the next stage of development. These crucial shifts occur throughout life, yet people consistently refuse to recognize that they possess an internal life system. Ask anyone who seems down, "Why are you feeling low?" Most will displace the inner message onto a marker event: "I've been down since we moved, since I changed jobs, since my wife went back to graduate school and turned into a damn social worker in sackcloth," and so on. Probably less than ten percent would say: "There is some unknown disturbance within me, and even though it's painful, I feel I have to stay with it and ride it out." Even fewer people would be able to explain that the turbulence they feel may have no external cause. And yet it may not resolve itself for *several years*.

During each of these passages, how we feel about our way   3
of living will undergo subtle changes in four areas of perception. One is the interior sense of self in relation to others. A second is the proportion of safeness to danger we feel in our lives. A third is our perception of time—do we have plenty of it, or are we beginning to feel that time is running out? Last, there will be some shift at the gut level in our sense of aliveness or stagnation. These are the hazy sensations that compose the background tone of living and shape the decisions on which we take action.

The work of adult life is not easy. As in childhood, each   4
step presents not only new tasks of development but requires a letting go of the techniques that worked before. With each passage some magic must be given up, some cherished illusion of safety and comfortably familiar sense of self must be cast off, to allow for the greater expansion of our own distinctiveness.

....

PULLING UP ROOTS

Before 18, the motto is loud and clear: "I have to get away from   5
my parents." But the words are seldom connected to action. Generally still safely part of our families, even if away at school,

we feel our autonomy to be subject to erosion from moment to moment.

After 18, we begin Pulling Up Roots in earnest. College, military service, and short-term travels are all customary vehicles our society provides for the first round trips between family and a base of one's own. In the attempt to separate our view of the world from our family's view, despite vigorous protestations to the contrary—"I know exactly what I want!"—we cast about for any beliefs we can call our own. And in the process of testing those beliefs we are often drawn to fads, preferably those most mysterious and inaccessible to our parents.

Whatever tentative memberships we try out in the world, the fear haunts us that we are really kids who cannot take care of ourselves. We cover that fear with acts of defiance and mimicked confidence. For allies to replace our parents, we turn to our contemporaries. They become conspirators. So long as their perspective meshes with our own, they are able to substitute for the sanctuary of the family. But that doesn't last very long. And the instant they diverge from the shaky ideals of "our group," they are seen as betrayers. Rebounds to the family are common between the ages of 18 and 22.

The tasks of this passage are to locate ourselves in a peer group role, a sex role, an anticipated occupation, an ideology or world view. As a result, we gather the impetus to leave home physically and the identity to *begin* leaving home emotionally.

Even as one part of us seeks to be an individual, another part longs to restore the safety and comfort of merging with another. Thus one of the most popular myths of this passage is: We can piggyback our development by attaching to a Stronger One. But people who marry during this time often prolong financial and emotional ties to the family and relatives that impede them from becoming self-sufficient.

A stormy passage through the Pulling Up Roots years will probably facilitate the normal progression of the adult life cycle. If one doesn't have an identity crisis at this point, it will erupt during a later transition, when the penalties may be harder to bear.

THE TRYING TWENTIES

The Trying Twenties confront us with the question of how to take hold in the adult world. Our focus shifts from the interior turmoils of late adolescence—"Who am I?" "What is truth?"—

and we become almost totally preoccupied with working out the externals. "How do I put my aspirations into effect?" "What is the best way to start?" "Where do I go?" "Who can help me?" "How did *you* do it?"

In this period, which is longer and more stable compared 12 with the passage that leads to it, the tasks are as enormous as they are exhilarating: To shape a Dream, that vision of ourselves which will generate energy, aliveness, and hope. To prepare for a lifework. To find a mentor if possible. And to form the capacity for intimacy, without losing in the process whatever consistency of self we have thus far mustered. The first test structure must be erected around the life we choose to try.

Doing what we "should" is the most pervasive theme of 13 the twenties. The "shoulds" are largely defined by family models, the press of the culture, or the prejudices of our peers. If the prevailing cultural instructions are that one should get married and settle down behind one's own door, a nuclear family is born. If instead the peers insist that one should do one's own thing, the 25-year-old is likely to harness himself onto a Harley-Davidson and burn up Route 66 in the commitment to have no commitments.

One of the terrifying aspects of the twenties is the inner 14 conviction that the choices we make are irrevocable. It is largely a false fear. Change is quite possible, and some alteration of our original choices is probably inevitable.

Two impulses, as always, are at work. One is to build a 15 firm, safe structure for the future by making strong commitments, to "be set." Yet people who slip into a ready-made form without much self-examination are likely to find themselves *locked in.*

The other urge is to explore and experiment, keeping any 16 structure tentative and therefore easily reversible. Taken to the extreme, these are people who skip from one trial job and one limited personal encounter to another, spending their twenties in the *transient* state.

Although the choices of our twenties are not irrevocable, 17 they do set in motion a Life Pattern. Some of us follow the locked-in pattern, others the transient pattern, the wunderkind pattern, the caregiver pattern, and there are a number of others. Such patterns strongly influence the particular questions raised for each person during each passage, and so the most common patterns will also be traced throughout the book.

Buoyed by powerful illusions and belief in the power of   18
the will, we commonly insist in our twenties that what we have
chosen to do is the one true course in life. Our backs go up at
the merest hint that we are like our parents, that two decades
of parental training might be reflected in our current actions
and attitudes.

"Not me," is the motto, "I'm different."   19

CATCH-30

Impatient with devoting ourselves to the "shoulds," a new vi-   20
tality springs from within as we approach 30. Men and women
alike speak of feeling too narrow and restricted. They blame all
sorts of things, but what the restrictions boil down to are the
outgrowth of career and personal choices of the twenties. They
may have been choices perfectly suited to that stage. But now
the fit feels different. Some inner aspect that was left out is
striving to be taken into account. Important new choices must
be made, and commitments altered or deepened. The work involves great change, turmoil, and often crisis—a simultaneous
feeling of rock bottom and the urge to bust out.

One common response is the tearing up of the life we   21
spent most of our twenties putting together. It may mean striking out on a secondary road toward a new vision or converting
a dream of "running for president" into a more realistic goal.
The single person feels a push to find a partner. The woman
who was previously content at home with children chafes to
venture into the world. The childless couple reconsiders children. And almost everyone who is married, especially those
married for seven years, feels a discontent.

If the discontent doesn't lead to divorce, it will, or should,   22
call for a serious review of the marriage and of each partner's
aspirations in their Catch-30 condition. The gist of that condition
was expressed by a 29-year-old associate with a Wall Street law
firm:

"I'm considering leaving the firm. I've been there four   23
years now; I'm getting good feedback, but I have no clients of
my own. I feel weak. If I wait much longer, it will be too late,
too close to that fateful time of decision on whether or not to
become a partner. I'm success-oriented. But the concept of being
55 years old and stuck in a monotonous job drives me wild. It
drives me crazy now, just a little bit. I'd say that 85 percent of
the time I thoroughly enjoy my work. But when I get a screwball

case, I come away from court saying, 'What am I doing here?' It's a *visceral* reaction that I'm wasting my time. I'm trying to find some way to make a social contribution or a slot in city government. I keep saying, 'There's something more.' "

Besides the push to broaden himself professionally, there   24
is a wish to expand his personal life. He wants two or three more children. "The concept of a home has become very meaningful to me, a place to get away from troubles and relax. I love my son in a way I could not have anticipated. I never could live alone."

Consumed with the work of making his own critical life-   25
steering decisions, he demonstrates the essential shift at this age: an absolute requirement to be more self-concerned. The self has new value now that his competency has been proved.

His wife is struggling with her own age-30 priorities. She   26
wants to go to law school, but he wants more children. If she is going to stay home, she wants him to make more time for the family instead of taking on even wider professional commitments. His view of the bind, of what he would most like from his wife, is this:

"I'd like not to be bothered. It sounds cruel, but I'd like   27
not to have to worry about what she's going to do next week. Which is why I've told her several times that I think she should do something. Go back to school and get a degree in social work or geography or whatever. Hopefully that would fulfill her, and then I wouldn't have to worry about her line of problems. I want her to be decisive about herself."

The trouble with his advice to his wife is that it comes out   28
of concern with *his* convenience, rather than with *her* development. She quickly picks up on this lack of goodwill: He is trying to dispose of her. At the same time, he refuses her the same latitude to be "selfish" in making an independent decision to broaden her own horizons. Both perceive a lack of mutuality. And that is what Catch-30 is all about for the couple.

ROOTING AND EXTENDING

Life becomes less provisional, more rational and orderly in the   29
early thirties. We begin to settle down in the full sense. Most of us begin putting down roots and sending out new shoots. People buy houses and become very earnest about climbing career ladders. Men in particular concern themselves with "making it." Satisfaction with marriage generally goes downhill

in the thirties (for those who have remained together) compared with the highly valued, vision-supporting marriage of the twenties. This coincides with the couple's reduced social life outside the family and the in-turned focus on raising their children.

THE DEADLINE DECADE

In the middle of the thirties we come upon a crossroads. We 30 have reached the halfway mark. Yet even as we are reaching our prime, we begin to see there is a place where it finishes. Time starts to squeeze.

The loss of youth, the faltering of physical powers we have 31 always taken for granted, the fading purpose of stereotyped roles by which we have thus far identified ourselves, the spiritual dilemma of having no absolute answers—any or all of these shocks can give this passage the character of crisis. Such thoughts usher in a decade between 35 and 45 that can be called the Deadline Decade. It is a time of both danger and opportunity. All of us have the chance to rework the narrow identity by which we defined ourselves in the first half of life. And those of us who make the most of the opportunity will have a full-out authenticity crisis.

To come through this authenticity crisis, we must re- 32 examine our purposes and reevaluate how to spend our resources from now on. "Why am I doing all this? What do I really believe in?" No matter what we have been doing, there will be parts of ourselves that have been suppressed and now need to find expression. "Bad" feelings will demand acknowledgment along with the good.

It is frightening to step off onto the treacherous footbridge 33 leading to the second half of life. We can't take everything with us on this journey through uncertainty. Along the way, we discover that we are alone. We no longer have to ask permission because we are the providers of our own safety. We must learn to give ourselves permission. We stumble upon feminine or masculine aspects of our natures that up to this time have usually been masked. There is grieving to be done because an old self is dying. By taking in our suppressed and even our unwanted parts, we prepare at the gut level for the reintegration of an identity that is ours and ours alone—not some artificial form put together to please the culture or our mates. It is a dark passage at the beginning. But by disassembling ourselves, we can glimpse the light and gather our parts into a renewal.

Women sense this inner crossroads earlier than men do.   34
The time pinch often prompts a woman to stop and take an all-
points survey at age 35. Whatever options she has already
played out, she feels a "my last chance" urgency to review
those options she has set aside and those that aging and biology
will close off in the *now foreseeable* future. For all her qualms and
confusion about where to start looking for a new future, she
usually enjoys an exhilaration of release. Assertiveness begins
rising. There are so many firsts ahead.

Men, too, feel the time push in the mid-thirties. Most men   35
respond by pressing down harder on the career accelerator. It's
"my last chance" to pull away from the pack. It is no longer
enough to be the loyal junior executive, the promising young
novelist, the lawyer who does a little *pro bono* work on the side.
He wants now to become part of top management, to be recognized as an established writer, or an active politician with his
own legislative program. With some chagrin, he discovers that
he has been too anxious to please and too vulnerable to criticism. He wants to put together his own ship.

During this period of intense concentration on external   36
advancement, it is common for men to be unaware of the more
difficult, gut issues that are propelling them forward. The survey that was neglected at 35 becomes a crucible at 40. Whatever
rung of achievement he has reached, the man of 40 usually feels
stale, restless, burdened, and unappreciated. He worries about
his health. He wonders, "Is this all there is?" He may make a
series of departures from well-established lifelong base lines,
including marriage. More and more men are seeking second
careers in midlife. Some become self-destructive. And many
men in their forties experience a major shift of emphasis away
from pouring all their energies into their own advancement. A
more tender, feeling side comes into play. They become interested in developing an ethical self.

RENEWAL OR RESIGNATION

Somewhere in the mid-forties, equilibrium is regained. A new   37
stability is achieved, which may be more or less satisfying.

If one has refused to budge through the midlife transition,   38
the sense of staleness will calcify into resignation. One by one,
the safety and supports will be withdrawn from the person who
is standing still. Parents will become children; children will become strangers; a mate will grow away or go away; the career

will become just a job—and each of these events will be felt as an abandonment. The crisis will probably emerge again around 50. And although its wallop will be greater, the jolt may be just what is needed to prod the resigned middle-ager toward seeking revitalization.

On the other hand . . .   39

If we have confronted ourselves in the middle passage and   40
found a renewal of purpose around which we are eager to build a more authentic life structure, these may well be the best years. Personal happiness takes a sharp turn upward for partners who can now accept the fact: "I cannot expect *anyone* to fully understand me." Parents can be forgiven for the burdens of our childhood. Children can be let go without leaving us in collapsed silence. At 50, there is a new warmth and mellowing. Friends become more important than ever, but so does privacy. Since it is so often proclaimed by people past midlife, the motto of this stage might be "No more bullshit."

THE WRITER'S THEMES

1. To what extent do you agree with Gail Sheehy's divisions of life into the different periods she describes? For example, is the writer being realistic when she emphasizes the significance of age thirty? Is the "Deadline Decade" really between thirty-five and forty-five, or could that important period be another decade in a person's life?
2. According to Gail Sheehy, what is the greatest danger to the individual at each stage of life? For example, at what stage is "standing still" a serious obstacle to a person's progress?
3. In her essay, Gail Sheehy does not discuss stages of childhood and early adolescence. Select one period from these years (the years in high school, for example) and show how this period is different from other stages in a person's life.

THE WRITER'S TECHNIQUE

In paragraph twenty-nine of her essay, Gail Sheehy describes the phenomenon she calls "Rooting and Extending." Here is that paragraph:

Life becomes less provisional, more rational and orderly in the early thirties. We begin to settle down in the full sense. Most of us begin putting down roots and sending out new shoots. People buy houses and become very earnest about climbing career ladders. Men in particular concern themselves with "making it." Satisfaction with marriage generally goes downhill in the thirties (for those who have remained together) compared with the highly valued, vision-supporting marriage of the twenties. This coincides with the couple's reduced social life outside the family and the in-turned focus on raising their children.

Gail Sheehy is describing "the early thirties" and she notes that during this period life becomes "less provisional, [and] more rational and orderly." It is at this time that people "settle down in the full sense." In the next sentence, the writer expands on this notion of settling down when she observes that people at this period in their lives "begin putting down roots and sending out new shoots." The remainder of the paragraph is made up of specific examples that support this statement.

At this point in the paragraph the writer concentrates on marriage as she begins to deal with both men and women. Marriage, the writer notes, "generally goes downhill in the thirties," and by the end of the paragraph we see men and women in relation to the family; it is in the thirties that the couple's "social life outside the family" is reduced and there is an "in-turned focus on raising their children."

The writer begins the paragraph with a very general statement about a person's early thirties, and continues by giving us some very specific details that help us to see what she calls the "roots and shoots" of this period in a person's life. The "roots" may be seen as the houses we buy and the careers we start to build, while the "shoots" are, presumably, the children that a couple concentrates on at this stage in life, as the husband and wife reduce their outside social life and begin to raise a family.

PARAGRAPH PRACTICE

Write a paragraph of your own, using Gail Sheehy's paragraph as your model. First, choose a specific time of life; it could be the mid-teens or the late teens, the early twenties, or any other period you wish to choose. Begin your paragraph by making a general statement about that period of a person's life. For example, Gail Sheehy tells us that in the early thirties life becomes "less provisional" and "more rational and orderly." What do you believe life becomes by the late teens (or any other period of life you have chosen)?

Follow this general opening with a more specific statement as to what people do during this period of their lives. For example, if you have chosen the early twenties, state what people begin to do at this time. Do most people generally finish their schooling and begin a career? Do they start to think seriously about marriage?

The remainder of your paragraph should contain your most specific examples that will support your main idea. Your paragraph will have increased strength and variety if you imitate Gail Sheehy's technique of including both men and women as examples. What do men especially engage in during the period you are describing? What do women do? For example, if you have chosen the mid-teens, you might wish to show the differences between the maturity of adolescent girls and that of boys of the same age. What does each group do that shows the differences between them?

Your paragraph will have a greater sense of direction if you carefully move from a general opening sentence to a more specific statement. In addition, the more specific your examples are, the stronger will be the impression on the reader. Your paragraph will also have a greater sense of variety if you are careful to share your examples between both males and females.

ESSAY PRACTICE

The following outline will help you plan a complete essay of at least five paragraphs. The theme of your essay will be closely related to the selection from *Passages*.

The following sentence may serve as your thesis sentence, and will also be the main idea of your introductory paragraph:

¶ 1. When important changes take place in life, they are often recognized by ourselves and our families, and also by society in general.

Each of the sentences below is the topic sentence for one of the paragraphs that you will write to develop your thesis.

You may use the suggested details to develop each paragraph, or you may supply details of your own.

¶ 2. When a person makes an important change in his or her life, that person is often aware of the significance of that change.

[DETAILS: Choose an important change that a person could make in life—marriage or a choice of careers, for example—and indicate the different ways that person could show how important that change is. Be sure to indicate whether or not the person might have conflicting emotions about this change. For example, a person about to accept a new job might feel excitement *and* apprehension because of this new position.]

¶ 3. The person's family and friends will also have definite reactions to this important change.

[DETAILS: Keeping the example you have chosen, indicate how the members of a person's family, along with his or her friends, might react to this change. Would all of the reactions be verbalized? What effect(s) would these reactions have on the person?]

¶ 4. As a result of this change, the person may find a different attitude on the part of society.

[DETAILS: Using the same example, describe how various institutions might react to this change in the person's life. In how many ways would society recognize the importance of this change? Your examples could range from a new category with the Internal Revenue Service, to a new attitude on the part of a local community group, such as a church or club.]

Be certain that you use transitions between paragraphs to make your writing flow smoothly. In addition, be sure that your conclusion gives your reader a clear signal that you have come to the end of your essay.

ESSAY TOPICS

1. a. In the "Pulling Up Roots" section of her essay, Gail Sheehy points out that one of the ways young people separate their "view of the world" from their families' view is to be "drawn to fads."

Classify some of the most common fads that young people are drawn to, in order to show their independence from their families. How is each type of fad "mysterious and inaccessible" to the parents?

b. Gail Sheehy notes that when we are in our twenties we reject "the merest hint that we are like our parents, that two decades of parental training might be reflected in our current actions and attitudes." In what way(s) are you very different from your parents? In what aspects of your personality do you find certain characteristics that you have inherited from either one, or both, of your parents?

2. When she is discussing "The Trying Twenties" Gail Sheehy observes that one of the "terrifying aspects" of this period is "the inner conviction that the choices we make are irrevocable. It is largely a false fear." Classify the types of choices people have to make in life. In each case, indicate whether the type of choice tends to be revocable or irrevocable.

3. a. What period in a person's life do you feel is the prime of life? Why is that particular period the best?

   b. When you consider your own life, what do you think was (or will be) the best period? Why do you look back on, or look forward to, this period?

☙ *Judith Viorst* ☙

Judith Viorst was born in Newark, New Jersey, and was educated at Rutgers University. She is a poet, a journalist, and the author of several books of fiction and nonfiction for children. She has also worked as a contributing editor at *Redbook* magazine and has written a syndicated column for the Washington Star Syndicate.

Among her published works for adults is a book of collected poems entitled *It's Hard to Be Hip Over Thirty, and Other Tragedies of Married Life,* and a volume of collected pieces, *Yes, Married: A Saga of Love and Complaint.* In 1970, Judith Viorst won an Emmy Award for her poetic monologues written for the CBS special "Annie, the Women in the Life of a Man."

In the following essay, which first appeared in *Redbook* magazine in April, 1970, Judith Viorst examines her changing attitudes toward friendship and provides us with detailed descriptions of the different types of friends she has known.

PREVIEWING THE WRITER

• Note the order in which the writer describes the various types of friends. Why, for example, has she followed "convenience friends" with "special-interest friends"?

• Note the writer's report on her change of attitude toward friendship. Why did the writer experience this change? How has her new attitude led to a deeper awareness of friendship?

• Note the different sources for the writer's evidence. How much of her evidence comes from her own personal experience? How much is drawn from the experience of others?

FRIENDS, GOOD FRIENDS—AND SUCH GOOD FRIENDS

WOMEN ARE FRIENDS, I once would have said, when 1 they totally love and support and trust each other, and bare to each other the secrets of their souls, and run—no questions asked—to help each other, and tell harsh truths to each other (no, you can't wear that dress unless you lose ten pounds first) when harsh truths must be told.

Women are friends, I once would have said, when 2 they share the same affection for Ingmar Bergman, plus train

rides, cats, warm rain, charades, Camus, and hate with equal
ardor Newark and Brussels sprouts and Lawrence Welk and
camping.

In other words, I once would have said that a friend is a 3
friend all the way, but now I believe that's a narrow point of
view. For the friendships I have and the friendships I see are
conducted at many levels of intensity, serve many different
functions, meet different needs and range from those as all-the-
way as the friendship of the soul sisters mentioned above to
that of the most nonchalant and casual playmates.

Consider these varieties of friendship: 4

1. Convenience friends. These are the women with whom, 5
if our paths weren't crossing all the time, we'd have no particular reason to be friends: a next-door neighbor, a woman in our
car pool, the mother of one of our children's closest friends or
maybe some mommy with whom we serve juice and cookies
each week at the Glenwood Co-op Nursery.

Convenience friends are convenient indeed. They'll lend 6
us their cups and silverware for a party. They'll drive our kids
to soccer when we're sick. They'll take us to pick up our car
when we need a lift to the garage. They'll even take our cats
when we go on vacation. As we will for them.

But we don't, with convenience friends, ever come too 7
close or tell too much; we maintain our public face and emotional distance. "Which means," says Elaine, "that I'll talk about
being overweight but not about being depressed. Which means
I'll admit being mad but not blind with rage. Which means I
might say that we're pinched this month but never that I'm
worried sick over money."

But which doesn't mean that there isn't sufficient value to 8
be found in these friendships of mutual aid, in convenience
friends.

2. Special-interest friends. These friendships aren't inti- 9
mate, and they needn't involve kids or silverware or cats. Their
value lies in some interest jointly shared. And so we may have
an office friend or a yoga friend or a tennis friend or a friend
from the Women's Democratic Club.

"I've got one woman friend," says Joyce, "who likes, as 10
I do, to take psychology courses. Which makes it nice for me—
and nice for her. It's fun to go with someone you know and it's
fun to discuss what you've learned, driving back from the
classes." And for the most part, she says, that's all they discuss.

"I'd say that what we're doing is *doing* together, not being together," Suzanne says of her Tuesday-doubles friends. "It's mainly a tennis relationship, but we play together well. And I guess we all need to have a couple of playmates." 11

I agree. 12

My playmate is a shopping friend, a woman of marvelous taste, a woman who knows exactly *where* to buy *what*, and furthermore is a woman who always knows beyond a doubt what one ought to be buying. I don't have the time to keep up with what's new in eyeshadow, hemlines and shoes and whether the smock look is in or finished already. But since (oh, shame!) I care a lot about eyeshadow, hemlines and shoes, and since I don't *want* to wear smocks if the smock look is finished, I'm very glad to have a shopping friend. 13

3. Historical friends. We all have a friend who knew us when . . . maybe way back in Miss Meltzer's second grade, when our family lived in that three-room flat in Brooklyn, when our dad was out of work for seven months, when our brother Allie got in that fight where they had to call the police, when our sister married the endodontist from Yonkers and when, the morning after we lost our virginity, she was the first, the only, friend we told. 14

The years have gone by and we've gone separate ways and we've little in common now, but we're still an intimate part of each other's past. And so whenever we go to Detroit we always go to visit this friend of our girlhood. Who knows how we looked before our teeth were straightened. Who knows how we talked before our voice got un-Brooklyned. Who knows what we ate before we learned about artichokes. And who, by her presence, puts us in touch with an earlier part of ourself, a part of ourself it's important never to lose. 15

"What this friend means to me and what I mean to her," says Grace, "is having a sister without sibling rivalry. We know the texture of each other's lives. She remembers my grandmother's cabbage soup. I remember the way her uncle played the piano. There's simply no other friend who remembers those things." 16

4. Crossroads friends. Like historical friends, our crossroads friends are important for *what was*—for the friendship we shared at a crucial, now past, time of life. A time, perhaps, when we roomed in college together; or worked as eager young singles in the Big City together; or went together, as my friend 17

Elizabeth and I did through pregnancy, birth and that scary first year of new motherhood.

Crossroads friends forge powerful links, links strong   18
enough to endure with not much more contact than once-a-year letters at Christmas. And out of respect for those crossroads years, for those dramas and dreams we once shared, we will always be friends.

5. Cross-generational friends. Historical friends and cross-   19
roads friends seem to maintain a special kind of intimacy— dormant but always ready to be revived—and though we may rarely meet, whenever we do connect, it's personal and intense. Another kind of intimacy exists in the friendships that form across generations in what one woman calls her daughter- mother and her mother-daughter relationships.

Evelyn's friend is her mother's age—"but I share so much   20
more than I ever could with my mother"—a woman she talks to of music, of books and of life. "What I get from her is the benefit of her experience. What she gets—and enjoys—from me is a youthful perspective. It's a pleasure for both of us."

I have in my own life a precious friend, a woman of 65   21
who has lived very hard, who is wise, who listens well; who has been where I am and can help me understand it; and who represents not only an ultimate ideal mother to me but also the person I'd like to be when I grow up.

In our daughter role we tend to do more than our share   22
of self-revelation; in our mother role we tend to receive what's revealed. It's another kind of pleasure—playing wise mother to a questing younger person. It's another very lovely kind of friendship.

6. Part-of-a-couple friends. Some of the women we call   23
our friends we never see alone—we see them as part of a couple at couples' parties. And though we share interests in many things and respect each other's views, we aren't moved to deepen the relationship. Whatever the reason, a lack of time or—and this is more likely—a lack of chemistry, our friendship remains in the context of a group. But the fact that our feeling on seeing each other is always, "I'm *so* glad she's here" and the fact that we spend half the evening talking together says that this too, in its own way, counts as a friendship.

(Other part-of-a-couple friends are the friends that came   24
with the marriage, and some of these are friends we could live without. But sometimes, alas, she married our husband's best

friend; and sometimes, alas, she *is* our husband's best friend. And so we find ourself dealing with her, somewhat against our will, in a spirit of what I'll call *reluctant* friendship.)

7. Men who are friends. I wanted to write just of women friends, but the women I've talked to won't let me—they say I must mention man-woman friendships too. For these friendships can be just as close and as dear as those that we form with women. Listen to Lucy's description of one such friendship:

"We've found we have things to talk about that are different from what he talks about with my husband and different from what I talk about with his wife. So sometimes we call on the phone or meet for lunch. There are similar intellectual interests—we always pass on to each other the books that we love—but there's also something tender and caring too."

In a couple of crises, Lucy says, "he offered himself, for talking and for helping. And when someone died in his family he wanted me there. The sexual, flirty part of our friendship is very small, but *some*—just enough to make it fun and different." She thinks—and I agree—that the sexual part, though small is always *some*, is always there when a man and a woman are friends.

It's only in the past few years that I've made friends with men, in the sense of a friendship that's *mine*, not just part of two couples. And achieving with them the ease and the trust I've found with women friends has value indeed. Under the dryer at home last week, putting on mascara and rouge, I comfortably sat and talked with a fellow named Peter. Peter, I finally decided, could handle the shock of me minus mascara under the dryer. Because we care for each other. Because we're friends.

8. There are medium friends, and pretty good friends, and very good friends indeed, and these friendships are defined by their level of intimacy. And what we'll reveal at each of these levels of intimacy is calibrated with care. We might tell a medium friend, for example, that yesterday we had a fight with our husband. And we might tell a pretty good friend that this fight with our husband made us so mad that we slept on the couch. And we might tell a very good friend that the reason we got so mad in that fight that we slept on the couch had something to do with that girl who works in his office. But it's only to our very best friends that we're willing to tell all, to tell what's going on with that girl in his office.

The best of friends, I still believe, totally love and support 30
and trust each other, and bare to each other the secrets of their
souls, and run—no questions asked—to help each other, and
tell harsh truths to each other when they must be told.

But we needn't agree about everything (only 12-year-old 31
girl friends agree about *everything*) to tolerate each other's point
of view. To accept without judgment. To give and to take without ever keeping score. And to *be* there, as I am for them and
as they are for me, to comfort our sorrows, to celebrate our joys.

THE WRITER'S THEMES

1. Trace the writer's changing attitudes toward friendship. At
   what point in her life did some of her attitudes change?
   What is her current thinking on the subject?
2. How is the writer's argument made stronger by the variety
   of the evidence she presents? Do her own experiences seem
   as convincing as the experiences of the other women she
   quotes?
3. What is the special value of the male friends the writer has
   recently made? What do these male friends offer that none
   of the writer's female friends seem to offer?

THE WRITER'S TECHNIQUE

In paragraph twenty-nine of her essay, Judith Viorst reviews
the various levels of friendship. Here is that paragraph:

> There are medium friends, and pretty good friends, and very
> good friends indeed, and these friendships are defined by their
> level of intimacy. And what we'll reveal at each of these levels
> of intimacy is calibrated with care. We might tell a medium friend,
> for example, that yesterday we had a fight with our husband.
> And we might tell a pretty good friend that this fight with our
> husband made us so mad that we slept on the couch. And we
> might tell a very good friend that the reason we got so mad in
> that fight that we slept on the couch had something to do with
> that girl who works in his office. But it's only to our very best
> friends that we're willing to tell all, to tell what's going on with
> that girl in his office.

Notice that in her opening sentence, the writer indicates three types of friends ("medium friends," "pretty good friends," and "very good friends") and she observes that these friendships "are defined by their levels of intimacy." In the next sentence she observes that at each level of friendship we are very careful about what we reveal to other people. She then gives examples of what she means, beginning with the first type ("medium friends") from her opening sentence, and proceeding to the second and third types. Throughout the paragraph the writer is careful to follow the order she established at the beginning of the paragraph.

We also notice that the writer develops a single example throughout the entire paragraph. She begins that example when she is discussing a "medium friend": "We might tell a medium friend, for example, that yesterday we had a fight with our husband." As she proceeds to the next type of friend, "a pretty good friend," the same example of the fight with her husband is given in more detail, showing that this is indeed a deeper level of friendship. Next, the writer describes the third level of friendship by providing further details about the same example, and by the time we get to this level ("a very good friend") these details are quite intimate: we are told "the reason we got so mad in that fight that we slept on the couch had something to do with that girl who works in his office."

So far, the writer's method has been predictable. The topic sentence has prepared us for three types of friends, and the example of the woman fighting with her husband seems to have been taken to its limits. But not quite. In the final sentence of the paragraph, Judith Viorst does something she has not prepared us for: she introduces still another type of friend, while she takes the example of the fight to its ultimate conclusion. "But," concludes the writer, "it's only to our very best friends that we're willing to tell all, to tell what's going on with that girl in his office."

In a single developed paragraph, Judith Viorst has shown us the range of friendships and she has carefully illuminated each one in the light of a single example.

PARAGRAPH PRACTICE

Write a paragraph of your own, using the Judith Viorst paragraph as your model. You might, for example, wish to describe three types of relatives you have known. You could begin your paragraph in the same way that Judith Viorst begins hers, but using your own method of division. The different kinds of relatives could be indicated in this way:

> There are stingy relatives, there are generous relatives, and there are overly generous relatives, and all of these relatives may be defined by how they treat the children of the family.

You could also choose as your subject three types of classmates, three types of neighbors, or three types of co-workers. No matter what subject you choose, develop your paragraph in the same manner as Judith Viorst developed hers, by selecting one central example and showing how each type of person you have listed can be defined according to that example. Judith Viorst uses the central example of a wife's fight with her husband to define the "level of intimacy" she enjoys with each type of friend. If you choose to describe three types of relatives, you could show the level of your relationship with each type by describing how your different relatives treated you each Christmas when you were a child. If you choose to write about three classmates, you could show how you relate to each of them by describing each one being helpful to you in a different way when you were experiencing a problem in a course.

No matter what you choose to write about, your paragraph will have unity and a sense of development when all three types of people you write about are related to one central example you have chosen to use. You might also want to save a fourth type until the end of your paragraph, to surprise your reader. This would make your paragraph a very close imitation of Judith Viorst's writing.

ESSAY PRACTICE

The following outline will help you plan a complete essay of at least five paragraphs. The theme of your essay will be closely related to the Judith Viorst essay.

The following sentence may serve as your thesis sentence, and will also be the main idea of your introductory paragraph:

¶ 1. When it comes to placing our confidence in friends or even acquaintances, we must carefully judge those whom we would trust.

Each of the sentences below is the topic sentence for one of the paragraphs that you will write to develop your thesis. You may use the suggested details to develop each paragraph, or you may supply details of your own.

¶ 2. There are some people in whom I would never confide.

[DETAILS: In what kind of person do you believe it is unwise to confide? Specifically, who are the people you know fairly well but to whom you would never confide anything important? In each case, indicate whether your decision is based on an intuition you have had about the person, or on some experience you had with that person.]

¶ 3. There are certain people in whom I can confide some of the time.

[DETAILS: Who are the people in your life you find yourself confiding in at certain times? Indicate at least two people in your life who fall into this category and describe an occasion when you found it necessary or desirable to confide in each of them. In this paragraph, you might also indicate the circumstances under which you would confide in someone who is not an especially close friend.]

¶ 4. There are very few people to whom I can confide my most private thoughts and concerns.

[DETAILS: How many people are so close to you that you could confide virtually anything to them? Help your reader to see how close these people are by describing what you have confided, or would confide, under the right circumstances.]

Be certain that you use transitions between paragraphs to make your writing flow smoothly. In addition, be sure that your conclusion gives your reader a clear signal that you have come to the end of your essay.

ESSAY TOPICS

1. a. Using Judith Viorst's essay as your model, classify the different types of friendships you enjoy. How many of the categories used by Judith Viorst can also be applied to your friendships? If you have friends who do not fit into any of these categories, indicate this in your essay and provide your own names for the different types of friends you have.

b. Using Judith Viorst's essay as your model, classify various types of people, or groups of people, that you know. You could, for example, describe different types of fathers or mothers, different types of news broadcasters, or different types of singing groups. Be sure that you develop your description of each type of person or group that you present. Your reader's ability to see each type will depend on the number and quality of your supporting details.

2. a. In her essay, Judith Viorst points out that ''the sexual part, though small is always *some,* is always there when a man and a woman are friends.''

Is it easier for you to make friends with someone of the same sex, or with someone of the opposite sex? How are the problems of making and maintaining a friendship different when your friend is of the opposite sex?

b. Judith Viorst's main concern in her essay is female friendship. How different would her essay have been if she had chosen to describe the male experience of friendship? Using Judith Viorst's approach to the subject, classify two or three types of friendships, or categories of friends, from the male point of view. For example, if you choose to write about ''convenience friends'' as one of your categories, describe how men help each other in a variety of everyday situations.

3. a. Our society is known for the mobility of its people; Americans are often on the move. With this in mind, how difficult is it for you to maintain old friendships? How easy or difficult is it to make new friends? To what extent do you believe that people's mobility affects their attitudes toward making new friends? For example, do some people decide not to bother making friends in a community if they know they will be living there only a year or two?

b. Once a person has a family, how much time or energy is left for friendship? What types of friends tend to become less visible or important in a person's life, once that person is married and has his or her own family? To what extent does a family tend to replace a person's friends after marriage?

🙠 *John Updike* 🙠

John Updike (1932–   ) was born in Shillington, Pennsylvania. He graduated from Harvard in 1954 and the following year began to write for the *New Yorker* magazine. Along with such favorably received novels as *Rabbit, Run* (1960) and *The Centaur* (1963), Updike is also well known as a short story writer. In 1959 he published *The Same Door,* and three years later his *Pigeon Feathers and Other Stories* appeared. Updike also has a considerable reputation as a poet, and in 1959 he received a Guggenheim fellowship for poetry. The writer is a regular contributor of poetry and short stories to national magazines. In 1982 he received a Pulitzer Prize and an American Book Award for his tenth novel, *Rabbit Is Rich.*

Updike's writing is admired for what critics have called its "stylistic virtuosity" and others have referred to the "crystalline style" of his work. He has also been called the master of the "distilled phrase." Updike himself has noted that he is "still running on energy laid down in childhood. Writing is a way of keeping up with that childhood."

The following selection first appeared in the book *Five Boyhoods,* a collection of short autobiographies. Among the other contributors to that volume were the writers Harry Golden and William Zinsser, along with the cartoonist Walt Kelly. In this selection from the book, John Updike not only describes some of his childhood experiences, he also gives a feeling for the texture of that childhood.

PREVIEWING THE WRITER

• Note the order in which Updike describes his three friends. Why is this order appropriate?

• Note the writer's relationship with each of his childhood friends. To what extent does his personality change, depending on the friend he is with at the time?

• Note the kinds of activities the writer engages in with each of his childhood friends. In each case, what do the activities reveal about the quality of that friendship?

THREE BOYS

A, B, AND C, I'll say, in case they care. *A* lived next   1
door; he *loomed* next door, rather. He seemed immense—a great
wallowing fatso stuffed with possessions; he was the son of a

full-fashioned knitter. He seemed to have a beer-belly; after several generations beer-bellies may become congenital. Also his face had no features. It was just a blank ball on his shoulders. He used to call me "Ostrich," after Disney's Ollie Ostrich. My neck was not very long; the name seemed horribly unfair; it was its injustice that made me cry. But nothing I could say, or scream, would make him stop. And I still, now and then—in reading, say, a book review by one of the apple-cheeked savants of the quarterlies or one of the pious gremlins who manufacture puns for *Time*—get the old sensations: my ears close up, my eyes go warm, my chest feels thin as an eggshell, my voice churns silently in my stomach. From *A* I received my first impression of the smug, chinkless, irresistible *power* of stupidity; it is the most powerful force on earth. It says "Ostrich" often enough, and the universe crumbles.

A was more than a boy, he was a force-field that could manifest itself in many forms, that could take the wiry, disconsolate shape of wide-mouthed, tiny-eared boys who would now and then beat me up on the way back from school. I did not greatly mind being beaten up, though I resisted it. For one thing, it firmly involved me, at least during the beating, with the circumambient humanity that so often seemed evasive. Also, the boys who applied the beating were misfits, periodic flunkers, who wore corduroy knickers with threadbare knees and men's shirts with the top button buttoned—this last an infallible sign of deep poverty. So that I felt there was some justice, some condonable revenge, being applied with their fists to this little teacher's son. And then there was the delicious alarm of my mother and grandmother when I returned home bloody, bruised, and torn. My father took the attitude that it was making a boy of me, an attitude I dimly shared. He and I both were afraid of me becoming a sissy—he perhaps more afraid than I.

When I was eleven or so I met *B*. It was summer and I was down at the playground. He was pushing a little tank with moving rubber treads up and down the hills in the sandbox. It was a fine little toy, mottled with camouflage green; patriotic manufacturers produced throughout the war millions of such authentic miniatures which we maneuvered with authentic, if miniature, militance. Attracted by the toy, I spoke to him; though taller and a little older than I, he had my dull straight brown hair and a look of being also alone. We became fast friends. He lived just up the street—toward the poorhouse, the east part of the street, from which the little winds of tragedy blew. He had just moved from the Midwest, and his mother was a widow. Beside wage war, we did many things together. We played marbles for days at a time, until one of us had won the other's entire coffee-canful. With jigsaws we cut out plywood animals copied from comic books. We made movies by tearing the pages from Big Little Books and coloring the drawings and pasting them in a strip, and winding them on toilet-paper spools, and making a cardboard carton a theatre. We rigged up telephones, and racing wagons, and cities of the future, using orange crates and cigar boxes and peanut-butter jars and such potent debris. We loved Smokey Stover and were always saying "Foo." We had an intense spell of Monopoly. He called me "Uppy"—the only person who ever did. I remember once, knowing he was coming down that afternoon to my house to play Monopoly, in order to show my joy I set up the board elaborately, with the Chance and Community Chest cards fanned painstakingly, like spiral staircases. He came into the room, groaned, "Uppy, what are you doing?" and impatiently scrabbled the cards together in a sensible pile. The older we got, the more the year between us told, and the more my friendship embarrassed him. We fought. Once, to my horror, I heard myself taunting him with the fact that he had no father. The unmentionable, the unforgivable. I suppose we patched things up, children do, but the fabric had been torn. He had a long, pale, serious face, with buckteeth, and is probably an electronics engineer somewhere now, doing secret government work.

So through *B* I first experienced the pattern of friendship. 4
There are three stages. First, acquaintance: we are new to each other, make each other laugh in surprise, and demand nothing beyond politeness. The death of the one would startle the other, no more. It is a pleasant stage, a stable stage; on austere rations of exposure it can live a lifetime, and the two parties to it always feel a slight gratification upon meeting, will feel vaguely confirmed in their human state. Then comes intimacy: now we laugh before two words of the joke are out of the other's mouth, because we know what he will say. Our two beings seem marvellously joined, from our toes to our heads, along tingling points of agreement; everything we venture is right, everything we put forth lodges in a corresponding socket in the frame of the other. The death of one would grieve the other. To be to-

gether is to enjoy a mounting excitement, a constant echo and amplification. It is an ecstatic and unstable stage, bound of its own agitation to tip into the third: revulsion. One or the other makes a misjudgment; presumes; puts forth that which does not meet agreement. Sometimes there is an explosion; more often the moment is swallowed in silence, and months pass before its nature dawns. Instead of dissolving, it grows. The mind, the throat, are clogged; forgiveness, forgetfulness, that have arrived so often, fail. Now everything jars and is distasteful. The betrayal, perhaps a tiny fraction in itself, has inverted the tingling column of agreement, made all pluses minuses. Everything about the other is hateful, despicable; yet he cannot be dismissed. We have confided in him too many minutes, too many words; he has those minutes and words as hostages, and his confidences are embedded in us where they cannot be scraped away, and even rivers of time cannot erode them completely, for there are indelible stains. Now—though the friends may continue to meet, and smile, as if they had never trespassed beyond acquaintance—the death of the one would please the other.

An unhappy pattern to which C is an exception. He was 5 my friend before kindergarten, he is my friend still. I go to his home now, and he and his wife serve me and my wife with alcoholic drinks and slices of excellent cheese on crisp crackers, just as twenty years ago he served me with treats from his mother's refrigerator. He was a born host, and I a born guest. Also he was intelligent. If my childhood's brain, when I look back at it, seems a primitive mammal, a lemur or shrew, his brain was an angel whose visitation was widely hailed as wonderful. When in school he stood to recite, his cool rectangular forehead glowed. He tucked his right hand into his left armpit and with his left hand mechanically tapped a pencil against his thigh. His answers were always correct. He beat me at spelling bees and, in another sort of competition, when we both collected Big Little Books, he outbid me for my supreme find (in the attic of a third boy), the first Mickey Mouse. I can still see that book, I wanted it so badly, its paper tan with age and its drawings done in Disney's primitive style, when Mickey's black chest is naked like a child's and his eyes are two nicked oblongs. Losing it was perhaps a lucky blow; it helped wean me away from hope of ever having possessions.

C was fearless. He deliberately set fields on fire. He en- 6 gaged in rock-throwing duels with tough boys. One afternoon he persisted in playing quoits with me although—as the hospital discovered that night—his appendix was nearly bursting. He was enterprising. He peddled magazine subscriptions door-to-door; he mowed neighbors' lawns; he struck financial bargains with his father. He collected stamps so well his collection blossomed into a stamp company that filled his room with steel cabinets and mimeograph machinery. He collected money—every time I went over to his house he would get out a little tin box and count the money in it for me: $27.50 one week, $29.95 the next. $30.90 the next—all changed into new bills nicely folded together. It was a strange ritual, whose meaning for me was: since he was doing it, I didn't have to. His money made me richer. We read Ellery Queen and played chess and invented board games and discussed infinity together. In later adolescence, he collected records. He liked the Goodman quintets but loved Fats Waller. Sitting there in that room so familiar to me, where the machinery of the Shilco Stamp Company still crowded the walls and for that matter the tin box of money might still be stashed, while my thin friend grunted softly along with that dead dark angel on "You're Not the Only Oyster in the Stew," I felt, in the best sense, patronized: the perfect guest of the perfect host. What made it perfect was that we had both spent our entire lives in Shillington.

THE WRITER'S THEMES

1. How do the activities John Updike engaged in with his friends reflect the quality of his relationship with each of the boys he describes? For example, to what extent does the military tank illustrate the quality of Updike's relationship with "B"?

2. Trace John Updike's changing attitudes toward possessions, as those attitudes are revealed in the course of his essay. What does "C" teach him about possessons that "A" and "B" do not?

3. What are the qualities in "C" that Updike most admires? What qualities does "C" possess that are conspicuously absent from the personalities of "A" and "B"?

THE WRITER'S TECHNIQUE

In paragraph four of his essay, John Updike describes what he calls "the pattern of friendship." In the paragraph, he observes that it was through his second friend, "B," that he first experienced this pattern. The writer then describes these three stages in detail.

The following excerpts from paragraph four of the essay trace Updike's description of these three stages of friendship:

> There are three stages. First, acquaintance: we are new to each other, make each other laugh in surprise, and demand nothing beyond politeness. The death of one would startle the other, no more. It is a pleasant stage, a stable stage . . .
>
> ....
>
> Then comes intimacy: now we laugh before two words of the joke are out of the other's mouth, because we know what he will say. Our two beings seem marvellously joined. . . . The death of one would grieve the other. . . . It is an ecstatic and unstable stage, bound of its own agitation to tip into the third: revulsion. One or the other makes a misjudgment. . . . Now everything jars and is distasteful.
>
> ....
>
> Now—though the friends may continue to meet, and smile, as if they had never trespassed beyond acquaintance—the death of one would please the other.

The writer points out that when people are acquaintances, the connections between them are slight. At this pleasant stage, "the death of one would startle the other, no more." At the next stage, intimacy, the two people seem "marvellously joined"; before, in the acquaintance stage, each would make the other "laugh in surprise," but now "we laugh before two words of the joke are out of the other's mouth . . ." At this stage, "the death of one would grieve the other." Finally comes what the writer calls "revulsion," when one of the friends makes a mistake of some kind. Now everything is "distasteful." At this final stage, "the death of the one would please the other." Updike is writing as an adult, and this last statement is undoubtedly his comment on the cruelty children sometimes feel toward each other.

PARAGRAPH PRACTICE

Write a paragraph of your own, using the above excerpts from the John Updike essay as your model. Your paragraph could describe three stages in a relationship with which you are familiar. For example, you could trace three different stages in a person's relationship with a friend, with a teacher, or with a parent.

Begin your paragraph with the initial period of the relationship you have chosen to describe. Is this a pleasant stage, or are there feelings of awkwardness? What does each person do for the other? What would be the reaction of each person if the relationship were to end at this point?

Develop your paragraph further by providing details about the next stage of the relationship. At this stage, how much closer or more comfortable are both people? What do they say to each other, or what do they do together, that indicates the relationship has become a closer one? End this section of your paragraph by noting what you think the reaction of each one would be if the relationship were to end at this point.

Finally, describe a third stage in the relationship. What are the characteristic signs of this stage? Is the relationship in any danger, or does this stage represent a strengthening of the relationship? Whether or not you choose to show the relationship coming to an end, conclude your paragraph by giving your opinion as to what each person's reaction would be if for any reason the relationship ended.

ESSAY PRACTICE

The following outline will help you plan a complete essay of at least five paragraphs. The theme of your essay will be closely related to the selection by John Updike.

The following sentence may serve as your thesis sentence, and will also be the main idea of your introductory paragraph:

¶ 1. Friendship is an organic part of our lives that grows as we grow, and our attitudes toward making friends should mature as we mature.

Each of the sentences below is the topic sentence for one of the paragraphs that you will write to develop your thesis.

You may use the suggested details to develop each paragraph, or you may supply details of your own.

¶ 2.   There are certain ways children make friends.

[DETAILS: Do children have their own ritual ways to make friends, or do they have a spontaneous way of making friends, a quality we lose as we get older?]

¶ 3.   As we get older, we not only have different ways of making friends, we also begin to have certain expectations for these friendships.

[DETAILS: Describe an incident in your own life when you first realized that you had a new attitude toward friendship. Did you have this realization at the same time that a friendship was beginning or ending for you?]

¶ 4.   By the time we are adults, we have established our methods of making friends and our ways of judging the quality of our friendships.

[DETAILS: How do you make friends now? At what point in a friendship do you begin to make serious judgments about the nature of that friendship? In this paragraph you could provide a detailed example of one of your own friendships, how it developed, and how your perceptions of it changed.]

Be certain that you use transitions between paragraphs to make your writing flow smoothly. In addition, be sure that your conclusion gives your reader a clear signal that you have come to the end of your essay.

ESSAY TOPICS

1.   Very often something happens to ruin the perfection of a relationship. Perhaps this incident even signals the end of the relationship. Classify the various occurrences that can damage or even end a relationship. Arrange these occurrences in order of increasing seriousness and illustrate each one by using specific examples, either from your own experience or the experience of others.

2.   Classify all of the friendships you have had (or now enjoy). What types of friends attract you the most? In each case, how strong did the relationship become, and how long did it last?

3. Write an essay in which you classify people according to
   their different attitudes toward possessions. Your examples
   may range from people you have observed who have a very
   sharing attitude toward what they own, to people who
   would never part with anything. Be sure to give a good
   range of examples by including several different types of
   people, and be sure to provide at least one specific example
   of each type.

Focus on Terms: Diction

Diction is your choice of words, either when you speak or when you write. This choice of diction involves making several decisions. Diction in a piece of writing is determined both by your audience and by your reasons for writing. Diction also involves slang (*bread* for *money*), colloquial expressions (calling *an untidy person* a *slob*), and an unnecessarily elevated choice of words (*living environment* instead of *home*).

In John Updike's essay "Three Boys," when the writer tells us that "A" was "immense" he is using a very standard word to describe the boy's size, but when he immediately adds that the boy was a "fatso," his level of diction becomes much more colloquial—"fatso" is the kind of word one would expect to hear in an informal conversation between two children.

Judith Viorst's essay on friendship was originally published in *Redbook*, and the writer's level of diction is appropriate for a popular magazine; the essay does not contain the level of diction one would expect in a sociological study of friendship. For example, in her opening sentence, when the writer points to women who "bare to each other the secrets of their souls," she is using a level of diction that is appropriate for her intentions and her audience. If this idea were to be expressed in a formal scientific study of the same subject, it might read as follows: women "choose to reveal to each other their most private and rarely discussed thoughts."

It sometimes happens that a writer will deliberately choose a level of diction that would ordinarily be inappropriate, but in a particular context does support what the writer is trying to say. Such an instance occurs at the end of the excerpt from Gail Sheehy's *Passages*. Writing about people who have reached the age of fifty, the author concludes by supplying what she calls "the motto of this stage," which she suggests might be, "No more bullshit." In most writing, and even in many personal encounters, such an expression might be considered completely inappropriate, but in this case the writer clearly felt that this was the proper way to sum up the feelings of someone who has reached fifty years of age.

In reviewing the level of diction you have used in any of your writing, you must ask yourself two questions. First, has your level of diction helped to express your thoughts for the audience you had in mind? Second, will your audience be puzzled or even offended by the level of diction you have used?

Student Essay ❧ ❧ *Lawrence Kent*

A favorite occupation of many of us is classifying the types of people we see around us every day, including the people who are a part of our lives. We recognize that we have different types of friends, different types of classmates, and we sometimes find ourselves putting our teachers into different classifications. The writer of the following essay has chosen to classify different types of parents. As you read the essay, compare the writer's report of parental types with your own observations. How many types of parents have you come across that the writer does not include?

• Examine the essay and make some judgments of your own as to its level of diction. What do you think this writer's attitude might be regarding the question of an appropriate level of diction for any piece of writing?

THOSE WHO GOVERN, THOSE WHO GUIDE

THE BIGGEST FACTOR in classifying types of parents is 1 the philosophy they use in raising their children. One could break these philosophies down into two main schools. There are those parents who govern their children and those who guide them. Those who guide leave a certain freedom of choice with the child while trying to push him or her toward a preferred path. The governing parent keeps a tighter rein on the child, making decisions for the child, and molding the child's personality more closely. As with all categories, there are degrees within each grouping, so more specific classification is necessary.

One form of the governing parent is the authoritarian type. 2 He or she is big on discipline. Many specific rules are set for the children and any infraction results in punishment. It's similar to the army. To complete the picture, the authoritarian parent may also include daily ''chores'' for the kids. This type of parent is dominating but not overwhelming. While the children do what they are told for fear of punishment, they are almost always willing to cheat behind the boss's back.

Then there are totalitarian parents. Just as our UN Secre- 3
tary Jeane J. Kirkpatrick distinguishes between the two, so do
I. Authoritarian parents are annoying, but their children usually
can maintain some individuality. Totalitarian parents are so in
command that their offspring seem to be absorbed into the will
and personality of the parent. The dictator can be either Mom
or Dad, but not both. The ruling parent controls practically all
aspects of the child's life because he or she is living through the
child. One example is Mr. Collins, a frustrated athlete trying to
succeed through his son by scheduling every free hour Greg
has in order to improve his tennis game. Or there is Mrs. Strom
who seems to feel her daughter's sex appeal is the reemergence
of that attraction she lost when she passed the thirty-five mark.
By encouraging, scheduling, threatening, and generally coer-
cing, Mrs. Strom is making sure that daughter Carrie is thinking
and acting just the way Mrs. Strom wishes she could think and
act. The totalitarian parents are able to control all aspects of the
child's life because they can control the child's mind. Junior
does just what Dad wants him to because his mind has been
trained to think just like Dad's.

Now we come to those parents who guide instead of gov- 4
ern. These parents place more value on freedom of choice and
individuality than on tough discipline. One form of the guiding
parent is the type that believes in these virtues but allows them
to exist in name only. Mrs. Stone says to her son, ''You are free
to choose any school you want, but if you don't pick Bergen
Catholic, your father and I will be heartbroken.'' She may also
praise honesty, but when Suzy tells her she went to the Mudd
Club last night, Mom will be so upset that the next time Suzy
goes out it will be much easier for her just to lie.

There is another type of parent, the kind that tries to be 5
guiding but doesn't succeed. This parent gives the child individuality and freedom of choice, but then does little to point
out the right direction. This parent is often unsuccessful because
he or she does not provide a good example. The parent whose
son uses as a defense when caught smoking hashish at school,
''I got it from Mom and Dad's room,'' has hardly provided a
proper example to guide that child's behavior. This type of parent usually has too many problems to spend time either governing or guiding a child.

There are some parents who are successful guiders. This 6
class of parent teaches through example and is able to point the

child in the right direction. This parent, however, does not compromise the child's freedom of choice and is willing to let the kid make a mistake. Mrs. Horton gives her sons Ed and Steve advice but then lets them do whatever they want. What Ed and Steve want usually follows along the lines of Mom's advice. The fact that their parent gives them freedom to choose seems to endow Ed and Steve with a responsibility which matures them and enables them to make right decisions. Mrs. Horton also allows for honesty in her family by being understanding, not upset, when her sons approach her with problems.

Although there could be other ways of classifying parents, such as single, working, unwed, or drinking, the best method is according to how they go about the job of raising their children. As we have seen, in this job some philosophies are better than others. However, the one ingredient that can override them all is what every parent needs, a deep and loving concern for the child.

7

Strategies for Writing

1. In paragraph two, the writer refers to "daily 'chores' for the kids." Why does he emphasize the word "chores" as he does?
2. Rewrite the opening paragraph of the essay, using a different level of diction. Review the paragraph before you begin to write. What key words or phrases should you be sure to revise, in order to change the level of diction?
3. Write an essay in which you classify different types of teachers, as you have observed them.
4. Write an essay in which you classify various types of sons or daughters (or both). Use either the Judith Viorst essay or the student essay above as your model.

7

MEN, WOMEN, AND LOVE

WRITING SKILL: Comparison and Contrast

It's Saturday. You hear your alarm clock and wonder if you should get up right away or sleep for another five minutes. When you finally do get up, you are faced with some further choices. You can enjoy a leisurely breakfast, or you can make a quick cup of coffee. You could start the term paper that is due on Monday, or you could wait until the afternoon. When you go to the library will you walk or take the bus?

Every day we make any number of such decisions and each one involves a comparison on our part. Most of our decisions are made quickly and without too much thought; others must be more carefully considered, with judgments made as to both the positive and negative aspects of the question. For example, at a certain point in your college career you may find yourself having to decide between two very different majors. Should you major in business or chemistry? Here the choice you make will have serious consequences for your career, and you will no doubt spend a good deal of time judging the many factors that will go into your decision.

In formal writing, this process of making a judgment between two or more things is known as comparison and contrast. We engage in *comparison* when we compare items that are similar; when we point out the differences between things, we are engaged in *contrast*. For example, you might be asked on a history exam to point out the similarities between a nineteenth-century army and a modern army; this would be an essay of comparison. Or you might be asked to do an anthropology report on the differences between the Lapps of northern Sweden and the Eskimos of Canada; this would be an essay of contrast. Later, in a job situation, you may find yourself being asked by your company to compare two products, one of which the company will eventually want to develop. Or, you might have to contrast two management methods. Your ability to use evidence to decide which choice is best could have important implications for your company and your own position in that company.

When we write an essay of comparison or contrast, we are not always trying to prove that one side is better than the other. We might be trying to make a well-known subject more understandable or provide an explanation for a subject that is not yet understood. For example, you may feel you already know a good deal about industrial management, but a study comparing American management practices with those of Switzerland might suggest business ideas you know have not yet been tried in this country. The same study might even confirm that established practices are best, after all. At the same time, such a study might serve to teach you about an area of your subject that you may not be familiar with, in this case what the Swiss do in industrial management.

The two methods that are most often used in comparison and contrast are the *block method* and the *alternating method*. When you use the block method, you present all of the information about one side of an issue or a problem and then you give all of the information about the other side. When you use the alternating method, you give a point from one side and immediately give a point from the other side. The alternating method is usually recommended for longer pieces of writing because the reader is more easily able to see the different points of the comparison as they are being made.

Each of the essays in this unit uses either comparison or contrast to make a point or to present an argument. For example, in "Courtship Through the Ages" James Thurber compares the mating habits of various birds and insects with the human male's attempts to court women. Thurber's purpose is to entertain us by pointing out the similarities between human beings and animals in the area of courtship, but the writer may also be making some subtle comments on some very human habits. For example, when Thurber compares the activities of the male bowerbird with those of a nightclub-goer, he concludes that ''A male bowerbird is as exhausted as a night-club habitué before he is out of his twenties.'' Much of the effect of Thurber's essay depends on this type of comparison; the writer finds one example after another from the world of nature to illustrate the human condition.

On the other hand, Margaret Mead's essay ''From Popping the Question to Popping the Pill'' discusses the differences between past courtship practices and those of today. The writer's purpose is not so much to entertain us (although we might be amused to find out how people in colonial New England acted when they were engaged) as to explain her subject as fully as she can.

In the ancient story of the Amazons, reported to us by Herodotus, we find a number of comparisons that are either made directly or implied by the writer. The events of the story make our comparison of the Amazon women and Scythian men inevitable, but we also find opportunities for contrast, as the Amazons point out the differences between themselves and the Scythian women the men have left behind. The way in which Herodotus presents the differences between the two cultures and both sexes may lead us to some amusing conclusions.

Katherine Anne Porter's essay ''The Necessary Enemy'' also deals with the relationship between men and women, but here the emphasis is surprising: what, the writer asks, is the connection between love and hate?

Comparison and contrast is a valuable way to convince your reader that your examination of an issue is a thorough analysis, and a convincing one. It is also important for you as a reader to know how writers use comparison and contrast to convince us to buy a product, vote for a candidate, or simply change our way of thinking about an issue.

🐚 *Herodotus* 🐚

Herodotus has a unique distinction among world writers: he was the first European writer to use prose as an art form. He is popularly known as "the father of history" because his book, the *Histories*, remains one of the greatest historical works in any language. He was born around 484 B.C. in the city of Halicarnassus in Asia Minor. From his earliest youth Herodotus traveled extensively through Greece, Asia Minor, and the rest of the known world. At each place of interest, he would stop for a time in order to absorb as many facts and local legends as he could. As a result, the *Histories* are a delightful blend of authoritative fact and pleasant story.

Herodotus was about thirty-five when he moved to Athens. There, the fame of his writings led him to be accepted into the best social and literary circles. He gave public readings from his *Histories*, and these were so well received that the Athenians rewarded him with a large sum of money. When in 443 B.C. Athens sent out a colony to settle Thurii in southern Italy, Herodotus was one of the founding members. From this point on we lose sight of Herodotus, but it seems likely that he spent his last years at Thurii, revising his writings. It is believed he died around 425 B.C.

The stated purpose of the *Histories* is to tell the story of the dispute between Greece and Persia, but in the process of describing this great struggle Herodotus traces the entire history of both nations. Furthermore, he gives some account of nearly all the other nations of the known world and gives a multitude of details—some factual, some fanciful—concerning their climates, their products, and their famous monuments.

The following selection is from Book Four of the *Histories*, where Herodotus describes the land and the people of Scythia. Part of his description includes the story of the conflict between the Greeks and the Amazons, a struggle that may have some basis in historical fact, but which is most likely a myth. The story is told in a very immediate, compelling way. As the translator Aubrey De Sèlincourt observes, when we read Herodotus he "invites us to walk by his side, to listen to his voice, to mark on his face the shifts of expression from grave to gay. . . . Herodotus' prose is a mirror of personality and character."

PREVIEWING THE WRITER

• Note what skills the Amazons have, what skills they lack, and what skills they acquire.

• Note the details of the plan formulated by the Scythians. How does that plan change?

• Note the details of the Amazons' plan. When does it first become clear that these women have a plan of their own?

THE AMAZONS

IN THE WAR between the Greeks and the Amazons, the Greeks, after their victory at the river Thermodon, sailed off in three ships with as many Amazons on board as they had succeeded in taking alive. Once at sea, the women murdered their captors, but, as they had no knowledge of boats and were unable to handle either rudder or sail or oar, they soon found themselves, when the men were done for, at the mercy of wind and wave, and were blown to Cremni—the Cliffs—on Lake Maeotis, a place within the territory of the free Scythians. Here they got ashore and made their way inland to an inhabited part of the country. The first thing they fell in with was a herd of horses grazing; these they seized, and, mounting on their backs, rode off in search of loot. The Scythians could not understand what was happening and were at a loss to know where the marauders had come from, as their dress, speech, and nationality were strange to them. Thinking, however, that they were young men, they fought in defence of their property, and discovered from the bodies which came into their possession after the battle that they were women. The discovery gave a new direction to their plans; they decided to make no further attempt to kill the invaders, but to send out a detachment of their youngest men, about equal in number to the Amazons, with orders to camp near them and take their cue from whatever it was that the Amazons then did: if they pursued them, they were not to fight, but to give ground; then, when the pursuit was abandoned, they were once again to encamp within easy range. The motive behind this policy was the Scythians' desire to get children by the Amazons. The detachment of young men obeyed their orders, and the Amazons, realizing that they meant no harm, did not attempt to molest them, with the result that every day the two camps drew a little closer together. Neither party had anything but their weapons and their horses, and both lived the same sort of life, hunting and plundering.

Towards midday the Amazons used to scatter and go off 2 to some little distance in ones and twos to ease themselves, and the Scythians, when they noticed this, followed suit; until one of them, coming upon an Amazon girl all by herself, began to make advances to her. She, nothing loth, gave him what he wanted, and then told him by signs (being unable to express her meaning in words, as neither understood the other's language) to return on the following day with a friend, making it clear that there must be two men, and that she herself would bring another girl. The young man then left her and told the others what had happened, and on the next day took a friend to the same spot, where he found his Amazon waiting for him and another one with her. Having learnt of their success, the rest of the young Scythians soon succeeded in getting the Amazons to submit to their wishes. The two camps were then united, and Amazons and Scythians lived together, every man keeping as his wife the woman whose favours he had first enjoyed. The men could not learn the women's language, but the women succeeded in picking up the men's; so when they could understand one another, the Scythians made the following proposal: 'We', they said, 'have parents and property. Let us give up our present way of life and return to live with our people. We will keep you as our wives and not take any others.' The Amazons replied: 'We and the women of your nation could never live together; our ways are too much at variance. We are riders; our business is with the bow and the spear, and we know nothing of women's work; but in your country no woman has anything to do with such things—your women stay at home in their waggons occupied with feminine tasks, and never go out to hunt or for any other purpose. We could not possibly agree. If, however, you wish to keep us for your wives and to behave as honourable men, go and get from your parents the share of property which is due to you, and then let us go off and live by ourselves.' The young men agreed to this, and when they came back, each with his portion of the family possessions, the Amazons said: 'We dread the prospect of settling down here, for we have done much damage to the country by our raids, and we have robbed you of your parents. Look now—if you think fit to keep us for your wives, let us get out of the country altogether and settle somewhere on the other side of the Tanais.' Once again the Scythians agreed, so they crossed the Tanais and travelled east for three days, and then north, for another three, from Lake Maeotis, until they reached the country where they are to-day, and settled down there. Ever since then the women of the Sauromatae have kept to their old ways, riding to the hunt on horseback sometimes with, sometimes without, their menfolk, taking part in war and wearing the same sort of clothes as men. The language of these people is the Scythian, but it has always been a corrupt form of it because the Amazons were never able to learn to speak it properly. They have a marriage law which forbids a girl to marry until she has killed an enemy in battle; some of their women, unable to fulfil this condition, grow old and die in spinsterhood.

THE WRITER'S THEMES

1. At the beginning of the story, we see the Amazons defeated and taken prisoner. Where do we first see the women gaining some control over their lives? In what respects are they seen as superior to the men they encounter?
2. In this contest between the Amazons and the Scythians, each side has a plan of action. Briefly review the stated plan of the Scythians. Then reconstruct the unstated, but just as real, plan of the Amazon women.
3. One of the most important points in the story is the communication that is established between the Amazons and the Scythians. On how many levels do the two groups communicate? Which group is superior in the art of communication?

THE WRITER'S TECHNIQUE

Shortly after the Amazon women have landed and stolen some horses, we see the Scythians bewildered by this unusual turn of events. Here, from the first paragraph of the selection, is Herodotus' description of the Scythians' reaction, and the events that followed:

> The Scythians could not understand what was happening and were at a loss to know where the marauders had come from, as their dress, speech, and nationality were strange to them. Thinking, however, that they were young men, they fought in defence

of their property, and discovered from the bodies which came into their possession after the battle that they were women. The discovery gave a new direction to their plans; they decided to make no further attempt to kill the invaders, but to send out a detachment of their youngest men, about equal in number to the Amazons, with orders to camp near them and take their cue from whatever it was that the Amazons then did: if they pursued them, they were not to fight, but to give ground; then, when the pursuit was abandoned, they were once again to encamp within easy range. The motive behind this policy was the Scythians' desire to get children by the Amazons.

Notice that Herodotus first shows the Scythians "at a loss" to know from where these strangers had come. Then, when they decide they must defend their property, the Scythians discover that the strangers are women; this leads them to make a careful, thought-out response: they will send out a group of their youngest men and have them camp near the Amazons. The thinking behind this plan was "the Scythians' desire to get children by the Amazons."

Note that Herodotus first shows the Scythians as being puzzled. Then we see that they have a theory about the intruders, but a discovery disproves that theory (the Amazons are really women) and they decide on a plan. This plan is outlined in detail, and the motive for the plan is given. Herodotus not only shows us how the Scythians react to the Amazons and what their plan is, but he also gives us their thinking. By the time we know what the Scythians are going to do, we also know why they are going to do it.

PARAGRAPH PRACTICE

Write a paragraph of your own, using the writing of Herodotus as your model. You might want to describe a time you were puzzled by something and you made a discovery that led you to change your plans or formulate a new plan. For example, in the course of a science experiment you might have discovered that your approach was not correct and you had to try a new approach. Or, you might have tried to repair something, and your original plan did not work. Or, you might have been puzzled by some change in a personal relationship and you decided to try and find out what could be done about the matter.

As you write your paragraph, use the order that Herodotus uses. For example, you could begin by writing:

I could not understand what was happening. (Explain why you were puzzled that something was not going according to plan, or why something was different from what you had hoped.)

By the middle of your paragraph, after you have described what you discovered that made you change your mind, describe what that change of mind led to:

This discovery gave a new direction to my plan . . . (Explain, in a step-by-step fashion, what you now planned to do.)

Conclude your paragraph by giving the reason you planned and acted the way you did:

My motive for this was . . .

ESSAY PRACTICE

The following outline will help you plan a complete essay of at least five paragraphs. The theme of your essay will be closely related to the selection from Herodotus.

The following sentence may serve as your thesis sentence, and will also be the main idea of your introductory paragraph:

¶ 1.   A man and a woman look for different qualities in a mate before marriage, and each recognizes other qualities in the mate after marriage; if they divorce, each one may look for still other qualities in the next relationship.

Each of the sentences below is the topic sentence for one of the paragraphs that you will write to develop your thesis. You may use the suggested details to develop each paragraph, or you may supply details of your own.

¶ 2.   In the period before marriage, women look for certain characteristics in a man, and men look for certain qualities in a woman.

[DETAILS: What is it that women look for in a man? What do men look for in a woman?]

¶ 3. During marriage, men and women acquire some new perspectives on each other.

[DETAILS: After a few years of marriage, what do most men and women discover to be the essential qualities they want in a marriage partner?]

¶ 4. In the event there is a divorce, a man and a woman have an even further change of perspective.

[DETAILS: At this point, with the marriage over, what new qualities emerge as essential for a new relationship?]

Be certain that you use transitions between paragraphs to make your writing flow smoothly. In addition, be sure that your conclusion gives your reader a clear signal that you have come to the end of your essay.

ESSAY TOPICS

1. The Amazon women knew they would not feel comfortable with the families of the Scythian men, so they solved the problem by insisting on moving away.

Because of economic pressures, many young people today are finding it increasingly difficult to establish their own homes. What are the advantages and disadvantages of being either single or married and living with parents, grandparents, or other relatives? What advantages could there be for the family as a whole to have more than one generation living together?

2. In how many ways have the lives of women changed in the course of a single generation? Compare the women of your mother's generation with the young women of today. What conclusions can you come to about the rights, duties, and achievements of each generation?

3. The Scythian men devise a plan to get the Amazon women, and the Amazons clearly have their own plan to get the Scythian men. Compare these plans with the most unusual courtship you have ever heard of or have ever observed.

❧ *James Thurber* ❧

James Thurber (1894–1961) was one of America's favorite humorists. He was born in Columbus, Ohio, educated at Ohio State University, and began his career as a newspaperman on the Columbus *Dispatch*. He also worked for a time in Paris, on the staff of the Chicago *Tribune*.

Thurber left Paris in 1926 and came to New York, where E. B. White helped him find a job with the *New Yorker* magazine. Some of Thurber's best-known essays and most famous cartoons appeared in the *New Yorker*, although he also produced several books of humor, including *Is Sex Necessary?* (with E. B. White), *My Life and Hard Times,* and *Fables for Our Times*. In 1940 he co-authored a play entitled *The Male Animal*.

As a writer, Thurber is deceptive. His books and essays give the impression that they were written with ease, but he would often rewrite a single piece as many as ten times and he once spent two years working on a short book.

In "Courtship Through the Ages" Thurber uses a factual encyclopedia article on animal behavior to compare people with animals. The result is Thurber at his humorous best. As we read the essay, we might also keep in mind the words of a *New York Times* reviewer, who wrote that Thurber "is not only a humorist; he is also a satirist who can toss a bomb while he appears to be tipping his hat."

PREVIEWING THE WRITER

- How does the introductory paragraph indicate that this will be a humorous essay?
- Note the author's technique of giving human qualities to the animals and insects he describes.
- Note each place in the essay where the author exaggerates his material. What word choices help us see Thurber's humor?

COURTSHIP THROUGH THE AGES

SURELY NOTHING in the astonishing scheme of life can have nonplussed Nature so much as the fact that none of the females of any of the species she created really cared very much for the male, as such. For the past ten million years Nature has been busily inventing ways to make the male attractive to the female, but the whole business of courtship, from the marine annelids up to man, still lumbers heavily along, like a complicated musical comedy. I have been reading the sad and absorbing story in Volume 6 (Cole to Dama) of the *Encyclopaedia Britannica*. In this volume you can learn all about cricket, cotton, costume designing, crocodiles, crown jewels, and Coleridge, but none of these subjects is so interesting as the Courtship of Animals, which recounts the sorrowful lengths to which all males must go to arouse the interest of a lady.

We all know, I think, that Nature gave man whiskers and   2
a mustache with the quaint idea in mind that these would prove attractive to the female. We all know that, far from attracting her, whiskers and mustaches only made her nervous and gloomy, so that man had to go in for somersaults, tilting with lances, and performing feats of parlor magic to win her attention; he also had to bring her candy, flowers, and the furs of animals. It is common knowledge that in spite of all these ''love displays'' the male is constantly being turned down, insulted, or thrown out of the house. It is rather comforting, then, to discover that the peacock, for all his gorgeous plumage, does not have a particularly easy time in courtship; none of the males in the world do. The first peahen, it turned out, was only faintly stirred by her suitor's beautiful train. She would often go quietly to sleep while he was whisking it around. The *Britannica* tells us that the peacock actually had to learn a certain little trick to wake her up and revive her interest: he had to learn to vibrate his quills so as to make a rustling sound. In ancient times man himself, observing the ways of the peacock, probably tried vibrating his whiskers to make a rustling sound; if so, it didn't get him anywhere. He had to go in for something else; so, among other things, he went in for gifts. It is not unlikely that he got this idea from certain flies and birds who were making no headway at all with rustling sounds.

One of the flies of the family Empidae, who had tried   3
everything, finally hit on something pretty special. He contrived to make a glistening transparent balloon which was even larger than himself. Into this he would put sweetmeats and tidbits and he would carry the whole elaborate envelope through the air to the lady of his choice. This amused her for a time, but she finally got bored with it. She demanded silly little colorful presents, something that you couldn't eat but that would look nice around

the house. So the male Empis had to go around gathering flower petals and pieces of bright paper to put into his balloon. On a courtship flight a male Empis cuts quite a figure now, but he can hardly be said to be happy. He never knows how soon the female will demand heavier presents, such as Roman coins and gold collar buttons. It seems probable that one day the courtship of the Empidae will fall down, as man's occasionally does, of its own weight.

The bowerbird is another creature that spends so much   4
time courting the female that he never gets any work done. If all the male bowerbirds became nervous wrecks within the next ten or fifteen years, it would not surprise me. The female bowerbird insists that a playground be built for her with a specially constructed bower at the entrance. This bower is much more elaborate than an ordinary nest and is harder to build; it costs a lot more, too. The female will not come to the playground until the male has filled it up with a great many gifts: silvery leaves, red leaves, rose petals, shells, beads, berries, bones, dice, buttons, cigar bands, Christmas seals, and the Lord knows what else. When the female finally condescends to visit the playground, she is in a coy and silly mood and has to be chased in and out of the bower and up and down the playground before she will quit giggling and stand still long enough even to shake hands. The male bird is, of course, pretty well done in before the chase starts, because he has worn himself out hunting for eyeglass lenses and begonia blossoms. I imagine that many a bowerbird, after chasing a female for two or three hours, says the hell with it and goes home to bed. Next day, of course, he telephones someone else and the same trying ritual is gone through with again. A male bowerbird is as exhausted as a night-club habitué before he is out of his twenties.

The male fiddler crab has a somewhat easier time, but it   5
can hardly be said that he is sitting pretty. He has one enormously large and powerful claw, usually brilliantly colored, and you might suppose that all he had to do was reach out and grab some passing cutie. The very earliest fiddler crabs may have tried this, but, if so, they got slapped for their pains. A female fiddler crab will not tolerate any caveman stuff; she never has and she doesn't intend to start now. To attract a female, a fiddler crab has to stand on tiptoe and brandish his claw in the air. If any female in the neighborhood is interested—and you'd be surprised how many are not—she comes over and engages

him in light badinage, for which he is not in the mood. As many as a hundred females may pass the time of day with him and go on about their business. By nightfall of an average courting day, a fiddler crab who has been standing on tiptoe for eight or ten hours waving a heavy claw in the air is in pretty sad shape. As in the case of the males of all species, however, he gets out of bed next morning, dashes some water on his face, and tries again.

The next time you encounter a male web-spinning spider, stop and reflect that he is too busy worrying about his love life to have any desire to bite you. Male web-spinning spiders have a tougher life than any other males in the animal kingdom. This is because the female web-spinning spiders have very poor eyesight. If a male lands on a female's web, she kills him before he has time to lay down his cane and gloves, mistaking him for a fly or a bumblebee who has tumbled into her trap. Before the species figured out what to do about this, millions of males were murdered by ladies they called on. It is the nature of spiders to perform a little dance in front of the female, but before a male spinner could get near enough for the female to see who he was and what he was up to, she would lash out at him with a flat-iron or a pair of garden shears. One night, nobody knows when, a very bright male spinner lay awake worrying about calling on a lady who had been killing suitors right and left. It came to him that this business of dancing as a love display wasn't getting anybody anywhere except the grave. He decided to go in for web-twitching, or strand-vibrating. The next day he tried it on one of the nearsighted girls. Instead of dropping in on her suddenly, he stayed outside the web and began monkeying with one of its strands. He twitched it up and down and in and out with such a lilting rhythm that the female was charmed. The serenade worked beautifully; the female let him live. The *Britannica*'s spider-watchers, however, report that this system is not always successful. Once in a while, even now, a female will fire three bullets into a suitor or run him through with a kitchen knife. She keeps threatening him from the moment he strikes the first low notes on the outside strings, but usually by the time he has got up to the high notes played around the center of the web, he is going to town and she spares his life.

Even the butterfly, as handsome a fellow as he is, can't always win a mate merely by fluttering around and showing off. Many butterflies have to have scent scales on their wings. Hepialus carries a powder puff in a perfumed pouch. He throws perfume at the ladies when they pass. The male tree cricket, Oecanthus, goes Hepialus one better by carrying a tiny bottle of wine with him and giving drinks to such doxies as he has designs on. One of the male snails throws darts to entertain the girls. So it goes, through the long list of animals, from the bristle worm and his rudimentary dance steps to man and his gift of diamonds and sapphires. The golden-eye drake raises a jet of water with his feet as he flies over a lake; Hepialus has his powder puff, Oecanthus his wine bottle, man his etchings. It is a bright and melancholy story, the age-old desire of the male for the female, the age-old desire of the female to be amused and entertained. Of all the creatures on earth, the only males who could be figured as putting any irony into their courtship are the grebes and certain other diving birds. Every now and then a courting grebe slips quietly down to the bottom of a lake and then, with a mighty "Whoosh!," pops out suddenly a few feet from his girl friend, splashing water all over her. She seems to be persuaded that this is a purely loving display, but I like to think that the grebe always has a faint hope of drowning her or scaring her to death.

　　I will close this investigation into the mournful burdens of ⁸ the male with *Britannica*'s story about a certain Argus pheasant. It appears that the Argus displays himself in front of a female who stands perfectly still without moving a feather. . . . The male Argus the *Britannica* tells about was confined in a cage with a female of another species, a female who kept moving around, emptying ashtrays and fussing with lampshades all the time the male was showing off his talents. Finally, in disgust, he stalked away and began displaying in front of his water trough. He reminds me of a certain male (Homo sapiens) of my acquaintance who one night after dinner asked his wife to put down her detective magazine so that he could read a poem of which he was very fond. She sat quietly enough until he was well into the middle of the thing, intoning with great ardor and intensity. Then suddenly there came a sharp, disconcerting *slap!* It turned out that all during the male's display, the female had been intent on a circling mosquito and had finally trapped it between the palms of her hands. The male in this case did not stalk away and display in front of a water trough; he went over to Tim's and had a flock of drinks and recited the poem to the fellas. I am sure they all told bitter stories of their own about how their displays had been interrupted by females. I am also sure that they all ended up singing "Honey, Honey, Bless Your Heart."

THE WRITER'S THEMES

1. Thurber calls "the age-old desire of the male for the female" a "bright and melancholy story." What parts of the story, as presented by Thurber, are "bright" (or humorous)? What parts of the story are essentially melancholy?
2. Is Thurber's primary intention in the essay serious or light-hearted?
3. What does Thurber's essay teach us about human relationships?

THE WRITER'S TECHNIQUE

In the second paragraph of his essay, James Thurber describes some of the things men have done to attract females. Here is the opening section of that paragraph:

> We all know, I think, that Nature gave man whiskers and a mustache with the quaint idea in mind that these would prove attractive to the female. We all know that, far from attracting her, whiskers and mustaches only made her nervous and gloomy, so that man had to go in for somersaults, tilting with lances, and performing feats of parlor magic to win her attention; he also had to bring her candy, flowers, and the furs of animals. It is common knowledge that in spite of all these "love displays" the male is constantly being turned down, insulted, or thrown out of the house.

Note that Thurber begins his paragraph by describing what should attract a woman (whiskers and a mustache) and then points out that this has just the opposite effect: "far from attracting her, whiskers and mustaches only made her nervous and gloomy . . ." The writer then provides a list of man's other activities, from somersaults to giving presents of candy and flowers. In spite of all of these attempts, the male is constantly being rejected; it seems that no matter how hard the male tries to please the female, his attempts are doomed to end in failure.

PARAGRAPH PRACTICE

Write a paragraph of your own, using James Thurber's writing as your model. You could, for example, write a paragraph on an aspect of modern society that once promised a great deal but did not fulfill those expectations. For example, owning a big car was once an American ideal, but now it is much more desirable to have a smaller, more fuel-efficient car. In fact, the large automobile is now considered undesirable. Another example would be the fashion industry. It was once believed that women's fashions could be dictated by designers every season. Today, however, women are refusing to follow this established practice, and quality and utility are now considered more important than mere fashion.

Your paragraph might begin with a statement of what *should* be desirable, or what was once thought to be desirable. You can then proceed to a description of the reality by writing at least three sentences in which you give details that show what that reality is. Then write a conclusion of one sentence.

ESSAY PRACTICE

The following outline will help you plan a complete essay of at least five paragraphs. The theme of your essay will be closely related to the James Thurber essay.

The following sentence may serve as your thesis sentence, and will also be the main idea of your introductory paragraph:

¶ 1.   Courtship is the serious business of each sex trying to impress the other, with sometimes comic results.

Each of the sentences below is the topic sentence for one of the paragraphs that you will write to develop your thesis. You may use the suggested details to develop each paragraph, or you may supply details of your own.

¶ 2.   When a man wants to impress a woman, he usually tries very hard.

[DETAILS: What do men do nowadays to attract the attention of females?]

¶ 3.   These days, there are a number of ways a woman can impress a man.

[DETAILS: What does a woman do today to impress a man?]

¶ 4. When a person tries too hard to impress a member of the opposite sex, the results can be very funny.

> [DETAILS: How can a person make himself or herself look foolish in a dating situation?]

Be certain that you use transitions between paragraphs to make your writing flow smoothly. In addition, be sure that your conclusion gives your reader a clear signal that you have come to the end of your essay.

ESSAY TOPICS

1. Compare Thurber's picture of dating practices with dating practices of today. In your essay, contrast the attitudes and actions of a young man of today with the attitudes and actions of the type of young man Thurber describes.
2. Compare the possible attitudes of two different kinds of women toward this essay. What might be the reaction of a modern feminist to Thurber's ideas? What might a more traditional woman feel? What parts of the essay would each woman use to support her point of view?
3. The following paragraph is taken from the *Encyclopaedia Britannica* entry on ''Courtship of Animals.''

> *Bowerbirds.*—In some ways the most remarkable courtship known is that of the bowerbirds. . . . These birds clear playgrounds, in which special bowers (quite unlike nests) are constructed by some species. In the playground (if a bower is made opposite its entrance) is deposited a collection of bright objects. The objects differ with the species; they may include silvery leaves, flowers, shells, berries, bones, etc. When the female visits the playground, the male pursues her amorously round it (through the bower, when present). Here it appears that the bright objects collected serve instead of the brilliant plumage of other male birds to stimulate the female.

Compare the above paragraph with the following section from paragraph four of the Thurber essay:

> The bowerbird is another creature that spends so much time courting the female that he never gets any work done. If all the male bowerbirds became nervous wrecks within the next ten or fifteen years, it would not surprise me. The female bowerbird insists that a playground be built for her with a specially con-

structed bower at the entrance. This bower is much more elaborate than an ordinary nest and is harder to build; it costs a lot more, too. The female will not come to the playground until the male has filled it up with a great many gifts: silvery leaves, red leaves, rose petals, shells, beads, berries, bones, dice, buttons, cigar bands, Christmas seals, and the Lord knows what else. When the female finally condescends to visit the playground, she is in a coy and silly mood and has to be chased in and out of the bower and up and down the playground before she will quit giggling and stand still long enough even to shake hands. The male bird is, of course, pretty well done in before the chase starts, because he has worn himself out hunting for eyeglass lenses and begonia blossoms.

How much of the material from the encyclopedia did Thurber use in his own writing? Which facts did he choose to exaggerate? How do his distortions of the factual material make his own writing humorous?

🐝 *Margaret Mead* 🐝

Margaret Mead (1901–1978) was one of the foremost anthropologists of our time. During the 1920s she attended Barnard College and Columbia University, and began her field work in 1925 when she went to the Samoan Islands to study adolescent girls and how they lived. In 1928 she was studying the lives of children in New Guinea, and the following year she turned her attention to the American Indian. Throughout the 1930s she continued her investigations of native peoples in Asia and the Pacific.

In the 1950s and 1960s she visited these places again, to study the changes that had taken place as these previously undisturbed societies began to cope with the problems of being absorbed into the modern world. In her later years, the anthropologist began to concentrate on contemporary Western society. With the knowledge she had gained from her studies of smaller and older societies, she was able to bring fresh insights to such areas of modern concern as education and culture, environmental problems, family life, and women's roles in society.

Among Margaret Mead's most famous published works are *Coming of Age in Samoa, Growing Up in New Guinea, Male and Female, The School in American Culture,* and *Childhood in Contemporary Culture.*

The following essay, originally published in *McCall's* magazine, represents one of Margaret Mead's final statements on an important American institution, that of dating and courtship. In the essay, published in the American bicentennial year of 1976, this close observer of many cultures looks with sensitivity and objectivity at her own society, as she points out how Americans have courted over the years and how these courtship practices have changed.

PREVIEWING THE WRITER

• Note how the author traces the history of courtship practices in this country. Note also how the different sections of her essay correspond to the different eras she is describing.

• Note how the author maintains her sense of objectivity. At what point(s) could she have taken her own position on a certain issue but did not do so?

• Note the writer's comments on future relations between the sexes.

FROM POPPING THE QUESTION TO POPPING THE PILL

THERE HAVE BEEN major changes in attitudes toward courtship and marriage among those middle-class, educated Americans who are celebrated in the media and who are style setters for American life. Courtship was once a regular part of American life; it was a long period, sometimes lasting for many years, and also a tentative one, during which a future husband or wife could still turn back but during which their relationship became more and more exclusive and socially recognized. Courtship both preceded the announcement of an engagement and followed the announcement, although a broken engagement was so serious that it could be expected to throw the girl into a depression from which she might never recover.

There were definite rules governing the courtship period, from the "bundling" permitted in early New England days, when young couples slept side by side with all their clothes on, to strict etiquette that prescribed what sort of gifts a man might give his fiancée in circles where expensive presents were customary. Gifts had to be either immediately consumable, like candy or flowers, or indestructible, like diamonds—which could be given back, their value unimpaired, if there was a rift in the relationship. Objects that could be damaged by use, like gloves and furs, were forbidden. A gentleman might call for a lady in a cab or in his own equipage, but it was regarded as inappropriate for him to pay for her train fare if they went on a journey.

How much chaperoning was necessary, and how much privacy the courting couple was allowed, was a matter of varying local custom. Long walks home through country lanes after church and sitting up in the parlor after their elders had retired for the night may have been permitted, but the bride was expected to be a virgin at marriage. The procedure for breaking off an engagement, which included the return of letters and photographs, was a symbolic way of stating that an unconsummated relationship could still be erased from social memory.

The wedding day was the highest point in a girl's life—a day to which she looked forward all her unmarried days and to which she looked back for the rest of her life. The splendor of her wedding, the elegance of dress and veil, the cutting of the cake, the departure amid a shower of rice and confetti, gave her an accolade of which no subsequent event could completely rob her. Today people over 50 years of age still treat their daughter's wedding this way, prominently displaying the photographs of the occasion. Until very recently, all brides' books prescribed exactly the same ritual they had prescribed 50 years before. The etiquette governing wedding presents—gifts that were or were not appropriate, the bride's maiden initials on her linen—was also specified. For the bridegroom the wedding represented the end of his free, bachelor days, and the bachelor dinner the night before the wedding symbolized this loss of freedom. A woman who did not marry—even if she had the alibi of a fiancé who had been killed in war or had abilities and charm and money of her own—was always at a social disadvantage, while an eligible bachelor was sought after by hostess after hostess.

Courtship ended at the altar, as the bride waited anxiously 5 for the bridegroom who might not appear or might have forgotten the ring. Suppliant gallantry was replaced overnight by a reversal of roles, the wife now becoming the one who read her husband's every frown with anxiety lest she displease him.

This set of rituals established a rhythm between the future 6 husband and wife and between the two sets of parents who would later become co-grandparents. It was an opportunity for mistakes to be corrected; and if the parents could not be won over, there was, as a last resort, elopement, in which the young couple proclaimed their desperate attraction to each other by flouting parental blessing. Each part of the system could be tested out for a marriage that was expected to last for life. We have very different ways today.

Since World War I, changes in relationships between the 7 sexes have been occurring with bewildering speed. The automobile presented a challenge to chaperonage that American adults met by default. From then on, except in ceremonial and symbolic ways, chaperonage disappeared, and a style of premarital relationship was set up in which the onus was put on the girl to refuse inappropriate requests, while each young man declared his suitability by asking for favors that he did not expect to receive. The disappearance of chaperonage was facilitated by the greater freedom of middle-aged women, who began to envy their daughters' freedom, which they had never had. Social forms went through a whole series of rapid changes: The dance with formal partners and programs gave way to occasions in which mothers, or daughters, invited many more young men than girls, and the popular girl hardly circled the dance floor twice in the same man's arms. Dating replaced courtship—not as a prelude to anything but rather as a way of demonstrating popularity. Long engagements became increasingly unfashionable, and a series of more tentative commitments became more popular. As college education became the norm for millions of young people, "pinning" became a common stage before engagement. The ring was likely to appear just before the wedding day. And during the 1950's more and more brides got married while pregnant—but they still wore the long white veil, which was a symbol of virginity.

In this conservative, security-minded decade love became 8 less important than marriage, and lovers almost disappeared from parks and riverbanks as young people threatened each other: "Either you marry me now, or I'll marry someone else." Courtship and dating were embraced by young people in lower grades in school, until children totally unready for sex were enmeshed by the rituals of pairing off. Marriage became a necessity for everyone, for boys as well as for girls: Mothers worried if their sons preferred electronic equipment or chess to girls and pushed their daughters relentlessly into marriage. Divorce became more and more prevalent, and people who felt their marriages were failing began to worry about whether they ought to get a divorce, divorce becoming a duty to an unfulfilled husband or to children exposed to an unhappy marriage. Remarriage was expected, until finally, with men dying earlier than women, there were no men left to marry. The United States became the most married country in the world. Children, your own or adopted, were just as essential, and the suburban lifestyle—each nuclear family isolated in its own home, with several children, a station wagon and a country-club membership—became the admired life-style, displayed in magazines for the whole world to see.

By the early sixties there were signs of change. We dis- 9 covered we were running out of educated labor, and under the heading of self-fulfillment educated married women were being tempted back into the labor market. Young people began to advocate frankness and honesty, rebelling against the extreme hypocrisy of the 1950s, when religious and educational institutions alike connived to produce pregnancies that would lead to marriage. Love as an absorbing feeling for another person was rediscovered, as marriage as a goal for every girl and boy receded into the background.

A series of worldwide political and ecological events facil- 10
itated these changes. Freedom for women accompanied agitation for freedom for blacks, for other minorities, for the Third
World, for youth, for gay people. Zero-population growth became a goal, and it was no longer unfashionable to admit one
did not plan to have children, or perhaps even to marry. The
marriage age rose a little, the number of children fell a little.
The enjoyment of pornography and use of obscenity became
the self-imposed obligation of the emancipated women. Affirmative action catapulted many unprepared women into executive
positions. Men, weary of the large families of the '50s, began
to desert them; young mothers, frightened by the prospect of
being deserted, pulled up stakes and left their suburban split-
levels to try to make it in the cities. "Arrangements," or public
cohabitation of young people with approval and support from
their families, college deans and employers, became common.

By the early 1970s the doomsters were proclaiming that 11
the family was dead. There were over 8,000,000 single-parent
households, most of them headed by poorly paid women. There
were endless discussions of "open marriages," "group marriages," communes in which the children were children of the
group, and open discussion of previously taboo subjects, including an emphasis on female sexuality. Yet most Americans
continued to live as they always had, with girls still hoping for
a permanent marriage and viewing "arrangements" as step-
ping-stones to marriage. The much-publicized behavior of small
but conspicuous groups filtered through the layers of society,
so that the freedoms claimed by college youth were being
claimed five years later by blue-collar youth; "swinging" (mate
swapping) as a pastime of a bored upper-middle-class filtered
down.

Perhaps the most striking change of all is that courtship is 12
no longer a prelude to consummation. In many levels of contemporary society, sex relations require no prelude at all; the
courtship that exists today tends to occur between a casual sex
encounter and a later attempt by either the man or the woman
to turn it into a permanent relationship. Courtship is also seen
as an act in which either sex can take the lead. Women are felt
to have an alternative to marriage, as once they had in the Middle Ages, when convent life was the choice of a large part of
the population. Weddings are less conventional, although new
conventions, like reading from Kahlil Gibran's *The Prophet*,

spread very quickly. There is also a growing rebellion against the kind of town planning and housing that isolate young couples from the help of older people and friends that they need.

But the family is not dead. It is going through stormy times, 13 and millions of children are paying the penalty of current disorganization, experimentation and discontent. In the process, the adults who should never marry are sorting themselves out. Marriage and parenthood are being viewed as a vocation rather than as the duty of every human being. As we seek more human forms of existence, the next question may well be how to protect our young people from a premature, pervasive insistence upon precocious sexuality, sexuality that contains neither love nor delight.

The birthrate is going up a little; women are having just 14 as many babies as before, but having them later. The rights of fathers are being discovered and placed beside the rights of mothers. Exploitive and commercialized abortion mills are being questioned, and the Pill is proving less a panacea than was hoped. In a world troubled by economic and political instability, unemployment, highjacking, kidnapping and bombs, the preoccupation with private decisions is shifting to concern about the whole of humankind.

Active concern for the world permits either celibacy *or* mar- 15 riage, but continuous preoccupation with sex leaves no time for anything else. As we used to say in the '20s, promiscuity, like free verse, is lacking in structure.

THE WRITER'S THEMES

1. How and when did dating replace courtship? What was lost when this change took place? What advantages came about as a result of this change?
2. According to Margaret Mead, what were the economic factors that led to a change in attitude toward courtship and marriage?
3. Margaret Mead notes that today's women feel they have an alternative to marriage. What are some of the alternatives to traditional marriage that are available to both men and women today?

THE WRITER'S TECHNIQUE

In the first paragraph of her essay, Margaret Mead states that there have been "major changes in attitudes toward courtship and marriage" among middle-class educated Americans. Here is that paragraph:

> There have been major changes in attitudes toward courtship and marriage among those middle-class, educated Americans who are celebrated in the media and who are style setters for American life. Courtship was once a regular part of American life; it was a long period, sometimes lasting for many years, and also a tentative one, during which a future husband or wife could still turn back but during which their relationship became more and more exclusive and socially recognized. Courtship both preceded the announcement of an engagement and followed the announcement, although a broken engagement was so serious that it could be expected to throw the girl into a depression from which she might never recover.

Notice that the writer begins with a topic sentence that introduces her subject, in this case an area of social change. She also identifies the group of people involved. First, we are given the fact that there have been "major changes in attitudes toward courtship and marriage . . ." We then are told that these changes have taken place among "middle-class educated Americans . . ."

The writer then tells us that courtship was once "long" and "tentative"; it was a time when the young man or woman could "still turn back," but it was also a time when the relationship became more and more "exclusive." Finally, the writer tells us that courtship was an integral part of the engagement; it "both preceded the announcement of an engagement and followed the announcement . . ." If an engagement were broken, the result could be very serious for the young woman; it could "throw the girl into a depression from which she might never recover."

Throughout the paragraph, the writer emphasizes different aspects of time as it is connected with past courtship practices: courtship "was once" a part of American life; it was "a long period, sometimes lasting for many years"; during courtship either the young man or the young woman could still "turn back;" and if an engagement was broken a girl could be so seriously affected that she might "never" recover from the shock.

PARAGRAPH PRACTICE

Write a paragraph of your own, using Margaret Mead's paragraph as your model. You could describe a social custom or a social attitude that has changed a great deal in recent years. For example, you might choose to describe a new fashion in dating, something that makes older customs seem old-fashioned. You might wish to describe some changing attitudes toward going to school. For example, many people today are returning to school after spending considerable periods of time taking care of a family or working at a job.

If you wish, you could begin your paragraph by imitating Margaret Mead's opening sentence:

There have been major changes in attitudes toward . . .

The second part of your opening sentence should identify the group of people who share this new attitude. The remainder of your paragraph (at least six or seven sentences) should contain several supporting details. You could make the first half of each sentence describe an old attitude, while the second half of the sentence could reflect what people are thinking now. For example:

In the past, if you were settled in a job it was expected that you would stay there, but today it is not unusual for people to change jobs depending on different circumstances.

ESSAY PRACTICE

The following outline will help you plan a complete essay of at least five paragraphs. The theme of your essay will be closely related to the Margaret Mead essay.

The following sentence may serve as your thesis sentence, and will also be the main idea of your introductory paragraph:

¶ 1. When people begin to date, they go through an initial stage, and then a period when their relationship deepens; sooner or later they may also have to go through a crisis in their relationship.

Each of the sentences below is the topic sentence for one of the paragraphs that you will write to develop your thesis.

You may use the suggested details to develop each paragraph, or you may supply details of your own.

¶ 2. When two people begin to date, they usually act in predictable ways.

[DETAILS: How do people act when they first go out together? What is each one very careful to do, and not to do, during this early stage?]

¶ 3. After a period of time, this relationship changes.

[DETAILS: How long does it take before the two people begin to look at each other differently? How do their actions reflect these new attitudes?]

¶ 4. It often happens that sooner or later the relationship is threatened by a crisis of some kind.

[DETAILS: What kinds of crises usually threaten a dating relationship? How can a couple overcome such crises?]

Be certain that you use transitions between paragraphs to make your writing flow smoothly. In addition, be sure that your conclusion gives your reader a clear signal that you have come to the end of your essay.

ESSAY TOPICS

1. Compare the best date you ever had with the worst date you ever had.

2. Should a couple get married soon after they have made a commitment to each other? Compare the advantages and the disadvantages of a long engagement.

3. Margaret Mead describes courtship and wedding customs, but she does not deal with the consequences of a marriage that fails.

    Discuss the changing American attitudes toward divorce. Compare people's attitudes toward divorce now with attitudes that were common in the past.

Katherine Anne Porter

Katherine Anne Porter (1890–1980) was born in Texas; she was raised there and in Louisiana. From her earliest years she thought of herself as a writer, and by the age of twenty-one she was working for a Chicago newspaper. Later, she played bit parts in the movies, and in 1921 she went to Mexico to study Aztec and Mayan art. Katherine Anne Porter was involved with her own writing all during this period. She wrote endlessly and discarded what she later described as "trunksful of manuscripts."

At the age of thirty she published her first short story, "Maria Concepcion." From this point on, and with the publication of more stories, she began to achieve a reputation. She was careful never to write in a hurry, and she never wrote for money. In addition to her many short stories, Katherine Anne Porter is well known for her three short novels, which were published under the single title of *Pale Horse, Pale Rider*. She also achieved fame from her novel *Ship of Fools*, a story that was made into a Hollywood film in 1965.

Katherine Anne Porter was first married at sixteen; in 1933 she married again, but the marriage ended in divorce in 1938. That same year she married for a third time, but four years later this marriage also ended in divorce.

Later in her life, Katherine Anne Porter was well known as a lecturer and teacher at writers' conferences. She was also writer in residence at several colleges and universities throughout the country, and in 1959 she became the first woman faculty member in the history of Washington and Lee University in Virginia.

Some critics have felt that Katherine Anne Porter was primarily a regional writer who was, in the words of one critic, "truly at home in only one place, the American Southwest of her childhood." Other critics, and the writer herself, saw the direction and purpose of her work in a broader perspective. "My whole attempt," Katherine Anne Porter wrote, "has been to discover and understand human motives, human feelings, to make a distillation of what human relations and experiences my mind has been able to absorb."

In the following essay, published in 1948, Katherine Anne Porter tries to understand and describe the often conflicting emotions associated with love. "The Necessary Enemy" shows the writer's honesty and directness as she makes some very frank statements about human relationships and the fact that love can often have more than one face.

PREVIEWING THE WRITER

- Note the writer's brief history of romantic love. How recently did the tradition of romantic love begin?
- Note the writer's attitude toward romantic love. Is romantic love something to be sought after, or is it something that should be approached with caution?
- Note the writer's emphasis on the connection between love and hate. How can love and hate be connected?

THE NECESSARY ENEMY

SHE IS A FRANK, charming, fresh-hearted young woman who married for love. She and her husband are one of those gay, good-looking young pairs who ornament this modern scene rather more in profusion perhaps than ever before in our history. They are handsome, with a talent for finding their way in their world, they work at things that interest them, their tastes agree and their hopes. They intend in all good faith to spend their lives together, to have children and do well by them and each other—to be happy, in fact, which for them is the whole point of their marriage. And all in stride, keeping their wits about them. Nothing romantic, mind you; their feet are on the ground.

Unless they were this sort of person, there would be not much point to what I wish to say; for they would seem to be an example of the high-spirited, right-minded young whom the critics are always invoking to come forth and do their duty and practice all those sterling old-fashioned virtues which in every generation seem to be falling into disrepair. As for virtues, these young people are more or less on their own, like most of their kind; they get very little moral or other aid from their society; but after three years of marriage this very contemporary young woman finds herself facing the oldest and ugliest dilemma of marriage.

She is dismayed, horrified, full of guilt and forebodings because she is finding out little by little that she is capable of hating her husband, whom she loves faithfully. She can hate him at times as fiercely and mysteriously, indeed in terribly much the same way, as often she hated her parents, her brothers and sisters, whom she loves, when she was a child. Even then it had seemed to her a kind of black treacherousness in her, her private wickedness that, just the same, gave her her only private life. That was one thing her parents never knew about her, never seemed to suspect. For it was never given a name. They did and said hateful things to her and to each other as if by right, as if in them it was a kind of virtue. But when they said to her, "Control your feelings," it was never when she was amiable and obedient, only in the black times of her hate. So it was her secret, a shameful one. When they punished her, sometimes for the strangest reasons, it was, they said, only because they loved her—it was for her good. She did not believe this, but she thought herself guilty of something worse than ever they had punished her for. None of this really frightened her: the real fright came when she discovered that at times her father and mother hated each other; this was like standing on the doorsill of a familiar room and seeing in a lightning flash that the floor was gone, you were on the edge of a bottomless pit. Sometimes she felt that both of them hated her, but that passed, it was simply not a thing to be thought of, much less believed. She thought she had outgrown all this, but here it was again, an element in her own nature she could not control, or feared she could not. She would have to hide from her husband, if she could, the same spot in her feelings she had hidden from her parents, and for the same no doubt disreputable, selfish reason: she wants to keep his love.

Above all, she wants him to be absolutely confident that   4
she loves him, for that is the real truth, no matter how un-reasonable it sounds, and no matter how her own feelings be-tray them both at times. She depends recklessly on his love; yet while she is hating him, he might very well be hating her as much or even more, and it would serve her right. But she does not want to be served right, she wants to be loved and for-given—that is, to be sure he would forgive her anything, if he had any notion of what she had done. But best of all she would like not to have anything in her love that should ask forgive-ness. She doesn't mean about their quarrels—they are not so bad. Her feelings are out of proportion, perhaps. She knows it is perfectly natural for people to disagree, have fits of temper, fight it out; they learn quite a lot about each other that way, and not all of it disappointing either. When it passes, her hatred seems quite unreal. It always did.

Love. We are early taught to say it. I love you. We are trained   5
to the thought of it as if there were nothing else, or nothing

else worth having without it, or nothing worth having which it could not bring with it. Love is taught, always by precept, sometimes by example. Then hate, which no one meant to teach us, comes of itself. It is true that if we say I love you, it may be received with doubt, for there are times when it is hard to believe. Say I hate you, and the one spoken to believes it instantly, once for all.

Say I love you a thousand times to that person afterward 6 and mean it every time, and still it does not change the fact that once we said I hate you, and meant that too. It leaves a mark on that surface love had worn so smooth with its eternal caresses. Love must be learned, and learned again and again; there is no end to it. Hate needs no instruction, but waits only to be provoked . . . hate, the unspoken word, the unacknowledged presence in the house, that faint smell of brimstone among the roses, that invisible tongue-tripper, that unkempt finger in every pie, that sudden oh-so-curiously *chilling* look— could it be boredom?—on your dear one's features, making them quite ugly. Be careful: love, perfect love, is in danger.

If it is not perfect, it is not love, and if it is not love, it is 7 bound to be hate sooner or later. This is perhaps a not too exaggerated statement of the extreme position of Romantic Love, more especially in America, where we are all brought up on it, whether we know it or not. Romantic Love is changeless, faithful, passionate, and its sole end is to render the two lovers happy. It has no obstacles save those provided by the hazards of fate (that is to say, society), and such sufferings as the lovers may cause each other are only another word for delight: exciting jealousies, thrilling uncertainties, the ritual dance of courtship within the charmed closed circle of their secret alliance; all *real* troubles come from without, they face them unitedly in perfect confidence. Marriage is not the end but only the beginning of true happiness, cloudless, changeless to the end. That the candidates for this blissful condition have never seen an example of it, nor ever knew anyone who had, makes no difference. That is the ideal and they will achieve it.

How did Romantic Love manage to get into marriage at 8 last, where it was most certainly never intended to be? At its highest it was tragic: the love of Héloïse and Abélard. At its most graceful, it was the homage of the trouvère for his lady. In its most popular form, the adulterous strayings of solidly married couples who meant to stray for their own good reasons, but at the same time do nothing to upset the property settlements or the line of legitimacy; at its most trivial, the pretty trifling of shepherd and shepherdess.

This was generally condemned by church and state and a word of fear to honest wives whose mortal enemy it was. Love within the sober, sacred realities of marriage was a matter of personal luck, but in any case, private feelings were strictly a private affair having, at least in theory, no bearing whatever on the fixed practice of the rules of an institution never intended as a recreation ground for either sex. If the couple discharged their religious and social obligations, furnished forth a copious progeny, kept their troubles to themselves, maintained public civility and died under the same roof, even if not always on speaking terms, it was rightly regarded as a successful marriage. Apparently this testing ground was too severe for all but the stoutest spirits; it too was based on an ideal, as impossible in its way as the ideal Romantic Love. One good thing to be said for it is that society took responsibility for the conditions of marriage, and the sufferers within its bounds could always blame the system, not themselves. But Romantic Love crept into the marriage bed, very stealthily, by centuries, bringing its absurd notions about love as eternal springtime and marriage as a personal adventure meant to provide personal happiness. To a Western romantic such as I, though my views have been much modified by painful experience, it still seems to me a charming work of the human imagination, and it is a pity its central notion has been taken too literally and has hardened into a convention as cramping and enslaving as the older one. The refusal to acknowledge the evils in ourselves which therefore are implicit in any human situation is as extreme and unworkable a proposition as the doctrine of total depravity; but somewhere between them, or maybe beyond them, there does exist a possibility for reconciliation between our desires for impossible satisfactions and the simple unalterable fact that we also desire to be unhappy and that we create our own sufferings; and out of these sufferings we salvage our fragments of happiness.

Our young woman who has been taught that an important part of her human nature is not real because it makes trouble and interferes with her peace of mind and shakes her self-love, has been very badly taught; but she has arrived at a most important stage of her re-education. She is afraid her marriage is going to fail because she has not love enough to face its diffi-

9

10

culties; and this because at times she feels a painful hostility toward her husband, and cannot admit its reality because such an admission would damage in her own eyes her view of what love should be, an absurd view, based on her vanity of power. Her hatred is real as her love is real, but her hatred has the advantage at present because it works on a blind instinctual level, it is lawless; and her love is subjected to a code of ideal conditions, impossible by their very nature of fulfillment, which prevents its free growth and deprives it of its right to recognize its human limitations and come to grips with them. Hatred is natural in a sense that love, as she conceives it, a young person brought up in the tradition of Romantic Love, is not natural at all. Yet it did not come by hazard, it is the very imperfect expression of the need of the human imagination to create beauty and harmony out of chaos, no matter how mistaken its notion of these things may be, nor how clumsy its methods. It has conjured love out of the air, and seeks to preserve it by incantations; when she spoke a vow to love and honor her husband until death, she did a very reckless thing, for it is not possible by an act of the will to fulfill such an engagement. But it was the necessary act of faith performed in defense of a mode of feeling, the statement of honorable intention to practice as well as she is able the noble, acquired faculty of love, that very mysterious overtone to sex which is the best thing in it. Her hatred is part of it, the necessary enemy and ally.

THE WRITER'S THEMES

1. Is there still a belief in romantic love in our society, or have people today become more practical? What is our modern concept of love?
2. According to Katherine Anne Porter, what is "the oldest and ugliest dilemma" of marriage? Do you agree that this dilemma can exist in a marriage that otherwise seems to be normal and happy?
3. According to the author, happiness is supposed to be the end and purpose of marriage. What do you believe should be the most important goal or end of marriage?

THE WRITER'S TECHNIQUE

In the first paragraph of her essay, Katherine Anne Porter gives us a detailed portrait of a modern young couple. Here is the major portion of that paragraph:

> She is a frank, charming, fresh-hearted young woman who married for love. She and her husband are one of those gay, good-looking young pairs who ornament this modern scene rather more in profusion perhaps than ever before in our history. They are handsome, with a talent for finding their way in their world, they work at things that interest them, their tastes agree and their hopes. They intend in all good faith to spend their lives together, to have children and do well by them and each other— to be happy, in fact, which for them is the whole point of their marriage.

Notice that the writer engages our attention by first giving us a description of the young woman. She is "frank, charming [and] fresh-hearted" and we are told that she "married for love." By the next sentence the writer is considering the couple together; "She and her husband," we are told, are one of those attractive young couples that are so often found in modern society.

The writer then gives a more detailed description of this representative young couple. They are handsome, talented, and hardworking, and their tastes and hopes "agree." We are also told about their intentions: they plan "to spend their lives together, to have children, and do well by them and each other . . ." Finally, we are told that they intend to be happy, "which for them is the whole point of their marriage."

The writer has taken us from a brief sketch of the woman, to a more detailed picture of the married couple with their talents, abilities, and hopes for the future.

PARAGRAPH PRACTICE

Write a paragraph of your own, using Katherine Anne Porter's writing as your model. You could, for example, write a description of a married couple you know well. Use your first sentence to briefly describe either the man or the woman, and then write at least three sentences in which you describe how the man and woman act together. In what areas of their life together do they agree? On what do they disagree? Finally, write a one-sentence conclusion in which you sum up, in your own words, "the whole point of their marriage." What do you see as the main point or purpose of this relationship?

ESSAY PRACTICE

The following outline will help you plan a complete essay of at least five paragraphs. The theme of your essay will be closely related to Katherine Anne Porter's "The Necessary Enemy."

The following sentence may serve as your thesis sentence, and will also be the main idea of your introductory paragraph:

¶ 1. The nature of a relationship inevitably changes and may even be in danger if a spirit of acceptance and understanding is lacking between the two people.

Each of the sentences below is the topic sentence for one of the paragraphs that you will write to develop your thesis. You may use the suggested details to develop each paragraph, or you may supply details of your own.

¶ 2. The first time one of the people in a relationship reveals a negative aspect of his or her personality, it is always unpleasant.

[DETAILS: What are some negative revelations that can come as an unpleasant surprise for the other person in a relationship? In this paragraph, you might want to support what you are saying by providing an example from your own experience, or the experience of someone you know.]

¶ 3. This revelation usually changes the nature of the relationship, sometimes in subtle ways.

[DETAILS: In such a situation, how does the relationship change? What does each person do or say that had not been done or said before?]

¶ 4. If the relationship is to continue, each person has to recognize the other's strengths and accept the other's weaknesses.

[DETAILS: How can a person use the strengths of the other person in a relationship? To what extent does a person have to accept the limitations of the other person in a relationship?]

Be certain that you use transitions between paragraphs to make your writing flow smoothly. In addition, be sure that your conclusion gives your reader a clear signal that you have come to the end of your essay.

ESSAY TOPICS

1. What are some of the issues and mutual concerns a young couple should try to resolve *before* marriage? For example, should a young couple try to agree on how they will handle their money after they are married? Should they agree on how they will handle possible problems with their relatives, especially in-laws?
2. What is your concept of a successful marriage? Describe your idea of what a successful marriage should be and what the relationship should provide for both partners.
3. a. Do young people today marry primarily for love? What are the other bases for marriage in today's society?
    b. Describe someone you know who married for a reason (or reasons) other than love. Why did this person marry? What was the outcome of the marriage?

Focus on Terms: Conclusions

A conclusion is the final part of a piece of writing that gives the reader the sense of a satisfying end. Whether it is a single sentence or one or more paragraphs, a conclusion should be designed to leave the reader with the sense that the essay or story has come to a genuine or logical ending, and is not simply stopping as the result of the writer's fatigue.

In planning a conclusion, a writer may choose from more than one approach. For example, the writer may decide to use a key word or phrase to signal that the end of the piece has been reached. The constructions "In closing," "To conclude," "To sum up," and even the single word "Finally," all indicate that a piece of writing is about to end. James Thurber concludes "Courtship through the Ages" by directly telling the reader that his conclusion has been reached: "I will close this investigation . . ."

Another method of telling your reader that you are approaching the end of your piece of writing is to restate your central thesis. The final sentence of Katherine Anne Porter's "The Necessary Enemy" is a restatement of the unusual thesis that she announced in her title, namely, that love and hate are necessary complements. The writer's final words are a direct echo of her title as she tells us that, for the woman she has described in her essay, hatred is a necessary part of her love, "the necessary enemy and ally."

Some writers prefer to end by quoting or paraphrasing a well-known saying or expression in order to emphasize what they have written. This is how Margaret Mead chose to end her survey of American courtship practices, by giving a paraphrase of a popular saying that the author remembered from the 1920s, to the effect that "promiscuity, like free verse, is lacking in structure." The idea is an appropriate conclusion to the essay because in a single sentence the author bridges the 1920s and the 1970s, showing that a comment about sexual mores made fifty years ago may still be relevant today.

An additional method favored by some writers is to directly point out the significance of what has been written, perhaps making a prediction as to what might happen in the future.

A conclusion is important because it announces to your reader that you have finished the development of your ideas. It also gives you a final opportunity to state your position or argue your point. A conclusion is worth a little extra attention on your part, if only because the last idea you express is the final impression your reader will take away from a reading of your essay.

Student Essay ⋅⋅ *Diane J. Allcroft*

The student writer of the following essay is similar to Katherine Anne Porter, in that she also questions the meaning of romantic love and compares it with other types of relationships which may be more important.

Notice how the writer achieves authority in this essay by referring to writers such as Harding to support her points. Notice also the range of the writer's examples, from Greek mythology to American soap operas. The student does not only point out differences; she makes judgments and gives advice.

• The writer signals her conclusion in the next to last paragraph, when she writes "My advice, then . . ." She continues this conclusion in the final paragraph as she urges her readers not to conclude "that romantic love has no place in our lives."

ROMANTIC LOVE OR SELF-DISCOVERY?

WHAT IS ROMANTIC LOVE? Is it glittering starlit nights, 1 dinner by flickering teasing candlelight, long gliding strolls on a moonswept beach, no mosquitos to poke at the nocturnal lovers, no greasy dishes to scrape after the dainty meal, not even a sandy beer can to clatter and pierce the "magic" of the oceanside evening?

What is romantic love? Society reveres it. Every day mil- 2 lions are mindlessly riveted to the television set as program after program reveals an endless variety of schemes on love's intricacies. "The Edge of Night," "All My Children," "As the World Turns" are all branches of the same tree that is badly in need of pruning. Or is it "All My Nights," "My Edgy Children," and "As the Stomach Churns"? No matter. The message is the same: romantic love is wonderful, and if you ain't got it, baby, you're a loser. Never mind that the gargantuan difficulties that result from these romances would sink the "Love Boat."

What is romantic love? Businesses profit by it: toothpaste, 3
mouthwash, soap, fashion, cosmetics, and food. Again the message is that gleaming teeth, the correct hem length, the "just-
for-you" scent will promptly draw true love. Vidal Sassoon
points the way, and we, hobbling in our Jordache jeans, do our
best to shop for that bottle of mineral water that will show how
much we care.

Greek mythology tells a tale of the famous and breath- 4
taking song of the beautiful Sirens, legendary women who from
their rocky ocean perch sang to the passing ships. Unsuspecting
sailors, lured by the haunting melodies, would abandon their
course to seek out the Sirens, only to meet their death. Ulysses,
to avoid this dismal fate, had himself tied to the mast of his
ship to resist the terrible temptation. It was that act that saved
him and allowed him to continue his journey. Romantic love,
with its alluring and lovely image, is the fateful song of the
Sirens. Many an unsuspecting relationship has met its demise
by stopping too long to listen. Enthralled and drunk on emotion
as well as amazement finally to have met "someone special,"
we are encouraged to believe that this heady state is the way
we are supposed to feel all the time, that to move beyond it is
to leave the relationship, not save it.

Elizabeth Harding, in her book *The Way of All Women*, deals 5
with the phenomenon of romantic love and its dangers. An
individual of either sex, she points out, possesses both masculine and feminine characteristics. The terms "masculine" and
"feminine" here are not used to denote sexuality, but rather to
symbolize certain human aspects. Assertiveness and aggression
are considered masculine traits, where passivity and intuition
are the feminine ones. This concept did not originate with Harding. Carl Jung, the Swiss psychiatrist, was among many in the
West who dealt with this concept extensively, and it is at the
core of most Eastern philosophies and religions. Harding suggests, however, that Western society places great emphasis on
the idea that only those attributes considered masculine belong
to the male and only those feminine traits belong to the female,
and never the twain shall meet. Unfortunately, in order to fulfill
society's subscription to the West, individuals must rigorously
repress those aspects of themselves not deemed acceptable to
society. Those traits then become hidden, not only from society
but from the individual's self as well. But alas, being hidden
does not mean the traits have disappeared. Because they are

out of our conscious awareness, they have increased power over our emotions and our actions.

Herein lies the first danger of romantic love. Harding 6 points out that it is precisely these repressed and therefore disassociated aspects of ourselves that we project onto each other. A woman, for instance, meeting an assertive and aggressive man, would become infatuated with him, not realizing the possibility that she is actually identifying with these long-repressed attributes in herself. In other words, she is in love with her projection of those qualities that she has kept herself from "owning." Not being able to separate her projection from who the person really is, she is swept away emotionally, only to discover later on that the fine young man was indeed far different from what she had initially perceived.

This woman cannot remain "in love" with her projection. 7 Eventually the reality of individual personality and its flaws will come into focus. Here is the second danger point in an emerging relationship. In some cases the dwindling excitement of infatuation evolves into a more lasting and deeper love. More frequently, however (and I believe this is more often the case with younger lovers who have not yet developed a clear sense of self), the let-down is interpreted as an indication that the relationship should be terminated. Oh, the songs that have been written over the loss of "love's sweet beauty!"

In order to avoid this unhappy pitfall, it is essential that 8 we embark on a journey of self-discovery. This means we need to be open to our own selves and be patient as well as nonjudgmental of what we may find. Integration is the key word here— integration of the many aspects, both masculine and feminine, that create who we are and who we can become. "Women's liberation" is, therefore, a liberation for us all since it encourages us to explore and even enjoy essential parts of ourselves that we never allowed ourselves to be in touch with before. So men can discover that they can indeed be very intuitive, and women can allow themselves to feel the growth that comes with being assertive.

As we become older, the tendency to project these un- 9 acknowledged traits that manifest themselves in "romantic love" is lessened. Maturity is not, of course, a guarantee that we will not do this, but generally speaking older persons by dint of their years of experience have had more time to discover who they are. Younger people, in contrast, have not yet developed psychic roots and are more easily swayed not only by passions, but also by the continual pounding of the pressures of society, of the media, and of peers.

My advice, then, to a person of any age entering into such a relationship that has its origins in "romantic love" is the Greeks' "Know thyself." Take time. Read. Study. Discuss. Explore. Try on parts of yourself that you've never tried and see how they fit. If you've never kissed a kitten, try it. If you've never disagreed with your boss, admit how you feel about a certain issue. Learn. Experiment. Accept. Decide what your boundaries are and how you will maintain them. Listen to that still small voice within.

Let us not conclude that romantic love has no place in our lives. On the contrary, recognized for what it is as a port of entry into a relationship, romantic love provides spontaneity and meaning, but only if we are the ones in control. We, like Ulysses, can tie ourselves to the mast and be engulfed but not swallowed. By so doing, we can move past the tempting dangers of romantic love into the calmer, deeper waters of trust, intimacy, and friendship.

Strategies for Writing

1. How does the writer use her conclusion to echo her opening?
2. Rewrite the conclusion of this essay, using one of the other methods (restating a thesis, using a key word or phrase, or quoting a well-known expression) discussed in "Focus on Terms."
3. Compare the various economic problems and social pressures young men face today with the problems and social pressures faced by their fathers a generation ago.
4. The writer points out that "assertiveness and aggression are considered masculine traits, where passivity and intuition are the female ones."

   Compare past attitudes toward this belief with today's attitudes. To what extent are people's attitudes changing with regard to the traditional definitions of "masculine" and "feminine"?

8

SELF AND SOCIETY

WRITING SKILL: *Definition and Analysis*

You have just been given a term paper assignment. Your instructor has made it a requirement that you define a concept and analyze it. How will you approach this assignment? You will want to begin with as precise a meaning of the word or concept as possible. Such precision is not easy to achieve, but if a definition is to satisfy us, it must be exact. Whether you are writing an answer for a biology quiz or writing an introduction for a term paper, the more precise your definitions are, the more convincing and authoritative your writing will be.

When we want to *analyze* a word or idea, we explore that concept as fully as we can, always looking for a broader understanding of the definition. Here, the boundaries are wide, and such analysis is often called extended definition. Your instructor may have required you to begin your term paper with a specific definition of a concept, but you will also be expected to analyze that concept (or a related one) throughout the rest of your paper. In effect, your paper will be an extended definition of your subject.

If we look for the definition of the word *insanity*, for ex-

288 ê& SELF AND SOCIETY

ample, we might first try to explain the term by means of a synonym: *craziness*, *lunacy*, and *madness* are all words that are loosely interchangeable with the term *insanity*. However, if we wanted a stricter definition of *insanity*, we would go to the dictionary entry for that word. The first part of the dictionary entry for *insanity* is, "Persistent mental disorder or derangement."[1] There are, in addition, other related definitions of *insanity* given in the same entry. The first additional meaning is the definition of the term as it applies to civil law. Here, *insanity* means "Unsoundness of mind sufficient, in the judgment of a court, to render a person unfit to maintain a contractual or other legal relationship or to warrant commitment to a mental hospital."

The second additional meaning of *insanity* applies to the area of criminal law. Although a strict definition of *criminal insanity* has never been agreed upon, the dictionary gives us at least a basic meaning of the term as it applies to criminal matters:

> In most jurisdictions, a degree of mental malfunctioning sufficient to prevent the accused from knowing right from wrong, as to the act he is charged with, or to render him unaware of the nature of the act when committing it.

There are additional ways to define the term *insanity* beyond the necessarily narrow limits of a dictionary entry. We could, for example, go to the article on *insanity* in the *Encyclopaedia Britannica*, which provides us with a further dimension to the definition, namely, some historical background to the term. In the article the *Britannica* concentrates on the meaning of the word in criminal law and provides information on the historical growth of the concept:

> Various legal tests of insanity have been put forward, none of which has escaped criticism. Anglo-American systems, including that of India, base the law of criminal responsibility primarily on the famous case of M'Naghten. In that case (1843) the English judges held that "to establish a defense of insanity, it must be clearly proved that, at the time of committing the act, the party accused was labouring under such a defect of reason, from disease of mind, as not to know the nature and quality of the act he was doing; or if he did know it, that he did not know he was doing what was wrong." Some U.S. courts went further and

also relieved from responsibility one moved by an "irresistible impulse."

....

The 1954 decision of *Durham* v. *United States* employed a new test: "simply that an accused is not criminally responsible if his unlawful act was the product of mental disease or mental defect." In simplicity, this test resembles the Japanese: "An act of an insane person is not punishable." Such a rule has been supported by some lawyers and judges and by many psychiatrists, but few U.S. courts have adopted it.

The concept may also be defined culturally: what is considered insane behavior in one culture may be quite acceptable in another. Furthermore, *insanity* could be defined in terms of its causes. For instance, does insanity have a chemical cause, or could it be the result of a single tragic event in the life of an individual? For these cultural, chemical, or psychological definitions, one would consult books in the fields of sociology, medicine, or psychology.

There is an even more extended method of defining a term such as *insanity*, and that is by the use of narration. In recent years there have been several book-length accounts of insanity, among them Ken Kesey's 1962 novel *One Flew Over the Cuckoo's Nest* and Hannah Green's *I Never Promised You a Rose Garden* (1964). Both of these books were later made into well-known motion pictures.

Definition that goes beyond the scope of a single entry or short analysis is often referred to as extended definition, a term that leads us directly to analysis. For example, the two novels mentioned above could be described as either extended definitions of *insanity* or as detailed analyses of the term. In the selections that follow in this unit the various writers define words and ideas in a number of ways, and each one is an extended definition. None of the writers depends on a dictionary definition, but they make use of description, examples, causes, historical analysis, and narration to arrive at an understanding of the concept that is being discussed.

In "Being Prohibited," Doris Lessing describes herself trying to enter the Union of South Africa. At the border, her national identity is brought into question and at one point a South African official gives his own definition of her nationality:

"You were born in Persia?"
"Yes."

"Then you are an Asiatic. You know the penalty for filling in the form wrongly?"

Doris Lessing uses her essay to argue against this method of defining nationality, and by the time we have finished reading the piece we realize we have been given an extended definition of another concept: racism.

In the excerpt from her book *The Death and Life of Great American Cities,* Jane Jacobs defines privacy by first pointing out its characteristic features and then describing how people maintain their privacy in a big city environment. In another essay on privacy, William Zinsser defines what privacy is by employing a different strategy, one that is often used to define a term: he defines it by telling what it is *not.* By the time we have read all the examples of the loss of privacy in our lives, we have an indirect definition of what privacy essentially is. It is the opposite of what the writer describes in his essay!

In the essay "The Nudist Idea," Margaret Mead and Rhoda Metraux use a number of approaches to arrive at a definition of nudism. First, they describe what the average nudist camp looks like; then they explain what kind of people come to nudist camps and what they do there. They explain the philosophy behind the nudist movement and they trace the history of that movement back to its beginnings in Europe. In addition, throughout the essay the writers also define nudism by showing what it is not, as they describe attitudes and actions from the world outside the nudist camp. A subject such as nudism usually produces strong emotional reactions from the general public. However, by using a wide variety of rhetorical techniques and by not interjecting their own personal attitudes or values into the essay, these writers have given us an understanding of nudism that is both objective and complete.

Clear definition and objective analysis are basic building blocks in all good writing, from a college term paper to a business report. When you pay close attention to these aspects of the writing process, you are helping your reader and you are helping yourself.

◄ Doris Lessing ◄

Doris Lessing was born in Persia, of British parents, in 1919. She was educated in Salisbury, Rhodesia, and left school at the age of fourteen. She then held various jobs, working as a nursemaid, a lawyer's secretary, and a typist.

At the age of eighteen, Doris Lessing began to write, and during this early period of her career she completed and destroyed some six full-length novels. In 1949 she left Rhodesia and went to England where the following year her first published novel, *The Grass Is Singing,* appeared. Since that time she has written a great many novels, short stories, and essays. Her frankness in analyzing social situations, especially relationships between men and women, has made her one of our most widely read and influential modern writers. Among her best-known works is *The Four-Gated City,* a series of five novels. Her latest novels are also being published as a series under the title *Canopus in Argos: Archives.*

The following essay appeared in Doris Lessing's 1976 book of essays, *A Small Personal Voice,* and describes her encounters with the world of rigid bureaucracy at the border between Rhodesia and the Union of South Africa.

PREVIEWING THE WRITER

• Note the details in the essay that help us form a picture of South African society. What impression do we have of that society?

• Note the different emotional reactions the writer has at each border crossing. When she crosses the border into South Africa for the last time, what is her attitude toward the border officials? How do her actions reveal her attitude?

• Note how the writer emphasizes her own isolation as she describes each of the border incidents, especially the last one. How do we see her isolation while she is in the compartment of the train with five other women? How does she reveal her isolation while she is being questioned in the office of the border officials?

BEING PROHIBITED

THE BORDER IS MAFEKING, a little dorp[1] with nothing interesting about it but its name. The train waits (or used to

[1] A village.

wait) interminably on the empty tracks, while immigration and customs officials made their leisurely way through the coaches, and pale gritty dust settled over everything. Looking out, one saw the long stretch of windows, with the two, three, or four white faces at each; then at the extreme end, the single coach for "natives" packed tight with black humans; and, in between, two or three Indians or Coloured people on sufferance in the European coaches.

Outside, on the scintillating dust by the tracks, a crowd of ragged black children begged for *bonsellas*.[2] One threw down sandwich crusts or bits of spoiled fruit and watched them dive and fight to retrieve them from the dirt.   2

I was sixteen. I was not, as one says, politically conscious; nor did I know the score. I knew no more, in fact, than on which side my bread was buttered. But I already felt uneasy about being a member of the Herrenvolk.[3] When the immigration official reached me, I had written on the form: *Nationality*, British, *Race*, European; and it was the first time in my life I had had to claim myself as a member of one race and disown the others. I remember distinctly that I had to suppress an impulse opposite *Race:* Human. Of course I *was* very young.   3

The immigration man had the sarcastic surliness which characterises the Afrikaans[4] official, and he looked suspiciously at my form for a long time before saying that I was in the wrong part of the train. I did not understand him. (I forgot to mention that where the form asked, Where were you born?, I had written, Persia.)   4

"Asiatics," said he, "have to go to the back of the train; and anyway you are prohibited from entry unless you have documents proving you conform to the immigration quota for Asians."   5

"But," I said, "I am not an Asiatic."   6

The compartment had five other females in it; skirts were visibly being drawn aside. To prove my bona fides[5] I should, of course, have exclaimed with outraged indignation at any such idea.   7

"You were born in Persia?"   8

---

[2] Treats.
[3] The ruling race.
[4] "Afrikaans" refers to the descendants of Dutch-speaking immigrants who began to settle in South Africa in the seventeenth century.
[5] Authenticity or genuineness (Latin).

"Yes."

"Then you are an Asiatic. You know the penalties for filling in the form wrongly?"

This particular little imbroglio involved my being taken off the train, escorted to an office, and kept under watch while they telephoned Pretoria for a ruling.

When next I entered the Union it was 1939. Sophistication had set in in the interval, and it took me no more than five minutes to persuade the official that one could be born in a country without being its citizen. The next two times there was no trouble at all, although my political views had in the meantime become nothing less than inflammatory: in a word, I had learned to disapprove of the colour bar.

This time, two weeks ago, what happened was as follows: one gets off the plane and sits for about fifteen minutes in a waiting room while they check the plane list with a list, or lists, of their own. They called my name first, and took me to an office which had two tables in it. At one sat a young man being pleasant to the genuine South African citizens. At the one where they made me sit was a man I could have sworn I had seen before. He proceeded to go through my form item by item, as follows: "You *say*, Mrs. Lessing, that, etc. . . ." From time to time he let out a disbelieving laugh and exchanged ironical looks with a fellow official who was standing by. Sure enough, when he reached that point on my form when he had to say: "You *claim* that you are British; you *say* you were born in Persia," I merely said "Yes," and sat still while he gave me a long, exasperated stare. Then he let out an angry exclamation in Afrikaans and went next door to telephone Pretoria. Ten minutes later I was informed I must leave at once. A plane was waiting and I must enter it immediately.

I did so with dignity. Since then I have been unable to make up my mind whether I should have made a scene or not. I never have believed in the efficacy of dignity.

On the plane I wanted to sit near the window but was made to sit by myself and away from the window. I regretted infinitely that I had no accomplices hidden in the long grass by the airstrip, but, alas, I had not thought of it beforehand.

It was some time before it came home to me what an honour had been paid me. But now I am uneasy about the whole thing: suppose that I owe these attentions, not to my political views, but to the accident of my birthplace?

THE WRITER'S THEMES

1. What evidence does Doris Lessing use to show the segregation in South African society? Begin with her opening description of the train that waits at the border. How does the waiting room there also show the segregation of the society that lies beyond that border? How does the writer's final description of her treatment on the airplane also illustrate this idea of segregation?

2. How does Doris Lessing's reaction to the border officials differ each time she enters (or tries to enter) South Africa? What do her reactions tell us about her growth as a person?

3. Point out the different places in the essay where people are deprived of their dignity, beginning with the "ragged black children" diving and fighting in the dirt for scraps of food, and ending with the writer's own final departure, which, she tells us, she made "with dignity."

   In view of all this, why does the writer say toward the end of her essay, "I never have believed in the efficacy of dignity"?

THE WRITER'S TECHNIQUE

In paragraph thirteen of her essay, the writer provides a detailed description of her last attempt to enter South Africa. Here is that paragraph:

> This time, two weeks ago, what happened was as follows: one gets off the plane and sits for about fifteen minutes in a waiting room while they check the plane list with a list, or lists, of their own. They called my name first, and took me to an office which had two tables in it. At one sat a young man being pleasant to the genuine South African citizens. At the one where they made me sit was a man I could have sworn I had seen before. He proceeded to go through my form item by item, as follows: "You *say*, Mrs. Lessing, that, etc. . . ." From time to time he let out a disbelieving laugh and exchanged ironical looks with a fellow official who was standing by. Sure enough, when he reached that point on my form when he had to say: "You *claim* that you are British; you *say* you were born in Persia," I merely said "Yes," and sat still while he gave me a long, exasperated stare. Then he let out an angry exclamation in Afrikaans and went next door to telephone Pretoria. Ten minutes later I was informed I must leave at once. A plane was waiting and I must enter it immediately.

Notice that the writer begins by describing what happens to everyone in this situation ("one gets off the plane and sits for about fifteen minutes . . .") and then describes what happened in her particular case: "They called my name first, and took me to an office . . ." She briefly describes the office and then shows the immigration official going through her form "item by item," while he exchanges "ironical looks with a fellow official who was standing by."

The writer then describes the exchange between the official and herself, ending with that official giving her "a long, exasperated stare." Finally, the official lets out "an angry exclamation" and goes next door to telephone the nearest city; ten minutes later Doris Lessing is told she "must leave at once."

The writer begins with a general description of the usual procedure in this situation, and then describes her particular situation in detail. When we hear the official actually talking to her, we begin to realize how negative this experience is becoming: the official's laugh is "disbelieving," the looks he exchanges with another man are "ironical," and the stare he gives the writer is "long" and "exasperated." Finally, the situation reaches its climax when the official lets out an "angry" exclamation; the only thing left is to order her to "leave at once."

PARAGRAPH PRACTICE

Write a paragraph of your own, using Doris Lessing's paragraph as your model. You could describe an experience you once had. If this experience is one that many people have been through, make your opening sentence reflect this, as Doris Lessing does when she notes that "one gets off the plane and sits . . ." Next, begin to describe what happened to you on one particular occasion. You could have been registering for school, or applying for a license of some kind, or any other situation where you found yourself in a bureaucratic atmosphere. Be sure to include another person in this situation, in the way Doris Lessing describes her encounter with the immigration official. If your experience was a positive one, indicate this by using appropriate adjectives to describe your conversation or interaction with this other person. Was the person helpful? Did he or she speak to you in a kind way? Next, note how you responded and indicate the high point (or low point) of the encounter. Finally, end your description by telling what happened last. What was your mood as you left?

ESSAY PRACTICE

The following outline will help you plan a complete essay of at least five paragraphs. The theme of your essay will be closely related to the selection you have just read.

The following sentence may serve as your thesis sentence, and will also be the main idea of your introductory paragraph:

¶ 1. When people find themselves in new situations, they need all the support and encouragement they can get.

Each of the sentences below is the topic sentence for one of the paragraphs that you will write to develop your thesis. You may use the suggested details to develop each paragraph, or you may supply details of your own.

¶ 2. When we are in an unfamiliar or alarming situation we are often unsure of ourselves. At such a time, the support of those around us is really important.

[DETAILS: Describe a situation where you were unsure of yourself, either because of a lack of knowledge or because of a lack of experience. You may have found yourself lost, or you may have suddenly felt ill. How did someone help you by showing support or encouragement? How important was this encouragement to you at the time?]

¶ 3. Even when we feel more secure in a situation, there are always times when we need the friendly support of those around us.

[DETAILS: Describe a situation when you felt secure in what you were doing, but you still needed some help and support from others. You may have been working on a term paper and needed the advice of a fellow student who knew a great deal about the subject, or you could have felt discouraged about a course you were taking. How did the support of other people help you?]

¶ 4. We know we are really sure of ourselves in a situation when we are able to help someone else who may not be so secure.

[DETAILS: When have you been in a position where you were able to help someone else? To what extent did your own earlier experience influence you in your decision to help this other person?]

Be certain that you use transitions between paragraphs to make your writing flow smoothly. In addition, be sure that your

conclusion gives your reader a clear signal that you have come
to the end of your essay.

ESSAY TOPICS

1. Define one of the following concepts: *justice, patriotism,* or
   nationality. You might begin by looking up the word in a
   dictionary or thesaurus, or by consulting an encyclopedia.
   You may want to give some historical background to the
   term, or you could put it in a cultural context. You could
   also bring in causes and effects, or explain what the term is
   not. In short, use whatever techniques will lead your reader
   to a deeper understanding of the term.
2. Analyze the concept of *prejudice.*
   a. When did you first become aware that some parts of
      society separate people because of age, or sex, or some
      other method of division? Describe the circumstances
      that led to this awareness on your part, and tell what
      your reactions were when you became conscious of this
      fact.
   b. Have you ever been unjustly denied something because
      of your age, or sex, or color? Describe the situation in
      which you found yourself. How were you treated? How
      did you react?
3. a. When is it better to remain silent in a difficult situation?
      When is it better to make a scene?
   b. Analyze a situation in which you found yourself in dif-
      ficult circumstances. The situation could have involved
      several other people, or only yourself. How did you
      react? Looking back on the situation, should you have
      acted differently?

❧ *Jane Jacobs* ❧

Jane Jacobs (1916–   ) was born in Scranton, Pennsylvania. After high school, she spent a year as a reporter on the *Scranton Tribune*. She then moved to New York where she worked as a stenographer; she also began to write magazine articles about conditions in the working districts of the city.

From 1952 to 1962, Jane Jacobs was an editor for *Architectural Forum*. While she was with this journal, she became increasingly skeptical of conventional urban planning. She concluded that the city building projects she was writing about for her magazine were neither safe nor economical, nor were they interesting or stimulating for the people who lived in them.

In addition to her work on *Architectural Forum*, Jane Jacobs contributed to *The Exploding Metropolis* (1958), and in 1969 she published *The Economy of Cities*. However, the most important result of Jane Jacobs' analysis of urban problems was the publication in 1961 of *The Death and Life of Great American Cities*. The book made an immediate impact in the area of urban studies, and it has been widely hailed as the most influential analysis of cities since Lewis Mumford's classic study, *The Culture of Cities*. According to one critic, the great value of Jane Jacobs' book lies in the fact that the writer ''has looked at cities not as inanimate conglomerations of buildings but as the intricate working mechanisms that they really are.''

In the following selection from *The Death and Life of Great American Cities*, Jane Jacobs gives us a portrait of a New York City neighborhood. In the process, the writer leads us to examine our own notions of what really defines a neighborhood.

PREVIEWING THE WRITER

• Note the different kinds of neighborhoods the writer describes in the essay. How does this variety of examples support the main point of the essay?

• How do city people maintain both their need for public contact and their need for privacy? What role do neighborhood merchants play in helping to meet these needs?

• Note the references to the suburbs and the country. In what way do these comments support the writer's main points about city neighborhoods?

from *THE DEATH AND LIFE OF GREAT AMERICAN CITIES*

PRIVACY IS PRECIOUS in cities. It is indispensable. Perhaps it is precious and indispensable everywhere, but most places you cannot get it. In small settlements everyone knows your affairs. In the city everyone does not—only those you choose to tell will know much about you. This is one of the attributes of cities that is precious to most city people, whether their incomes are high or their incomes are low, whether they are white or colored, whether they are old inhabitants or new, and it is a gift of great-city life deeply cherished and jealously guarded.

Architectural and planning literature deals with privacy in terms of windows, overlooks, sight lines. The idea is that if no one from outside can peek into where you live—behold, privacy. This is simple-minded. Window privacy is the easiest commodity in the world to get. You just pull down the shades or adjust the blinds. The privacy of keeping one's personal affairs to those selected to know them, and the privacy of having reasonable control over who shall make inroads on your time and when, are rare commodities in most of this world, however, and they have nothing to do with the orientation of windows.

Anthropologist Elena Padilla, author of *Up from Puerto Rico*, describing Puerto Rican life in a poor and squalid district of New York, tells how much people know about each other—who is to be trusted and who not, who is defiant of the law and who upholds it, who is competent and well informed and who is inept and ignorant—and how these things are known from the public life of the sidewalk and its associated enterprises. These are matters of public character. But she also tells how select are those permitted to drop into the kitchen for a cup of coffee, how strong are the ties, and how limited the number of a person's genuine confidants, those who share in a person's private life and private affairs. She tells how it is not considered dignified for everyone to know one's affairs. Nor is it considered dignified to snoop on others beyond the face presented in public. It does violence to a person's privacy and rights. In this, the people she describes are essentially the same as the people of the mixed, Americanized city street on which I live, and essentially the same as the people who live in high-income apartments or fine town houses, too.

A good city street neighborhood achieves a marvel of balance between its people's determination to have essential privacy and their simultaneous wishes for differing degrees of contact, enjoyment or help from the people around. This balance is largely made up of small, sensitively managed details, practiced and accepted so casually that they are normally taken for granted. 4

Perhaps I can best explain this subtle but all-important balance in terms of the stores where people leave keys for their friends, a common custom in New York. In our family, for example, when a friend wants to use our place while we are away for a week end or everyone happens to be out during the day, or a visitor for whom we do not wish to wait up is spending the night, we tell such a friend that he can pick up the key at the delicatessen across the street. Joe Cornacchia, who keeps the delicatessen, usually has a dozen or so keys at a time for handing out like this. He has a special drawer for them. 5

Now why do I, and many others, select Joe as a logical custodian for keys? Because we trust him, first, to be a responsible custodian, but equally important because we know that he combines a feeling of good will with a feeling of no personal responsibility about our private affairs. Joe considers it no concern of his whom we choose to permit in our places and why. 6

Around on the other side of our block, people leave their keys at a Spanish grocery. On the other side of Joe's block, people leave them at the candy store. Down a block they leave them at the coffee shop, and a few hundred feet around the corner from that, in a barber shop. Around one corner from two fashionable blocks of town houses and apartments in the Upper East Side, people leave their keys in a butcher shop and a bookshop; around another corner they leave them in a cleaner's and a drug store. In unfashionable East Harlem keys are left with at least one florist, in bakeries, in luncheonettes, in Spanish and Italian groceries. 7

The point, wherever they are left, is not the kind of ostensible service that the enterprise offers, but the kind of proprietor it has. 8

A service like this cannot be formalized. Identifications . . . questions . . . insurance against mishaps. The all-essential line between public service and privacy would be transgressed by 9 institutionalization. Nobody in his right mind would leave his key in such a place. The service must be given as a favor by someone with an unshakable understanding of the difference between a person's key and a person's private life, or it cannot be given at all.

Or consider the line drawn by Mr. Jaffe at the candy store   10
around our corner—a line so well understood by his customers and by other storekeepers too that they can spend their whole lives in its presence and never think about it consciously. One ordinary morning last winter, Mr. Jaffe, whose formal business name is Bernie, and his wife, whose formal business name is Ann, supervised the small children crossing at the corner on the way to P.S. 41, as Bernie always does because he sees the need; lent an umbrella to one customer and a dollar to another; took custody of two keys; took in some packages for people in the next building who were away; lectured two youngsters who asked for cigarettes; gave street directions; took custody of a watch to give the repair man across the street when he opened later; gave out information on the range of rents in the neighborhood to an apartment seeker; listened to a tale of domestic difficulty and offered reassurance; told some rowdies they could not come in unless they behaved and then defined (and got) good behavior; provided an incidental forum for half a dozen conversations among customers who dropped in for oddments; set aside certain newly arrived papers and magazines for regular customers who would depend on getting them; advised a mother who came for a birthday present not to get the ship-model kit because another child going to the same birthday party was giving that; and got a back copy (this was for me) of the previous day's newspaper out of the deliverer's surplus returns when he came by.

After considering this multiplicity of extra-merchandising   11
services I asked Bernie, "Do you ever introduce your customers to each other?"

He looked startled at the idea, even dismayed. "No," he   12
said thoughtfully. "That would just not be advisable. Sometimes, if I know two customers who are in at the same time have an interest in common, I bring up the subject in conversation and let them carry it on from there if they want to. But oh no, I wouldn't introduce them."

When I told this to an acquaintance in a suburb, she   13
promptly assumed that Mr. Jaffe felt that to make an introduc-

tion would be to step above his social class. Not at all. In our neighborhood, storekeepers like the Jaffes enjoy an excellent social status, that of businessmen. In income they are apt to be the peers of the general run of customers and in independence they are the superiors. Their advice, as men or women of common sense and experience, is sought and respected. They are well known as individuals, rather than unknown as class symbols. No; this is that almost unconsciously enforced, well-balanced line showing, the line between the city public world and the world of privacy.

This line can be maintained, without awkwardness to anyone, because of the great plenty of opportunities for public contact in the enterprises along the sidewalks, or on the sidewalks themselves as people move to and fro or deliberately loiter when they feel like it, and also because of the presence of many public hosts, so to speak, proprietors of meeting places like Bernie's where one is free either to hang around or dash in and out, no strings attached. 14

Under this system, it is possible in a city street neighborhood to know all kinds of people without unwelcome entanglements, without boredom, necessity for excuses, explanations, fears of giving offense, embarrassments respecting impositions or commitments, and all such paraphernalia of obligations which can accompany less limited relationships. It is possible to be on excellent sidewalk terms with people who are very different from oneself, and even, as time passes, on familiar public terms with them. Such relationships can, and do, endure for many years, for decades; they could never have formed without that line, much less endured. They form precisely because they are by-the-way to people's normal public sorties. 15

THE WRITER'S THEMES

1. What are the different kinds of privacy, as Jane Jacobs describes them in the opening paragraphs of her essay?
2. How many different sources of evidence does Jane Jacobs use to support her points? How does her essay achieve authority by her use of these different sources?
3. To what extent does the writer include herself in the description of her neighborhood? To what extent does she sim-

ply remain a reporter? What effect does her presence (or lack of it) have on the description of her neighborhood?

THE WRITER'S TECHNIQUE

In paragraph ten of her essay, Jane Jacobs describes a typical day in one of the stores in her neighborhood. Here is the major portion of that paragraph:

> . . . One ordinary morning last winter, Mr. Jaffe, whose formal business name is Bernie, and his wife, whose formal business name is Ann, supervised the small children crossing at the corner on the way to P.S. 41, as Bernie always does because he sees the need; lent an umbrella to one customer and a dollar to another; took custody of two keys; took in some packages for people in the next building who were away; lectured two youngsters who asked for cigarettes; gave street directions; took custody of a watch to give the repair man across the street when he opened later; gave out information on the range of rents in the neighborhood to an apartment seeker; listened to a tale of domestic difficulty and offered reassurance; told some rowdies they could not come in unless they behaved and then defined (and got) good behavior; provided an incidental forum for half a dozen conversations among customers who dropped in for oddments; set aside certain newly arrived papers and magazines for regular customers who would depend on getting them; advised a mother who came for a birthday present not to get the ship-model kit because another child going to the same birthday party was giving that; and got a back copy (this was for me) of the previous day's newspaper out of the deliverer's surplus returns when he came by.

Notice that after he helps the children cross the street, Bernie Jaffe lends an umbrella and a small amount of money to some customers, while he keeps some items for other people of the neighborhood. The store owner's services now extend to some of the younger members of the community as he lectures "two youngsters who asked for cigarettes"; he also gives street directions and provides an apartment seeker with "information on the range of rents in the neighborhood . . ." The remainder of the paragraph shows the candy store owner performing similar neighborhood services. The paragraph concludes with the description of a service done for the writer herself: Bernie has obtained for her a copy of the previous day's newspaper.

We notice that the writer has deliberately combined the different kinds of services performed by the storekeeper. At the beginning of the paragraph, Bernie "took custody of two keys," and after taking in some packages and lecturing the two youngsters who tried to buy cigarettes, he "took custody of a watch" to give to another businessman later in the day. In addition, Bernie gives out information to various people and even offers reassurance to "a tale of domestic difficulty," and then we see him lecturing again as he tells "some rowdies that they could not come in unless they behaved." One effect of this mixture of details is that the reader has a real sense of the remarkable variety of Bernie Jaffe's activities in the course of an "ordinary morning."

We also notice that most of the activities described in the paragraph have little if anything to do with Mr. Jaffe's business. Unless we were told, we would hardly know the activities of a candy store owner were being described. In fact, the few times that candy store items are mentioned, they are not presented as examples of Mr. Jaffe's business transactions. For example, he does not sell the cigarettes to the two youngsters, he advises the mother who came to buy a birthday present *not* to buy the ship model kit, and when he does sell something connected with his business, it is a *back copy* of a newspaper. The author seems to deliberately avoid showing us Mr. Jaffe as a businessman, and even the details in the paragraph that do relate to the candy store are presented as examples of the owner's services to the community.

PARAGRAPH PRACTICE

Write a paragraph of your own, using the above portion of the Jane Jacobs paragraph as your model. Your paragraph could be a description of a typical morning, afternoon, or evening in the life of someone you know—or, if you prefer, in your own life. For example, you could describe the different morning activities of your own neighborhood candy store owner, or what your local grocer (or some other merchant) does every afternoon, or the usual tasks you find yourself doing every evening.

In your paragraph, imitate Jane Jacobs' technique by including a number of very specific details. The activities of the person you are describing will be more vivid and immediate for your reader when you are careful to include a representative sampling of those activities. You can also give greater interest to your paragraph if the first two or three details you include are unrelated to the person's occupation; the final detail could be one that is related to what the person does for a living. For example, if you choose to describe what your local mail deliverer does each morning, you might wish to include the fact that he or she reminds a merchant that his car is parked illegally, then brings a message from another merchant to an elderly person who cannot get out of the house, and then, last but not least, delivers the mail to the people of the neighborhood.

No matter what local person you choose to describe, your paragraph will gain strength from your choice of details and interest from the variety of those details.

ESSAY PRACTICE

The following outline will help you plan a complete essay of at least five paragraphs. The theme of your essay will be closely related to the Jane Jacobs selection.

The following sentence may serve as your thesis sentence, and will also be the main idea of your introductory paragraph:

¶ 1. Being a good neighbor means cooperating with others and watching out for them.

Each of the sentences below is the topic sentence for one of the paragraphs that you will write to develop your thesis. You may use the suggested details to develop each paragraph, or you may supply details of your own.

¶ 2. There are many ways that people who live in the same neighborhood can be helpful to each other.

[DETAILS: From your own experience, what are some of the ways the people of a neighborhood can show concern for each other? For example, how do some people in a neighborhood look after the special needs of older people in the area? How do some people help look after their neighbors' children in the course of a typical day? In this paragraph, you could combine examples from your own experience with examples of what you would consider an ideal neighborhood.]

¶ 3. In the process of helping each other, people can also help maintain the quality of their neighborhood.

[DETAILS: How does cooperation among the people of a neighborhood enhance the quality of that neighborhood? You could develop this paragraph by including the obvious signs of a well-maintained neighborhood, including clean sidewalks, freshly painted doors and windows, and perhaps even flowers and shrubs. How does each detail you have chosen reveal the people's sense of caring for their neighborhood?]

¶ 4. These days, helping your neighborhood is not only worthwhile, it is absolutely necessary.

[DETAILS: In this paragraph you could describe the real need for maintaining a sense of community. How necessary is this for protection against crime? How important is this sense of community in obtaining better local services?]

Be certain that you use transitions between paragraphs to make your writing flow smoothly. In addition, be sure that your conclusion gives your reader a clear signal that you have come to the end of your essay.

ESSAY TOPICS

1. You are about to move into a new area. Analyze your prospective neighborhood. Base your analysis on the factors you consider most important for a good neighborhood.
2. Analyze your relationship with the people who work in the stores where you shop. How well do these people know you? Are you just another customer to them, no matter how long you have shopped there, or have you become friendly with at least a few of your local merchants?
3. a. Analyze why some people want to live in a big city neighborhood where few people know them. What kind of person is attracted to this kind of lifestyle?
   b. Analyze the advantages and disadvantages of living in a small town or rural area. What features does a small town or rural area have that a city cannot offer?

◄§ *Margaret Mead and Rhoda Metraux* ◊◙

Margaret Mead (1901–1978) was one of the most famous anthropologists America has produced. After graduation from Barnard College and Columbia University, she did extensive field work in New Guinea. Later, Dr. Mead studied many different kinds of societies, from Asia to the United States, and some of her final studies involved a close examination of our own American customs. The following essay, written with her associate Rhoda Metraux, is a good example of Margaret Mead's ability to make a close study of her culture and report her perceptions objectively.[1]

Rhoda Metraux (1914–) is an anthropologist who has studied people and their cultures in Europe, Haiti, the West Indies, and Mexico. "The Nudist Idea" is taken from *A Way of Seeing*, a book Professor Metraux and Margaret Mead published in 1970. The essay gives us a closeup view of a part of our culture that has not generally received much exposure.

PREVIEWING THE WRITER

• Note the history of the nudist movement. In what ways are nudist camps today similar to the first nudist camps? In what ways are they different?

• Note the details of life in a nudist camp. In what ways are the regulations in nudist camps very much like those of any other social club or organization?

• Note the writers' predictions regarding the future of nudism in our culture. What aspects of modern society seem to have helped prepare the way for a wider acceptance of nudist ideas?

THE NUDIST IDEA

SOME OF THE pleasanter parts of the country shelter   1
resorts that are carefully screened from public view and firmly barricaded against invasion by unfriendly or merely curious sight-seers and strangers. Externally there is little to distinguish these resorts from others to which Americans flock for weekend

[1]For additional details on Margaret Mead's life and career, see the introduction to her essay "From Popping the Question to Popping the Pill," p. 264.

and holiday outings. Why, then, the barriers? Essentially they are a safeguard both for those inside and those who stay outside.

For in these enclosed resorts members of nudist clubs 2 gather, mostly in family groups, to swim and sunbathe, play volleyball, stroll, picnic or just relax in the warm sunshine and tan their bodies from head to toe. They are the outdoor settings in which enthusiasts carry out their conviction that wearing clothes is a hindrance to the health and well-being of men and women and children, their belief that social nudism is truly the way to a new morality and a new democracy in human relations.

In fact, nudists don't object to functional articles of cloth- 3 ing. Sunbathers wear hats to shield their heads from glaring light and sandals to protect their feet. Other modifications of nudity are permitted, and still others are insisted upon. Newcomers are allowed a period of grace, for instance, before they take the final plunge. Untrained toddlers must wear diapers. Teen-agers, who are welcome only in the company of their parents, may wear clothes if they want to. But the belief that social nudity is natural, good and wholesome sets the style of people's appearance and governs their rules of behavior at each of the resorts.

There are a thousand or more nudist parks across the 4 country. Although each seems to have its own identity and local atmosphere, the parks do have certain things in common. One is the big swimming pool, with a wide sunbathing area around it where people gather to chat in relaxed comfort. Another is a volleyball court—perhaps several courts—for this is the one game most sunbathers seem to enjoy. There is also their protected seclusion. Nudists, as individuals and as organized groups, have had to fight innumerable legal battles for the right to live according to their ideal, but they are still a group set apart.

In other respects there are variations among parks. Some 5 resemble more-familiar kinds of resorts for the well-to-do, with spacious grounds and facilities for many kinds of outdoor recreation. Members may have cottages or cabins. There may be a central lodge with a dining room, a recreation hall, and a great fireplace for chilly hours. At the other extreme are parks that are laid out as campgrounds, with trailer and tent sites and a simple snack canteen. Some parks operate only during the warm summer-holiday season. Others, in milder climates, may be open the year round, and some invite attendance by vacationing nudist club members who live far away. But by and large each resort draws for its membership on an area within which people can travel comfortably for a weekend or for a day's outing.

Clubs also share in their basic rules of membership and behavior. Only adults can join and membership is generally in family units: husbands and wives and their children. The number of "singles" accepted is relatively small. First names only are used in introductions; generally, only as much is known about a person's background and occupation as the individual chooses to confide. This is in keeping with the belief that by divesting themselves of artificial distinctions along with their clothes, people can meet on more natural and equal terms. But partial anonymity also serves as one more protective device for those who feel that they may be ridiculed or even persecuted for their beliefs at any time by a prejudiced outside world. Similarly there is a taboo on religious and political discussions, as inherently divisive and emotion-ridden topics. Much more fundamental is the taboo on touching and body contact. At dances everyone puts on clothes. 6

The plunge into nudism by novices is reported to be a pretty violent one. But once newcomers catch their breath, they find themselves taking part in a life of domestic bliss where husbands and wives walk about naked and as unconscious of each other as in the days before the serpent entered the Garden. This at least is the hope, and, in some nudist camps, the rule. 7

Two things seem to make this possible. One is the sense of congenial companionship among the sunbathing families who meet at nudist resorts. The other is the members' firm adherence to accepted practice. Although there have been modifications over time, arising from more general changes in American tastes, nudist groups retain the austere rules and moral attitudes that characterized the movement when it was imported into this country. 8

Social nudism had its beginnings in Germany around the turn of the century, and the idea spread as a kind of secular cult in the years immediately following World War I. Initially it had strong overtones of righteous rebellion against a society that was conceived of as hypocritical, corrupt and coercive. The nudist idea was combined with a belief in the healthful value of body-building exercises; converts not only swam and sunbathed but also took part in energetic calisthenics. Similarly they de- 9 nounced the use of stimulants and intoxicants, and many became vegetarians. For social nudists, however, the central aim was—and still is—a new morality based on a shame-free acceptance of the whole human body.

As the movement has grown and spread in the United   10
States over the last forty years most of the faddist characteristics, including the emphasis on exercise, have been lost. There is smoking in many parks, and in some the rules have been modified to permit a modest bar on the premises. At the same time, however, true believers still tend to see themselves as pioneers in a potentially—and sometimes even actively—hostile world.

Yet in the same period we have lived through an almost   11
worldwide revolution in standards of publicly acceptable dress and behavior. There is almost no limit to what can be shown on the stage or screen. And few voices are raised in condemnation as people of all ages, dressed in costumes that combine the barest concession to decency with an almost total surrender to seduction, lie entwined on beaches or romp in the water, touching and tumbling, teasing and courting each other.

Why, then, do nudist resorts continue to multiply and   12
nudist clubs to increase their membership? And why, on the other hand, do outsiders continue to regard social nudism with suspicion and antipathy?

In thinking about this I turn back to New Guinea, where   13
I once lived with a people who wore hardly any clothes, just a G string for the men and a little apronlike grass skirt for the women. Nearby there were a people who went stark naked except for beautiful ornaments of fur and bird-of-paradise feathers that they wore on their heads. Very frequently I saw the stark-naked men striding, heads high and unashamed, through the village of their slightly clothed neighbors. But I also saw the air of disdain with which my own villagers looked on those who had not yet imported the right to dress, and I heard them snicker with squeamish superiority. Lightly clad as they were, they felt shame in the presence of nakedness.

Elsewhere in New Guinea I have lived among a people,   14
wearing as few clothes, who were so puritanical that no woman would completely remove her grass skirt in the presence of another woman even during childbirth. And when a widow ceremonially walked naked into the sea, accompanied by a row of clothed women, all men had to remain inside the houses behind

barred doors. Among these prudish and puritanical people, men told salacious stories of hiding, in order to watch, by the paths along which naked women from inland villages walked.

Certainly one function of dress is to create a state of indiscriminate sexual awareness that is unrelated to the individual as such, so that the very idea of taking off whatever is normally worn in public makes a woman—any woman—desirable in fantasy, if not in reality. Such fantasies in turn foster shame and fears of exposure. No doubt the more that women are covered up, the greater are real ignorance and also the artificial excitement and anxieties that fantasies of exposure generate. 15

Early nudists rebelled against the excesses of Victorian prudery and the burdensome taboos that stifled the human spirit the way distorting layers of clothes stifled the human body. Other rebels advocated other kinds of freedom—free verse and free love and a freer enjoyment of the good things in life. But the nudists, in breaking down one major taboo, had to give up much else. The price they had to pay for the right to strip off the concealing envelope of clothing was the maintenance of a rigid puritanism in other respects, including the taboo on body contact. 16

Today we have substituted for Victorian obsessive prudery an equally obsessive and doubtfully healthier exhibitionism. Those things that once were hidden are not merely revealed but publicly flaunted. This reversal—and an emphasis on transparency—goes far beyond dress. Picture windows reveal the life going on inside the home, and vast expanses of glass expose to the outer world men at work in banks and other businesses. Plastic chairs not only contain but also display the persons sitting in them. The "glass lady" exhibited in museums reveals the inner organs of the body, and sound-taped operations give us a surgeon's view of the body's interior. In clothing styles we accentuate all that remains unrevealed. The young wife buys a mother-to-be dress to advertise her otherwise as-yet-unobservable pregnancy when her grandmother or even her mother wore a maternity dress in some hope of concealing her state. 17

Early social nudists were extreme and cultist precursors of the present situation. But perhaps nudism is coming to have a new contemporary significance in a world that has moved from concealment to transparency and accentuated revelation. What nudists have tried and are still trying to do is break the links between dress and fantasy and shame, by turning what has 18 been shameful and therefore a subject of fantasy into acceptable everyday experience.

It may be that we *are* moving in this direction. But most people have very little opportunity for experimentation. In vast urban areas there is no escape from possibly censorious neighbors. People may hear about the "free" European beaches where bathers of both sexes sunbathe and swim together matter-of-factly and without the slightest embarrassment. And faintly Freudian echoes of the ill effects on children of never seeing human bodies of both sexes and all ages filter through to parents in books and articles. But most adults are still too shy to attempt radical innovations on their own initiative. 19

Nudist parks, registered, legal and sheltered, give them a chance to make the trial. Here they can depend on the experience of older practitioners and gain assurance through the system of protective rules. Though most new arrivals seem to have last-minute doubts, when they do take their clothes off they make two comforting discoveries. The first is that nothing at all happens; their anxieties were quite needless. The second is that their new companions are families very much like their own. 20

Although it has been said by some psychiatrists that social nudists do not differ much from their contemporaries in their fantasy life, nudists themselves feel that they have been freed from disturbing fantasies. They feel more relaxed. Of course, even the most convinced advocates can practice what they so firmly believe only on a part-time basis. The rest of the time they live within the larger community, and some of their own rules reflect beliefs they share with the rest of the community. What they have demonstrated is that within limited settings, such as swimming and sunbathing, people can learn to accept their own bodies and the bodies of others of both sexes and all ages without embarrassment. 21

In the long run it may be that the acceptance of a limited range of social situations in which children can run free and adults can enjoy unexciting relaxation without wearing clothes will be the end result both of the nudist movement and the plastic transparency of everyday life. Mixed swimming under controlled conditions probably is not far away. And swimming and sunbathing are the two activities in which total nudity really makes sense in a temperate climate. Some clothing is necessary most of the time, simply for reasons of sanitation and safety. But not in the water. Beaches and lake shores could be the safe 22 and sensible setting within which everyone could learn relaxed acceptance of the human body as it really is.

This could mean a reduction in puritanism and prudery 23 that would ultimately lead to a decrease in neuroses and certain kinds of crime—but it will not come about overnight. The legacy of prudery is a long one, and fantasies that are fostered in early childhood are hard to outgrow or overcome. The sense of freedom gained in the puritanical setting of nudist resorts is one step away from prudery, but it is also a retreat from the freedom to express affection in public.

Wearing clothes has been one of the conditions necessary 24 for unembarrassed and easy physical contact between human beings in public situations. What we need is both freedom from prudery and the freedom to express our feelings.

THE WRITERS' THEMES

1. What is the nudist philosophy? What were the early nudists reacting against? Are today's nudists reacting against the same things, or do they have different reasons for following the nudist philosophy?
2. In what ways are the rules that govern nudist camps the same as rules that govern other organizations? Why have nudist clubs made up special rules for themselves?
3. According to the writers, in how many ways are we exposed to public view in our daily lives? How does this type of exposure differ from nudism? What does it have in common with nudism?

THE WRITERS' TECHNIQUE

In paragraph six of their essay, Margaret Mead and Rhoda Metraux describe some of the basic rules and regulations of nudist camps. Here is that paragraph:

> Clubs also share in their basic rules of membership and behavior. Only adults can join and membership is generally in family units: husbands and wives and their children. The number of "singles" accepted is relatively small. First names only are used in introductions; generally, only as much is known about a person's

background and occupation as the individual chooses to confide. This is in keeping with the belief that by divesting themselves of artificial distinctions along with their clothes, people can meet on more natural and equal terms. But partial anonymity also serves as one more protective device for those who feel that they may be ridiculed or even persecuted for their beliefs at any time by a prejudiced outside world. Similarly there is a taboo on religious and political discussions, as inherently divisive and emotion-ridden topics. Much more fundamental is the taboo on touching and body contact. At dances everyone puts on clothes.

Notice that in the topic sentence, the writers announce that they will describe the ''basic rules of membership and behavior'' of the clubs. They then note that only adults can join, and that people usually join as a family; the number of single people who are accepted for membership is ''relatively small.''

The writers then describe how the people at the camps treat each other. When they are introduced, only first names are used, and people know only as much about an individual as that person ''chooses to confide.'' Two reasons are given for this practice. By using only first names, nudists believe that ''people can meet on more natural and equal terms''; the custom also serves ''as one more protective device'' for those who are afraid of possible harassment from ''a prejudiced outside world.''

Finally, the writers deal with some of the ''taboos'' that exist in nudist camps. Religious and political discussions are avoided, but even ''more fundamental'' is the taboo on ''touching and body contact.'' As proof of this, the writers note in their last sentence that at nudist dances, ''everyone puts on clothes.''

PARAGRAPH PRACTICE

Write a paragraph of your own, using the above paragraph as your model. Your paragraph could describe a club or organization you belong to, or that you know very well. First, indicate the extent to which you are going to describe the rules and regulations of this particular organization. Then, give an idea of the membership by describing who can join this organization. What kind of people make up most of the membership? What other types of people may be found among the members?

Next, describe how the people in this club act toward each other. How do the members address each other, formally or informally? Does everyone in the club know everyone else, or does the organization consist of a number of small groups, each of which tends to keep to itself?

Finally, point out one or two things that are either not allowed or not encouraged in this club. What are the taboos of the club you are describing? Why do the members of this club agree on these points?

ESSAY PRACTICE

The following outline will help you plan a complete essay of at least five paragraphs. The theme of your essay will be closely related to "The Nudist Idea."

The following sentence may serve as your thesis sentence, and will also be the main idea of your introductory paragraph:

¶ 1. The control of crime depends on the degree of strictness (or the degree of liberalism) in a society.

Each of the sentences below is the topic sentence for one of the paragraphs that you will write to develop your thesis. You may use the suggested details to develop each paragraph, or you may supply details of your own.

¶ 2. There is a connection in our society between social permissiveness and certain kinds of crime.

[DETAILS: To what extent does violence on television and in films lead to the violence we hear about in the news every day? Do you believe that the availability of pornographic material is related to the likelihood of increased sexual assaults on people? Does easy access to guns encourage violence?]

¶ 3. These kinds of crimes increase (or decrease) depending on the degree of control we exercise over certain areas of our lives.

[DETAILS: Would a loosening of restrictions in certain areas, such as fashions and television programming, lead to an increase in crime, or in your opinion would such a loosening of restrictions actually lessen the crime rate? In your view, what individuals should be allowed to have guns?]

¶ 4. This increase (or decrease) in social controls is likely (or unlikely) to happen because . . .

[DETAILS: Tell why you believe these controls will or will not be increasingly important in our society, at least in the foreseeable future. In your opinion, will our society be more or less liberal in the future?]

Be certain that you use transitions between paragraphs to make your writing flow smoothly. In addition, be sure that your conclusion gives your reader a clear signal that you have come to the end of your essay.

ESSAY TOPICS

1. Define and analyze the terms "liberal" and "conservative." Show how these terms apply to politics, religion, morality, dress, and a conservative or liberal philosophy of life. In each case, provide specific examples based on your own experience, the experience of our culture today, or based on a particular period of history that you have studied.

2. We can define ourselves and others in many ways. For example, we could define a friend as a Democrat, a Protestant, and an animal lover. Each term helps us to define the person, and the more details we provide the sharper our definition will be.

   Choose several terms that would define yourself or someone you know well. With each term you use, provide an extended definition of that term that will help your reader understand how you are using the term. For example, it is not enough to simply say that a person is a Democrat; there are liberal Democrats and conservative Democrats. Many people are animal lovers, but if you write about a friend as an active conservationist, deeply committed to the preservation of endangered species, your reader will have a better picture of the person after knowing these facts.

3. For most people, nudism is a radical idea. What other philosophies or ways of living do you consider radical, or even dangerous for our society? Provide an extended definition of one or more of these philosophies. For example, if you decided to write about punk rock, you could provide a definition of the term by first giving your own one-sentence definition (such a modern phenomenon would not usually be found in a dictionary or other standard reference work). You could make this definition by putting the term into a larger class where it belongs (in this case, popular music), and then give its distinguishing characteristics.

For your extended definition or analysis, you may want to include some historical background, causes and effects of the phenomenon, the psychology of punk rock, or even a personal experience when you heard that type of music for the first time. You could also give examples of particular groups and how they are examples of punk rock.

Note the elements of extended definition that are described in the introduction to this unit and use as many of these elements as you can to form your extended definition of the term you have chosen.

🍃 *William Zinsser* 🍃

William Zinsser (1922–   ) is a writer and professor who began his career as a journalist. In 1959, after thirteen years with the *New York Herald Tribune,* he left journalism to become a freelance writer, and for some years he was a regular contributor to major national magazines.

In 1970 William Zinsser was asked to design and teach the first nonfiction writing course at Yale University. In his own words, this work at Yale gave him the opportunity to "give back some of the things I had learned." One result of this course was *On Writing Well: An Informal Guide to Writing Nonfiction,* a widely used book of expert advice on the writer's craft. In 1979 the writer became executive editor of the Book-of-the-Month Club. He also continues to write for magazines, including the *New Yorker.*

William Zinsser is the author of several books, including *Seen Any Good Movies Lately?* (1958), *The City Dwellers* (1962), and *The Lunacy Boom* (1970). His most recent book is *Writing with a Word Processor.* "Whatever Happened to Privacy?" is an examination of a growing problem in our society. It appeared in *The Haircurl Papers,* a book of essays William Zinsser published in 1964.

PREVIEWING THE WRITER

- Note the writer's analysis of the different ways our privacy has been eroded in modern society. How many of these erosions are funny? How many of them do you believe the writer considers serious erosions of our privacy?
- Note the ways in which people from all walks of life seem to cooperate in the invasions of their own privacy.
- Note the writer's frequent references to television. Why is the writer's use of television appropriate in a discussion of privacy?

WHATEVER HAPPENED TO PRIVACY?

THE EXACT MOMENT when privacy began going out of   1
American life has never been fixed by scholars. Perhaps it was the day when Chic Young, creator of "Blondie," first put Dagwood in the bathtub. Since then countless children and dogs,

trooping in and out of Dagwood's bathroom, have sailed little boats in the water where he sat soaping. And countless real children (and dogs) have copied the custom, assuming it to be common behavior. Thus one of modern man's last sanctuaries has been invaded and despoiled.

Invading other people's privacy is now a big pursuit—and big business—in America. So is the voluntary surrender of privacy, judging by the large number of men and women who seem driven to make an outward show of their inner selves. Newspapers, magazines and televison programs are battening as never before on the personal lives of the famous, and no detail is too intimate to be made public, as President Eisenhower found during his recovery from a heart attack. In fact, anyone who tries to guard his privacy is regarded as somewhat odd and un-American.

Certainly a man's home is no longer his castle, or, if it is, the moat is dry and the portcullis[1] is always up. Nothing can stanch the daily tide of impersonal mail posing as personal mail, of salesmen at the door and strangers on the telephone. In the hands of the inconsiderate the telephone is a deadly weapon, but if a man dons armor against it by refusing to have his number listed in the directory, he must now pay a penalty. The New York Telephone Company has almost half a million of these diehards on its rolls—a figure which suggests that the urge for privacy is still alive, even if the respect for it is not. A few years ago the company became impatient with its unlisted patrons and put an extra charge on their monthly bill, hoping thereby to force them back into the listed world of good fellowship.

Modern architecture has also done its share to abolish privacy. The picture window was first designed by men like Frank Lloyd Wright to frame a scene of natural beauty. Today millions of Americans look out of picture windows into other picture windows and busy streets. The contractor has no sooner finished installing the picture window than the decorator is summoned to cover it with expensive curtains against an inquisitive world. Even then, privacy is uncertain. In many modern houses the rooms have yielded to "areas" that merge into each other, so that the husband trying to work in the "reading area" (formerly den) is naked to the blasts from the "recreation area" (formerly rumpus room) a few feet away.

2

3

4

---

[1] A sliding grille, suspended in the gateway of a castle or other fortified place, that could be quickly lowered in case of an attack.

If privacy is hard to find at home, it is almost extinct out- 5
side. Strangers in the next seat on trains and planes are seldom
given to vows of silence, and certainly the airline pilot is no
man to leave his passengers to their thoughts. His jovial voice
crackles out of the intercom whenever the customers are in any
danger of dropping off to sleep. Airplanes have also been infested by canned music, leaving the captive listener only one
method of escape—and no method if he wants to live to tell the
tale.

Unwanted music is privacy's constant enemy. There is 6
hardly an American restaurant, store, railroad station or bus
terminal that doesn't gurgle with melody from morning to night,
nor is it possible any longer to flee by boarding the train or bus
itself, or even by taking a walk in the park. Transistor radios
have changed all that. Men, women and children carry them
everywhere, hugging them with the desperate attachment that
a baby has for its blanket, fearful that they might have to generate an idea of their own or contemplate a blade of grass.
Thoughtless themselves, they have no thought for the sufferers
within earshot of their portentous news broadcasts and raucous
jazz. It is hardly surprising that RCA announced a plan that
would pipe canned music and pharmaceutical commercials to
25,000 doctors' offices in eighteen big cities—one place where a
decent quietude might be expected. This raises a whole new
criterion for choosing the family physician. Better to have a sec-
ond-rate healer content with the sounds of his stethoscope than
an eminent specialist poking to the rhythms of Gershwin.

If Americans no longer think twice about invading the privacy 7
of others, it is because popular example has demolished the very
concept, as anyone with a TV set will attest. The past decade
of television has been an orgy of prying and catharsis. Mike
Wallace first achieved fame as a TV inquisitor who left no question unasked. To Drew Pearson,[2] for instance, he said, "President Roosevelt once called you a chronic liar; President Truman
called you an S.O.B. at one time and a vicious liar at another
time. Could it be that you *are* a liar?" Wallace explained why
such questions are tolerated: "People's thresholds are lower
than they used to be."

Nor does TV fix its peeping eye only on the famous. Pro- 8
gram hosts ooze familiarity, no matter who comes into their

[2] Drew Pearson (1897–1969) was a widely known journalist.

net, and sooner or later almost everybody does. How many wretched women were induced to bare their miseries on "Queen for a Day"? How many couples exposed their marital troubles to dissection on "Divorce Court"? Small legions allowed such retrospective shows as "This Is Your Life" and "It Could Be You" to conjure up spirits from their unhappy past. Dr. Joyce Brothers had a program on which she answered questions on the sexual problems of her listeners, and Jack Paar in his long tenure on the "Tonight" show[3] frequently wheedled the audience's sympathy with tearful complaints about his personal woes. Who can forget his lachrymose return from exile after NBC suspended him? Jabbing at his various enemies, he had a special riposte for Walter Winchell,[4] who, he said, had defamed him and even questioned his virility. "As a moral man," Paar declaimed, "only my wife knows about my virility," and with this touching domestic vignette he routed the foe from darkest Hearstland.

Even more symbolic of the new age was Ed Murrow's "Person to Person." In its seven years more than 550 men and women welcomed this program's 19 million viewers into their homes. They included four Cabinet members, two Supreme Court justices, three college presidents, three bishops, many visiting heads of government, foreign diplomats of highest rank, governors and mayors, Congressmen and judges, generals and admirals, one ex-President and one ex-King of England.

"It was very rare of people to refuse on the grounds that it was an invasion of their privacy," says Jesse Zousmer, former producer of the show. "It became a question of prestige to be on it—sort of like being invited to the White House."

While TV programs thus invaded the privacy of men and women as a whole, TV commercials have gone after them limb by limb, and by now they have eroded most of the defenses that once surrounded the human body. When a toddler is old enough to turn a knob, he can see women flexing in girdles or "undies," or rejoicing in the thrust of a new brassiere. He can watch them spray deodorants or dab depilatories on themselves in a state of unaccountable rapture, or affix corn plasters to their tortured feet. Meanwhile, inside their transilluminated systems, little Mr. Aspirin is knocking at the door of the duodenum, Mr.

[3] Jack Paar was the host of TV's "Tonight" show from 1957 to 1962.

[4] Walter Winchell (1897–1972) was a widely read gossip columnist who also broadcast news items on his own radio program.

Laxative is dutifully hurrying toward the colon, and Mr. Nasal
Decongestant is flushing the eight sinus cavities.

In such an enlightened age, no wonder President Eisen-   12
hower's intestinal functions were front-page news. Three days
after the President's heart attack James C. Hagerty told a news
conference, "He had a good bowel movement," and Dr. Paul
Dudley White hurried to explain why he had included this extraordinary detail: "The country will be very pleased—the country is so bowel-minded anyway—to know that the President had
a good bowel movement this morning, and it is important."

Although assaults on privacy come from many sides, it is amaz-   13
ing how many are self-inflicted. Celebrities now disgorge their
blackest secrets in print, as if hoping to banish their private
demons by serving them at a public feast. From three such
confessions an industrious scribe named Gerold Frank has
mined one of the richest veins in recent literary annals. Frank
is the ghost who put to paper Lillian Roth's "I'll Cry Tomorrow," Diana Barrymore's "Too Much Too Soon" and Sheilah
Graham's "Beloved Infidel," books which together have sold 6
million copies and earned more than $750,000, including foreign
editions and royalties from the movies that Hollywood avidly
made from all three.[5]

In their books Miss Roth and Miss Barrymore told explic-   14
itly how an overdose of husbands and liquor reduced them to
squalid depths. "I told him things I wouldn't have told a priest,"
Miss Barrymore said, and Frank obviously had the same powers
of exorcism over Miss Graham. In her book she confessed that
her real name was Lily Sheil, which she loathed, and that her
upbringing was far shabbier than the one she had invented to
conceal it. "The whole of my childhood has been something
dark and secret to me," she said, "and the name I was born
with is tied up with the years I have kept hidden so long."

Miss Graham could have kept those years secret forever.   15
They are her business, or at least they would have been so
regarded in any era but this one, when there's no business like
everybody's business. As for Frank, he moved on to Zsa Zsa
Gabor, who promised to tell all, and "McCall's" had no doubt
that she would, for the magazine paid $100,000 for the rights,

---

[5] Singer Lillian Roth (1910–1980), who appeared in films and on stage;
actress Diana Barrymore (1921–1960), daughter of the actor John Barrymore;
writer and columnist Sheilah Graham (1908 [?]–), whose book *Beloved Infidel*
describes her relationship with the writer F. Scott Fitzgerald.

thereby giving new momentum to the wave of confessional journalism that has made "McCall's" rich—and has forced competitors like the "Ladies' Home Journal" to throw dignity to the winds and join the profitable game of disrobing the great.

This undressing has even taken literal form. The mother-in-law 16 of painter Larry Rivers once posed for him in the nude, and he exhibited the full-length portrait with the subject identified. During their marriage Tyrone Power and Linda Christian not only had themselves painted nude to the waist, but hung the portraits in their house and invited "Look" to publish photographs of them, which "Look" gladly did.

Such exhibitionism is not uncommon in people of artistic 17 bent. What *is* uncommon is for a country's leaders to drop their mask in public and help a photographer perform a stunt, as dozens did in Philippe Halsman's "Jump Book." Halsman persuaded his renowned subjects—including Richard Nixon, Adlai Stevenson, J. Robert Oppenheimer, Learned Hand and John J. McCloy—to jump for him. "One of our deepest urges," he says, "is to find out what the other person is like." But could he have persuaded America's illustrious men to take to the air ten or fifteen years ago?

Perhaps the snooping instinct has been sharpened by the 18 kind of magazine reporting that digs as deeply into a man as gall and tenacity will permit. "Time" boasts that its writers and researchers spend weeks trailing the subject of a cover story, detecting mannerisms that the subject's husband or wife never noticed. These techniques have undoubtedly inspired countless newspapermen, especially those who intrude on a family in their moment of grief after a tragedy. Sidney Skolsky is only being true to modern journalism's creed when he asks every Hollywood star if she (or he) sleeps in pajama tops, bottoms, or neither, and usually gets neither for an answer.

Serious writing has also suffered strange inroads. Before 19 television, authors generally worked in seclusion while publishers tried to sell their books. Now it is necessary to sell the man as well as the book, and publishers try hard to get their writers onto "Today," "Tonight" and other shows moderated by popular hosts, who have thus become literary arbiters with considerable influence. Rare is the author, like J. D. Salinger, who refuses to undergo this kind of promotion. Meanwhile all sorts of entertainers have suddenly blossomed into "authors"—and best-selling authors, too. They go from show to show, touting their "books" and each other's books, which accounts for the success of these volumes, unaccountable by literary standards.

The decline of privacy coincides—by no accident—with the rise of the "public relations consultant," one of the high priests of modern American life. (Manhattan listed ten public relations firms in 1935; today there are at least 1,200 in the United States.) His original purpose was to knead the public image of his client, like a lump of clay, into a fresh and attractive shape. In some cases this means a lot of kneading, for he is often called upon to repair a reputation that was damaged almost beyond mortal help.   20

Today the function of the "p.r." man has grown far beyond these mere overhauls. Now the task is not so much to shine an image that has tarnished as to create one where none existed before. Hitherto faceless and nameless corporation presidents, bankers and other executives by the hundreds allow themselves to be converted into "personalities" by such puppeteers as Ben Sonnenberg, on the theory that a company is more lovable if its officers are, too. To help sell the man is to help sell the product.   21

One of privacy's last preserves used to be "Society," and it still is in most countries. Society is founded, after all, on the principle of excluding almost everybody else. "Not to attract attention to oneself in public," declared Emily Post, "is one of the fundamental rules of good breeding." This fundamental rule is still observed by those who already belong to the aristocracy—and is doggedly broken by those who are trying to get there, aided by the public relations consultant. Most ladies in this category now hire a press agent to get their name and picture into print as often as possible, and they invite the press to their private social affairs in such volume that they seem, judging by the subsequent accounts, to have invited none of their private social friends.   22

"I'm asked to many parties," says Eugenia Sheppard, the New York "Herald Tribune's" lively columnist, "for no reason except that the hostesses expect me to write about them, and when I go I meet all the other fashion and society reporters." Certain ladies do indeed turn up with astonishing frequency in the New York papers, and it doesn't take a puzzle expert to locate them in print roughly once a day.   23

So far have the barriers fallen that Americans seldom think of invoking their moral and legal rights to privacy. As a people we   24 are endearingly nice to strangers who pester us at the door or on the phone, apologizing elaborately for not doing what they so unfeelingly ask. We can rarely bring ourselves to ask a cab driver to turn off his radio or his voice. Not to call a man "Jim" or "Jack" from the first handshake is to sully the notion that we are all old pals together in the great Waring Blendor called America.

The legal case for privacy was eloquently stated by Louis D. Brandeis as far back as 1890, and his words are, needless to say, infinitely more pressing today: "The intensity and complexity of life, attendant upon advancing civilization, have rendered necessary some retreat from the world, and man, under the refining influence of culture, has become more sensitive to publicity, so that solitude and privacy have become more essential to the individual; but modern invention and enterprise have, through invasions upon his privacy, subjected him to mental pain and distress, far greater than could be inflicted by mere bodily injury."

Yet only rarely does a knight rise in full view to hurl back the enemy—so rarely that it is always a memorable moment when he does. One such moment was Randolph Churchill's reply to John Wingate when that TV interviewer asked a nosy question on his "Night Beat" program about "the arrest of your sister Sarah in California." Churchill snapped: "I do not intend to discuss it with you. I never discuss matters relating to my family with total strangers. I wouldn't think of asking you about your sister. Why the hell should I let myself be bullied around and kicked around by you? Your shame is on your own head."

Equally stern was Steven Rockefeller's answer to reporters angry at being barred from his church wedding in a small town in Norway. "You represent the freedom of the press and I represent the privacy of an individual," he said. "To me this church service is a religious occasion and I am not a public figure."

What other oases of privacy remain? They can be almost counted on the fingers of a first baseman's mitt. One, paradoxically, is the commuter train. Though it is densely packed with men on its morning and evening journey, the man in the next seat occupies an inviolate island of silence, even if he is a close friend. Another oasis is the gentlemen's club. In that temple Emily Post brooks nothing but spartan self-control. "It is one of the unbreakable rules not to speak to anybody who is reading or writing," she says, and she might have added sleeping. "If a new member happens to find at the club no one whom he knows, he goes about his own affairs. He either reads, writes, or looks out the window, or plays solitaire, or occupies himself as he would if he were alone in a hotel.''

Sometimes in the strangling streets of Manhattan, a relic ²⁹ of privacy's golden age comes purring by and gives the heart a brief lift. It is a shiny cabriolet, its rear seat windowless and almost hidden from view. But in those dark shadows a bright object occasionally glitters. Is it the diamond choker of a very old lady going to tea with a girlhood friend? Is it the stickpin of a very old tycoon bound for his bank vault? Nobody on the sidewalk knows, and nobody every will.

THE WRITER'S THEMES

1. Trace the writer's use of military images in the opening paragraphs of his essay. For example, at the end of the first paragraph we are told that one of modern man's last sanctuaries "has been invaded and despoiled." Find at least four or five other words or phrases in the first three paragraphs that show these military images. What does the writer emphasize by using such words and phrases?
2. Review all of the writer's references to the world of television. How does the writer's frequent use of television strengthen the main point that he develops throughout the essay?
3. Toward the end of his essay, William Zinsser points to some of the people who have defended the individual's right to privacy. How is this defense of privacy strengthened by the fact that the three individuals the writer uses are Emily Post, a member of the Churchill family, and a Rockefeller?

THE WRITER'S TECHNIQUE

In paragraph twenty-eight of his essay, William Zinsser examines those few areas (he calls them "oases") of our lives where privacy still exists. Here is that paragraph:

> What other oases of privacy remain? They can be almost counted on the fingers of a first baseman's mitt. One, paradoxically, is the commuter train. Though it is densely packed with

men on its morning and evening journey, the man in the next seat occupies an inviolate island of silence, even if he is a close friend. Another oasis is the gentlemen's club. In that temple Emily Post brooks nothing but spartan self-control. "It is one of the unbreakable rules not to speak to anybody who is reading or writing," she says, and she might have added sleeping. "If a new member happens to find at the club no one whom he knows, he goes about his own affairs. He either reads, writes, or looks out the window, or plays solitaire, or occupies himself as he would if he were alone in a hotel."

The writer begins with a question ("What other oases of privacy remain?") and then answers it humorously: the remaining areas of privacy can almost be counted "on the fingers of a first baseman's mitt." He then proceeds to give examples of these few oases, and begins with the commuter train. He proves that the train provides privacy when he notes that, even though it is crowded morning and evening, "the man in the next seat occupies an inviolate island of silence, even if he is a close friend."

The writer then proceeds to his second example, that of "the gentleman's club." In that oasis (and here the writer quotes a famous authority on etiquette, Emily Post) it is "one of the unbreakable rules not to speak to anyone who is reading or writing." If a person finds himself alone in such a club "he goes about his own affairs."

Notice that after the writer has announced that there are very few "oases of privacy" remaining in our world, he makes sure that he proves his point by using only two examples, the commuter train and the gentleman's club. In each case, however, the example that supports the writer's point is presented in detail. We see the commuter train "densely packed with men" both "morning and evening," and we see men sitting next to each other but not speaking to each other, even if they are friends.

The writer's second example is also presented in detail, and in this case the details are from Emily Post, one of the most respected observers of social customs and manners. The quotation from Emily Post, which makes up most of the remainder of the paragraph, is filled with specific details: if a man finds himself alone at a club, he either "reads, writes, or looks out the window, or plays solitaire, or occupies himself as he would if he were alone in a hotel." In choosing this excerpt from Emily

Post, William Zinsser lends authority to his paragraph. We are convinced by the number of details in the paragraph and the quality of those details, and we respect their source.

PARAGRAPH PRACTICE

Write a paragraph of your own, using William Zinsser's paragraph as your model. In your paragraph describe two "oases of privacy" that are left in our lives. Your examples could range from driving alone in a car to studying in a secluded part of a library.

Even though you will use only two examples to illustrate the point that there is little privacy these days, provide several details to support each point. If you choose driving alone in a car, you could make your example more convincing by showing yourself alone in the car, surrounded by other cars with many of those drivers also traveling alone. If you choose the example of studying alone in a library, you could emphasize your solitude by describing the sound (or absence of sound) as you study, along with the fact that many people can walk by and not bother you.

No matter which examples you choose, your paragraph will be a more convincing description of oases of privacy if you show yourself surrounded by other people who either cannot disturb you, or choose not to bother you. When you provide several specific details to illustrate your examples, you help your reader see you in these situations, in much the same way that we are able to see the man in William Zinsser's paragraph as he goes about his own affairs in the club.

ESSAY PRACTICE

The following outline will help you plan a complete essay of at least five paragraphs. The theme of your essay will be closely related to the William Zinsser essay.

The following sentence may serve as your thesis sentence, and will also be the main idea of your introductory paragraph:

¶ 1. The entire concept of privacy is under attack in our society, and we maintain our privacy only with difficulty.

Each of the sentences below is the topic sentence for one of the paragraphs that you will write to develop your thesis.

You may use the suggested details to develop each paragraph, or you may supply details of your own.

¶ 2. I find that nowadays my privacy is very often invaded.

[DETAILS: How is your privacy invaded? For example, do you find yourself receiving unwanted letters and phone calls from salespeople? What are some other areas of your life (at school or at work) where you have also noticed erosions of your privacy? How have you reacted to these instrusions on your privacy?]

¶ 3. People in many areas of public life seem to have virtually no privacy these days.

[DETAILS: Describe how the lives of people in politics and in the world of show business are exposed to public view. What kinds of newspapers and magazines devote a great deal of attention to this kind of reporting? In your opinion, how many of these public figures really want to avoid this publicity? How many of them do you believe actually look for any kind of publicity?]

¶ 4. It may be difficult, but if a person really wants privacy there are ways to get it.

[DETAILS: Despite the lack of privacy in many areas of our lives, what steps can we take to protect that privacy? In this paragraph include specific details that show what a person can do to preserve or regain needed privacy. Would an unlisted telephone number help prevent unwanted calls? Should unwanted letters and other material that comes in the mail be sent back through the post office, marked "refused"?]

Be certain that you use transitions between paragraphs to make your writing flow smoothly. In addition, be sure that your conclusion gives your reader a clear signal that you have come to the end of your essay.

ESSAY TOPICS

1. Each person has a different definition of what constitutes privacy. Choose three types of people and examine what each type of person's definition of privacy might be. For example, you could choose an entertainer, a single person living in a small town, a very wealthy businessman, or yourself. Using these examples, or others you can think of, define what privacy means to each one. For example, why would a wealthy businessman with an important art collec-

330 ?● SELF AND SOCIETY

tion not want any publicity about his collection? Why would an entertainer who is marrying for the eighth time want national coverage of the latest wedding? Why would a student want a single room, rather than a double room, in a dormitory?

2. a. Imagine possible responses to the following situation: a friend of yours has invaded your privacy in some way. You may have been asked to buy housewares, hardware, or cosmetics that your friend was selling, or you may have been asked by a neighbor to buy a magazine subscription. Do you consider such situations or requests to be invasions of your privacy? How do you handle such situations?

   b. We hear a great deal about people who go to great lengths, including legal action, if they feel their privacy has been invaded. What would you consider a serious invasion of your privacy? Under what circumstances would you consider suing an individual or an institution for an invasion of your privacy?

3. a. All of us have felt uncomfortable at one time or another when a stranger begins talking to us in a public place. What are your reactions when a stranger begins talking to you under such circumstances? To what extent does your reaction depend on where you are at the time? Analyze one or two actual situations where your response to a stranger's remarks led to some good (or unfortunate) results for you.

   b. When do you feel comfortable beginning a conversation with a stranger? Describe any rules you have made for yourself that help you decide when to speak to a stranger.

Focus on Terms: Point of View

Point of view is the position a writer takes in relation to the material being presented. Point of view is important because, depending on the view the writer chooses, the reader's view of the subject will be altered. For example, in the selection from *The Death and Life of Great American Cities,* Jane Jacobs is writing as a resident of her neighborhood. Her report would have a very different effect if she wrote simply as a visitor to that neighborhood. On the other hand, when Margaret Mead and Rhoda Metraux write about "The Nudist Idea," our belief in their objectivity is strengthened by the fact that they do not present their findings as either believers or nonbelievers in nudism. By placing themselves as impartial observers outside the world of nudism, they lend authority to their point of view.

When Doris Lessing describes her experience in "Being Prohibited," we are aware that the writer is giving a highly subjective first-person report of a potentially dangerous situation. If we were to read a description of the same sequence of events from the point of view of, for example, the border official who interrogated her, we would have a very different account indeed.

When you are about to write an essay, you should consider your own point of view as a writer. Are you writing a science report as a person who actually performed the experiments you are describing, or have you assembled the results of other people's experiments? When you write an argument for or against a certain proposal, are you writing as a neutral reporter, or do you have some interest in the eventual outcome? If you are an authority on your subject, you should make that fact clear. Your relationship toward your subject is an important factor in how your reader will receive your work.

Student Essay ◂◂ ◂◂ Ellen Palombi

In recent years the great interest in rediscovering one's roots has resulted in some dramatic descriptions of the search for self. Alex Haley's *Roots* is probably the most famous example of this kind of search, but throughout America people in all walks of life are quietly reconstructing their past in order to find out where they have come from and to help define who they are.

The following essay analyzes what it means to belong to an ethnic group and what it means to rediscover one's connection to that group. By the end of the essay the writer is able to show us that the new direction of her life has added still another link to the chain that is her heritage.

• As you read the author's analysis of her childhood, notice that the writer uses the first-person point of view. Because of this, we are able to see through her eyes the various incidents she describes.

THE UNBREAKABLE CHAIN

I THINK it is pretty safe to say that, in the fifties, 1 Brooklyn was Jewish. I mean, it was all around you. You couldn't walk down the street without your nostrils being assaulted by the indescribable essence of the potato knishes sitting in the window of any one of a hundred delicatessens. Or pass the kosher butcher without a neighbor bellowing, "So how's your mama?"

On Friday nights, the roast chicken and matzoh ball soup 2 would be there at the table as sure as your own presence. And on Saturdays you sat quietly at home, not being able to write or cut or watch televison. You were only allowed the "privilege" of waiting for the grandparents to arrive with the dusk of evening and for the dinner of roast beef and oven-browned potatoes to begin.

Grandma always brought chocolates. Immediately after 3 dinner large bars of Nestle's would appear; one plain, one with almonds, and of course the semi-sweet kind for Dad, a son-in-law surprisingly appraised as "good enough" by the family matriarch. To me, this was the way of all families, and I assumed I would grow up and get married and roast chickens on Friday nights.

In 1959, we fled Brooklyn for the "better life" the suburbs 4 offered. But while my parents may have enjoyed the quality of their new location, I lived each day with insecurity and confusion. There were no knishes, no neighbors who knew me, and not many Jews. There were churches and CYO basketball games and bowling leagues on Saturday. Instead of Rosens and Steins there were Cappolettis and O'Neils. But ethnic as they were, a Jew was a different story.

My first day of school, a young sixth grader turned to me and, eyeing my Star of David, looked me in the eye and commanded that I "shut up . . . We don't like your kind around here!" To this day I cannot imagine what there was about me at ten years of age that another ten-year-old would so vehemently oppose.

High school was not much better. I was called by various nicknames and was often the butt of many a bad joke. One young man found it necessary to occasionally pull me from the lunch line, announcing to all present that I could not possibly eat food that was not kosher. These kinds of days were the worst, and I would run home after school longing for the security of my room, a place that belonged to me, understood me, and was empty without me.

Suddenly, I felt this compelling need to find out what being a Jew was really all about. I began to go to synagogue regularly, eventually becoming president of the junior congregation. I begged to be enrolled in Hebrew school and became the Rabbi's "pet" because his other students were there under duress! I joined a Jewish youth group in another town and became one of its most ardent members. I was insatiable. In retrospect, I suspect that my parents were more than proud; I believe I brought back into their home something they, too, had lost.

So what did I find out? What did I learn? Something ironic, actually. I learned that the identity that for so many years had been taken for granted was something that should never be taken for granted. It should be nourished, respected, admired, loved, and kept alive. Being a Jew, to me, does not require a scheduled speaking with God or a Star of David around your neck. It is remembering what man and many years have done to your ancestry. It is remembering people like Golda Meir who devoted their lives to a freedom state that should not have to be. And it is a proudness that becomes a source of strength; a strength that is fed by a sense of belonging to an unbreakable chain.

Times may change, but the pieces that make up your heart remain intact and represent the basics that are you. The family matriarch now accepts a new member of our family: the fine Italian man that I married. And that fine Italian man accepts and respects what I am: a nice Jewish girl from Brooklyn!

334 ᨠ SELF AND SOCIETY

Strategies for Writing

1. Rewrite paragraph seven of the essay, from the Rabbi's point of view. How different do the same details appear, now that they are being told by a different narrator? What details, if any, would have to be left out or added to the paragraph in order to make the Rabbi's description consistent and believable?
2. Rewrite paragraph five of the essay, but either from the point of view of the sixth grader described in the paragraph, or from the point of view of one of the teachers who could have witnessed the encounter.
3. In the essay, the writer points out that the identity she had assumed "was something that should never be taken for granted." Write an essay in which you analyze something that you once took for granted, but no longer assume must be yours. What happened that made for a change in your attitude?
4. Write an essay in which you analyze certain privileges and luxuries that you feel we as a society can no longer assume will be ours. What are these privileges that you feel we can no longer take for granted?

OUR ENDURING VALUES

WRITING SKILL: Cause and Effect

We have all heard children ask endless questions such as, Why is the sky blue? Adults never seem able to provide answers. However, they too ask themselves questions about the causes of a great many things around them. Why are there different shapes to the moon in the course of a month? Why are there earthquakes? Why is there evil in the world?

Ancient societies often answered these kinds of questions by creating myths and legends. Some of these stories, especially those from ancient Greece, were very imaginative and quite beautiful. Our modern world, however, seeks to answer questions in a scientific manner. In fact, most scientific writing is a strict expression of a way of thinking we call cause and effect.

The need to ask why, and the need to find reasons, is basic to our human nature, as individuals and as societies. When we try to understand connections, and when we attempt to make connections of our own, we are dealing with cause and effect.

There is more than one good reason to use cause and effect. The first is to gather information that helps us control the world around us. Why do bridges freeze in winter before the nearby roads freeze? Why do many businesses fail? As soon as we have found the answers to our questions, we are more in control of the circumstances of our daily lives.

Another reason for using the cause-and-effect approach is to enable us to speculate about possible answers to our questions. Why has crime increased at such an alarming rate in the past few years? Why do people cheat on their income taxes? In cases such as these, our answers may not be based on scientific proof, but our exploration of these questions may lead us to reasonable conclusions as to why certain events take place, or why certain attitudes are held by some people.

Most political analysis also deals with cause and effect. Why did a particular section of the city vote Republican for the first time in over forty years? Why did the people of a suburban town vote against the school budget in the last election? Proper causal analysis in the area of politics can make all the difference for a political party trying for a comeback after a major defeat.

When you are looking for causes, it is not enough to accept the most obvious or immediate explanation. Often, such an explanation is very superficial. A more complete answer demands a search for underlying causes or long-term effects. Your analysis will have greater authority when you show not only the immediate but also the underlying causes of an event. For example, a child spills a glass of juice and her mother screams at her. Why did the mother scream? We assume that the immediate cause of the mother's losing her temper was the child's carelessness, but she has often cleaned up after the child before and has not become so upset. Why has she done so now? The underlying cause for losing her temper could be anxiety about money, or upset over an argument she may have had with someone else. If we could find the underlying cause for her being upset, we would know the real reason why she lost her temper with the child.

The selections in the unit that follows contain examples of both causes and effects. For example, in Isak Dinesen's "The Oxen," the writer analyzes the brutal conditions under which those animals have to work near her home in Africa. The immediate cause of the animals' discomfort is that when the oxen pull the carts down the hills, the drivers do not put on the brakes. However, the writer is not content merely to point out this immediate, physical cause for the animals' situation; she investigates further and discovers an underlying reason those brakes are not used. By taking us this further step, Isak Dinesen helps us to better understand a situation that otherwise would have remained one-dimensional.

In her essay "Thoughts on Peace in an Air Raid," Virginia Woolf also deals with causes; the writer uses her experiences in World War II to analyze the causes of war in general. When the writer mentions Adolf Hitler as the person responsible for the war, she is echoing a popular belief. Her determination to find a deeper cause, however, leads her to point to "Hitlerism in the hearts of men" as an even greater cause of war.

In "The Electronic Revolution," Arthur C. Clarke discusses the many effects of an important area of modern technology. The writer points out, for example, the effects of telephone communication on today's society. Thanks to the telephone we now have the power to project our thoughts to other people at incredible speed. He also points out many future effects of the transistor, among them the rather striking possibility that in the future transistors will cause cities to lose their traditional importance as cultural centers. Furthermore, the writer suggests that we can never predict the ultimate effects of scientific knowledge and research. His final picture of our future in a world of increasing technology is not an altogether positive one.

Cause and effect can also provide the basis for an argument. If you examine a proposal and give its effects, you are providing an argument for or against what is being proposed. For example, in the final essay in this unit, Kenneth Watt presents an argument in favor of diversity in our world. He does this by pointing out the effects of our loss of this diversity. His argument is convincing partly because of the sheer number of his examples, and partly because of the range of those examples. The essay is an especially good example of cause and effect because the writer probes deeply, searching for the long-term effects of the loss of diversity he describes.

When you are working with cause and effect, be certain that you have sufficiently investigated the causes that are involved. Do not use coincidence as a true cause, and do not conclude that simply because one event follows another, they are connected. For example, if you take some medication in the morning and by lunch time you find yourself becoming sleepy, you cannot assume that the medicine has made you tired. You *may* be sleepy because of the medication, but there could also be any number of other reasons for your fatigue.

The ability to discover not only the obvious causes of something but also the underlying causes, not only the immediate effects but also the long-term effects, will help a person to reason carefully and make intelligent judgments. This search requires thoroughness that may demand extensive research.

❧ *Isak Dinesen* ❧

Isak Dinesen (1885–1962) grew up in the Danish countryside. She studied painting in Copenhagen, and went on to further art studies in Paris and Rome. It was during this period of her life that she also had her first short stories published.

In 1914 she married one of her cousins, Baron Blixen, and went to live with him in British East Africa (now Kenya). There her family had purchased and given the newly married couple a large coffee plantation. The marriage did not work out, and in 1921 Isak Dinesen was divorced from her husband. However, she continued to manage the coffee plantation until 1931, when the world economic situation became so bad that she was forced to sell her property and return to Denmark.

Isak Dinesen turned to writing during her years in Africa. "I began to write there to amuse myself in the rainy season," she later recalled. The results of this solitary literary activity were a number of well-known books of fiction and nonfiction. *Seven Gothic Tales* appeared in 1934, and *Winter's Tales* was published in 1942. Her first book of impressions of life in Kenya appeared in 1937 in her volume *Out of Africa;* her last book, *Shadows on the Grass* (1960) also describes the people of Africa as she knew them.

The following selection from *Out of Africa* describes the oxen on her farm in Kenya.

PREVIEWING THE WRITER

• Note how the writer's opening description provides us with a picture of the working lives of the people and the animals on the farm. How do both groups live and work?

• Where in the essay does the writer make a transition from a description of her farm to an analysis of the working relationships between people and animals in general?

• Where in the essay does the writer consciously describe the oxen in human terms?

THE OXEN

SATURDAY AFTERNOON was a blessed time on the farm. 1 First of all, there would now be no mail in till Monday afternoon, so that no distressing business letters could reach us till then, and this fact in itself seemed to close the whole place in, as within an enceinte.[1] Secondly, everybody was looking forward to the day of Sunday, when they would rest or play all the day, and the Squatters could work on their own land. The thought of the oxen on Saturday pleased me more than all other things. I used to walk down to their paddock at six o'clock, when they were coming in after the day's work and a few hours' grazing. To-morrow, I thought, they would do nothing but graze all day.

We had one hundred and thirty-two oxen on the farm, which meant eight working teams and a few spare oxen. Now in the golden dust of the sunset they came wandering home across the plain in a long row, walking sedately, as they did all things; while I sat sedately on the fence of the paddock, smoking a cigarette of peace, and watching them. Here came Nyose, Ngufu and Faru, with Msungu,—which means a white man. The drivers also often give to their teams the proper names of white men, and Delamere is a common name in an ox. Here came old Malinda, the big yellow ox that I liked best of the lot; his skin was strangely marked with shadowy figures, like starfishes, from which pattern perhaps he had his name, for Malinda means a skirt.

As in civilized countries all people have a chronic bad conscience towards the slums, and feel uncomfortable when they think of them, so in Africa you have got a bad conscience, and feel a pang, when you think of the oxen. But towards the oxen on the farm, I felt as, I suppose, a king will be feeling towards his slums: "You are I, and I am you."

The oxen in Africa have carried the heavy load of the advance of European civilization. Wherever new land has been broken they have broken it, panting and pulling kneedeep in the soil before the ploughs, the long whips in the air over them. Where a road has been made they have made it; and they have trudged the iron and tools through the land, to the yelling and shouting of the drivers, by tracks in the dust and the long grass of the plains, before there ever were any roads. They have been inspanned[2] before daybreak, and have sweated up and down the long hills, and across dungas and river-beds, through the

2

3

4

[1] An enclosure of any kind, such as a fence or a wall.

[2] The joining together of two animals, in this case oxen, that have been matched according to size and strength.

burning hours of the day. The whips have marked their sides, and you will often see oxen that have had an eye, or both of them, taken away by the long cutting whip-lashes. The waggon-oxen of many Indian and white contractors worked every day, all their lives through, and did not know of the Sabbath.

It is a strange thing that we have done to the oxen. The bull is in a constant stage of fury, rolling his eyes, shovelling up the earth, upset by everything that gets within his range of vision,—still he has got a life of his own, fire comes from his nostrils, and new life from his loins; his days are filled with his vital cravings and satisfactions. All of that we have taken away from the oxen, and in reward we have claimed their existence for ourselves. The oxen walk along within our own daily life, pulling hard all the time, creatures without a life, things made for our use. They have moist, limpid, violet eyes, soft muzzles, silky ears, they are patient and dull in all their ways; sometimes they look as if they were thinking about things.

There was in my time a law against bringing a waggon or cart on the roads without a brake, and the waggon-drivers were supposed to put on the brakes down all the long hills of the country. But the law was not kept; half the waggons and carts on the roads had no brakes to them, and on the others the brakes were but rarely put on. This made downhill work terribly hard on the oxen. They had to hold the loaded waggons up with their bodies, they laid their heads back under the labour until their horns touched the hump on their backs; their sides went like a pair of bellows. I have many times seen the carts of the firewood merchants which came along the Ngong Road, going into Nairobi the one after the other, like a long caterpillar, gain speed down the hill in the Forest Reserve, the oxen violently zig-zagging down in front of them. I have also seen the oxen stumble and fall under the weight of the cart, at the bottom of the hill.

The oxen thought: "Such is life, and the conditions of the world. They are hard, hard. It has all to be borne,—there is nothing for it. It is a terribly difficult thing to get the carts down the hill, it is a matter of life and death. It cannot be helped."

If the fat Indians of Nairobi, who owned the carts, could have brought themselves to pay two Rupees and have the brakes put in order, or if the slow young Native driver on the top of the loaded cart, had had it in him to get off and put on the brake, if it was there, then it could have been helped, and the oxen could have walked quietly down the hill. But the oxen did not know, and went on, day after day, in their heroic and desperate struggle, with the conditions of life.

THE WRITER'S THEMES

1. Where does the writer seem to be more positive about the oxen who work on the farm than she is about the people who work in the surrounding area? At what points in the essay do we see her descriptions favoring one group over the other?
2. Which details in the essay provide us with the most vivid pictures of life in Kenya? As the writer describes it, what is Kenyan society like and how does it operate?
3. Trace the writer's practice of giving the oxen an almost human personality, from the beginning of the essay where she tells us their names, to the concluding paragraphs where she imagines them actually speaking to us. What is the effect of this technique? How does it support what the writer is saying in the essay?

THE WRITER'S TECHNIQUE

In the first paragraph of her essay, Isak Dinesen describes a particular afternoon on the farm and she tells us why that day of the week was such a special time. Here is the paragraph:

> Saturday afternoon was a blessed time on the farm. First of all, there would now be no mail in till Monday afternoon, so that no distressing business letters could reach us till then, and this fact in itself seemed to close the whole place in, as within an enceinte. Secondly, everybody was looking forward to the day of Sunday, when they would rest or play all the day, and the Squatters could work on their own land. The thought of the oxen on Saturday pleased me more than all other things. I used to walk down to their paddock at six o'clock, when they were coming in after the day's work and a few hours' grazing. To-morrow, I thought, they would do nothing but graze all day.

Notice that as soon as she has indicated that Saturday afternoon was "a blessed time" on the farm, the writer begins to give reasons to prove her point. First, since there would be no mail delivery on Sunday, no unpleasant letters could reach them until Monday afternoon. In addition, on Saturday the people could look forward to having a choice on Sunday: they could either "rest or play all the day," and the squatters "could work on their own land" if they chose to do so.

Having described the people on the farm, the writer now devotes the second part of her paragraph to the animals. "The thought of the oxen on Saturday," we are told, pleased her "more than all other things." In the evening the writer would walk down to where the oxen were kept and think that, on Sunday, the oxen "would do nothing but graze all day."

The writer has used the first part of her paragraph to describe the people and their weekend activities on the farm; in the second part of the paragraph she has concentrated on the oxen. The fact that the oxen are seen "coming in after the day's work" and are described as being able to "do nothing but graze all day" on Sunday makes them full participants in the life of the farm: along with the people, the oxen are creatures that work and that can enjoy periods of leisure in the working week of the farm.

PARAGRAPH PRACTICE

Write a paragraph of your own, using Isak Dinesen's paragraph as your model. First, choose a day of the week that is either especially relaxed or especially frantic for you. Then provide two or three specific reasons why this particular day is either so calm or so frantic. In the next part of your paragraph, describe the same day as you believe it appears to the people around you. How do they react to this calm or hurried day?

Finally, describe what it is about that day that pleases you "more than all other things." If you have chosen a relaxed day, point out the best feature of that day; if you have chosen to describe a frantic day, indicate something that happens that at least makes that day bearable.

When you include other people in your description, be sure to indicate what they are doing. Do they act or react the same way you do? Your paragraph will have an effective conclusion if you are able to show other people in agreement (or disagreement) with your attitudes and actions. By describing everyone together, you will emphasize your connection with those around you, as all of you share a positive or negative experience.

ESSAY PRACTICE

The following outline will help you plan a complete essay of at least five paragraphs. The theme of your essay will be closely related to the Isak Dinesen essay.

The following sentence may serve as your thesis sentence, and will also be the main idea of your introductory paragraph:

¶ 1. When a person takes a job, the presence or absence of certain working conditions will have definite effects on that worker's well-being.

Each of the sentences below is the topic sentence for one of the paragraphs that you will write to develop your thesis. You may use the suggested details to develop each paragraph, or you may supply details of your own.

¶ 2. When a person takes a job, he or she should be guaranteed certain conditions.

[DETAILS: What should a person ask an employer about a job that he or she is about to accept? What are the working conditions that should always be clearly understood before a person takes a job?]

¶ 3. If these job conditions should change, or if guarantees are taken away, there will be serious effects on the worker.

[DETAILS: What happens when a person discovers that conditions on the job are changing? What kinds of changes are more serious than others?]

¶ 4. In any job, there comes a point where conditions become so intolerable that a worker has to leave.

[DETAILS: At what point in a deteriorating work situation should a person make the decision to leave? Give specific examples of work situations that would be intolerable to you. In this part of your essay you could use your own experience, or the experience of someone you know, to illustrate an intolerable work situation.]

Be certain that you use transitions between paragraphs to make your writing flow smoothly. In addition, be sure that your conclusion gives your reader a clear signal that you have come to the end of your essay.

ESSAY TOPICS

1. a. How much vacation time do you feel people should have every year? What are the effects on a person who does not take time off on a regular basis?
    b. Describe how you spend your free time on the weekend. When the weekend comes, what can you put off doing? What can you look forward to at that time?
2. Many communities have laws that do not permit shopping of any kind on Sunday, while in other communities shopping on Sunday is permitted, but with certain restrictions.
    a. What are the effects of such laws on the economy of a community? What are the different effects of such laws on the people of a community?
    b. Write an essay in which you support or oppose restrictions on Sunday shopping. What would be the effects on your community if your ideas were to be adopted?
3. In recent years, the concept of the minimum wage has been questioned by some government agencies, and it has been suggested that unemployed young people be allowed to work for less than the minimum wage. Some fast food restaurant chains have even been exempted from having to pay the legal minimum wage to their employees.
    a. What would be the effects of a reduction in the minimum wage, if such a reduction actually became law?
    b. What do you believe are the effects on those restaurant workers who have to work for less than the minimum wage? What effect(s) do you think this has on workers in other jobs or in other industries?

⅋ *Arthur C. Clarke* ⅋

Arthur C. Clarke was born in England in 1917. From 1936 to 1944 he worked in the British civil service, and in 1951 he became a full-time writer. He has published more than three hundred articles in such journals and magazines as *Life, Vogue,* and *Horizon.*

His nonfiction books include *The Exploration of Space* (1951), *The Challenge of the Spaceship* (1959), and *The First Five Fathoms* (1960). Clarke is also the author of several books of fiction, among them *The Other Side of the Sky* (1958) and *Tales of Ten Worlds* (1962). The writer is perhaps best known as the co-author of *2001: A Space Odyssey.* In 1982, Arthur C. Clarke published *2010: Odyssey II,* a continuation of this earlier book.

The following essay first appeared as an article in the *New York Times* in 1962.

PREVIEWING THE WRITER

- Note the writer's history of our use of electricity, including the discovery of the electron.
- Note the writer's discussion of the present implications of the electronic revolution. How have our lives already changed as a result of this revolution?
- Note the author's predictions as to what our future will be like as a result of the electronic revolution. What does the writer hint may be the ultimate goal of this revolution?

THE ELECTRONIC REVOLUTION

THE ELECTRON is the smallest thing in the universe; it would take thirty thousand million, million, million, million of them to make a single ounce. Yet this utterly invisible, all but weightless object has given us powers over nature of which our ancestors never dreamed. The electron is our most ubiquitous slave; without its aid, our civilization would collapse in a moment, and humanity would revert to scattered bands of starving, isolated savages.

We started to use the electron fifty years before we discovered it. The first practical application of electricity (which is nothing more than the ordered movement of electrons) began with the introduction of the telegraph in the 1840's. With really astonishing speed, a copper cobweb of wires and cables spread across the face of the world, and the abolition of distance had begun. For over a century we have taken the instantaneous transfer of news completely for granted; it is very hard to believe that when Lincoln was born, communications were little faster than in the days of Julius Caesar.

Although the beginning of "electronics" is usually dated ،3 around the 1920's, this represents a myopic view of technology. With the hindsight of historical perspective, we can now see that the telegraph and the telephone are the first two landmarks of the electronic age. After Alexander Graham Bell had sent his voice from one room to another in 1876, society could never be the same again. For the telephone was the first electronic device to enter the home and to affect directly the lives of ordinary men and women, giving them the almost godlike power of projecting their personalities and thoughts from point to point with the speed of lightning.

Until the closing years of the nineteenth century, men used 4 and handled electricity without knowing what it was, but in the 1890's they began to investigate its fundamental nature, by observing what happened when an electric current was passed through gases at very low pressures. One of the first, and most dramatic, results of this work was the invention of the X-ray tube, which may be regarded as the ancestor of all the millions of vacuum tubes which followed it. A cynic might also argue that it is the only electronic device wholly beneficial to mankind—though when it was invented many terrified spinsters, misunderstanding its powers, denounced poor Röntgen as a violator of privacy.

There is an important lesson to be learned from the X-ray 5 tube. If a scientist of the late Victorian era had been asked "In what way could money best be spent to further the progress of medicine?" he would never by any stretch of the imagination have replied: "By encouraging research on the conduction of electricity through rarefied gases." Yet that is what would have been the right answer, for until the discovery of X rays doctors and surgeons were like blind men, groping in the dark. One can never predict the outcome of fundamental scientific research, or guess what remote and unexpected fields of knowledge it will illuminate.

X rays were discovered in 1895—the electron itself just one 6 year later. It was then realized that an electric current consists of myriads of these submicroscopic particles, each carrying a minute negative charge. When a current flows through a solid conductor such as a piece of copper wire, we may imagine the electrons creeping like grains of sand through the interstices between the (relatively) boulder-sized copper atoms. Any individual electron does not move very far, or very fast, but it jostles its neighbor and so the impulse travels down the line at speeds of thousands of miles a second. Thus when we switch on a light, or send a Morse dash across a transatlantic cable, the response at the other end is virtually instantaneous.

But electrons can also travel *without* wires to guide them, when they shoot across the empty space of a vacuum tube like a hail of machine-gun bullets. Under these conditions, no longer entangled in solid matter, they are very sensitive to the pull and tug of electric fields, and as a result can be used to amplify faint signals. You demonstrate the principle involved every time you hold a hose-pipe in your hand; the slightest movement of your wrist produces a much greater effect at the far end of the jet. Something rather similar happens to the beam of electrons crossing the space in a vacuum tube; they can thus multiply a millionfold the feeble impulses picked up by a radio antenna, or paint a flourescent picture on the end of a television screen.

Until 1948, electronics was almost synonymous with the vacuum tube. The entire development of radio, talkies, radar, television, long-distance telephony, up to that date depended upon little glass bottles containing intricate structures of wire and mica. By the late 1940's the vacuum tube had shrunk from an object as large as (and sometimes almost as luminous as) an electric light bulb, to a cylinder not much bigger than a man's thumb. Then three scientists at the Bell Telephone Laboratories invented the transistor and we moved from the Paleoelectronic to the Neoelectronic Age.

Though the transistor is so small—its heart is a piece of crystal about the size of a rice grain—it does everything that a radio tube can do. However, it requires only a fraction of the power and space, and is potentially much more reliable. Indeed, it is hard to see how a properly designed transistor can ever wear out; think of little Vanguard I, still beeping away up there in space, and liable to continue indefinitely until some exasperated astronaut scoops it up with a butterfly net.

The transistor is of such overwhelming importance because it (and its still smaller successors) makes practical hundreds of electronic devices which were previously too bulky, too expensive or too unreliable for everyday use. The pocket radio is a notorious example; whether we like it or not, it points the way inevitably to a day when person-to-person communications is universal. Then everyone in the world will have his individual telephone number, perhaps given to him at birth and serving all the other needs of an increasingly complex society (driving license, social security, credit card, permit to have additional children, etc.). You may not know where on Earth your friend Joe Smith may be at any particular moment; but you will be able to dial him instantly—if only you can remember whether his number is 8296765043 or 8296756043.

Obviously, there are both advantages and disadvantages   11
in such a "personalized" communication system; the solitude which we all need at some time in our lives will join the vanished silences of the pre-jet age. Against this, there is no other way in which a really well-informed *and* fast-reacting democratic society can be achieved on the original Greek plan—with direct participation of every citizen in the affairs of the state. The organization of such a society, with feedback in both directions from the humblest citizen to the President of the World, is a fascinating exercise in political planning. As usual, it is an exercise that will not be completed by the time we need the answers.

A really efficient and universal communications system,   12
giving high-quality reception on all bands between all points on the Earth, can be achieved only with the aid of satellites. As they come into general use, providing enormous information-handling capacity on a global basis, today's patterns of business, education, entertainment, international affairs will change out of all recognition. Men will be able to meet face to face (individually, or in groups) without ever leaving their homes, by means of closed circuit television. As a result of this, the enormous amount of commuting and traveling that now takes place from home to office, from ministry to United Nations, from university to conference hall will steadily decrease. There are administrators, scientists and businessmen today who spend about a third of their working lives either traveling or preparing to travel. Much of this is stimulating, but most of it is unnecessary and exhausting.

The improvement of communications will also render ob-   13
solete the city's historic role as a meeting place for minds and a center of social intercourse. This is just as well anyway, since

within another generation most of our cities will be strangled to death by their own traffic.

But though electronics will ultimately separate men from their jobs, so that (thanks to remote manipulation devices) not even a brain surgeon need be within five thousand miles of his patient, it must also be recognized that few of today's jobs will survive long into the electronic age. It is now a cliché that we are entering the Second Industrial Revolution, which involves the mechanization not of energy, but of thought. Like all clichés this is so true that we seldom stop to analyze what it means. 14

It means nothing less than this: There are no routine, non-creative activities of the human mind which cannot be carried out by suitably designed machines. The development of computers to supervise industrial processes, commercial transactions and even military operations has demonstrated this beyond doubt. Yet today's computers are morons compared to those that they themselves are now helping to design. 15

I would not care to predict how many of today's professions will survive a hundred years from now. What happened to the buggywhip makers, the crossing sweepers, the scriveners, the stonebreakers of yesteryear? (I mention the last because I can just remember them, hammering away at piles of rock in the country lanes of my childhood.) Most of our present occupations will follow these into oblivion, as the transistor inherits the earth. 16

For as computers become smaller, cheaper and more reliable they will move into every field of human activity. Today they are in the office; tomorrow they will be in the home. Indeed, some very simple-minded computers already do our household chores; the device that programs a washing machine to perform a certain sequence of operations is a specialized mechanical brain. Less specialized ones would be able to carry out almost all the routine operations in a suitably designed house. 17

Because we have so many more pressing problems on our hands, only the science-fiction writers—those trail-blazers of the future—have given much thought to the social life of the later electronic age. How will our descendants be educated for leisure, when the working week is only a few hours? We have already seen, on a worldwide scale, the cancerous growths resulting from idleness and lack of usable skills. At every street corner in a great city you will find lounging groups of leather- 18 jacketed, general-purpose bioelectric computers of a performance it will take us centuries and trillions of dollars to match. What is their future—and ours?

More than half a century ago H. G. Wells described, in 19 *The Time Machine,* a world of decadent pleasure lovers, bereft of goals and ambitions, sustained by subterranean machines. He set his fantasy eight hundred thousand years in the future, but we may reach a similar state of affairs within a dozen generations. No one who contemplates the rising curve of technology from the Pilgrim fathers to the Apollo Project dare deny that this is not merely possible, but probable.

For most of history, men have been producers; in a very 20 few centuries, they will have to switch to the role of consumers devoting their energies 100 per cent to absorbing the astronomical output of the automated mines, farms and factories.

Does this *really* matter, since only a tiny fraction of the 21 human race has ever contributed to artistic creation, scientific discovery or philosophical thought, which in the long run are the only significant activities of mankind? Archimedes and Aristotle, one cannot help thinking, would still have left their marks on history even if they had lived in a society based on robots instead of human slaves. In any culture, they would be consumers of goods, but producers of thought.

We should not take too much comfort from this. The elec- 22 tronic computers of today are like the subhuman primates of ten million years ago, who could have given any visiting Martians only the faintest hints of their potentialities, which included the above mentioned Archimedes and Aristotle. Evolution is swifter now; electronic intelligence is only decades, not millions of years, ahead.

And *that*—not transistor radios, automatic homes, global 23 TV—is the ultimate goal of the Electronic Revolution. Whether we like it or not, we are on a road where there is no turning back; and waiting at its end are our successors.

THE WRITER'S THEMES

1. According to the author, what effects will the electronic revolution have on people's personal lives? How many of these changes will bring problems with them?

2. According to the essay, what changes will take place in society as a result of the electronic revolution? For example, what effects will this revolution have on the concepts of work and leisure?
3. According to the writer, what is the "ultimate goal" of the electronic revolution?

THE WRITER'S TECHNIQUE

The following quotations are from the opening sentences of paragraphs nine, ten, and eleven of "The Electronic Revolution." Here, the writer is describing the size of transistors, their importance in the future of communication, and the advantages and disadvantages of this kind of communication.

> Though the transistor is so small . . . it does everything that a radio tube can do.

> The transistor is of such overwhelming importance . . .

> Obviously, there are both advantages and disadvantages in such a . . . system . . .

After the writer points out what the transistor can do despite its size, he goes on to indicate its importance while he provides several examples that prove its importance for future communication. For example, the day will come when each person will have an individual telephone number, and everyone will be able to speak with everyone else anywhere in the world.

The writer then points out some of the advantages and disadvantages this system will bring. We will, for example, have virtually no privacy. On the other hand, it will be possible to arrange for what Clarke calls "the direct participation of every citizen in the affairs of the state."

PARAGRAPH PRACTICE

Write a paragraph of your own, using the above quotations from "The Electronic Revolution" as your guide for your paragraph. Your paragraph could describe virtually any object you own or use, from a calculator or other machine you use regularly at home or at work, to a car that you use every day.

Begin your paragraph by providing a physical description of the object you have chosen. Indicate the size of the object and provide at least two or three additional details that will help your reader visualize the object.

Next, indicate the importance of the object. Why is it important to you? Would it be just as important to other people, or do you believe they would think differently about it?

Finally, use the last part of your paragraph to present both the advantages and disadvantages of having or using the object you have described. What exactly are the advantages? How many disadvantages are there? By pointing out these advantages and disadvantages, you will give your reader the strong impression of your fairness, and the effect of your writing will be strengthened.

ESSAY PRACTICE

The following outline will help you plan a complete essay of at least five paragraphs. The theme of your essay will be closely related to Arthur C. Clarke's "The Electronic Revolution."

The following sentence may serve as your thesis sentence, and will also be the main idea of your introductory paragraph:

¶ 1. The use of electronics in nearly every area of our lives has brought with it a concern about the effects of technology on our society.

Each of the sentences below is the topic sentence for one of the paragraphs that you will write to develop your thesis. You may use the suggested details to develop each paragraph, or you may supply details of your own.

¶ 2. There is hardly a part of our everyday lives that is not affected in some way by electronics.

[DETAILS: What are some of the obvious, and perhaps not so obvious, areas of our lives where electronics plays an important role? In writing this paragraph use a wide variety of examples, including the areas of sport and play, to support the idea that the use of electronics is indeed widespread.]

¶ 3. Many electronic conveniences we have today seem to bring with them added responsibilities of some kind.

[DETAILS: What are the personal and social responsibilities that go along with modern electronics? Your examples could range from parents' concern about the popularity of video games to the government's responsibility not to misuse confidential information about individual citizens.]

¶ 4. Life would be truly less complicated if the number of electronic gadgets we use could somehow be made smaller.

[DETAILS: How could we reduce the number of gadgets we depend on, without giving up the many advantages of our electronic conveniences? If we did decide to simplify this area of our lives, what would be some of the results?]

Be certain that you use transitions between paragraphs to make your writing flow smoothly. In addition, be sure that your conclusion gives your reader a clear signal that you have come to the end of your essay.

ESSAY TOPICS

1. a. Arthur C. Clarke predicts that computers will "soon be in the home," a prediction that is already coming true. What would you like to see computers be able to do for you in your own home? What tasks would you still have to do for yourself, even if you had a computer?
    b. What effects of the computer revolution are already noticeable, either directly or indirectly, in our lives?
2. Clarke predicts a future when people "will be able to meet face to face . . . without ever leaving their homes, by means of closed circuit television."
    Imagine a world in which you will be able to visit friends and perhaps even attend school without ever leaving your home. Would you enjoy living in such a world? What would be the effects of such a system of communication on your life?
3. a. Clarke predicts that several of the professions we know today will probably not be around a hundred years from now. Which of today's professions do you believe will have disappeared a century from now? Which professions do you believe will almost certainly remain? How will present-day professions change?
    b. Clarke notes the problems that come with increased leisure and predicts a future when people will have to work only a few hours in the week. What are some of the problems that can come about with increased amounts of leisure? What must people do in order to, in Clarke's words, be "educated for leisure"?

✒ *Virginia Woolf* ✒

Virginia Woolf was born in London in 1882. She was a frail and lonely child, and the fact that she was educated at home only added to her feeling of being different from other children. The death of her mother in 1895 increased her sense of loneliness.

Virginia Woolf first gained attention as a writer in 1915 with her novel *The Voyage Out*, but she achieved more fame in the following decade with such novels as *Mrs. Dalloway* (1925) and *To the Lighthouse* (1927).

Throughout her career Virginia Woolf was an outspoken champion of women's rights in England. One of her earliest expressions of this concern was a volume of essays she entitled *A Room of One's Own* (1929). The following essay is one of the last pieces she wrote before her death in 1941. "Thoughts on Peace in an Air Raid" was written in August 1940 for delivery before an American symposium on matters concerning women. World War II had begun in Europe in 1939, and while the setting of the essay is a German air attack on Britain, Woolf's purpose is much larger than a single battle in a single war. Instead, the author investigates man's nature, woman's nature, and the tensions that so often result from the differences in our natures.

In the essay, Woolf presents us with the external world and the inner landscape of the narrator's own mind. One critic described Virginia Woolf's effect on her readers by noting that she used "a series of significant images, both visual and aural" to hold the reader's attention. The critic was referring to her early novels, but he could just as easily have been describing the essay that follows.

PREVIEWING THE WRITER

• Note the author's constant use of "dark" and "darkness." In how many instances is she using the word literally, to mean the simple absence of light? At what points in the essay do you believe she wants us to think of "darkness" as something else, such as a state of mind?

• Note the different references in the essay to battles. How many of these confrontations are military? How many of them are mental fights?

• How many of the writer's points about men, women, and power could be applied to society in peacetime as well as in war?

THOUGHTS ON PEACE IN AN AIR RAID

THE GERMANS were over this house last night and the 1
night before that. Here they are again. It is a queer experience,
lying in the dark and listening to the zoom of a hornet, which
may at any moment sting you to death. It is a sound that interrupts cool and consecutive thinking about peace. Yet it is a
sound—far more than prayers and anthems—that should com-
pel one to think about peace. Unless we can think peace into
existence we—not this one body in this one bed but millions of
bodies yet to be born—will lie in the same darkness and hear
the same death rattle overhead. Let us think what we can do to
create the only efficient air-raid shelter while the guns on the
hill go pop pop pop and the searchlights finger the clouds and
now and then, sometimes close at hand, sometimes far away,
a bomb drops.

Up there in the sky young Englishmen and young German 2
men are fighting each other. The defenders are men, the at-
tackers men. Arms are not given to Englishwomen either to
fight the enemy or to defend herself. She must lie weaponless
tonight. Yet if she believes that the fight going on up in the sky
is a fight by the English to protect freedom, by the Germans to
destroy freedom, she must fight, so far as she can, on the side
of the English. How far can she fight for freedom without fire-
arms? By making arms, or clothes or food. But there is another
way of fighting for freedom without arms; we can fight with
the mind. We can make ideas that will help the young Englishman who is fighting up in the sky to defeat the enemy.

But to make ideas effective, we must be able to fire them 3
off. We must put them into action. And the hornet in the sky
rouses another hornet in the mind. There was one zooming in
The Times this morning—a woman's voice saying, 'Women have
not a word to say in politics.' There is no woman in the Cabinet;
nor in any responsible post. All the idea-makers who are in a
position to make ideas effective are men. That is a thought that
damps thinking, and encourages irresponsibility. Why not bury
the head in the pillow, plug the ears, and cease this futile activity of idea-making? Because there are other tables besides
officer tables and conference tables. Are we not leaving the
young Englishman without a weapon that might be of value to

him if we give up private thinking, tea-table thinking, because it seems useless? Are we not stressing our disability because our ability exposes us perhaps to abuse, perhaps to contempt? 'I will not cease from mental fight', Blake wrote. Mental fight means thinking against the current, not with it.

That current flows fast and furious. It issues in a spate of words from the loudspeakers and the politicians. Every day they tell us that we are a free people, fighting to defend freedom. That is the current that has whirled the young airman up into the sky and keeps him circling there among the clouds. Down here, with a roof to cover us and a gas-mask handy, it is our business to puncture gas-bags and discover seeds of truth. It is not true that we are free. We are both prisoners tonight— he boxed up in his machine with a gun handy; we lying in the dark with a gas-mask handy. If we were free we should be out in the open, dancing, at the play, or sitting at the window talking together. What is it that prevents us? 'Hitler!' the loudspeakers cry with one voice. Who is Hitler? What is he? Aggressiveness, tyranny, the insane love of power made manifest, they reply. Destroy that, and you will be free.

The drone of the planes is now like the sawing of a branch overhead. Round and round it goes, sawing and sawing at a branch directly above the house. Another sound begins sawing its way in the brain. 'Women of ability'—it was Lady Astor speaking in *The Times* this morning—'are held down because of a subconscious Hitlerism in the hearts of men.' Certainly we are held down. We are equally prisoners tonight—the Englishmen in their planes, the Englishwomen in their beds. But if he stops to think he may be killed; and we too. So let us think for him. Let us try to drag up into consciousness the subconscious Hitlerism that holds us down. It is the desire for aggression; the desire to dominate and enslave. Even in the darkness we can see that made visible. We can see shop windows blazing; and women gazing; painted women; dressed-up women; women with crimson lips and crimson fingernails. They are slaves who are trying to enslave. If we could free ourselves from slavery we should free men from tyranny. Hitlers are bred by slaves.

A bomb drops. All the windows rattle. The anti-aircraft guns are getting active. Up there on the hill under a net tagged with strips of green and brown stuff to imitate the hues of autumn leaves guns are concealed. Now they all fire at once. On the nine o'clock radio we shall be told 'Forty-four enemy planes were shot down during the night, ten of them by anti-aircraft fire'. And one of the terms of peace, the loudspeakers say, is to be disarmament. There are to be no more guns, no army, no navy, no air force in the future. No more young men will be trained to fight with arms. That rouses another mind-hornet in the chambers of the brain—another quotation. 'To fight against a real enemy, to earn undying honour and glory by shooting total strangers, and to come home with my breast covered with medals and decorations, that was the summit of my hope. . . . It was for this that my whole life so far had been dedicated, my education, training, everything. . . .

Those were the words of a young Englishman who fought   7
in the last war. In the face of them, do the current thinkers honestly believe that by writing 'Disarmament' on a sheet of paper at a conference table they will have done all that is needful? Othello's occupation will be gone; but he will remain Othello. The young airman up in the sky is driven not only by the voices of loudspeakers; he is driven by voices in himself—ancient instincts, instincts fostered and cherished by education and tradition. Is he to be blamed for those instincts? Could we switch off the maternal instinct at the command of a table full of politicians? Suppose that imperative among the peace terms was: 'Child-bearing is to be restricted to a very small class of specially selected women', would we submit? Should we not say, 'The maternal instinct is a woman's glory. It was for this that my whole life has been dedicated, my education, training, everything. . . .' But if it were necessary, for the sake of humanity, for the peace of the world, that childbearing should be restricted, the maternal instinct subdued, women would attempt it. Men would help them. They would honour them for their refusal to bear children. They would give them other openings for their creative power. That too must make part of our fight for freedom. We must help the young Englishmen to root out from themselves the love of medals and decorations. We must create more honourable activities for those who try to conquer in themselves their fighting instinct, their subconscious Hitlerism. We must compensate the man for the loss of his gun.

The sound of sawing overhead has increased. All the   8
searchlights are erect. They point at a spot exactly above this roof. At any moment a bomb may fall on this very room. One, two, three, four, five, six . . . the seconds pass. The bomb did

not fall. But during those seconds of suspense all thinking stopped. All feeling, save one dull dread, ceased. A nail fixed the whole being to one hard board. The emotion of fear and of hate is therefore sterile, unfertile. Directly that fear passes, the mind reaches out and instinctively revives itself by trying to create. Since the room is dark it can create only from memory. It reaches out to the memory of other Augusts—in Bayreuth, listening to Wagner; in Rome, walking over the Campagna; in London. Friends' voices come back. Scraps of poetry return. Each of those thoughts, even in memory, was far more positive, reviving, healing and creative than the dull dread made of fear and hate. Therefore if we are to compensate the young man for the loss of his glory and of his gun, we must give him access to the creative feelings. We must make happiness. We must free him from the machine. We must bring him out of his prison into the open air. But what is the use of freeing the young Englishman if the young German and the young Italian remain slaves?

The searchlights, wavering across the flat, have picked up the plane now. From this window one can see a little silver insect turning and twisting in the light. The guns go pop pop pop. Then they cease. Probably the raider was brought down behind the hill. One of the pilots landed safe in a field near here the other day. He said to his captors, speaking fairly good English, 'How glad I am that the fight is over!' Then an Englishman gave him a cigarette, and an Englishwoman made him a cup of tea. That would seem to show that if you can free the man from the machine, the seed does not fall upon altogether stony ground. The seed may be fertile.   9

At last all the guns have stopped firing. All the searchlights have been extinguished. The natural darkness of a summer's night returns. The innocent sounds of the country are heard again. An apple thuds to the ground. An owl hoots, winging its way from tree to tree. And some half-forgotten words of an old English writer come to mind: 'The huntsmen are up in America. . . .' Let us send these fragmentary notes to the huntsmen who are up in America, to the men and women whose sleep has not yet been broken by machine-gun fire, in the belief that they will rethink them generously and charitably, perhaps shape them into something serviceable. And now, in the shadowed half of the world, to sleep.   10

THE WRITER'S THEMES

1. Throughout the essay, Virginia Woolf describes a world at war. However, she indicates that there is an ideal world in which she would like to live. Using various details found in the essay, describe as fully as you can the environment Virginia Woolf would consider ideal.
2. Virginia Woolf frequently describes people as being either free or imprisoned. What kind of prison exists for each person the writer describes?
3. At the end of her essay, Virginia Woolf says farewell from "the shadowed half of the world." Using all of the references to "dark" and "darkness" that you have noted in the essay, how many meanings can you find for the "shadowed half of the world"?

THE WRITER'S TECHNIQUE

In paragraph nine of her essay, Virginia Woolf makes a distant nameless enemy seem as close and human as a next-door neighbor. Here is that paragraph:

> The searchlights, wavering across the flat, have picked up the plane now. From this window one can see a little silver insect turning and twisting in the light. The guns go pop pop pop. Then they cease. Probably the raider was brought down behind the hill. One of the pilots landed safe in a field near here the other day. He said to his captors, speaking fairly good English, 'How glad I am that the fight is over!' Then an Englishman gave him a cigarette, and an Englishwoman made him a cup of tea. That would seem to show that if you can free the man from the machine, the seed does not fall upon altogether stony ground. The seed may be fertile.

The writer begins the paragraph by describing a scene that includes searchlights "wavering" across her apartment. Then she describes the enemy plane: it is something nonhuman, and is like "a little silver insect." After the British guns have done their work, it disappears from sight, probably "down behind the hill." However, the writer will not allow us to forget that the "little silver insect" actually contains a part of humanity, namely the pilot who flew that plane. She describes another enemy pilot who had landed "the other day" and who had been captured by the British. She then reports his greeting to his captors ("How glad I am that the fight is over!"), and then she notes the kindness of the people as they bring him tea and cigarettes. Finally, she comes to a conclusion: "That would seem to show that if you can free the man from the machine, the seed does not fall upon altogether stony ground."

In the paragraph, Virginia Woolf begins with a description of the general scene and indicates the enemy in the distance, but when we see the enemy up close we see that he smokes and drinks tea, and we realize that he is capable of a friendly remark. From these specific examples, the writer draws a general conclusion, suggesting that what she has described may have a universal application; the seed (referring to the pilot) "may be fertile," and there may yet be hope for peace.

PARAGRAPH PRACTICE

Write a paragraph of your own, using Virginia Woolf's paragraph as your model. In your paragraph give your initial view of a person as you see that person from a distance; then describe the person as he or she appears when closer. Some possible subjects for your paragraph could be:

—a person you see across the room at a party, and later meet at that party.

—your first impression of a professor on the opening day of class, and later in the semester.

—the first time you saw a person, and later when he or she became a good friend.

Begin your description as Virginia Woolf begins her paragraph, by indicating in a sentence or two the scene you are presenting to your reader. For example, if the setting you are describing is a party, help your reader see what kind of party it is, where it is held, and how many people are there. If you are describing the first time a class meets, indicate the course, the number of students who were present when you came in, and the atmosphere of the room.

Next, concentrate on the person you have chosen to describe. Begin by describing the person's appearance and then proceed to point out one or two of the person's actions. Finally, report what the person said. You could choose either the first words you heard the person say, or you could select something the person said at a later time. Choose a quotation you feel was especially characteristic of that person, or simply memorable to you.

Conclude your paragraph by writing one or two sentences in which you give your judgment of the person you have described. You could base your conclusion on what the person said, or you might wish to use both the person's appearance and what was said to form your judgment. When you finally met that person at the party, did that person's words confirm your first impression or were you surprised when the person spoke? Did the professor's remarks on that first day of class agree with your other impressions of him or her?

ESSAY PRACTICE

The following outline will help you plan a complete essay of at least five paragraphs. The theme of your essay will be closely related to the Virginia Woolf essay.

The following sentence may serve as your thesis sentence, and will also be the main idea of your introductory paragraph:

¶ 1. Sometimes experiences in a person's life may seem insignificant when they happen, but they can have some important immediate and long-range effects.

Each of the sentences below is the topic sentence for one of the paragraphs that you will write to develop your thesis. You may use the suggested details to develop each paragraph, or you may supply details of your own.

¶ 2. It is possible for a single incident to change the direction of our lives.

[DETAILS: Your incident could be a time you went to a party, or were introduced to someone, or when you answered an advertisement of some kind. In this paragraph make it clear to your reader that this was an incident that you did not think was important at the time.]

¶ 3. The immediate effects of this incident were . . .

[DETAILS: Using the incident you chose, recall your immediate reactions. What were the immediate changes in your life or your way of thinking as a result of this experience?]

¶ 4.   The long-range effects of this incident were . . .

[DETAILS: Using the same example, describe the long-range effects of your experience. For example, if you married the person you met, the effects could be described as long term.]

Be certain that you use transitions between paragraphs to make your writing flow smoothly. In addition, be sure that your conclusion gives your reader a clear signal that you have come to the end of your essay.

ESSAY TOPICS

1. Describe a situation in which you found yourself fighting against some aspect of popular or current thinking. Was it enough for you to struggle only in your mind? How did you make other people aware of your struggle?

2. a. When Virginia Woolf wrote this essay in 1940 it was extremely rare for a woman to exercise political power. Since that time women in several countries have achieved positions of power. What difference, if any, has this new direction in politics made in the modern world?

   b. What effects would there be on the power structure of our country, and on our institutions, if the United States elected a woman president?

3. In her essay, Virginia Woolf presents the stereotype of women as passive and men as aggressive. Based on your observation of men and women, what are some other stereotypes that still exist in our society? How do these stereotypes affect people's behavior? In your opinion, do people tend to act the way they have been stereotyped?

⏴ *Kenneth E. F. Watt* ⏴

Kenneth E. F. Watt was born in Toronto, Canada, in 1929. He received his B.A. from the University of Toronto and his Ph.D. from the University of Chicago. From 1954 to 1957 he worked for the Ontario Department of Lands and Forests, and from 1957 to 1960 he was senior biometrician for the Canadian Department of Agriculture at Ottowa. He also worked in the research division of the Canadian Department of Forestry.

Since 1963, Professor Watt has been with the Zoology and Environmental Studies Department of the University of California at Davis. He has written and contributed to several books, including *The Unsteady State: Growth, Culture, and Environmental Problems*. He has published over a hundred articles in professional journals and in such popular magazines as *Natural History* and *Saturday Review*.

The following essay appeared in *Natural History* magazine in 1972.

PREVIEWING THE WRITER

• Note the advantages of diversity, as outlined by the writer. Is there any one advantage that seems to be more convincing than the others?

• Note how the writer uses several different areas of our lives to argue in favor of diversity. How does the variety of his examples help to support his argument? What is the effect of the order in which the writer presents his examples?

• How does diversity benefit the individual, both physically and emotionally?

MAN'S EFFICIENT RUSH TOWARD DEADLY DULLNESS

IS DIVERSITY OF CONCERN to people interested in nat-   1
ural history, conservation, and the environment? To answer the question fully, one must understand the exact meaning of diversity, the ubiquitous loss of diversity in the world today, and the reasons for the value of diversity.

An argument for preserving anything, particularly some-   2
thing rare, often turns out to be an argument in disguise for

diversity. Thus, it seems worthwhile to provide natural historians with a handy kit of powerful arguments for variety because all too often they feel defenseless when confronted with the arguments of developers, which are clearly supported by short-term economic benefits, at least for a few investors.

The rapid loss of diversity in the world is a serious and 3 pervasive phenomenon. Everywhere we look, we see examples of a large number of diverse entities being replaced by a small number of similar entities. We all know about endangered species such as birds of prey and large mammals, including all species of whales. Most of the world's commercial fish stocks are in danger, shell collectors are depleting tropical beaches and coral reefs, and pollution will annihilate commercial shellfish populations, resulting in simplification of our diets. But progressive environmental simplification is far more widespread than this. Half the butterfly species have disappeared in Holland in the last few decades. Conversion of the Russian steppe from wild plants to wheat fields has cut the number of insect species there by 58 percent.

In the economic sphere, there has been a tremendous reduction in the number of manufacturers (think of the number of automobile manufacturers in the United States in 1910). Our numerous corner grocery stores have been replaced by a small number of huge supermarkets. In many fields, large numbers of small businesses have been replaced by small numbers of large businesses, to the point where we now have close to a monopoly in the manufacture of automobiles, aircraft, and computing equipment. Similarly, in agriculture large numbers of small farms have been replaced by small numbers of gigantic farm corporations.

Textural and cultural diversity has declined in our cities, 5 whether you compare different parts of the same city or different cities in different countries. Driving from an airport to the downtown section of a city, the signs tend to be in the same language (English) and to advertise the same products, whether one is in Rome, Beirut, or Singapore. Stores and banks seem to be stamped from a common mold.

Remarkably, the same process has occurred in the human 6 population. An extraordinarily high proportion of the world's population is now very young. The variety once found when many human age classes coexisted in approximately equal numbers has gone.

There are too many examples of the decline of diversity [7] for this situation to have come about by chance. There is indeed an underlying explanation: we live in an age, and a culture, that puts tremendous emphasis on efficiency and productivity as desiderata for mankind. Since variety is inimical to these goals, variety has suffered and will continue to suffer. Unless powerful and compelling arguments can be offered to stop this loss of diversity, we will soon be living in a homogeneous—and boring—world.

The large number of specific arguments for maintaining [8] the diversity of particular sets of plants, animals, or other items, all fall into four categories: (1) diversity promotes stability; (2) it insures against risks; (3) it utilizes more completely the sun's energy; and (4) it promotes the mental well-being of humans.

There are only two basic elements in all theoretical argu- [9] ments as to why diversity promotes stability. The first is the idea of spreading the risk (the same idea applies when you buy insurance from the largest insurance company). If an organism feeds on many different species, the chances of all its food sources being wiped out in some catastrophe are less than if the organism feeds on a few, or only one, species. The second idea is that a system functions more harmoniously if it has more elements because it then has more homeostatic feedback loops.

This abstract language can be translated into concrete ex- [10] amples. The greater the variety of foods the human population has available for harvesting, hunting, or fishing, the less the likelihood of human catastrophe due to a disaster befalling a particular food species. A most chilling example was the potato famine in Ireland, where an entire human population was excessively dependent on one food species. The situation is fundamentally the same when an Indian tribe depends greatly on salmon at a certain time of year, and then something happens to the salmon population (pollution or modification of the environment in the spawning stream due to a hydroelectric installation, for example). What few people realize is that the entire human population is now setting itself up for the same situation. For example, as we rapidly deplete the stocks of more and more oceanic species through overfishing and pollution, we cut off optional food sources that we might need desperately in the future. The larger the human population becomes and the more the sources of food decline, the more precarious is our situation.

Our great preoccupation with productivity and efficiency   11
and our lack of concern about diversity increase the precarious-
ness of our economic lives, as well as our food. Consider what
happens when we try to maximize the manufacturing efficiency
of aircraft. We are led, inexorably, to a situation in which a small
group of corporations manufacture all aircraft in the United
States. Each corporation is so large that it dominates the econ-
omies of the communities in which its plants are located. Thus,
if a corporation meets with disaster, the community is in deep
trouble. This is the case in Seattle, where Boeing sales slackened
with saturation of the international aircraft market. Architectural writer Jane Jacobs discovered this principle of relating the
economic stability of cities to their corporate diversity when she
applied current ecological theories about the relation between
diversity and stability to her urban studies.

In a most curious way, diversity appears to affect our eco-   12
nomic, social, cultural, and political processes. For example, a
slowly growing or nongrowing human population has a greater
evenness of numbers in different age classes than a rapidly
growing population. In a rapid-growth situation, young people
are being added to the population so quickly that their numbers
become unusually high relative to the numbers of older people.
This strains society's ability to generate adequate educational
taxes from the older group for the large younger group. It also
is difficult for a rapidly growing society to create new jobs at
the rate at which young people want to enter the labor force.

The more even the numbers of people in different age   13
classes, the easier it is to maintain good communication between
generations. Thus, all the present discussion about a ''generation gap'' has its ultimate origin in the lack of diversity in human age classes.

Many similar arguments relating diversity and different   14
forms of stability could be put forth. But the fundamental structure of all such arguments would be the same, whether the
subject is a human society or a rare plant. The reason for preserving it is that it may, in some unknown fashion, be important
to the maintenance of stability in a part of the planetary eco-
system.

The second class of arguments for maintaining diversity is   15
similar to the argument for buying life insurance. You don't
really want or expect to use it, but you buy it just in case.
Similarly, a civilization does not expect its acts to harm the

world, but just in case they are destructive it would be nice to have at hand other things to fall back on. For example, when we develop new strains of plants and animals, we do not plan on producing lines that will deteriorate in the future. We do not plan on producing strains of collie dogs in which the females will have progressively more difficulty bearing viable offspring, or strains of wheat that will succumb to rust, or berries that after many generations will no longer have much flavor. When these unintended events occur, we fall back on our "insurance policy," either by backcrossing our domestic strains to wild strains or by shifting our attention to new strains or species. But what if there are no new strains or species to replace the unsatisfactory ones?

The insurance value of diversity applies to more than just 16 individual species or strains of plants and animals. Suppose a civilization irrigated farmland in such a fashion that long-term, irreversible destruction of the soil only showed up after a century. Suppose, further, that the entire landscape of this civilization had been managed in an identical fashion. Then when the entire landscape lost its fertility, the civilization would be without land to produce food. Further, it wouldn't even have any unmanaged land to compare with the managed lands for scientific investigations. A simple example of the importance of such comparisons is the few forest areas in Greece from which goats have been excluded. The contrast between the grazed and ungrazed lands is so startling that no argument from goat-lovers could withstand visual comparison of forested areas with and without goats.

It is tremendously important for any civilization to set aside 17 areas where common cultivation practices are not adopted. If the same techniques are used everywhere, we can never know the long-term results of the practice. Thus, we can never know if intensive annual pesticide sprayings have long-term deleterious effects on orchards, forests, or woodlots unless we have unsprayed areas for comparison.

In short, a prudent civilization maintains the landscape 18 under many different management strategies, including parcels of each soil and climate zone that are not managed at all. This landscape diversity has two values. First, we have a yardstick for determining if something unexpected or odd is gradually showing up in a managed area. Without the unmanaged areas, the odd or unexpected effect could be ascribed to something else, to a change in climate, for example. The unsettled arguments as to whether the changes in the landscape of the Mediterranean basin, the Middle East, North Africa, and northern India were due to climatic change or man's activities show clearly the importance of having unmanaged areas for checking. The second value of landscape diversity is that if a civilization unwittingly destroys its managed lands, it has other places on which to raise food while the destroyed areas are gradually rebuilt to productivity.

A generalization of this argument holds that an extremely 19
prudent civilization would try to maintain other civilizations with different ideas about land use. Over the short term, the ideas of civilization A might appear vastly superior to those of civilization B. But over the long term it could turn out that the apparently "primitive" practices of civilization B were based on millennia of trial and error and incorporated deep wisdom that was unintelligible to civilization A.

The third argument for diversity originates in the theory 20
of modern ecologists that any habitat contains a set of "niches," or functions, that may be filled. If only part of the niches are filled, then the sun's energy that is captured by, and flows through, a system will be less than if all the niches were filled.

Perhaps the best-known and most convincing illustration 21
of this argument comes from Africa. Research shows that a mix of native animal species uses the landscape more economically than imported livestock. Each of the different types of antelope and other game consume slightly different mixes of food plants or parts of plants, so that a whole assemblage of different species uses the landscape more efficiently than, say, beef cattle would by themselves.

The same point has been demonstrated repeatedly in anal- 22
yses of the fish production per year per acre from different mixes of fish species. The more fish species there are in a body of water, the greater the gross production. Human understanding of this principle reaches its pinnacle in Oriental fish farming, where up to nine different species of carp are grown together in the set of proportions that makes best use of the resources in a pond.

Humanity has given far too little thought to the fourth 23
argument for preserving diversity. How much diversity in the world around us is optimal for the human mind? Might the extent of environmental diversity have any relationship to the

average level of mental health in a population? Could a certain level of diversity be most satisfying—emotionally and esthetically—to the human mind because of the conditions during human evolution? Diversity in an environment may have a much deeper significance for man than is generally recognized. We know that human beings tend to hallucinate when kept in confined quarters and deprived of sensory stimuli. This could be interpreted as a protective device by the mind to provide an otherwise unavailable need. Reports have been published indicating that extremely refractory mental patients, who had not spoken to anyone in years, showed an almost miraculous response when taken to wilderness areas.

The recent popularity of skin diving as recreation may convey a deep message. It may be that the rate of incoming sensory stimuli while skin diving is optimal for the human mind. I know that after several hours of constant interruption by the phone and visitors, I almost jump with each new phone call. But I also know that I can become bored amid all this stimuli. The extremely deep satisfaction I derive from exploring the ocean edge of a tropical island may be telling me something important about my mind and all our minds. We have evolved over a very long period so that our minds can cope handily with a certain rate of incoming sensory stimuli. We find the stimuli rate we can cope with in nature because we evolved there. Either sharply higher or sharply lower rates of incoming sensory stimuli are bad for our nervous systems.

This is only anecdotal evidence, but more carefully designed and measured research leads to the same conclusion. For some years, Professor J. Lee Kavanau of UCLA has been conducting experiments on small mammal behavior in heavily instrumented cages. These cages are wired, enabling the animal to change its environment and recording every move the animal makes and every detail of the conditions in the cage. The animals learn to control their environment by pressing levers. Kavanau has discovered that animals will press levers to select other than optimal conditions. In other words, confronted with a choice of living constantly in an optimal world but being bored or of living in a world that is only optimal part of the time and experiencing variety, even a small rodent will opt for variety. It is reasonable to assume that humans would opt even more strongly for variety rather than constant optimality. Perhaps diversity is not merely a luxury for us. It may be something we need.

If, upon reflection, you agree with my general line of ar- 26
gument as to the intrinsic value of diversity, then important
implications follow for many aspects of our lives. Particularly,
the argument has important political implications.

For example, if diversity breeds stability, then it is worth- 27
while for a government to regulate the rate at which different
interest groups acquire wealth and power. Undue concentration
of power and wealth allows a small group of people to change
the landscape to suit themselves, even though the change may
not suit others. For example, wilderness mountaintops and
tropical islands have been overdeveloped for second homes because the prospective profits for developers were very large relative to the total costs for society. Costs were small for the developers because they were not equitably divided within the
society. If something went sour with the development—the lots
didn't sell after trees were bulldozed—or if subsequent sewage
and pollution control costs spiraled, then someone else, not the
developer, absorbed the costs. Thus, the developer reaped a
great gain from subdividing, and someone else paid the price.
Given this situation, it is scarcely surprising that so much of the
world is being destroyed or that diversity is diminishing so rapidly.

A comparable situation exists with respect to the oceans, 28
which our culture treats as an international "common property
resource." Since no one or no one nation owns the oceans or
their contents, no one has a motive for perpetuating the living
diversity of the oceans. Consequently, the precious living treas-
ures of two-thirds of the earth may be less diverse or even de-
pleted in a short time. And there are too many links between
oceanic and terrestial life for such a loss to occur without profoundly affecting humanity.

THE WRITER'S THEMES

1. Review the title the writer chose for his essay. In view of
   the points made throughout the essay, how do you think
   the author intended us to understand the words "efficient"
   and "deadly"? What are the possible implications of "dullness," for both society and the individual?
2. What are the different kinds of evidence the writer uses to
   support the various parts of his argument? What kind of

evidence (personal, scientific, or historical) is the most convincing?
3. Watt tells us that the loss of diversity in the world is "serious." What are the most serious consequences of this loss of diversity?

THE WRITER'S TECHNIQUE

In the third paragraph of his essay, Kenneth Watt discusses the results of what he calls the "rapid loss of diversity in the world." Here is that paragraph:

> The rapid loss of diversity in the world is a serious and pervasive phenomenon. Everywhere we look, we see examples of a large number of diverse entities being replaced by a small number of similar entities. We all know about endangered species such as birds of prey and large mammals, including all species of whales. Most of the world's commercial fish stocks are in danger, shell collectors are depleting tropical beaches and coral reefs, and pollution will annihilate commercial shellfish populations, resulting in simplification of our diets. But progressive environmental simplification is far more widespread than this. Half the butterfly species have disappeared in Holland in the last few decades. Conversion of the Russian steppe from wild plants to wheat fields has cut the number of insect species there by 58 percent.

Notice that the writer begins his paragraph by announcing his subject with a topic sentence. In that topic sentence he also indicates his attitude toward that subject by referring to the "loss of diversity" in the world as "a serious and pervasive phenomenon." In the next sentence the writer indicates that he will provide examples of this ("Everywhere we look, we see examples . . ."), and in his third sentence he begins to provide them. His first examples are the commonly known "endangered species," such as birds of prey and large mammals, including whales; the writer does not go into details because he assumes we "all know about" these species.

However, the examples that follow are not so familiar. Most of the world's "fish stocks" are in danger, and "shell collectors are depleting tropical beaches and coral reefs" while shellfish are in danger because of pollution. So far the writer's examples have been restricted to marine life; the paragraph takes a new direction as we are told that the ongoing "simplification" of our environment "is far more widespread than this." From this point on, the writer deliberately avoids examples of marine life and draws his examples from a wide geographical area: in Holland, half of the butterfly species "have disappeared . . . in the last few decades" and on the Russian steppes the change "from wild plants to wheat fields" has reduced the number of insect species there "by 58 percent."

The writer's examples have clearly supported his thesis statement; we have been given examples that range from birds, to whales, to insects, and we also note that the examples range from the air and oceans of the world to the lands of Holland and Russia. We also observe that, in developing his paragraph, the writer has been careful to pay attention to each part of his topic sentence. The "rapid" loss of diversity is noted by the fact that half the butterfly species have disappeared in Holland "in the last few decades"; the fact that the writer is describing our world is clear from his use of the air ("birds of prey"), the oceans (whales and fish stock), and such different environments as the lowlands of Holland and the higher steppes of Russia. Finally, the fact that the situation is a "serious" one is also made clear when we are told that "all species of whales" are in danger, and that "pollution will annihilate commercial shellfish populations, resulting in simplification of our diets." The writer has not only proved his point, but by his careful choice of example we see the widespread implications of his point.

PARAGRAPH PRACTICE

Write a paragraph of your own, using the above paragraph as your model. Your paragraph could be an analysis of a current social or environmental problem. Some of these problems are:

Toxic waste dumping
Pollution from cars
Use of chemical pesticides
Noise pollution

Begin your paragraph by writing a clear thesis sentence, one that tells your reader what you are going to write about and that also reveals your attitude toward your subject. Next, indicate where examples to support your thesis may be found. Are examples easy to find, or does a person have to search for a long time to find the proper ones? Then provide at least two or three well-chosen examples to support your thesis. At this point in your paragraph, you should anticipate possible objections to your point of view and answer them briefly. Finally, give one additional piece of evidence to support your point of view. This final example should be just as specific as your earlier ones, and you should present it as your strongest point.

ESSAY PRACTICE

The following outline will help you plan a complete essay of at least five paragraphs. The theme of your essay will be closely related to the theme of the essay you have just read.

The following sentence may serve as your thesis sentence, and will also be the main idea of your introductory paragraph:

¶ 1.　Many institutions in our society do not encourage change, and the effects of this can be felt by individuals as well as by society at large.

Each of the sentences below is the topic sentence for one of the paragraphs that you will write to develop your thesis. You may use the suggested details to develop each paragraph, or you may supply details of your own.

¶ 2.　Despite the growing sense of personal liberation in recent years, many institutions still seem to prefer sameness rather than variety.

[DETAILS: What are the institutions that seem to prefer this sameness? In your opinion, why do they prefer to remain the same? Do these institutions lose by being so conservative? In this paragraph you might wish to give an example from the world of school or the world of work. For example, did you or someone you know ever try to make a change, only to be met by resistance?]

¶ 3.　This often leads to a real loss for the individual.

[DETAILS: How is an individual affected by a society or institution that discourages variety and individualism?]

¶ 4.　If variety is not encouraged, there are implications for the future of our society.

[DETAILS: What kind of society do you see for our future if variety is discouraged? Will we have a more or less interesting society in which to live?]

Be certain that you use transitions between paragraphs to make your writing flow smoothly. In addition, be sure that your conclusion gives your reader a clear signal that you have come to the end of your essay.

ESSAY TOPICS

1. How can Watts' ideas of the importance of diversity be applied to an individual's life? How could you apply his arguments in favor of diversity to areas of your own life?
2. The writer observes that undue concentration of power and wealth "allows a small group of people to change the landscape to suit themselves," and he also notes that it is good if a government regulates "the rate at which different interest groups acquire wealth and power."

   Describe a wealthy and powerful group or organization that is visible and active in our country today. How does such a group try to change things to suit itself? In your opinion, is the government doing enough to regulate this group? Do the activities of the group lead to benefits only for the group itself, or for society in general?
3. a. Assuming that the writer's argument in favor of diversity is correct, apply what he says to our political life. Should we encourage the growth of more political parties in our country, beyond the current two-party system? What effects would the appearance of new political parties have on the political life of our country?
   b. Choose another area of modern life where you feel that more diversity would have good results. Your choices could range from the world of sports, to the automobile industry, to more lifestyles that would be accepted by society. What specific benefits would there be for the individual and society if diversity were encouraged and accepted?

Focus on Terms: Concrete and Abstract

Concrete words or ideas are those we can observe with our senses; *abstract* ideas are those we are not able to observe so directly. Abstract ideas have their place in writing, but if a writer uses too many of them the reader will find it difficult to understand what was intended. Good writing always combines the concrete and the abstract into an interesting and compelling whole.

For example, in "Thoughts on Peace in an Air Raid," Virginia Woolf deals with a number of abstract concepts, such as "the desire to dominate and enslave," but the writer is careful also to show us concrete objects that illustrate her ideas. The writer immediately follows these twin desires by noting that "even in the darkness we can see that made visible. We can see shop windows blazing; and women gazing . . ." Virginia Woolf also includes the concepts of "peace" and "freedom" in her essay, but again she provides very concrete details of people able to do what they want to, in an atmosphere free of fear.

In Kenneth E. F. Watt's essay, "Man's Efficient Rush toward Deadly Dullness," the writer is very conscious of the need to present concrete examples of his argument. At one point in the essay, the writer is discussing the "two basic elements in all theoretical arguments as to why diversity promotes stability." He discusses these, and then begins his next paragraph by noting that this "abstract language can be translated into concrete examples" and proceeds to do just that.

A good basic plan for writing an essay that combines abstract examples with concrete examples is to present first the abstract and then without delay give concrete details and examples. These will make clear the abstract concept for the reader. If you stay too long in the area of the abstract and do not provide concrete examples quickly enough, you will risk losing your reader's attention. Few writing techniques will keep your reader with you as surely as a series of well-chosen concrete examples.

Student Essay \ \ Colleen Brosnan

The facts of our current economic situation have led many people to make changes in their working lives and in their family lives. Husbands and wives have discovered that if both of them are going to work and if the marriage is going to succeed, they will have to be more flexible at home.

The following essay is a report on this new situation. The writer looks at the many effects of today's economic situation on the modern family and concludes that these effects are being felt in the office as well as in the home.

• Notice that the writer of this essay makes such abstract terms as "inflation," "stagflation," and "recession" concrete for her readers by using several very specific examples, many of which we can recognize in our own lives or in the lives of people we know.

GOODBYE, MOM'S APPLE PIE

INFLATION. STAGFLATION. RECESSION. No matter what 1 you call the current state of our economy, virtually all of us have been touched by its effects. Rising prices and the shrinking dollar have made two-income families, once a rarity, now almost the norm. Besides fattening the family pocketbook (if only to buy necessities), how else has this phenomenon changed our lives?

The most noticeable change for most families is that Mom 2 is no longer home during the day—not there to fix hot lunches or to soothe scraped knees and bruised egos. So who does? The answer, unfortunately, often is "No one." Countless numbers of children have become "latchkey children," left to fend for themselves after school because there aren't enough dependable, affordable babysitters or after-school programs for them. Some children are able to handle this early independence quite well and may even become more resourceful adults because of it, but many are not. Vandalism, petty thievery, alcohol and drug abuse may all be products of this unsupervised life, problems that society in general must deal with eventually. Some companies (although too few) have adapted to this changing lifestyle by instituting on-site childcare facilities and/or "flextime" schedules for working mothers and fathers. Schools have begun to provide low-cost after-school activities during the school year, and summer day camps are filling the need during those months.

Another effect of Mom's absence from the home is that 3

businesses are discovering that she is no longer available to let meter readers in, accept furniture deliveries, take children to the doctor and dentist, or take care of banking needs. Just as many supermarkets have changed to a twenty-four-hour selling day, retail stores and service industries are beginning to realize that they must also adapt if they want to keep the working woman's business.

Even when Mom comes home in the evening, life is still 4 not "normal." Housecleaning is becoming a shared activity, when it gets done at all. Dad's duties are no longer confined to mowing the lawn and taking out the garbage. He is now expected to vacuum, wash dishes, bathe children, fold laundry— chores that no self-respecting man of a generation ago would have done. Has Dad's ego suffered? Maybe. But possibly, just possibly, his sense of being part of a family unit, not just the breadwinner and disciplinarian, has increased. Because he is now forced to deal with his children on a less exalted level, he may find that he is closer to them and they to him. Certainly, both parent and child will be affected by this more active fathering.

So now we have Dad helping with the household chores 5 and with the children. What about meals? Again, Dad may be asked to help out, but many men (and women) still feel the kitchen is the woman's domain. Enter time-saving appliances, such as the microwave oven and convenience foods such as boil-in-the-bag frozen entrees. Mom simply doesn't have the time or the energy to prepare traditional meals, including apple pie and home-baked bread. "Instant" meals are no longer considered a luxury and the food industry is cashing in on the demand. Even old standby items on the grocery shelves now proclaim that they are "microwavable," a fact that is not hurting their sales one bit. However, even with quickie meals Mom is sometimes just too tired to cook. At those times fast-food restaurants enjoy the family's business. They offer no fuss, no muss, and someone to clean up after the meal. And "clean up" the restaurants have. At a time when food prices were rising almost daily and supermarket sales were dropping, fast-food restaurants were enjoying even higher sales. Maybe part of the reason was that women were beginning to realize that their time was valuable too and if food prices were high anyway, they reasoned, they might as well eat out and not have to spend their few precious hours at home in the kitchen.

So far we have discussed only how Mom's absence from 6

the home has changed family life. How has Mom's presence in the workforce affected the business world? Most employers have found that older women are more dedicated, are more reliable than their younger unmarried counterparts, and are more mature in their attitudes toward work. An added benefit is that many women, having found that they are being challenged by their jobs and are being appreciated for more than their deftness at changing diapers and cleaning toilet bowls, are viewing their jobs as careers rather than just "a little job to make pin money." They are eager to learn more and to advance in their companies. To this end, many are returning to college, attending evening and Saturday classes. Colleges are delighted to have them. Not only do they help fill empty classrooms in a time of declining enrollment, they also are more serious about their studies and are able to contribute more to classroom discussions because of their life experiences.

How does the family feel about Mom as a late bloomer? 7 Dad may feel somewhat threatened, especially if he was raised to believe that woman's place is in the home. He may resent her working even more when the financial need is severe because he feels it announces to the world that he cannot provide for his family. Sometimes in marriages that are not solid to begin with, this perceived loss of dominance by the husband may even lead to divorce. In other instances, women who may have been unhappy in their marriages could now find that being in the world of work has given them the self-confidence and financial resources to enable them to end the marriage. However, most marriages survive these changes and the partners gain even greater respect for each other as they gain insight into the other's world. Children, once they learn to accept that their mother is no longer at their beck and call, begin to see her as an individual. They may also gain greater respect for her.

Yes, the two-income family has played havoc with our 8 lifestyles but it hasn't been all bad. There are problems that must be solved, changes that are difficult to accept, priorities that must be rearranged. However, with increased pressure from the growing number of two-income families, these problems will be addressed. Hopefully, society in general and individual families in particular will find even better ways to deal with these changes regarding how we raise our children, how we care for our homes, and how we view our marriages and ourselves.

Strategies for Writing

1. Review the essay and note those places where, in your view, the writer could have been more concrete. Rewrite at least one paragraph or section using as many of your own concrete details as you can supply.
2. Analyze paragraph six of the writer's essay from the point of view of concrete and abstract expression of ideas. How many of the ideas expressed in the paragraph are abstract? How many are concrete? How does this mixture help give strength and variety to the paragraph?
3. In your opinion, what are the causes for the recent dramatic increase in the numbers of women returning to school and the world of work? How many of these causes are purely economic?
4. Write an essay in which you discuss the effects of increased numbers of working women on today's business world. Has this increase led to any significant changes in business policies and attitudes?

10

THE SHAPING OF A
BETTER SOCIETY

WRITING SKILL: *Argumentation*

If you have ever seen a baseball player disagree vigorously with an umpire, if you have seen and heard a star tennis player shouting at an official on nationwide television, or if you have witnessed a couple fighting, you know what is commonly meant by the word *argument*. Formal argumentation, however, is a more structured matter that uses evidence in an organized and rational way.

Argumentation as a form of rhetoric has been in use for thousands of years. Originally, such formal arguments were heard in the law courts of ancient Athens to settle disputes, and the legal function of argument is still basic to our judicial system today. A written argument, in the rhetorical sense, is a structured attempt to convince another person of the truth of your position on a particular subject. Your aim may be simply to change that person's mind, or your argument may have as its ultimate aim a specific action that you want that person to take. In either case, your approach to the presentation of your argument is structured, orderly, and unemotional. You direct your thinking to the issue at hand, and when you write about your opposition you discuss only ideas, not personalities. Each part of your argument must be reasoned and rational; there should never be any room in your argument for words that have been chosen only for their emotional impact.

No matter what you are arguing for (or against), certain essential rules are basic to every argument. First, the problem must be clearly stated, along with an equally clear statement of your proposed solution. As you give the detailed evidence to support your argument, be sure that each of your points is clear to your reader. You should put those different points into an effective sequence, ending with your strongest point. Also essential in a good argument is your presentation of possible objections from your opponents. By noting these objections and answering them in advance, you gain an advantage over those who are on the opposite side of the argument. Another important part of an effective argument is explaining to your audience that your proposal is indeed practical and one that could realistically be adopted and put into action.

The major portion of most arguments is the presentation of evidence, and that evidence will be based on either inductive or deductive reasoning. When you use induction, your approach is very similar to that of a person solving a mystery. There are suggestions, facts, and clues of various kinds all around; your job is to put all those fragments together and arrive at a conclusion that will be convincing. If you use deduction, your approach is just the opposite. Deductive reasoning begins with a general statement and then places a specific example in the context of that general statement. For example, if you were to observe that all of your friends who worked in such places as restaurants, banks, and amusement parks were unhappy because of the way the public treated them, you might conclude that it is not desirable to work directly with the public. That is an example of induction. If, on the other hand, you began with the belief—a belief that you could have for any number of reasons—that working with the public is not pleasant, and then someone offered you a job in a supermarket, you might well decide that it would not be a pleasant atmosphere in which to work. That is deduction.

Each of the essays in this unit is an example of argumentation, and each one illustrates in slightly different ways the principles of a good argument. For example, the Marya Mannes essay "The Child before the Set" is an argument against television, although the writer is not so much arguing against what is on television as she is arguing *for* what is missing from that medium. A good deal of the writer's evidence is drawn from her own experience, but she is also careful to use an outside source that clearly supports her position. At one point the writer is close to admitting that the proponents of television watching have a valid argument—television *could* be worthwhile—but when the rest of her essay clearly reveals that it is not worthwhile, her own point of view is strengthened and the opposition's case suffers from lack of evidence.

In Erich Fromm's argument that "Our Way of Life Makes Us Miserable," the writer's point of view is clear from the moment we read his title, and the evidence of this point of view is clearly stated in a well-planned order. The writer deals with many sensitive areas of our lives, and he makes some penetrating comments about each of them. We notice, however, that he does not conclude his argument without proposing a solution to the problems he has raised. He also points the way toward achieving the goal of a renaissance of human values.

An additional prerequisite for a good argument is that the writer clearly show the need for what is being proposed. In Aldous Huxley's essay "The Scientist's Role," this need is described in detail. Huxley devotes a good deal of attention to proving his point that food and power are the two main problems facing the modern world. The writer is just as specific when he proposes his solutions to these problems.

Some arguments encourage controversy and discussion while others are intended to put an end to discussion and remove any doubts that there is only one correct solution. When Mayra Mannes wrote her essay, one of her intentions was to open up the whole area of discussion about television and its effects. This opening up of discussion is also one of Erich Fromm's purposes as he analyzes modern materialism, and we see the same thinking behind the Aldous Huxley essay. The essay by Paul and Percival Goodman, on the other hand, is a different kind of argument, one that has as its intention the *closing* of any further discussion. With its detailed plan of action and its answers to virtually any objection, "Banning Cars from Manhattan" is the kind of argument that seeks to prevent any kind of disagreement. It also contains many elements of the classic essay of argument. The writers begin with their proposed solution to the problem of congestion in New York City and they state why there is a problem. The writers then provide five specific reasons why any opposing plan would not work, and along with the many advantages of their plan, they carefully indicate the possible disadvantages. Finally, they give us specific details as to how their plan could be implemented and they conclude by emphasizing what the effects would be if their plan became reality.

Whether it tries to make us think in a new way, or act in a way that shows we have changed our minds about something, an argument is intended to persuade us that we should not only see a certain question in a new way, we should perhaps even act on this new perception. When you write an argument, you should use the classical techniques of argumentation and keep as your aim some kind of change in the minds of your audience.

✺ *Paul Goodman and Percival Goodman* ✺

Paul Goodman (1911–1972) was variously described as a lecturer, a psychotherapist, a humorist, an essayist, a poet, a novelist, and a social critic. Born and raised in New York City, Goodman graduated from City College (CCNY) in 1931, and began to support himself by reading movie scripts for Metro-Goldwyn-Mayer. During this period Goodman managed to get his first articles and short stories published.

From the 1930s to the 1950s Goodman wrote a great deal, but much of what he produced remained unpublished. For a while in the 1950s the writer worked as a lay psychotherapist with an institute in New York. Until the late 1950s Paul Goodman remained poor and was always close to failure as a writer, but in 1960 he won widespread acclaim as the author of *Growing Up Absurd: Problems of Youth in the Organized System,* a book which has been described as "a bristling indictment of American society and a spirited defense of the youth who drop out of it." After the publication of this book, Goodman was in constant demand as a lecturer and consultant to a wide variety of governmental and private institutions.

The following essay is taken from Paul Goodman's 1962 book, *Utopian Essays and Practical Proposals.* "Banning Cars from Manhattan" was written with his brother Percival, a noted architect.

PREVIEWING THE WRITERS

• Note the advantages and disadvantages of the plan that the authors present. How complete is this list of advantages and disadvantages?

• Note the kind of city that would result if the writers' suggestions were to be adopted.

• How many of the authors' suggestions could be used in communities other than Manhattan?

BANNING CARS FROM MANHATTAN

WE PROPOSE banning private cars from Manhattan Island. Permitted motor vehicles would be buses, small taxis, vehicles for essential services (doctor, police, sanitation, vans, etc.), and the trucking used in light industry.

Present congestion and parking are unworkable, and other   2
proposed solutions are uneconomic, disruptive, unhealthy,
nonurban, or impractical.

It is hardly necessary to prove that the actual situation is   3
intolerable. "Motor trucks average less than six miles per hour
in traffic, as against eleven miles per hour for horse drawn vehicles in 1911." "During the ban on nonessential vehicles during the heavy snowstorm of February 1961, air pollution
dropped 66 per cent." (*New York Times,* March 13, 1961.) The
street widths of Manhattan were designed, in 1811, for buildings of one to four stories.

By banning private cars and reducing traffic, we can, in   4
most areas, close off nearly nine out of ten crosstown streets
and every second north–south avenue. These closed roads plus
the space now used for off-street parking will give us a handsome fund of land for neighborhood relocation. At present over
35 per cent of the area of Manhattan is occupied by roads. Instead of the present grid, we can aim at various kinds of enclosed neighborhoods, in approximately 1200-foot to 1600-foot
superblocks. It would be convenient, however, to leave the existing street-pattern in the main midtown shopping and business areas, in the financial district, and wherever the access for
trucks and service cars is imperative. Our aim is to enhance the
quality of our city life with the minimum of disruption of the
existing pattern.

The disadvantages of this radical proposal are small. The   5
private cars are simply not worth the nuisance they cause. Less
than 15 per cent of the people daily entering Manhattan below
Sixty-first Street come by private car. Traffic is congested, speed
is slow, parking is difficult or impossible and increasingly expensive. It is estimated that the cost of building new garaging
is $20,000 per car; parking lots are a poor use of land in the
heart of a metropolis, and also break the urban style of the
cityscape.

The advantages of our proposal are very great. Important   6
and immediate are the relief of tension, noise, and anxiety; pu-
rifying the air of fumes and smog; alleviating the crowding of
pedestrians; providing safety for children. Subsequently, and
not less importantly, we gain the opportunity of diversifying
the gridiron, beautifying the city, and designing a more integrated community life.

The problem and our solution to it are probably unique to   7
Manhattan Island, though the experiment would provide valuable lessons elsewhere. Manhattan is a world center of business, buying, style, entertainment, publishing, politics, and light
manufacture. It is daily visited in throngs by commuters to work,
seekers of pleasure, shoppers, tourists, and visitors on business.
We have, and need, a dense population; and the area is small
and strictly limited. Manhattan does not sprawl. It can easily be
a place as leisurely as Venice, a lovely pedestrian city. But the
cars must then go.
....

Manhattan has been losing population to the suburbs and   8
near countryside, with a vast increase of daily commutation. A
more desirable center would reduce and perhaps eliminate this
trend. Indeed, within the city itself, it is possible to decrease
commutation. The I.L.G.W.U. housing near the garment district points the way. It would be useful, also, to establish a
municipal agency to facilitate people's living near their work if
they so choose, by arranging exchanges of residence advantageous to all parties. This should be possible in many thousands
of cases and is certainly worth trying.

1. PERIPHERAL PARKING

The banned private cars can be accommodated by various kinds   9
of peripheral parking . . .

At present many thousands of commuters' cars are left at   10
suburban railway stops and at more or less convenient subway
stations in Queens, Brooklyn, and the Bronx. This is because of
the obvious undesirability, from the motorists' point of view,
of driving them into Manhattan. We propose simply to gener-
alize this common-sense decision in order to use it as a basis
for important further advantages.

In addition, we propose the construction of multipurpose   11
parking piers in the Hudson and East Rivers for cars entering
by the main bridges and tunnels. These piers could be developed for promenade, recreational, and even residential use . . .

The piers would be served by bus and taxi. Consider a   12
particular case. A large emporium, e.g., Macy's, could provide
pier-limousines for commuting shoppers, including the service
of delivering packages to the parked cars.

2. ROADS

We keep the broad commercial cross streets—Greenwich Ave-   13
nue, Fourteenth Street, Twenty-third, Forty-second, Fifty-sev-
enth, Fifty-ninth, etc.—as two-way bus and taxi arteries; and
also First, Third, Fifth, Seventh, Broadway, Ninth, and Elev-
enth Avenues. These should provide adequate circulation for
the residual traffic (but this would have to be experimented).
As indicated above, we would keep the existent street pattern
in midtown—from Twenty-third to Fifty-ninth Streets—to serve
the shops, theaters, etc.; and also wherever there is a special
case. (Every street would have to be studied individually.)

All other streets become pedestrian walks broad enough   14
to serve as one-way roads for servicing: fire, garbage, mail, and
so forth.

The proposed grid of through arteries is such that the max-   15
imum walk to the nearest bus stop would always be less than
one-fifth of a mile. Subway entrances exist as at present. In
general, bus service throughout Manhattan is expanded, and
the two-deck buses are brought back. We must bear in mind
that with the ending of congestion and the immense diminishing of pedestrian cross-overs, the speed limit for taxis and express buses could be raised to twenty-five or even thirty miles
an hour. Since there is less need to cross, it is possible to eliminate jay walking, and perhaps provide pedestrian bridges and
tunnels. By and large, *given the improvement of the bus service,
most travel about town would be swifter and more convenient than it
is at present with private cars.*

There would be more taxis. We conceive of these as small,   16
half the present length. They might well be electrics. It is absurd
for taxis in a limited-speed metropolis to be the same cars designed for family travel on super highways.

If opened out and if its blocks are enlarged, the gridiron   17
plan is practical and has a sort of grandeur. To avoid the boredom of endless vistas, however, we should recommend bridg-
ing certain streets with buildings and creating other spatial effects. Every street and avenue should be studied as an individual
artistic problem.

3. NEIGHBORHOOD AND COMMUNITY

The ideal for New York or any other vast city is to become a   18
large collection of integral neighborhoods sharing a metropolitan center and metropolitan amenities. The neighborhoods dif-

fer since they comprise a wide variety of inhabitants and community functions, which could be administered with relative independence by each neighborhood. There is no reason for them to look alike. A basically family-residential neighborhood, for instance, might have nearly autonomous control of its local school, with much of the school-tax administered by the local Parent-Teacher Association. The central Board of Education could dictate minimum standards and see to it that underprivileged neighborhoods get a fair share of the total revenue; but it need not stand in the way, as it does at present, of variation and experimentation. The hope is to diminish sharply the amount of ''administration''—at present there are more school administrators in the New York City system than in all of France. Our idea too is that local exercise of political initiative on local problems like schooling, housing, and planning would educate the electorate and make real democracy possible. A neighborhood should be planned to increase mutual acquaintance of the neighbors and to increase their responsibility for school, market, playground, zoning, and so forth. Such a complex could well serve as the primary municipal electoral unit. Meantime, all the integral neighborhoods share in the great city of the big shops, theaters, hotels, museums, and national enterprises. *The aim of integral planning is to create a human-scale community, of manageable associations, intermediary between the individuals and families and the metropolis; it is to counteract the isolation of the individual in the mass society.* Naturally, in a vast region like New York there will be many thousands of persons who choose precisely to be isolated individuals—that might be why they came here—but these too form a distinctive and valuable element in the federal whole, and they can be provided for in the center, perhaps in apartment hotels, or in characteristic neighborhoods of their own. It is curious, on this point, that the ''individualistic'' persons who came to New York to escape conformist small-town mores found that precisely they themselves had much in common and formed a famous community, the intellectual and artistic stratum of Greenwich Village.

Toward the ideal of a city of federated communities, the ¹⁹ simple device of banning the cars and replanning the gridiron is a major step. The new road-pattern allows for superblocks of from six to nine acres. (For comparison, Stuyvesant Town covers sixteen acres.) With plastic invention aiming at the maximum variety of landscaping, land use and building height, there is here an unexampled opportunity for dozens of eventual solutions that could surpass in urbanity and amenity the squares and crescents of eighteenth-century London. There is space for recreation and play. E.g., the length of a tennis court fits across Ninth Avenue; an occasional corner is big enough for a softball field. Given the large fund of newly available land, now wasted on largely unnecessary and always inconvenient traffic and parking, it is possible to develop new neighborhoods in a leisurely fashion, with careful study and without problems of relocation, or dislocation of such neighborhood ties as exist. *We would especially recommend competitions and public referenda, in order to avoid bureaucratic imposition and to educate the community to concern for its proper business.*

4. MEANS, ETC.

The legal execution of the proposed ban should not be difficult. 20
Streets are at present closed off for play and other purposes. The Mayor banned all traffic in the emergency of snow clearance—though his right to do so has been disputed. We have had a vehicle tax; it could be so pegged as to be prohibitive. A prohibitive entry fee could be charged.

Such a ban should, or course, be leniently interpreted to 21
allow for special cases and emergency use. E.g., a family starting on a trip could use its car to load. Likewise, there must be provision for cars to pass across Manhattan, east and west.

It is likely that the ban on cars could be lifted on weekends, 22
when the truck and bus traffic is much diminished. Especially during the warm months this would be convenient for weekend trippers.

5. CONCLUSION

This proposal seems to us to be common sense. The cars have 23
caused many and increasingly severe evils, and the situation is admittedly critical. The proposed solutions, however—new traffic regulations, new highways, multilevels, underground parking—all bear the typical earmark of American planning: to alleviate an evil by remedies that soon increase the evil. But in the special case of Manhattan, the elementary radical remedy, to get rid of the cars, would cause little hardship and have immense and beautiful advantages. (Naturally, in sprawling cities like Los Angeles or Cleveland, one cannot get rid of the cars. Correspondingly, such places lack center and urbanity.)

The chief advantage of this proposal is that it provides 24

opportunity. It does not merely remedy an evil or provide a way to do the same things more efficiently, but it opens the possibility to think about ideal solutions, human values, and new ways to do basic things. Most big-scale planning, however, and most of what passes for Urban Renewal, are humanly indifferent. The quality of life in our cities will not be improved by such planning, but by some elementary social psychiatry and common sense.

Finally, conceive that one of our mayoral candidates were convinced of the advantages of this proposal and made it a part of his program in campaigning for office. This is hard to conceive, for it is just such concrete issues that are never offered to the voters—they are left to special "experts," and indeed to special interests. The voters do not have real choices to think about, therefore they never learn to think. Instead, they vote for personalities and according to ethnic and party groupings. The rival programs are both vague and identical. 25

If such a plan as this, however, were offered as an important issue, our guess is that the candidate would lose on the first try, because he would be considered radical and irresponsibly adventurous; but he would win the next time around, when people had had the chance to think the matter through and see that it made sense. 26

THE WRITERS' THEMES

1. Many plans for community renewal are concerned only with improving life for a certain part of a community. Would the type of proposal the writers present be of benefit to everyone in a city such as New York, or would it benefit only certain parts of society?
2. To what extent does effective neighborhood planning for Manhattan depend upon acceptance of the writers' proposal to ban cars from Manhattan? According to the authors, what is the connection between planning for the transportation needs of a community and neighborhood planning?
3. The writers describe their proposal as part of a larger vision of an ideal community. Where in the essay do we have indications of this larger vision? According to the writers, what is the aim of all integrated urban planning?

THE WRITERS' TECHNIQUE

In the opening paragraphs of their essay, the writers state a specific proposal and then point out its advantages and disadvantages. They state their proposal at the beginning of the first paragraph:

> We propose banning private cars from Manhattan Island.

At this point in any written argument, the writer should try to convince the reader that the proposal is necessary. Here, the writers do this when they indicate in the next paragraph that the "present congestion and parking are unworkable," while other proposed solutions are "uneconomic, disruptive, unhealthy, nonurban, or impractical."

Having dismissed any other solutions to the problem, the authors now provide (in paragraphs three and four) several supporting facts and statistics that prove the real need for their plan. Then they begin their fifth paragraph with this statement:

> The disadvantages of this radical proposal are small.

The paragraph that follows includes several disadvantages, but we notice that they all relate to the present situation where cars are used in Manhattan; the only real disadvantage to this proposal, and one that is never mentioned directly in the paragraph, seems to be that people would not be free to drive their cars on Manhattan Island. An important part of any argument is paying at least some attention to the disadvantages of one's own proposal; here the writers do just this, but we are reminded that they have already described the disadvantages as "small."

The authors now devote paragraph six to the advantages of their proposal, and again their opening sentence is a clear and direct topic sentence:

> The advantages of our proposal are very great.

The paragraph then supports the proposal by pointing out the specific advantages if banning cars were to become reality: there would be immediate "relief of tension, noise, and anxiety," not to mention the fact that the city would be beautified. In addition, it would be possible to design "a more integrated community life." This paragraph also demonstrates a further characteristic of a good argument, namely, that the proposal is a practical one; we can realistically expect that it could be accomplished.

The writers began with a clear statement of their argument, and after providing a number of strong supporting facts, they deal with both the disadvantages and advantages of their proposal. As we have seen, the paragraph that was supposed to describe the disadvantages actually contained a further list of advantages; the writers seemed unable to find, or could not bring themselves to include, anything that did not support their argument. However, the fact that they at least indicated the idea of disadvantages, as well as the actual advantages, shows that no matter which side of an argument you happen to be on it is important to deal with both sides. In addition, by anticipating arguments you feel your opposition is likely to make, you show that you are able to see both sides of the issue, and thus your side of the argument is strengthened.

PARAGRAPH PRACTICE

Write a paragraph of your own, using the above approach as the model for the development of your paragraph. Your paragraph should be an argument in which you make a proposal, state why you believe that proposal is valid, take care to point out some possible disadvantages to your proposal, and then point out some of the most important advantages to what you have proposed. For example, if you argue that students should not have to take required courses in college, your paragraph would have the following structure:

> I propose that college students should not be forced to take any required courses. [Here you would state why you think this idea is valid.] The disadvantages of this proposal are . . . The most important advantages would be . . .

Some other possible topics for your paragraph could be an argument for or against learning a foreign language, for or against having alcoholic beverages on campus, or for or against a national law that would set a legal drinking age.

ESSAY PRACTICE

The following outline will help you plan a complete essay of at least five paragraphs. The theme of your essay will be closely related to the theme of the essay you have just read.

The following sentence may serve as your thesis sentence, and will also be the main idea of your introductory paragraph:

¶ 1. I believe my community should seriously consider a new project [here, briefly identify the project], one that will become even more needed as time goes on.

Each of the sentences below is the topic sentence for one of the paragraphs that you will write to develop your thesis. You may use the suggested details to develop each paragraph, or you may supply details of your own.

¶ 2. Here is how the project would work.

[DETAILS: Describe the project or course of action you have proposed. For example, your proposal could call for workers sharing in the decision-making process with management or could argue for the establishment of a needed facility, such as a day-care center, in your neighborhood. Be sure to consider such factors as cost, time needed for construction, organization, personnel needed, and the number of people or families it would affect.]

¶ 3. There are a few disadvantages to this proposal.

[DETAILS: Describe at least one or two possible objections to your idea. In this paragraph you should anticipate your opposition and at the same time present your answers to these objections.]

¶ 4. There are several long-term effects that make this project significant.

[DETAILS: What are the benefits you believe would result if your proposal became reality? Arrange these benefits in such a manner that the greatest is last.]

Be certain that you use transitions between paragraphs to make your writing flow smoothly. In addition, be sure that your conclusion gives your reader a clear signal that you have come to the end of your essay.

ESSAY TOPICS

1. The writers point out that while "the problem and our solution to it are probably unique to Manhattan Island" the proposal "would provide valuable lessons elsewhere."

   What lesson(s) can this essay provide for your own community? In an essay, you could argue for the banning of all vehicles from the main street of your community, or you could argue for the creation of a pedestrian area where cars or trucks would not be allowed. What is the need for the adoption of such a proposal in your community? What are some of the disadvantages to your idea? In your view, what would be the greatest benefit to your community if your idea became reality?

2. a. "Banning Cars from Manhattan" was published in a book entitled *Utopian Essays and Practical Proposals*. Keeping in mind the dictionary definition of "utopian" as "excellent or ideal but existing only in visionary or impractical thought or theory," discuss the authors' proposal as either utopian or practical. In your opinion, is the idea of eliminating all private cars from the center of a major city such as New York only an "impractical thought or theory," or could it really become a practical way to solve a number of urban problems?

   b. Discuss a proposal for the solution of a current problem in your community. Your problem could range from the local parking situation, to a declining school population, to the need for new or renovated housing in the area. After describing the problem and its possible solution, analyze your proposal as either practical or utopian. Who would see your idea as a good solution but an impractical one? Who would view your proposal as not only something desirable, but practical as well?

3. Today our cities are facing more serious problems than at any other time in our history. What do you believe are our most serious urban problems? In your opinion, what must be done to make our cities more attractive places to live?

❧ *Marya Mannes* ❧

Marya Mannes (1904–) was born in New York City, the daughter of David and Clara Mannes, two performing musicians who later founded the Mannes College of Music in New York. Marya Mannes attended a private school where, in her own words, she obtained "a solid acquaintance with Latin and French [and] an attitude towards the English language compounded equally of respect and love." She also indulged in her favorite extracurricular activities, which included "reading, fantasy, play-acting, writing poetry, and worshipping heroes, living and dead."

After graduation, she tried a career in the theatre but soon decided to devote herself to writing. Throughout the 1920s and 1930s, Marya Mannes was a frequent contributor to such well-known periodicals as *Vogue*, *Theatre Arts*, and *Harper's* Magazine.

During World War II, Marya Mannes worked as an intelligence analyst for the government. She returned to journalism after the war, becoming a feature editor at *Glamour* magazine. Later, she became a staff writer for the *Reporter*, and for some years each issue of that magazine contained examples of her essays, articles, television reviews, or satirical verse.

Marya Mannes drew upon these various *Reporter* pieces when she came to write her 1958 book *More in Anger*. The following essay appeared in that book and gives us several insights into the writer's attitude toward television. The essay is also a good example of what Marya Mannes herself has declared to be her intention in writing: to "communicate clearly and honestly what I see and what I believe about the world I live in."

PREVIEWING THE WRITER

• Note the adjectives the writer uses in the opening paragraph of her essay. How does the writer's choice of adjectives reveal her attitude toward television viewing?

• Note the writer's use of both her own experience and the experience of an outside authority to support her argument.

• Note the writer's emphasis on the commercial aspect of our society. Is her position on modern commerce realistic or idealistic?

THE CHILD BEFORE THE SET

I AM SORRY for the children who are brought up on   1
television; not so much for the fare they receive, which is often
of abysmal quality, as for the hours they lose. For while it is

grotesque enough that healthy adults be "entertained" for three hours a day for six days a week (the seventh being mercifully reserved for enlightenment) it is an act of destruction that children should kill time, which is the most precious thing they possess: time to dream, time to imagine, time to make. Until a child can meet reality, he must live in fantasy. But he must create his own fantasy. And it is television's primary damage that it provides ten million children with the same fantasy, ready-made and on a platter. Nor is this, with very rare exceptions, the fruitful fantasy of poets or artists but the unreal world of television itself, which bears no relation to that of a child but which envelops him, willy-nilly, in a false adult vision which, in turn, is not even truly adult. And on this infinitely sensitive and apparently unerasable recording-tape of the child's mind is printed a shadow world of blurred values, where the only reality is the product Mom must buy.

This need not be so. Television could be the great teacher   2
and the great revealer to children, and I hope I live till the day when it fulfills its miraculous function as a third eye. But now I can think only of the killing of hours, and remember the hours of one child who grew before television pre-empted them.

In my childhood the days were not regimented. After   3
school and before a homework evening, the time was our own, for us to fill as we chose. In school we were groups, at home we were single; and it never occurred to my parents to arrange my social day with organized activity. They felt that a good school, an affectionate home, and a consistent standard of ethics were enough. The rest was up to us, my brother and me.

I cannot presume that our life was typical, because my   4
parents were making music all day, teaching or playing together or rehearsing for concerts, my mother at the piano, my father with the violin. In time my brother used the piano when it was free, and there were very few hours in my childhood when the air in our home was dead, or empty of meaning. Because of this, the advent of radio, miraculous as we thought it, left us indifferent. What could it give us then that our life could not? What need was there to turn on its scratchy blatancies when musicians like Cortot and Casals and Thibaud[1] came to the apartment and joined my parents in the quintets and trios of Brahms, in Schubert quartets? I remember clearly the exaltation

[1] Alfred Cortot (1877–1962), a famous French pianist; Pablo Casals (1876–1973), reknowned Spanish cellist; Jacques Thibaud (1880–1953), famous French violinist.

this music brought me, a sense of excitement and glory that often impelled me to tears. And I remember sitting in a corner of the living room watching these musicians play and noticing the transfiguration of their faces, which, a moment before had been—to my childish eyes—neither handsome nor extraordinary. I saw what music did to them and I felt great awe.

This was not, I repeat, a typical home; rather it was a rarely fortunate one. Yet there were still those hours in the afternoon when my parents were teaching or on tour, when my brother, whose five-year seniority then kept us worlds apart, was out or away, and when I fended for myself, often alone. And I know that if televison had been in the house I would not have done what I did. I read, voraciously and indiscriminately, nearly a book a day, alternating the *Golden Bough* with *Dotty Dimple*, *Kidnapped* with the *St. Nicholas* magazine. I wrote very bad poems with very deep emotion. I studied Swahili phrases in African adventure stories. I made peculiar figures out of plastecine, I painted messy water-colors of flowers in vases, I practiced the role, patterned on John Barrymore,[2] of Richard III, I tried leaping like Nijinsky[3] in *Spectre de La Rose*, and I spent a considerable amount of time hanging by my knees from a trapeze set in my bedroom door. I liked the feeling.

When I was not engaged in any of these pursuits, I was out on Riverside Drive with a friend, usually standing on a bridge where the freight trains came through beneath in a hissing cloud of white steam, or walking along the Hudson smelling the dampness of rotting piers, or climbing granite mountains blazing with mica. The hours were long and the sun was bright and our heads full of crazy thoughts. Even in our teens, nobody told us to join anything, nobody arranged subscription dances so that we could meet the right boys, and, in fact, we never thought of meeting boys. We were in love with Peter Ibbetson.[4]

What is more—and what I believe to be most relevant of all to the age before television and mass communication in general—I do not remember in all my childhood any commerical

---

[2] John Barrymore (1882–1942), famous American stage and film actor.

[3] Vaslav Nijinsky (1890–1950), legendary Russian ballet dancer and choreographer.

[4] *Peter Ibbetson*, a novel by George du Maurier, was published in 1892. Peter Ibbetson avoids the harsh reality of his life by escaping into his own dream world.

preoccupation. We bought what we needed, but nobody sold anything to us. My parents worried, often, about money, for they made little and lived gracefully. But the talk was of meeting bills, not of buying new things. And we were brought up, if not with frugality, then with a stern sense of the value of money and the sin of waste. To want things without needing them was an impulse to be scorned, and the word "material" in describing a person, an epithet.

Listen then to this excerpt from a well-known woman newspaper columnist, Sylvia Porter, writing last year about her eight-year old daughter:

> I began to think carefully about her [she wrote] and the millions of children like her, who are extravagant. It is not an extravagance encouraged by us. Rather, it is an extravagance stimulated by the TV shows they see and radio shows they hear— shows which cajole them into buying things and food on a scale which can be believed only by those living the experience. To Cris and all the boys and girls of her age who are allowed to watch TV during the pre-supper hour, the commercials are often more intriguing than the performances themselves.
>
> They feel they must obey when they are told to "go right out and buy" something. They ask and they nag—and finally, most of us give in.
>
> Again, we are not developing the brand name devotion in the youngsters. It is being pounded into them by the ads they see and hear on every side. They don't eat "a" cereal: they eat such-and-such cereal; they don't drink "a" soft drink; they name it by brand name.
>
> In all seriousness, Cris will tell me that a certain food is "good for me"—and she will tell me why in words that obviously come right out of a commercial. I recall my own childhood; I never asked for a food or drink because it would "help me grow."
>
> [Speaking of her own childhood, Miss Porter wrote:] I think I ate some food in the packages which came with the prizes. Not so with Cris and her friends. They grab the package, extract the prize or cut out the gimmick, etc., and that's the end of it. At times, I think that if all the half-consumed boxes of cereal on Americans' pantry shelves right now were collected and shipped overseas, we could solve the hunger problem of a fair-sized nation.
>
> [Then, later] Cris and her friends will actually coo over the color and style of a new car or appliance. In fact I think they're snobbish about it.

After this curdling tale, Miss Porter ends on a happy note. 9
"In short," she concludes, "one decade from today, Cris and
her contemporaries will be creating a market in our land, lush
and luxurious beyond anything ever seen."

While this may delight the country's economists and the 10
makers of goods, it horrifies me. For it is in effect producing a
race which believes that a high standard of living is the final
aspiration. I would be more inclined to call it the last ditch.

I am sorry for the children who grow up on television. 11
They don't know what they've missed, or how rich life can be,
in the real and imagined world.

THE WRITER'S THEMES

1. According to Marya Mannes, what is wrong with TV? What
   does she believe TV could accomplish? Is she optimistic that
   TV will reach this stage of development?
2. The writer tells us that her childhood was not typical. What
   aspects of her childhood do you feel support that statement?
3. Why does the writer use the long quotation by the newspaper columnist Sylvia Porter? In what ways has the columnist used objective and subjective evidence in much the
   same way that Marya Mannes presents her evidence?

THE WRITER'S TECHNIQUE

In the third paragraph of her essay, Marya Mannes describes
what her life was like as a child. Here is that paragraph:

> In my childhood the days were not regimented. After school and
> before a homework evening, the time was our own, for us to fill
> as we chose. In school we were groups, at home we were single;
> and it never occurred to my parents to arrange my social day
> with organized activity. They felt that a good school, an affec-
> tionate home, and a consistent standard of ethics were enough.
> The rest was up to us, my brother and me.

The writer's topic sentence announces that her concern will be
her childhood. She also tells us the predominant quality of that
childhood when she reports that it was "not regimented." All
of the details that follow support this impression. After school,

if there was no homework to do on a particular evening, "the time was our own . . ." If there was any sense of regimentation at all, it could be found only in school, where the children were seen as "groups"; at home, however, "we were single . . ." The writer's parents never thought of arranging her "social day" with any organized activity. Her life outside of school was truly without regimentation.

The writer concludes her paragraph with a final picture of the social informality allowed by her parents. They felt that "a good school, an affectionate home, and a consistent standard of ethics were enough." The rest was up to the children themselves.

The writer has not only consistently developed her topic sentence, she has also written a paragraph that holds our interest because of the variety of details she includes. In the second sentence the writer refers directly to "school" and indirectly refers to home when she mentions "a homework evening." She makes these references more direct in the following sentence: "In school we were groups, at home we were single . . ." By alternating between home and school in the paragraph, the writer gives movement and variety to her details. This in turn adds interest to her writing.

PARAGRAPH PRACTICE

Write a paragraph of your own, using the Marya Mannes paragraph as your model. Your paragraph could be a description of your own childhood, or you could choose to describe another period of your life. Use the first half of your topic sentence to indicate the period you are going to describe; in the second part of your opening sentence indicate your judgment as to the quality of that period of your life. For example, if you choose to describe your childhood, you could construct your topic sentence according to this pattern:

> In my childhood, the days were filled with family activities.

If, for example, you choose to describe your early adolescence, your topic sentence could read as follows:

> During my early teen years, my days were filled with a variety of new activities.

Develop your paragraph by providing details that illustrate the period of your life you have chosen to describe. Provide at least three or four specific examples that will help your reader see what you did during that time. No matter which part of your life you write about, the more specific your details, the more persuasive your paragraph will be. In addition, you will hold your reader's interest if you deliberately choose a variety of examples for your paragraph. For example, if you are writing about the family activities you enjoyed as a child, plan to include both indoor and outdoor activities. If you describe what you did during your early adolescence, show the variety of those activities by pointing them out in alternating fashion: go from your school activities, to your activities with a church group, to what you did close to your home. Specific details, along with a variety of details, will help to make your paragraph enjoyable and interesting to your reader.

ESSAY PRACTICE

The following outline will help you plan a complete essay of at least five paragraphs. The theme of your essay will be closely related to the theme of the Marya Mannes essay.

The following sentence may serve as your thesis sentence, and will also be the main idea of your introductory paragraph:

¶ 1.   Many television commercials are so misleading, so tasteless, or so personally irritating, that we should actively campaign against the current television advertisement policies.

Each of the sentences below is the topic sentence for one of the paragraphs that you will write to develop your thesis. You may use the suggested details to develop each paragraph, or you may supply details of your own.

¶ 2.   Television commercials are misleading; they encourage people to buy products that either are not needed or are not good for them.

   [DETAILS: Choose at least two or three examples of television commercials and describe how the advertisers try to convince us that we need their products. How many of these products are not really necessary? How many of these products are not good for people?]

¶ 3. Television commercials are tasteless.

[DETAILS: Give an example of the most offensive television commercial you ever saw. Why did it offend you?]

¶ 4. People should try to do something to improve the quality of the commercials they must see on television.

[DETAILS: Provide specific details of the course of action you would encourage. Would you recommend letters? Would you support a boycott of some kind?]

Be certain that you use transitions between paragraphs to make your writing flow smoothly. In addition, be sure that your conclusion gives your reader a clear signal that you have come to the end of your essay.

ESSAY TOPICS

1. Marya Mannes points out that it never occurred to her parents to arrange her "social day with organized activity."

Write an essay in which you argue that parents should (or should not) arrange their children's after-school activities. What are the advantages for both parents and children if these activities are highly organized? What are the dangers if there is too much organization? (If you choose the opposite point of view, point out what you feel are the advantages and dangers of a very liberal attitude on the part of parents toward their children's after-school activities.)

2. a. Is TV a waste of time? Argue for or against TV by pointing out the good and bad effects of TV watching. If you choose to argue against TV, be sure to choose those TV programs that will best prove your case. If you argue in favor of TV watching, be sure that the programs you use as examples will be seen as worthwhile by a majority of your readers.

   b. Discuss an activity that many people engage in, but that you consider a waste of time. Your example could be sports or stamp collecting, or anything in between. Why is the activity a waste of time? Did you ever engage in an activity that you liked at first, but that you later decided was a waste of time?

3. a. Write an essay in which you argue that people should support educational TV stations because the program-

ming on those stations is more creative and of a higher quality than the programming on commercial television.

b. Write an essay in which you argue that, because of such innovations as cable TV and Home Box Office, many of the arguments Marya Mannes makes against commercial television are no longer valid. How have these newer methods of TV broadcasting changed our perception of TV? How have these innovations affected different age groups?

♣ Erich Fromm ♣

Erich Fromm (1900–   ) was born in Frankfort, Germany. After receiving his Ph.D. from the University of Heidelberg in 1922, Fromm began his career as a psychoanalyst, philospher, and writer. He came to the United States in 1934 and became a naturalized citizen in 1940. For the next several years he taught and engaged in research in several institutes and universities in the United States and Mexico.

Erich Fromm is the author of many books and articles, among them *Escape from Freedom* (1941), *The Sane Society* (1955), and *The Art of Loving* (1956). This last book, in which the author maintains that "love is the only sane and satisfactory answer to the problem of human existence," is perhaps his most famous work.

In the following essay, which appeared in the *Saturday Evening Post* in 1964, Erich Fromm examines our affluent modern society and points out in detail what we are lacking, despite our unprecedented material wealth.

PREVIEWING THE WRITER

• Note the writer's disagreement with the popular view of happiness. What evidence does the writer give in the opening paragraphs of his essay to support his point of view?

• Note the writer's attitude toward our mechanized world. How many areas of our lives have been affected by our mechanical society? What is the writer's opinion of this trend?

• Note Fromm's emphasis on our society's habit of consumption. According to the writer, in how many areas of our lives is this habit of consumption to be found? What are the results of all this consumption?

OUR WAY OF LIFE MAKES US MISERABLE

MOST AMERICANS believe that our society of consumption-happy, fun-loving, jet-traveling people creates the greatest happiness for the greatest number. Contrary to this view, I believe that our present way of life leads to increasing anxiety, helplessness and, eventually, to the disintegration of our culture. I refuse to identify fun with pleasure, excitement with joy, business with happiness, or the faceless, buck-passing "organization man" with an independent individual.

From this critical view our rates of alcoholism, suicide and divorce, as well as juvenile deliquency, gang rule, acts of violence and indifference to life, are characteristic symptoms of our "pathology of normalcy." It may be argued that all these pathological phenomena exist because we have not yet reached our aim, that of an affluent society. It is true, we are still far from being an affluent society. But the material progress made in the last decades allows us to hope that our system might eventually produce a materially affluent society. Yet will we be happier then? The example of Sweden, one of the most prosperous, democratic and peaceful European countries, is not very encouraging: Sweden, as is often pointed out, in spite of all its material security has among the highest alcoholism and suicide rates in Europe, while a much poorer country like Ireland ranks among the lowest in these respects. Could it be that our dream that material welfare per se leads to happiness is just a pipe dream? . . .

Certainly the humanist thinkers of the eighteenth and nineteenth centuries, who are our ideological ancestors, thought that the goal of life was the full unfolding of a person's potentialities; what mattered to them was the person who *is* much, not the one who *has* much or *uses* much. For them economic production was a means to the unfolding of man, not an end. It seems that today the means have become ends, that not only "God is dead," as Nietzsche[1] said in the nineteenth century, but also man is dead; that what is alive are the organizations, the machines; and that man has become their slave rather than being their master.

Each society creates its own type of personality by its way of bringing up children in the family, by its system of education, by its effective values (that is, those values that are rewarded rather than only preached). Every society creates the type of "social character" which is needed for its proper functioning. It forms men who *want* to do what they *have* to do. What kind of men does our large-scale, bureaucratized industrialism need?

It needs men who cooperate smoothly in large groups, who want to consume more and more, and whose tastes are standardized and can be easily influenced and anticipated. It needs men who feel free and independent, yet who are willing

[1] The German philosopher, poet, and critic Friedrich Nietzsche (1844–1900).

to be commanded, to do what is expected, to fit into the social machine without friction; men who can be guided without force, led without leaders, prompted without an aim except the aim to be on the move, to function, to go ahead.

Modern industrialism has succeeded in producing this kind   6
of man. He is the "alienated" man. He is alienated in the sense that his actions and his own forces have become estranged from him; they stand above him and against him, and rule him rather than being ruled by him. His life forces have been transformed into things and institutions, and these things and institutions have become idols. They are something apart from him, which he worships and to which he submits. Alienated man bows down before the works of his own hands. He experiences himself not as the active bearer of his own forces and riches but as an impoverished "thing," dependent on other things outside of himself. He is the prisoner of the very economic and political circumstances which he has created.

Since our economic organization is based on continuous   7
and ever-increasing consumption (think of the threat to our economy if people did not buy a new car until their old one was really obsolete), contemporary industrial man is encouraged to be consumption-crazy. Without any real enjoyment, he "takes in" drink, food, cigarettes, sights, lectures, books, movies, television, any new kind of gadget. The world has become one great maternal breast, and man has become the eternal suckling, forever expectant, forever disappointed.

Sex, in fact, has become one of the main objects of con-   8
sumption. Our newsstands are full of "girlie" magazines; the percentages of girls having premarital sexual relations and of unwed mothers are on a steep incline. It can be argued that all this represents a welcome emancipation from Victorian morality, that it is a wholesome affirmation of independence, that it reflects the Freudian principle that repression may produce neurosis. But while all these arguments are true to some extent, they omit the main point. Neither independence nor Freudian principle is the main cause of our present-day sexual freedom. Our sexual mores are part and parcel of our *cult of consumption*, whose main principle was so succinctly expressed by Aldous Huxley in *Brave New World:* "Never put off till tomorrow the fun you can have today." Nature has provided men and women with the capacity for sexual excitement; but excitement in consumption, whether it is of sex or any other commodity, is not the same as aliveness and richness of experience.

In general, our society is becoming one of giant enterprises 9
directed by a bureaucracy in which man becomes a small, well-
oiled cog in the machinery. The oiling is done with higher
wages, fringe benefits, well-ventilated factories and piped music, and by psychologists and "human-relations" experts; yet
all this oiling does not alter the fact that man has become powerless, that he does not wholeheartedly participate in his work
and that he is bored with it. In fact, the blue- and the white-
collar workers have become economic puppets who dance to
the tune of automated machines and bureaucratic management.

The worker and employee are anxious, not only because 10
they might find themselves out of a job (and with installment
payments due); they are anxious also because they are unable
to acquire any real satisfaction or interest in life. They live and
die without ever having confronted the fundamental realities of
human existence as emotionally and intellectually productive,
authentic and independent human beings.

Those higher up on the social ladder are no less anxious. 11
Their lives are no less empty than those of their subordinates.
They are even more insecure in some respects. They are in a
highly competitive race. To be promoted or to fall behind is not
only a matter of salary but even more a matter of self-esteem.
When they apply for their first job, they are tested for intelligence as well as for the right mixture of submissiveness and
independence. From that moment on they are tested again and
again—by the psychologists, for whom testing is a big business,
and by their superiors, who judge their behavior, sociability,
capacity to get along, etc., their own and that of their wives.
This constant need to *prove* that one is as good as or better than
one's fellow-competitor creates constant anxiety and stress, the
very causes of unhappiness and psychosomatic illness.

The "organization man" may be well fed, well amused 12
and well oiled, yet he lacks a sense of identity because none of
his feelings or his thoughts originates within himself; none is
authentic. He has no convictions, either in politics, religion,
philosophy or in love. He is attracted by the "latest model" in
thought, art and style, and lives under the illusion that the
thoughts and feelings which he has acquired by listening to the
media of mass communication are his own.

He has a nostalgic longing for a life of individualism, ini- 13
tiative and justice, a longing that he satisfies by looking at West-
erns. But these values have disappeared from real life in the
world of giant corporations, giant state and military bureaucra-

cies and giant labor unions. He, the individual, feels so small before these giants that he sees only one way to escape the sense of utter insignificance: He identifies himself with the giants and idolizes them as the true representatives of his own human powers, those of which he has dispossessed himself. His effort to escape his anxiety takes other forms as well. His pleasure in a well-filled freezer may be one unconscious way of reassuring himself. His passion for consumption—from television to sex— is still another symptom, a mechanism which psychiatrists often find in anxious patients who go on an eating or buying spree to evade their problems.

The man whose life is centered around producing, selling   14 and consuming commodities transforms himself into a com- modity. He becomes increasingly attracted to that which is man- made and mechanical, rather than to that which is natural and organic. Many men today are more interested in sports cars than in women; or they experience women as a car which one can cause to race by pushing the right button. Altogether they ex- pect happiness is a matter of finding the right button, not the result of a productive, rich life, a life which requires making an effort and taking risks. In their search for the button, some go to the psychoanalyst, some go to church and some read ''self- help'' books. But while it is impossible to find the button for happiness, the majority are satisfied with pushing the buttons of cameras, radios, televison sets, and watching science fiction becoming reality.

One of the strangest aspects of this mechanical approach   15 to life is the widespread lack of concern about the danger of total destruction by nuclear weapons; a possibility people are consciously aware of. The explanation, I believe, is that they are more proud of than frightened by the gadgets of mass de- struction. Also, they are so frightened of the possibility of their personal failure and humiliation that their anxiety about per- sonal matters prevents them from feeling anxiety about the pos- sibility that everybody and everything may be destroyed. Per- haps total destruction is even more attractive than total insecurity and never-ending personal anxiety.

Am I suggesting that modern man is doomed and that we   16 should return to the preindustrial mode of production or to nineteenth-century ''free enterprise'' capitalism? Certainly not. Problems are never solved by returning to a stage which one has already outgrown. I suggest transforming our social system from a bureaucratically managed industrialism in which maximal production and consumption are ends in themselves (in the Soviet Union as well as in the capitalist countries) into a humanist industrialism in which man and the full development of his potentialities—those of love and of reason—are the aims of all social arrangements. Production and consumption should serve only as means to this end, and should be prevented from ruling man.

To attain this goal we need to create a Renaissance of Enlightenment and of Humanism. It must be an Enlightenment, however, more radically realistic and critical than that of the seventeenth and eighteenth centuries. It must be a Humanism that aims at the full development of the total man, not the gadget man, not the consumer man, not the organization man. The aim of a humanist society is the man who loves life, who has faith in life, who is productive and independent. Such a transformation is possible if we recognize that our present way of life makes us sterile and eventually destroys the vitality necessary for survival.   17

Whether such transformation is likely is another matter. But we will not be able to succeed unless we see the alternatives clearly and realize that the choice is still ours. Dissatisfaction with our way of life is the first step toward changing it. As to these changes, one thing is certain: They must take place in all spheres simultaneously—in the economic, the social, the political and the spiritual. Change in only one sphere will lead into blind alleys, as did the purely political French Revolution and the purely economic Russian Revolution. Man is a product of circumstances—but the circumstances are also his product. He has a unique capacity that differentiates him from all other living beings: the capacity to be aware of himself and of his circumstances, and hence to plan and to act according to his awareness.   18

THE WRITER'S THEMES

1. According to Fromm, a century or two ago people's goals were very different from what they are today. What are these two visions of life as the writer describes them in paragraph three?

2. According to Fromm, in what areas of their lives have people lost their freedom?

3. What is Fromm's solution to all of the problems he describes? Is his vision realistic?

THE WRITER'S TECHNIQUE

In paragraph nine of his essay, Erich Fromm presents a detailed observation regarding the direction of our society and the individual's position in that society. Here is that paragraph:

> In general, our society is becoming one of giant enterprises directed by a bureaucracy in which man becomes a small, well-oiled cog in the machinery. The oiling is done with higher wages, fringe benefits, well-ventilated factories and piped music, and by psychologists and "human-relations" experts; yet all this oiling does not alter the fact that man has become powerless, that he does not wholeheartedly participate in his work and that he is bored with it. In fact, the blue- and the white-collar workers have become economic puppets who dance to the tune of automated machines and bureaucratic management.

In the first sentence, which is also the topic sentence, the writer combines his observation of society (it is becoming a giant bureaucracy) with his view of the position of human beings in that society: man is "a small, well-oiled cog in the machinery." The writer then provides a series of examples that show man as a well-oiled cog in this giant machine. The "oiling is done with higher wages, fringe benefits, well-ventilated factories and piped music, and by psychologists and 'human-relations' experts . . ."

In the remainder of the paragraph, the writer continues to use the image of the machine as he observes that "all this oiling does not alter the fact that man has become powerless." He notes that the workers are really "puppets" who must "dance to the tune of automated machines and bureaucratic management."

Throughout the paragraph the writer has shown us the rather unnatural combination of people and machines. This combination is made possible by the use of a special "oil," the wages and other fringe benefits that keep people a part of the machinery of society. Throughout the paragraph the writer emphasizes the inhumanity of the machine by showing people as small parts of that machine. They are mere cogs.

Notice that the writer carefully combines details that relate to people with details that relate to machines. "Higher wages" and "fringe benefits" can only refer to people, while "well-ventilated factories and piped music" refer to the mechanical side of our society. The writer emphasizes the inhumanity of the machines by showing those machines being oiled by human elements. The writer proves his point by showing us the machine being served by people, when it should be the other way around.

PARAGRAPH PRACTICE

Write a paragraph of your own, using Erich Fromm's paragraph as your model. Your paragraph could be your analysis of a particular aspect of our society. When you analyze this aspect of society or a particular institution, you could adapt Fromm's opening by starting your paragraph in this way:

In general, our society is becoming more fearful . . .

In general, large corporations are becoming much too powerful . . .

In general, professional sports are becoming much too concerned with large amounts of money . . .

In the second part of your opening sentence, place people in the situation you are describing. Here are the statements given above, but now expanded into complete sentences:

In general, our society is becoming more fearful, and one result is that people have less trust in each other.

In general, large corporations are becoming much too powerful, and the people who work for them are feeling more and more alienated.

In general, professional sports are becoming much too concerned about large amounts of money, and people are losing sight of the real value of sports.

Notice that, in each case, the sentence is made up of two related parts: a general opening statement and an additional statement that focuses on how people are related to the situation being described.

After you have constructed your opening sentence, develop your paragraph by providing a number of specific details that support your opening statement. In what ways are people trusting each other less? Exactly how do people who work for large corporations show their feelings of alienation? How can you prove that the emphasis on money in sports is making people lose sight of the real value of sports?

As you develop your paragraph, keep in mind that your choice of examples will determine whether or not your reader is convinced of the truth of your opening statement.

ESSAY PRACTICE

The following outline will help you plan a complete essay of at least five paragraphs. The theme of your essay will be closely related to the theme of the Erich Fromm essay.

The following sentence may serve as your thesis sentence, and will also be the main idea of your introductory paragraph:

¶ 1.   Competition has a definite place in our lives, and competitive situations can be either positive or negative, depending on our attitude.

Each of the sentences below is the topic sentence for one of the paragraphs that you will write to develop your thesis. You may use the suggested details to develop each paragraph, or you may supply details of your own.

¶ 2.   In most situations, competition acts as a positive force.

   [DETAILS: How is competition a positive force in athletics? Do people increase their academic efforts when there is competition? How important is competition among large companies? For example, what are the positive effects of an American industry finding itself in competition with foreign industries?]

¶ 3.   It is true, however, that problems can arise if competitive situations become too intense.

   [DETAILS: In this paragraph provide at least three or four examples of situations in which competition can become a destructive force. You might describe two fathers shouting at each other over a Little League baseball game, or you could describe an incident where a company steals trade secrets from a rival company.]

¶ 4.   If a person finds himself or herself in an unhealthy situation where there is clearly too much competition, there is often more than one way to handle it.

   [DETAILS: What are the different attitudes a person can have in such situations? In this paragraph, you might argue for or against a person's fleeing from such a situation immediately.]

Be certain that you use transitions between paragraphs to make your writing flow smoothly. In addition, be sure that your conclusion gives your reader a clear signal that you have come to the end of your essay.

ESSAY TOPICS

1. Write an argument for or against the teaching of specific values, or a whole value system, as part of the school curriculum. For example, should schools advocate particular attitudes in sex education courses? Should prayer be allowed in public schools? Should schools be allowed to teach that one political system is better than another? In your essay be sure to describe the advantages for society if your ideas were to become reality.

2. Write an essay in which you argue for or against continued buildup of nuclear weapons. Choose one of the following groups as the intended audience for your essay:
   a group of politicians;
   a group of high school or college students;
   a church organization;
   a group of industrialists.

3. a. Early in his essay, Erich Fromm asks the question, "Could it be that our dream that material welfare . . . leads to happiness is just a pipe dream?" Now, nearly twenty years after Fromm's essay was published, our awareness as consumers has changed a great deal.

   In what way(s) are we changing our habits as consumers? Write an essay based on your own experience or your observation of others, in which you point out how people are becoming more aware of their choices in today's marketplace. Your examples could range from the current housing situation, to how people are buying cars (or keeping their older ones), to the growing popularity of consumer-oriented books and magazines.

   b. Write an essay in which you argue for the use of a more natural approach in an important area of our lives. For example, you might wish to argue in favor of more natural foods, or you might wish to describe the advantages of natural childbirth. You could even write an argument in favor of a more natural lifestyle, involving a move to a rural area, away from the problems of cities or suburbs.

As you develop your argument, be sure to point out how both society and the individual would benefit from the adoption of your idea.

Aldous Huxley

Aldous Huxley (1894–1963) was born in England and received his B.A. from Oxford University in 1916. During World War I Huxley worked for the British government; after the war he spent a few years teaching and writing, and it was at this time that he decided to become a full-time writer. He soon became well known as a novelist, short story writer, playwright, and writer of nonfiction.

When Aldous Huxley was sixteen, he suffered from an eye disease that temporarily blinded him. Although this forced him to abandon his plan to become a doctor, Huxley never lost his interest in science and its implications for our world. As one of Huxley's biographers has stated, all of the writer's work was "touched by his scientific and analytic processes of thought and sense of detail."

Perhaps Huxley's most famous book is *Brave New World* (1932), a picture of future society that has often been compared with George Orwell's grim prediction of the future, *1984*. Huxley later revised his novel, and this new version appeared in 1958 under the title *Brave New World Revisited*.

A good deal of Huxley's later writing emphasizes the connection between science and the future of humanity. The following essay, first published in 1946, shows Huxley's concern with how we will use our scientific knowledge. The writer begins by referring to Thomas Malthus (1766–1834), an English economist who formulated a famous theory of population growth. Malthus believed that if population were allowed to expand without any control, it would increase in a geometrical ratio (1–3–9–27–81, etc.), while food production can only increase arithmetically (1–2–3–4, etc.). The result, according to Malthus, would be worldwide disaster. In the opening section of his first paragraph, Huxley examines our modern views of the ideas Malthus put forward over a century ago. The writer indicates that even though twentieth-century technology has modified the theories Malthus formulated, there are other factors at work in our modern world that could just as surely lead us to disaster.

PREVIEWING THE WRITER

• Note the writer's description of today's growing food problem. How is the production and transport of food related to international politics and the sharing of power among countries?

• Note Huxley's analysis of the problem of our power needs. Is there a single solution to this serious international problem, or does the writer see a variety of solutions in the future?

• Note the writer's emphasis on the future role of the scientist. What are the directions scientific research can take in the future?

THE SCIENTIST'S ROLE

IT IS FASHIONABLE nowadays to say that Malthus was wrong, because he did not foresee that improved methods of transportation can now guarantee that food surpluses produced in one area shall be quickly and cheaply transferred to another, where there is a shortage. But first of all, modern transportation methods break down whenever the power politicians resort to modern war, and even when the fighting stops they are apt to remain disrupted long enough to guarantee the starvation of millions of persons. And, secondly, no country in which population has outstripped the local food supply can, under present conditions, establish a claim on the surpluses of other countries without paying for them in cash or exports. Great Britain and the other countries in western Europe, which cannot feed their dense populations, have been able, in times of peace, to pay for the food they imported by means of the export of manufactured goods. But industrially backward India and China—countries in which Malthus' nightmare has come true with a vengeance and on the largest scale—produce few manufactured goods, consequently lack the means to buy from underpopulated areas the food they need. But when and if they develop mass-producing industries to the point at which they are able to export enough to pay for the food their rapidly expanding populations require, what will be the effect upon world trade and international politics? Japan had to export manufactured goods in order to pay for the food that could not be produced on the overcrowded home islands. Goods produced by workers with a low standard of living came into competition with goods produced by the better paid workers of the West, and undersold them. The West's retort was political and consisted of the imposition of high tariffs, quotas and embargoes. To these restrictions on her trade Japan's answer was the plan for creating a vast Asiatic empire at the expense of China and of the Western imperialist powers. The result was war.[1] What will happen when India and China are as highly industrialized as prewar Japan and seek to exchange their low-priced manufactured goods for food, in competition with Western powers, whose standard of living is a great deal higher than theirs? Nobody can foretell the future; but undoubtedly the rapid industrialization of Asia (with equipment, let it be remembered, of the very latest and best postwar design) is pregnant with the most dangerous possibilities.

It is at this point that internationally organized scientists and technicians might contribute greatly to the cause of peace by planning a world-wide campaign, not merely for greater food production, but also (and this is the really important point) for regional self-sufficiency in food production. Greater food production can be obtained relatively easily by the opening up of the earth's vast subarctic regions at present almost completely sterile. Spectacular progress has recently been made in this direction by the agricultural scientists of the Soviet Union; and presumably what can be done in Siberia can also be done in northern Canada. Powerful ice-breakers are already being used to solve the problems of transportation by sea and river; and perhaps commercial submarines, specially equipped for traveling under the ice may in the future insure a regular service between arctic ports and the rest of the world. Any increase of the world's too scanty food supply is to be welcomed. But our rejoicings must be tempered by two considerations. First, the surpluses of food produced by the still hypothetical arctic granaries of Siberia and Canada will have to be transferred by ship, plane and rail to the overpopulated areas of the world. This means that no supplies would be available in wartime. Second, possession of food producing arctic areas constitutes a natural monopoly, and this natural monopoly will not, as in the past, be in the hands of politcally weak nations, such as Argentina and Australia, but will be controlled by the two great power systems of the postwar period—the Russian power system and the Anglo-American power system. That their monopolies of food surpluses will be used as weapons in the game of power

2

---

[1] Huxley is referring to World War II. Part of that war was fought in the Pacific between the United States and Japan, from 1941 to 1945.

politics seems more than probable. "Lead us not into temptation." The opening up of the Arctic will be undoubtedly a great
good. But it will also be a great temptation for the power politicians—a temptation to exploit a natural monopoly in order to
gain influence and finally control over hitherto independent
countries, in which population has outstripped the food supply.

It would seem, then, that any scientific and technological 3
campaign aimed at the fostering of international peace and political and personal liberty must, if it is to succeed, increase the
total planetary food supply by increasing the various regional
supplies to the point of self-sufficiency. Recent history makes it
abundantly clear that nations, as at present constituted, are quite
unfit to have extensive commercial dealings with one another.
International trade has always, hitherto, gone hand in hand
with war, imperialism and the ruthless exploitation of industrially backward peoples by the highly industrialized powers.
Hence the desirability of reducing international trade to a minimum, until such time as nationalist passions lose their intensity
and it becomes possible to establish some form of world government. As a first step in this direction, scientific and technical
means must be found for making it possible for even the most
densely populated countries to feed their inhabitants. The improvement of existing food plants and domestic animals; the
acclimatization in hitherto inhospitable regions of plants that
have proved useful elsewhere; the reduction of the present
enormous wastes of food by the improvement of insect controls
and the multiplication of refrigerating units; the more system-
atic exploitation of seas and lakes as sources of food; the development of entirely new foods, such as edible yeasts; the synthesizing of sugars as a food for such edible yeasts; the
synthesizing of chlorophyll so as to make direct use of solar energy in food production—these are a few of the lines along which
important advances might be made in a relatively short time.

Hardly less important than regional self-sufficiency in food 4
is self-sufficiency in power for industry, agriculture and transportation. One of the contributing causes of recent wars has
been international competition for the world's strictly localized
sources of petroleum, and the current jockeying for position in
the Middle East, where all the surviving great powers have
staked out claims to Persian, Mesopotamian and Arabian oil,
bodes ill for the future. Organized science could diminish these
temptations to armed conflict by finding means for providing

all countries, whatever their natural resources, with a sufficiency of power. Water power has already been pretty well exploited. Besides, over large areas of the earth's surface there are no mountains and therefore no sources of hydroelectric power. But across the plains where water stands almost still, the air often moves in strong and regular currents. Small windmills have been turning for centuries; but the use of large-scale wind turbines is still, strangely enough, only in the experimental stage. Only recently the direct use of solar power has been impracticable, owing to the technical difficulty of constructing suitable reflectors. A few months ago, however, it was announced that Russian engineers had developed a cheap and simple method for constructing paraboloid mirrors of large size, capable of producing superheated steam and even of melting iron. This discovery could be made to contribute very greatly to the decentralization of production and population and the creation of a new type of agrarian society making use of cheap and inexhaustible power for the benefit of individual small holders or self-governing, co-operative groups. For the peoples of such tropical countries as India and Africa the new device for directly harnessing solar power should be of enormous and enduring benefit—unless, of course, those at present possessing economic and political power should choose to build mass-producing factories around enormous mirrors, thus perverting the invention to their own centralistic purposes, instead of encouraging its small-scale use for the benefit of individuals and village communities. The technicians of solar power will be confronted with a clear-cut choice. They can work either for the completer enslavement of the industrially backward peoples of the tropics, or for their progressive liberation from the twin curses of poverty and servitude to political and economic bosses.

The storage of the potentialities of power is almost as important as the production of power. One of the most urgent tasks before applied science is the development of some portable source of power to replace petroleum—a most undesirable fuel from the political point of view, since deposits of it are rare and unevenly distributed over the earth's surface, thus constituting natural monopolies which, when in the hands of strong nations, are used to increase their strength at the expense of their neighbors and, when possessed by weak ones, are coveted by the strong and constitute almost irresistible temptations to imperialism and war. From the political and human point of view, the most desirable substitute for petroleum would be an efficient battery for storing the electric power produced by water, wind or the sun. Further research into atomic structure may perhaps suggest new methods for the construction of such a battery.

Meanwhile it is possible that means may be devised, within the next few years, for applying atomic energy to the purposes of peace, as it is now being applied to those of war. Would not this technological development solve the whole problem of power for industry and transportation? The answer to this question may turn out to be simultaneously affirmative and negative. The problems of power may indeed be solved—but solved in the wrong way, by which I mean in a way favorable to centralization and the ruling minority, not for the benefit of individuals and co-operative, self-governing groups. If the raw material of atomic energy must be sought in radioactive deposits, occurring sporadically, here and there, over the earth's surface, then we have natural monopoly with all its undesirable political consequences, all its temptations to power politics, war, imperialistic aggression and exploitation. But of course it is always possible that other methods of releasing atomic energy may be discovered—methods that will not involve the use of uranium. In this case there will be no natural monopoly. But the process of releasing atomic energy will always be a very difficult and complicated affair, to be accomplished only on the largest scale and in the most elaborately equipped factories. Furthermore, whatever political agreements may be made, the fact that atomic energy possesses unique destructive potentialities will always constitute a temptation to the boy gangster who lurks within every patriotic nationalist. And even if a world government should be set up within a fairly short space of time, this will not necessarily guarantee peace. The Pax Romana was a very uneasy affair, troubled at almost every imperial death by civil strife over the question of succession. So long as the lust for power persists as a human trait—and in persons of a certain kind of physique and temperament this lust is overmasteringly strong—no political arrangement, however well contrived, can guarantee peace. For such men the instruments of violence are as fearfully tempting as are, to others, the bodies of women. Of all instruments of violence, those powered by atomic energy are the most decisively destructive; and for power lovers, even under a system of world government, the temptation to resort to these all too simple and effective means for gratifying their lust will be great indeed. In view of all this, we must conclude that atomic energy is, and for a long time is likely to remain, a source of industrial power that is, politically and humanly speaking, in the highest degree undesirable.

It is not necessary in this place, nor am I competent, to enter any further into the hypothetical policy of internationally organized science. If that policy is to make a real contribution toward the maintenance of peace and the spread of political and personal liberty, it must be patterned throughout along the decentralist lines laid down in the preceding discussion of the two basic problems of food and power. Will scientists and technicians collaborate to formulate and pursue some such policy as that which has been adumbrated here? Or will they permit themselves, as they have done only too often in the past, to become the conscious or unconscious instruments of militarists, imperialists and a ruling oligarchy of capitalistic or governmental bosses? Time alone will show. Meanwhile, it is to be hoped that all concerned will carefully consider a suggestion made by Dr. Gene Weltfish in the September, 1945, issue of the *Scientific Monthly*. Before embarking upon practice, all physicians swear a professional oath—the oath of Hippocrates—that they will not take improper advantage of their position, but always remember their responsibilities toward suffering humanity. Technicians and scientists, proposes Dr. Weltfish, should take a similar oath in some such words as the following: "I pledge myself that I will use my knowledge for the good of humanity and against the destructive forces of the world and the ruthless intent of men; and that I will work together with my fellow scientists of whatever nation, creed or color for these our common ends." 7

THE WRITER'S THEMES

1. According to Huxley, how could countries become more self-sufficient in terms of energy and the production of food? How likely is this to happen?
2. Huxley indicates that if the more powerful nations control the sources of food and energy, they will then be able to dominate the smaller nations politically. Is there any way these less powerful countries could prevent this from happening?

3. Huxley's essay was published in 1946. How much of what he describes in the essay is still valid? How many of his predictions have already come true, or are in the process of becoming true at the present time?

THE WRITER'S TECHNIQUE

In the opening section of his first paragraph, Aldous Huxley notes that a century-old theory of economic and population growth, a theory developed by Malthus, is now in disfavor. Here is the opening section of that paragraph:

> It is fashionable nowadays to say that Malthus was wrong, because he did not foresee that improved methods of transportation can now guarantee that food surpluses produced in one area shall be quickly and cheaply transferred to another, where there is a shortage. But first of all, modern transportation methods break down whenever the power politicians resort to modern war, and even when the fighting stops they are apt to remain disrupted long enough to guarantee the starvation of millions of persons. And, secondly, no country in which population has outstripped the local food supply can, under present conditions, establish a claim on the surpluses of other countries without paying for them in cash or exports.

The writer begins by reporting what the current attitudes are toward the theories of Malthus: it is "fashionable nowadays" to say that those theories are wrong because Malthus could not have seen that improved technology would permit the efficient transport of food. Huxley now points out weaknesses in this objection. First, we are told, "modern transportation methods break down" whenever there is a war; even when that war ends, communications will be sufficiently disrupted "to guarantee the starvation of millions of persons."

Huxley then suggests a second reason why the current disbelief in the theories of Malthus may be wrong. If a country cannot feed its own population with its own food supply, then that country can only obtain food surpluses from other countries by paying for them in cash or exports.

In presenting modern criticism of Malthus, Aldous Huxley begins by noting that it is now fashionable to criticize the English theorist, and he indicates why Malthus is criticized, but then he gives two reasons to suggest that these criticisms may not be justified.

PARAGRAPH PRACTICE

Write a paragraph of your own, using the above section from Huxley's paragraph as your model. Begin your paragraph by pointing out some opinion that is currently fashionable and indicate why this opinion is so widely accepted. Then give at least two reasons why you personally disagree with this popular opinion. For example, you could write about the fashionable idea that test scores are real indications of academic achievement, or that it is better to have a small family, with no more than one or two children. Why do you disagree with the popular idea you have chosen to describe? Introduce your first objection by imitating Aldous Huxley's approach: "But first of all . . ." Then provide at least one additional reason why you disagree with this popular idea. The more detailed your reasons, and the more fully you expand each one, the more convincing your position will be to your reader.

ESSAY PRACTICE

The following outline will help you plan a complete essay of at least five paragraphs. The theme of your essay will be closely related to the theme of the Aldous Huxley essay.

The following sentence may serve as your thesis sentence, and will also be the main idea of your introductory paragraph:

¶ 1. America is a powerful and generous nation, but we have to recognize that generosity cannot be endless and that power has its limits.

Each of the sentences below is the topic sentence for one of the paragraphs that you will write to develop your thesis. You may use the suggested details to develop each paragraph, or you may supply details of your own.

¶ 2. The United States is both powerful and generous in its dealings with other nations.

   [DETAILS: Choose two or three examples from current events that show the United States using its power and/or being generous with other nations.]

¶ 3. In recent years, however, our country has begun to recognize that power must be used with caution and that there are limits to any country's generosity.

[DETAILS: What are some of the factors in today's international situation that seem to limit the power of the United States? For example, to what extent does our dependence on foreign oil supplies place limitations on our country's power?]

¶ 4. In the future, the United States will have to reconsider its attitudes toward other nations, and reconsider the extent of its responsibilities toward them.

[DETAILS: What are some current international events that are making our country reconsider some of its traditional attitudes toward other countries, and the people of those countries? For example, to what extent are we reconsidering our policies toward immigrants and refugees? How will these policies have to change in the future?]

Be certain that you use transitions between paragraphs to make your writing flow smoothly. In addition, be sure that your conclusion gives your reader a clear signal that you have come to the end of your essay.

ESSAY TOPICS

1. a. Should America increase its tariffs, embargoes, and quotas on goods that are imported from other countries and that compete directly with American products? To what extent should the United States take direct action to control what is sold in its home market? Use specific, current examples to support your argument.

   b. In paragraph three of his essay, Huxley speaks of the "ruthless exploitation of industrially backward peoples by the highly industrialized powers." Who are the nations being "exploited" by the industrial nations, and how are they being exploited? Write an argument for or against this system of industrial production. In your argument, point out how this system does or does not result in exploitation. How could the system be structured so as to benefit the peoples of these nonindustrial countries?

2. a. What is the future of nuclear power? Should we continue to develop nuclear power plants or should we look for other, more locally produced, sources of energy? Write an argument for or against the use of nuclear power in our society and in societies elsewhere.

    b. Several parts of Huxley's essay deal with the self-suffi- ciency of countries. To what extent can an *individual* be self-sufficient in today's society? Discuss the extent to which you are self-sufficient now. In what areas of your life are you still dependent on others? In how many of these areas could you, realistically speaking, become more self-sufficient?

3. a. Keeping the points of Huxley's essay in mind, write an argument in which you speak directly to a class of sci- ence majors about their role in the future of society. What will their roles be? To what extent will they be responsible for all of our futures? In writing your ar- gument, use Huxley's ideas in addition to your own information about current events.

    b. At the conclusion of his essay, Huxley quotes a sugges- tion that technicians and scientists should take an oath similar to the Hippocratic oath taken by doctors before they begin work in their profession. Choose at least two professions that you feel should also have professional oaths for their members. What would be the wording of each oath? Why do you feel that each of the profes- sions you have chosen needs such an oath? What do you believe would be the effect(s) of such oaths on the members of the professions you have chosen?

Focus on Terms: Emphasis

*E*mphasis is the weight a writer gives to a certain part of a piece of writing in order to make that part stand out for the reader. A writer can place this most important part at the beginning or at the end of a piece. Keep in mind that it is not usually a good idea to place the point you wish to emphasize in the middle sections of an essay, where the emphasis tends to be lost.

When a writer devotes a major part of an essay to a specific point, the writer is emphasizing that point. For example, in her essay "The Child before the Set," Marya Mannes clearly wishes us to see how she lived through her own childhood without a television set. She therefore devotes a good deal of her essay to a description of how she entertained herself as she was growing up. By doing this, the writer indirectly invites us to consider possible alternatives to television.

There are other ways to emphasize a point. A writer can use an exclamation mark after an especially important point, or the writer can decide to *italicize* (as we have done here) a word or a sentence to call attention to what is being emphasized.[1] These techniques should not be used very often, however, or their effectiveness will tend to be lost. For example, it is only at the most important points in their essay on "Banning Cars from Manhattan" that Paul and Percival Goodman emphasize suggestions or conclusions by placing them in italics. At one point, when the writers are arguing that travel in the city would be speeded up by the elimination of cars, they end a paragraph by placing their conclusion in italics:

> By and large, *given the improvement of the bus service, most travel about town would be swifter and more convenient than it is at present with private cars.*

Finally, you could tell your reader what you are emphasizing simply by stating that one or more of your points should be considered the most important in your essay. For example, in the second paragraph of "The Scientist's Role," Aldous Huxley argues that scientists and technicians could plan "a worldwide campaign, not merely for greater food production, but also (and this is the really important point), for regional self-suffi-

---

[1] However, when you write by hand or use a typewriter, you simply underline the word, phrase, or sentence you wish to emphasize. In this case, underlining is the equivalent of italics.

ciency in food production.'' Here, the writer uses his parenthetical remark to emphasize for us the ''really important point.''

Used with care, emphasis helps your reader see the points
that you want to stand out in your writing. The total meaning
of your essay is also enhanced by the proper use of emphasis.

Student Essay ❧ ❧ *Ellen Palombi*

There have always been arguments between the sexes, and men
and women have always disagreed about the extent of their obligations to each other. In recent years women have been arguing
the question of mutual responsibilities more openly, and several
women writers have made direct challenges to some traditional
male rights. They have also begun to question some long-accepted
male hobbies and leisure activities.

In the following essay we hear a woman's voice arguing
against the traditional male interest in sports. The writer concentrates on the male who tunes in to the world of sports and tunes
out everything else, including her. The woman's voice in this
essay combines humor and protest, and her protest is loud
enough to be clearly heard over the voice of any TV sportscaster.

• In the following essay, the writer uses more than one
method to emphasize her points. In paragraph two, for example, she emphasizes the husband's comment by using exclamation marks, and in the next paragraph she provides her own
emphasis when she argues that the man should pay attention
to his wife ''*during* an inning . . .''

A WORLD OF SPORTS

IT'S HER HUSBAND'S BIRTHDAY and at 8 p.m. she is   1
ready for his arrival home from a hard day at the office. His
favorite red wine—a cabernet—is ''breathing'' on the beautifully
set table, right next to the $60 long-stemmed red roses. As she
lights the candles, she is careful not to hold the match too near
the favorite silk dress that she is wearing. And though her cu-
linary talents are usually lacking, dinner smells divine. The evening is one he will be sure to remember.

At 8:10, his key fits into the door. She glides into his arms, only to receive lips that miss her own and land somewhere between her ear and her hairline. As he runs by she hears an "Oh, damn! I missed the first inning already!" And as her husband removes his jacket and tie, his eyes are so riveted to the television set that he does not see her blow out the candles, turn off the oven, and change into her ratty old bathrobe.

"Listen, darling, be happy he's home with you and not running around," is what mother offers as consolation. And, "He's a real 'man's man'," comes at her more times than she cares to mention. But doesn't this "man's man" realize that he could hit a homerun with her just by smiling in her direction *during* an inning, rather than at the call for the "seventh inning stretch"?

Sports Illustrated is delivered weekly, and three different newspapers are delivered daily, so that the results of any given sports event can be reviewed from four different perspectives. And when asked, instead of handing her the lettuce that has been draining in the sink, her in-house Joe Namath grabs the lettuce and fades back for a twenty-foot pass. And will a basketball net ever be passed by without an imaginary lay-up shot being practiced?

Gentlemen, please. Why make a woman a sports widow at so young an age? Why make a woman go through life knowing that she has her son and daughter thanks to two rained-out games?

Marriage is a relationship between two people who have decided to share their lives together. Interests that are not shared equally by both partners need not be discontinued, but should instead be indulged in with moderation. So, while your wife is having her nails manicured on a Saturday afternoon, go right ahead and watch twenty-two college heroes mangle each other while chasing a football. But do you have to see twenty-two more heroes do the same thing during Sunday's pro game, and again Monday night with Howard Cosell's Game of the Week? How many "But sweetheart, this is the one special game of the season I've been waiting for" are you going to hand us?

Confessing that as a young boy your fantasy was to grow up to be seven foot two and score 150 points in one basketball game (breaking, of course, Wilt Chamberlain's record of 100 points), and that you only grew to be five foot nine with bad knees, does not make a woman who has been waiting three

months to see a formerly new movie understand why it is crucial that you see the Saturday night basketball game—in which
your favorite team is not even playing. And when her absolutely, all-time, most favorite movie which is on television maybe
once every two years is on, why does she have to go and watch
it next door on her girlfriend's second television while you sulk
over ten men trying to hit a little hockey puck into a net?

This is not another cry for women's rights, gentlemen. It 8
is a cry for the companionship for which we married you. It is
a plea that you not force the lady in your life to find other
interests while you are immersed in the season's ratings; those
other interests may grow and become more important than the
sharing relationship you once wanted so badly.

You do not have to be one of those fat-bellied, beer-drink- 9
ing, cigar-smoking creatures that has been symbolic of the
American sports-minded male in order to own a worn-out re-
clining chair that can be sat in only by yourself, positioned just
so in front of the television. You may be fit and trim, have all
your hair, and not even own an undershirt without sleeves, and
still "make the cut." But we women know that you are not
breaking your necks to retain that youthful body so that you
can look good for us. Oh, no! We know very well it is so that
you can still get around on that golf swing of yours for the entire
eighteen holes.

And no thanks—we do not want to caddy! 10

Strategies for Writing

1. Rewrite paragraph six of the essay, adding at least three
different emphases in three different places. One of these
emphases should be an exclamation mark, a second emphasis should be an italicized (underlined) word, and the
third emphasis should be your addition of a parenthetical
phrase, such as: "and this is the really important point," to
signal the emphasis for the reader.
2. Review the essay and point out where the writer uses emphasis to strengthen her argument. Pay particular attention
to the final paragraphs.
3. Write an essay in which you argue for or against a couple
cultivating the same interests. Should two people try to en-

gage in the same activities, even if one of them does not have quite the degree of interest the other one has, for the sake of the relationship?

4. Write an essay in which you argue for or against the idea that, at some point in a relationship, an interest held by one person can actually begin to damage the relationship.

11

 **AN ENVIRONMENT FOR ALL**

WRITING SKILL: Argumentation

In Unit 10 you learned that there are certain essential parts to any good argument. You may or may not use all of these strategies when you write your own arguments; your approach will depend on the purpose you have in mind when you write. For example, not all arguments contain suggestions for the practical implementation of a solution, and you may simply want your readers to change their minds about a particular problem.

You will encounter many written and verbal arguments that are not based on logic but which try to convince us solely on their appeal to the emotional side of an issue. For example, it sometimes happens that one political candidate will try to argue against an opponent by stating that "A vote for Joe Smith is a vote to let criminals roam our streets!" Here, the politician is playing on people's fears by strongly implying that the opposition is soft on criminals. Such a slogan is far from any coherent political platform and is simply an appeal to emotion—in this case, fear. The world of advertising also makes constant use of emotional appeals. For example, car manufacturers openly try to appeal to people's sense of status or longing for adventure by naming their products after exotic animals or far-away places. Hundreds of other types of products, from cosmetics to vacations, are also sold on the basis of an appeal to our emotional reactions rather than to any sense of logic.

Although these kinds of appeals to emotion are not considered appropriate for a good argument, some of the most effective arguments contain both appeals to rational thinking as well as appeals to our emotions. In fact, few writers use either logic or emotion exclusively. In this unit, for example, the essays by Marjorie Kinnan Rawlings and Rachel Carson show how a writer may reveal a personal involvement in a subject and still present a factual, coherent argument, one that involves us on an emotional level and that convinces us by an intelligent presentation of facts. The emotional part of such an argument is a supporting element of that argument, but there is no cheap appeal to an emotion, such as we saw in the political and advertising examples given above. When Marjorie Kinnan Rawlings attempts to answer the question "Who Owns Cross Creek?" she argues her point by describing in detail her feelings about the world of nature, as she observes it in her community. Her concern about the fate of her environment is even more convincing because the writer is using her own environment as her example. Because Cross Creek itself is her context, we understand her bias and her reasons for using that bias as she does.

Rachel Carson's essay "The Obligation to Endure" is one of the most famous essays of the past several years. It is also one of the most influential pieces on the environment that has ever been published. The writer uses general concepts and carefully chosen details to present an argument that few would dare dispute.

One of the most important parts of an argument is the way the evidence is presented. The more specific a writer is with the facts, the greater the impression those facts will make. For example, in "Lightning Water" by Joseph Wood Krutch, the author argues for a greater sense of responsibility toward our environment and presents, as part of his evidence, a description of rainfall in the desert. Writing about Death Valley in California, Krutch observes:

> Average rainfall is about 1.5 inches and more than a year has been known to pass without a measurable trace. Yet in July, 1950, a cloudburst (a convenient but not very meaningful term) produced a flood which cut a 6-foot-deep gully across the main road and rolled along boulders 5 feet in diameter. In Arizona more

434 ε& AN ENVIRONMENT FOR ALL

than 5 inches of rain has fallen in a twenty-four-hour period; as much as 11 inches in the course of one storm. These are
exceptional figures, but very heavy downpours within a short
time are usual.

Notice the variety of evidence the writer uses, and his
careful presentation of that evidence. We are told that the average rainfall is "about" one and a half inches; we are told the
month and the year (July 1950) of a dramatic cloudburst; and
we are told some of the specific results of that event. We are
also given some additional evidence of dramatic rainfalls, this
time from the state of Arizona. The writer's caution with his
material is also seen in his carefully balanced final sentence: the
figures he has just given are indeed "exceptional," but he wants
us to realize that it is certainly "usual" to experience such "very
heavy downpours within a short time . . ." The writer is trying
to persuade us by not exaggerating an honest presentation of
specific facts. At the same time he just as carefully anticipates
some possible objections from those who might disagree with
the quality of those facts, or the direction the argument takes
because of those facts. Notice that at no point in his essay does
Joseph Wood Krutch resort to sweeping generalizations to prove
his point. The writer's argument is always based upon a careful
analysis of specific, established facts.

The remaining selection in the unit, Garrett De Bell's essay
"Energy," is a very logical analysis of an ongoing problem that
has worldwide implications. The writer uses an orderly, factual
approach to the problem of our future energy supply, and we
notice that his entire essay is an extended support of his opening argument that "All power pollutes." Although the writer
clearly intended us to think of the physical pollution that results
from use of power, by the time we finish reading the essay we
may have formed in our minds a different concept of pollution.
Garrett De Bell's essay is not only a description of a growing
physical problem, it is also an analysis of what we must do in
order to change our way of thinking about energy.

In composing arguments, always avoid the use of broad
generalizations or sweeping statements that cannot be proven.
In addition, do not include irrelevant information in any part of
your argument; this will merely distract and possibly annoy
your reader. Finally, if you do include your own personal attitudes or opinions in your argument, be certain that your reader
will be readily able to see which parts of your writing are objective report and which parts are subjective opinion.

✺ *Marjorie Kinnan Rawlings* ✺

Marjorie Kinnan Rawlings (1896–1953) was born in Washington, D.C., and graduated from the University of Wisconsin in 1918. She became a publicity writer for the YMCA and during the 1920s she also worked for a number of newspapers.

In 1928 she bought a seventy-two-acre orange grove near Hawthorne in central Florida, where she devoted all of her time to writing fiction. Her most successful book, which won the Pulitzer Prize for fiction in 1939, was *The Yearling,* the story of a young boy and his pet deer.

In *Cross Creek,* published in 1942, the author tells of her life in Florida and her close relationship with the people of her local community. The following selection is the conclusion to that book. It reveals the writer at her graceful and sensitive best. The passage also shows that, although Marjorie Kinnan Rawlings is generally considered to be a regional writer who emphasized her immediate surroundings in her work, she was also able to bring out the larger implications of her material. As the writer shares the deeper meaning of her environment with us, we realize that Cross Creek could be any neighborhood anywhere.

PREVIEWING THE WRITER

• Note all of the human and nonhuman inhabitants that live and work at Cross Creek.

• Note all of the constructive and destructive acts the writer reports as occurring at Cross Creek. In each case, is the act done by a human or an animal?

• Note each point in the essay where the author refers to past, present, and future time. Which period receives the most attention from the writer?

WHO OWNS CROSS CREEK?

THE QUESTION ONCE AROSE, "Who owns Cross   1
Creek?" It came to expression when Mr. Marsh Turner was turning his hogs and cattle loose on us and riding drunkenly across the Creek bridge to drive them home. Tom Morrison, who does not own a blade of corn at the Creek, but is yet part and parcel to it, became outraged by Mr. Marsh Turner's arro-

gance. Tom stood with uplifted walking stick at the bridge, a Creek Horatio,[1] and turned Mr. Marsh Turner back.

"Who do you think you are?" he demanded. "How come you figure you can turn your stock loose on us, and then ride up and down, whoopin' and hollerin'? You act like you own Cross Creek. You don't. Old Boss owns Cross Creek, and Young Miss owns it, and old Joe Mackay. Why, you don't own six feet of Cross Creek to be buried in."

Soon after this noble gesture was reported to me by Martha, I went across the Creek in April to gather early blackberries. I had not crossed the bridge for some weeks and I looked forward to seeing the magnolias in full bloom. The road is lined with magnolia trees and is like a road passing through a superb park. There were no magnolia blossoms. It seemed at first sight that there were no magnolia trees. There were only tall, gray, rose-lichened trunks from which the branches had been cut. The pickers of magnolia leaves had passed through. These paid thieves come and go mysteriously every second or third year. One week the trees stand with broad outstretched branches, glossy of leaf, the creamy buds ready for opening. The next, the boughs have been cut close to the trunks, and it will be three years before there are magnolia blossoms again. After long inquiry, I discovered the use for the stripped leaves. They are used for making funeral wreaths. The destruction seemed to me a symbol of private intrusion on the right of all mankind to enjoy a universal beauty. Surely the loveliness of the long miles of magnolia bloom was more important to the living than the selling of the bronze, waxy leaves for funerals of the dead.

I had a letter from a friend at this time, saying, "I am a firm believer in property rights."

The statement disturbed me. What is "property" and who are the legitimate owners? I looked out from my veranda, across the acres of grove from which I had only recently been able to remove the mortgage. The land was legally mine, and short of long tax delinquency, nothing and nobody could take it from me. Yet if I did not take care of the land lovingly, did not nourish and cultivate it, it would revert to jungle. Was it mine to abuse or to neglect? I did not think so.

I thought of the countless generations that had "owned" land. Of what did that ownership consist? I thought of the great

[1] In ancient Roman legend, Horatio was a hero who singlehandedly held a bridge against an enemy army until Roman reinforcements could arrive.

earth, whirling in space. It was here ahead of men and could conceivably be here after them. How should one man say that he "owned" any piece or parcel of it? If he worked with it, labored to bring it to fruition, it seemed to me that at most he held it in fief. The individual man is transitory, but the pulse of life and of growth goes on after he is gone, buried under a wreath of magnolia leaves. No man should have proprietary rights over land who does not use that land wisely and lovingly. Steinbeck raised the same question in his *Grapes of Wrath*. Men who had cultivated their land for generations were dispossessed because banks and industrialists believed they could make a greater profit by turning over the soil to mass, mechanized production. But what will happen to that land when the industrialists themselves are gone? The earth will survive bankers and any system of government, capitalistic, fascist or bolshevist. The earth will even survive anarchy.

7 I looked across my grove, hard fought for, hard maintained, and I thought of other residents there. There are other inhabitants who stir about with the same sense of possession as my own. A covey of quail has lived for as long as I have owned the place in a bramble thicket near the hammock. A pair of blue-jays has raised its young, raucous-voiced and handsome, year after year in the hickory trees. The same pair of redbirds mates and nests in an orange tree behind my house and brings its progeny twice a year to the feed basket in the crepe myrtle in the front yard. The male sings with a *joie de vivre*[2] no greater than my own, but in a voice lovelier than mine, and the female drops bits of corn into the mouths of her fledglings with as much assurance as though she paid the taxes. A black snake has lived under my bedroom as long as I have slept in it.

8 Who owns Cross Creek? The red-birds, I think, more than I, for they will have their nests even in the face of delinquent mortgages. And after I am dead, who am childless, the human ownership of grove and field and hammock is hypothetical. But a long line of red-birds and whippoorwills and blue-jays and grove doves will descend from the present owners of nests in the orange trees, and their claim will be less subject to dispute than that of any human heirs. Houses are individual and can be owned, like nests, and fought for. But what of the land? It seems to me that the earth may be borrowed but not bought. It may be used, but not owned. It gives itself in response to love

[2] "Joy of life" (French).

438 ~~ AN ENVIRONMENT FOR ALL

and tending, offers its seasonal flowering and fruiting. But we are tenants and not possessors, lovers and not masters. Cross Creek belongs to the wind and the rain, to the sun and the seasons, to the cosmic secrecy of seed, and beyond all, to time.

THE WRITER'S THEMES

1. Which people at Cross Creek act lovingly toward the area? Which people act like the possessors of Cross Creek?
2. The author describes in some detail the activities of both humans and animals at Cross Creek. Which group does the writer present with more sympathy? What are the best details from the essay to support your choice?
3. At what point(s) in the essay does the writer compare herself with the other inhabitants (human and nonhuman) of Cross Creek?

THE WRITER'S TECHNIQUE

In paragraph seven of her essay, Marjorie Kinnan Rawlings provides us with a detailed picture of her house and land, seen from her own point of view. Here is the paragraph:

> I looked across my grove, hard fought for, hard maintained, and I thought of other residents there. There are other inhabitants who stir about with the same sense of possession as my own. A covey of quail has lived for as long as I have owned the place in a bramble thicket near the hammock. A pair of blue-jays has raised its young, raucous-voiced and handsome, year after year in the hickory trees. The same pair of red-birds mates and nests in an orange tree behind my house and brings its progeny twice a year to the feed basket in the crepe myrtle in the front yard. The male sings with a *joie de vivre* no greater than my own, but in a voice lovelier than mine, and the female drops bits of corn into the mouths of her fledglings with as much assurance as though she paid the taxes. A black snake has lived under my bedroom as long as I have slept in it.

Notice that the writer first establishes her personal point of view ("I looked"; "I thought") and immediately moves to a detailed description of the "other residents," which includes various birds and a black snake. Throughout the description of these creatures, the writer herself is nearly always visible: the quail have lived there "as long as I have owned the place"; the red-birds mate and nest "behind my house"; the male red-bird sings with a joy of life "no greater than my own"; and when the female red-bird feeds her young, the writer is reminded of her own position as the taxpayer of the property. The paragraph ends with a picture of the black snake living under her bedroom "as long as I have slept in it."

The writer uses the presence of all these animals to emphasize the harmony of life that is possible at Cross Creek; even the snake directly under her bedroom is not a threat. Humans and animals together give variety and texture to life at Cross Creek.

PARAGRAPH PRACTICE

Write a paragraph of your own, using the paragraph from *Cross Creek* as your model. Your paragraph could be a description of one of your classes, a restaurant you know well, or it could be a view of a vacation spot.

Some possible openings for your paragraph might be:

I looked at the other members of the class . . .

I looked at the other people sitting in the restaurant . . .

I looked at all the people relaxing on the beach . . .

Notice that Marjorie Kinnan Rawlings begins with a general view across her grove, but she uses her house as a constant point of reference. In the course of the paragraph she mentions the hammock, the area behind the house, the front yard, and her bedroom. In your paragraph it would be helpful to the reader if you would use a similar point of reference. If you describe one of your classes, for example, you might want to use your own desk as the point of reference; if you choose a restaurant setting, it could be your own table; if you are describing a beach as the setting, you could use your own blanket.

ESSAY PRACTICE

The following outline will help you plan a complete essay of at least five paragraphs. The theme of your essay will be closely related to the theme of the Marjorie Kinnan Rawlings selection.

The following sentence may serve as your thesis sentence, and will also be the main idea of your introductory paragraph:

¶ 1. When people harm the environment, there should be consequences for their actions.

Each of the sentences below is the topic sentence for one of the paragraphs that you will write to develop your thesis. You may use the suggested details to develop each paragraph, or you may supply details of your own.

¶ 2. In recent years we have become more aware of the many ways people are harming their environment.

[DETAILS: Your general examples of people harming the environment could range from individuals writing graffiti in public places, to large corporations ignoring their responsibilities. In this paragraph you could also include a specific example that you are personally aware of and that you can describe in some detail.]

¶ 3. This kind of action intrudes on my right to an unspoiled environment.

[DETAILS: How is your enjoyment affected by these actions? What happens to the quality of your life when other people spoil the environment?]

¶ 4. Therefore, if people insist on acting in this way, there should be consequences.

[DETAILS: What do you feel should be done to those people and corporations that spoil the environment?]

Be certain that you use transitions between paragraphs to make your writing flow smoothly. In addition, be sure that your conclusion gives your reader a clear signal that you have come to the end of your essay.

ESSAY TOPICS

1. Some people feel that they can be careless or even destructive with something they are renting or using but do not own. Write an argument in which you disagree with people who have this attitude. For example, you could argue with a roommate who feels that, since you do not own the dormitory you are living in, it does not matter what you do to it. You could also argue with a student who justifies stealing

a book from the school library by saying that college tuition fees are so high that students deserve a free book now and then.

2. Has there ever been a time when you were responsible for something you did not own? What was your attitude toward your responsibility? Would your attitude have been any different if you had actually been the owner?

3. a. Marjorie Kinnan Rawlings writes that "No man should have proprietary rights over land who does not use that land wisely and lovingly." In view of our concern today over those who do not always use the land "wisely and lovingly," write an argumentative essay in which you try to persuade a group of people (campers, for example) to treat the land with care.

   b. Many people today still believe in traditional property rights. Write an argumentative essay in which you attempt to persuade the head of a corporation that property rights also carry with them the need for a sense of responsibility toward the land and all forms of life that depend on that land.

🍂 *Garrett De Bell* 🍂

Garrett De Bell is an ecologist and environmentalist with a diverse background and long experience in his field. His interest in ecology began when he accompanied professors from the University of California on field trips to various natural environments in that state. De Bell received his B.A. in Biology from Stanford University and holds a graduate degree from the University of California. Upon leaving the academic world in 1969, he devoted his career to solving the environmental crisis that was becoming recognized as a critical issue in the world.

In November 1969, at the request of David Brower, president of Friends of the Earth, Garrett De Bell began work on a compilation of essays and other materials that would provide people with what De Bell himself calls "the insights, information, and synthesis necessary to bring the environmental concerns of the day into focus." The result was *The Environmental Handbook*, which was completed in six weeks and which immediately became an authoritative sourcebook for the environmental movement. One critic praised the book by calling attention to one of its most important messages, namely, the "love of life and earth which alone makes possible a true approach to the central problems of our time." De Bell has written two other books and numerous articles, and for the past eight years he has been a corporate executive in charge of environmental quality in Yosemite National Park in California.

In the following essay, taken from *The Environmental Handbook*, Garrett De Bell argues for a new way of thinking about our use of energy resources. The writer makes it clear that such rethinking on our part will mean radical changes in many areas of our lives.

PREVIEWING THE WRITER

• According to the writer, how much control do people have over their use of energy sources? How likely is it that people will exercise this self-control?

• Note the writer's analysis of the rate of America's power use compared with other nations of the world. Do Americans use a fair proportion of the world's energy supply?

• What are the consequences of the "greenhouse effect," as the writer describes it? How likely is it that the world will someday experience this "greenhouse effect"?

ENERGY

ALL POWER POLLUTES. 1

Each of the major forms of power generation does its own 2
kind of harm to the environment. Fossil fuels—coal and oil—
produce smoke and sulfur dioxide at worst; even under ideal
conditions they convert oxygen to carbon dioxide. Hydroelectric
power requires dams that cover up land, spoil wild rivers, increase water loss by evaporation, and eventually produce valleys full of silt. Nuclear power plants produce thermal and radioactive pollution and introduce the probability of disaster.

We are often told that it is essential to increase the amount 3
of energy we use in order to meet demand. This "demand,"
we are told, must be met in order to increase or maintain our
"standard of living." What these statements mean is that if
population continues to increase, and if per capita power continues to increase as in the past, then power generation facilities
must be increased indefinitely.

Such statements ignore the environmental consequences 4
of building more and more power generation facilities. They
ignore the destruction of wild rivers by dams, the air pollution
by power plants, the increasing danger of disease and disaster
from nuclear power facilities.

These effects can no longer be ignored, but must be di- 5
rectly confronted. *The perpetually accelerating expansion of power
output is not necessary.*

It is assumed by the utilities that the demand for power is 6
real because people continue to purchase it. However, we are
all bombarded with massive amounts of advertising encouraging us to buy appliances, gadgets, new cars, and so on. There
is no comparable public service advertising pointing up the
harmful effects of over-purchase of "convenience" appliances
that increase use of power. Public utilities aggressively advertise
to encourage increasing use of power. For instance, Pacific Gas
and Electric advertises: "Beautify America—use electric clothes
dryers." The unbeautifying results of building more power
plants is, of course, not mentioned.

For the lopsided advertising, public utilities use public 7
monies, paid in by the consumer. This is allowed by the regulatory agencies on the theory that increasing use of power low-
ers the per unit cost, which is beneficial to the consumer. How-

ever, the consumer is also the person who breathes the polluted air and has his view spoiled by a power plant. Therefore, this sort of advertising should be prohibited.

But perhaps it is unrealistic to expect the power companies 8 and the appliance and car builders to call a halt, to flatly say, "This is where we stop. The limits have been reached, even exceeded." The limits can, and must, be set by the consumer. It is the consumer, ultimately, who must decide for himself what appliances he needs and which he can forego. The producers of power and power-using appliances will feel the pinch but they will, ultimately, cease to produce that which will not *sell*.

We *can* control our population and thus decrease our per 9 capita use of power. Population may be stabilized, and use of power reduced to what is necessary for a high quality of life. But population control will take time. We can begin now by ceasing to use power for trivial purposes.

Power use is presently divided about as follows in the 10 United States: household and commercial, 33 percent; industrial, 42 percent; transportation, 24 percent. We must decide which uses, within each category, improve the quality of people's lives sufficiently to justify the inevitable pollution that results from power generation and use.

HOUSEHOLD AND COMMERCIAL

The term "standard of living" as used by utility spokesmen in 11 the United States today generally means abundant luxuries, such as the following, for the affluent: electric blenders, toothbrushes and can openers, power saws, toys and mowers, dune buggies, luxury cars and golf carts, electric clothes dryers and garbage grinders, air conditioners, electric blankets and hair dryers.

Are these necessary for a high quality of life? We must 12 realize that a decision made to purchase one of these "conveniences" is also a decision to accept the environmental deterioration that results from the production, use and disposal of the "convenience." Hand-operated blenders, toothbrushes, can openers and saws, clotheslines, blankets, bicycles, and feet produce much less pollution than the powered equivalents.

We can make the ecologically sensible decision to reject 13 the concept of increasing perpetually the "standard of living" regardless of the human or ecological consequences. We can replace the outmoded industrial imperative—the "standard of living" concept—by the more human "quality of life" concept.

Many of us feel that the quality of our lives would be   14 higher with far less use of energy in this country. We would be happy to do with fewer cars, substituting a transportation system that can make us mobile without dependence on the expensive, polluting, and dangerous automobile. We would be happy to see the last of glaring searchlights, neon signs, noisy power mowers and private airplanes, infernally noisy garbage trucks, dune buggies, and motorcycles. The quality of our lives is improved by each power plant not constructed near our homes or recreation areas, by each dam not constructed on a river used for canoeing. Quality of life is a positive ethic. Peace and quiet and fresh air are positive values; noisy smoking machines are negative ones.

INDUSTRY

Industry has been rapidly increasing its use of energy to in-   15 crease production. An *Electrical World* pamphlet cheerfully describes this trend as follows:

> Industry's use of electric power has been increasing rapidly, too. The index of consumer use of electricity is kilowatts-per-hour. Industry's use is measured as the amount used per employee. Ten years ago, American industry used 24,810 kilowatt hours per year for each person employed. Today, the figure is estimated at 37,912. As industry finds more ways to use power to improve production, the output and wages of the individual employee rise.

Since unemployment is a problem and power use causes pollution, perhaps automation which uses energy to replace workers isn't a very good idea. Of course we could have full employment, a shorter work week, and less power use if we just wouldn't bother producing things that don't really improve the quality of life—pay for, and that complicate our lives.

TRANSPORTATION

If you wanted to design a transportation system to waste the   16 earth's energy reserves and pollute the air as much as possible, you couldn't do much better than our present system dominated by the automobile. Only by following the advice of the popular science journals, placing in every garage a helicopter (using three times as much gasoline per passenger mile as a car) could you manage to do greater environmental damage.

Compared to a bus, the automobile uses from four to five times as much fuel per passenger mile. Compared to a train, it uses ten times as much. Walking and bicycling, of course, require no fuel at all.* [17]

Switching from the system of automobilism to a system of rapid transit, with more bicycling and walking in cities, would reduce fossil fuel consumption for transportation by a factor of almost 10. As transportation now accounts for 24 percent of the fuel expended, a saving of even 50 percent in this category would be helpful in reducing the rapid consumption of fossil fuels. Added benefits would be fewer deaths and injuries by automobiles, which have much higher injury rates than any form of public transportation; the liberation of much of the cities' space presently dedicated to the automobile; and less smog. [18]

The term "standard of living" usually seems to apply only to Americans, and usually just to the present generation. It is important to think of all people in the world, and of future generations. The question must be asked whether it is fair to the rest of the world for the United States to use up such a disproportionate share of the world's energy resources. Even looking solely to United States interests, is it the best policy to use up our allotment as fast as possible? [19]

If the whole world had equal rights and everyone burned fuel as fast as the U.S., the reserves would be gone very soon. The U.S. per capita rate of use of fossil fuels is from ten to a hundred times as great as the majority of people (the Silent Majority?) who live in the underdeveloped countries. [20]

Each person in India uses only 1/83 as much power as an American. India now has 500,000,000 people or 2½ times the population of the U.S. Yet since each person uses so much less power, India's total use is only 1/33 of that of the U.S. Its fair share would be 2½ times as much power as the U.S. The same argument, with somewhat different figures, holds for China, Southeast Asia, Pakistan, the Middle East, South America and Africa. [21]

Not only does the burning of fossil fuels produce local [22]

* Driesback, R., *Handbook of the San Francisco Region.* Environmental Studies, Palo Alto, California, p. 322.

pollution, but it also increases the carbon dioxide-to-oxygen ratio in the atmosphere. This occurs because each molecule of oxygen consumed in burning fuels results in the production of a carbon dioxide molecule (CH_2O plus O_2 yields CO_2 plus H_2O). This has the doubly adverse effect of taking oxygen out of the atmosphere, and putting carbon dioxide in, in equal amounts. The latter effect is of most concern to us because the CO_2 percentage in the atmosphere is minute compared to the huge reservoir of oxygen. While the atmosphere contains 20 percent oxygen, it has only 0.02 percent CO_2. Thus, fuel combustion reducing the O_2 concentration by only 1 percent would simultaneously increase the CO_2 concentration *tenfold*.

23   Each year the burning of fossil fuels produces an amount of carbon dioxide equal to about 0.5 percent of the existing carbon dioxide reservoir in the atmosphere. Of this production, half stays in the atmosphere, resulting in a 0.25 percent increase in atmospheric CO_2 per year. Of the other half, some becomes bound up with calcium or magnesium to become limestone, some becomes dissolved in the sea, and some is stored as the bodies of plants that fall to the deep, oxygen-poor sediments of the ocean and do not decompose.

24   If no CO_2 were being disposed of by the physical and biological processes in the ocean, then the CO_2 concentration of the atmosphere would increase by twice the present rate, because all of the CO_2 produced each year would remain in the atmosphere.

25   Burning all the recoverable reserves of fossil fuels would produce three times as much carbon dioxide as is now present in the atmosphere. If the present rate of increase in fuel use continues, and the rate of CO_2 dispersal continues unchanged, there will be an increase of about 170 percent in the CO_2 level in the next 150 years (which is the minimum estimate of the amount of time our fossil fuels will last). If the fuels last longer, say up to the "optimistic" 400 years that some predict, we will have that much more CO_2 increase, with the attendant smog and oil spills.

26   Scientists are becoming worried about increasing CO_2 levels because of the greenhouse effect, with its possible repercussions on the world climate. Most of the sun's energy striking the earth's surface is in the form of visible and ultraviolet rays from the sun. Energy leaves the earth as heat radiation or infrared rays. Carbon dioxide absorbs infrared rays more strongly

than visible or ultraviolet rays. Energy coming toward the earth's surface thus readily passes through atmospheric carbon dioxide, but some escaping heat energy is absorbed and trapped in the atmosphere by carbon dioxide, much as heat is trapped in a greenhouse. This effect of carbon dioxide on the earth's climate has, in fact, been called the "greenhouse effect." Scientists differ in their opinions as to the eventual result this will have on our climate. Some believe that the earth's average temperature will increase, resulting in the melting of polar ice caps with an accompanying increase of sea levels and inundation of coastal cities. Others feel that there will be a temporary warming and partial melting of polar ice, but then greater evaporation from the open Arctic seas will cause a vast increase in snowfall, with an ensuing ice age.

Many people believe that green plants can produce a sur- 27 plus of oxygen to compensate for that converted to CO_2 in burning fuels. This is not true. A plant produces only enough oxygen for its own use during its life plus enough extra for the oxidation of the plant after death to its original building blocks (CO_2 plus H_2O). Whether this oxidation occurs by fire, by bacterial decay, or by respiration of an animal eating the plant, has no effect on the ultimate outcome. When the plant is totally consumed by any of these three means, all of the oxygen it produced over its life is also consumed. The only way a plant leaves an oxygen surplus is if it fails to decompose, a relatively rare occurrence.

The important point is that fossil fuel combustion results 28 in a change in the ratio of carbon dioxide to oxygen in the atmosphere, whereas use of oxygen by animals does not. This point is not generally understood, so two examples are discussed below.

First, since 70 percent of the world's oxygen is produced 29 in the ocean, it has been forecast that death of the plankton in the ocean would cause asphyxiation of the animals of the earth. This is not the case because oxygen and carbon dioxide cycle in what is called the carbon cycle. A plant, be it a redwood tree or an algal cell, produces just enough oxygen to be used in consuming its carcass after death. The ocean plankton now produce 70 percent of the oxygen, but animals in the ocean use it up in the process of eating the plants. Very little of it is left over. The small amount that is left over is produced by plankton that have dropped to the oxygen-poor deep sediments and are essentially forming new fossil fuel.

If the plankton in the ocean were all to die tomorrow, all 30 of the animals in the ocean would starve. The effect of this on the world's oxygen supply would be very small. The effect on the world's food supply, however, would be catastrophic. A large number of nations rely significantly on the ocean for food, particularly for high-quality protein. Japan, for example, is very heavily dependent on fisheries to feed itself.

....

Second, fears about reducing the world's oxygen supply 31 have been expressed in reference to the cutting down of large forest areas, particularly in the tropics, where the soil will become hardened into bricklike laterite and no plant growth of any sort will be possible in the future. It will be a disaster if the Amazon rain forest is turned into laterite because the animals and people dependent on it could not exist. But this would have no effect on the world's oxygen balance. If the Amazon Basin were simply bricklike laterite, the area would produce no oxygen and consume no oxygen. At present the Amazon Basin is not producing surplus organic material. The same amount of organic material is present in the form of animal bodies, trees, stumps, and humus from year to year; therefore no net production of oxygen exists. The oxygen produced in the forest each year, which obviously is a large amount, is used up by the animals and microorganisms living in the forest in the consumption of the plant material produced over the preceding year.

In summary, I suggest that one goal of the environmental 32 movement should be the reduction of total energy use in this country by 25 percent over the next decade. By doing this, we will have made a start toward preventing possibly disastrous climatic changes due to CO_2 buildup and the greenhouse effect. We will so reduce the need for oil that we can leave Alaska as wilderness and its oil in the ground. We will be able to stop offshore drilling with its ever-present probability of oil slick disasters, and won't need new supertankers which can spill more oil than the *Torrey Canyon* dumped on the beaches of Britain and France.[1] We will be able to do without the risks of disease and accident from nuclear power plants. We won't need to dam more rivers for power. And perhaps most important, we can liberate the people from the automobile, whose exhausts turn

---

[1] This accident occurred on March 18, 1967.

the air over our cities oily brown (which causes 50,000 deaths a year) and which is turning our landscape into a sea of concrete.

Many of the steps needed to reduce energy consumption are clear. We can press for: 33

1. Bond issues for public transit
2. Gas tax money to go to public transportation, not more highways
3. Ending of oil depletion allowance, which encourages use of fuel
4. More bicycle and walking paths
5. Better train service for intermediate length runs
6. A reverse of the present price system for power use where rates are lower for big consumers. Put a premium on conserving resources. Give householders power for essential needs at cost with heavy rate increases for extra energy for luxuries.

THE WRITER'S THEMES

1. Note the amount of space the writer devotes to each major area of our energy consumption. What does this emphasis tell you about the writer's view of the energy situation and its related problem of pollution?
2. In the essay, the writer asserts that it is the consumer "who must decide for himself what appliances he needs and which he can forego." He also states that, if the consumer makes these decisions, those who produce power and power-using appliances will "cease to produce that which will not sell." Do you agree with this analysis of consumer power? What do you believe is the extent of our influence on those who sell power and power-using products?
3. To what extent does the writer's use of strictly scientific facts help convince us of the points he is making? Where in the essay does the writer translate these facts into specific examples that help to convince us of the truth of his argument?

THE WRITER'S TECHNIQUE

In paragraph six of his essay, Garrett De Bell discusses the demand for more power in our society and gives some indication that there is another side to the argument. Here is the paragraph:

> It is assumed by the utilities that the demand for power is real because people continue to purchase it. However, we are all bombarded with massive amounts of advertising encouraging us to buy appliances, gadgets, new cars, and so on. There is no comparable public service advertising pointing up the harmful effects of over-purchase of "convenience" appliances that increase use of power. Public utilities aggressively advertise to encourage increasing use of power. For instance, Pacific Gas and Electric advertises: "Beautify America—use electric clothes dryers." The unbeautifying results of building more power plants is, of course, not mentioned.

The writer begins by noting an assumption that is made by the opposition: power companies assume that "the demand for power is real because people continue to purchase it." The writer then suggests that people may be buying "appliances, gadgets, new cars, and so on" because we are all "bombarded with massive amounts of advertising" that encourage us to make these purchases. The writer then complains that there is no "public service advertising" that would give the opposite point of view, showing the "harmful effects of over-purchase of 'convenience' appliances that increase use of power."

Notice that the writer began his paragraph by referring to the utility companies in the most general sense ("the utilities"), but by the end of the paragraph he not only names a particular company, he also gives a specific example of what those utilities can do that is harmful to the environment. One of the major points the writer is making is that it is difficult for the public to see the reality behind all of the advertising. In this case, when Pacific Gas and Electric urges people to use electric clothes dryers, they neglect to mention what the author calls the "unbeautifying effects" of building additional power plants.

PARAGRAPH PRACTICE

Write a paragraph of your own, using the above paragraph from "Energy" as your model. Your paragraph could deal with a popular assumption that is held by many people but that you do not agree is true. For example, if you do not agree that using air conditioners is a good idea, the first sentence of your paragraph might read as follows:

Many people believe that air conditioning is a necessity in our lives today simply because it is already so widely used.

You could then argue the opposite point of view. First, show that there is very little, if any, information available to suggest possible disadvantages to owning and using air conditioning. Here in your paragraph you could mention that the media actively promote only the positive aspects of air conditioning, and you could quote (or make up) a typical example of the kind of advertising we so often see: "Air conditioning is . . ." However, the final sentence of your paragraph should present the opposite point of view. As you restate your position, indicate a flaw in such advertising: "What these companies fail to admit is . . ."

You could also write a paragraph that might deal with a more controversial issue such as public school prayer. In such a paragraph, the structure of your argument might be as follows:

It is assumed by many people that the practice of public school prayer is [or is not] a good idea because . . .

Certain groups, such as ——— are for [or against] this idea. For example, one particular group believes . . .

However, a major point of the opposition that is seldom mentioned is . . .

Some other possible subjects for your paragraph might be arguments for or against harsh penalities for drunken driving, public aid for crime victims, or the reestablishment of the draft. No matter what subject you choose, present your argument in your first sentence by pointing out what is popularly assumed and then noting that certain other people are for or against this position. Your paragraph will gain in strength if you follow all three parts of Garrett De Bell's paragraph, taking care to use specific examples as part of your writing.

ESSAY PRACTICE

The following outline will help you plan a complete essay of at least five paragraphs. The theme of your essay will be closely related to the theme of Garrett De Bell's essay.

The following sentence may serve as your thesis sentence, and will also be the main idea of your introductory paragraph:

¶ 1.   Today in our country we are going through some drastic changes in our traditional attitudes toward the standard of living we can hope to achieve.

Each of the sentences below is the topic sentence for one of the paragraphs that you will write to develop your thesis. You may use the suggested details to develop each paragraph, or you may supply details of your own.

¶ 2.   I could describe my parents' standard of living as . . .

[DETAILS: Describe your parents' standard of living, either when you were a child or at the present time. Provide several details that will help your reader define that standard of living. For example, when did your parents buy their first car? When did they buy a color television set? Do they own their own home?]

¶ 3.   My own standard of living at the present time is . . .

[DETAILS: How would you describe your present standard of living? What are the items you have recently bought which you have needed or wanted for some time? What items have you not yet bought that you would like to have?]

¶ 4.   Judging by the rapid changes in the economic situation these days, I think that my standard of living five or ten years from now will be . . .

[DETAILS: Do you think that your standard of living will go up or down in the next five or ten years? If you think it will go up, what do you see yourself buying then that you cannot afford now? If you see it going down, what do you see yourself still waiting to buy years from now? In either case, how do you see yourself adjusting to your future economic situation?]

Be certain that you use transitions between paragraphs to make your writing flow smoothly. In addition, be sure that your conclusion gives your reader a clear signal that you have come to the end of your essay.

ESSAY TOPICS

1. a. Argue with a friend who is about to buy an appliance that you feel would result in an unnecessary use of energy. Your friend could be planning to buy anything

from an electric pencil sharpener to an air conditioning unit for a car. How would you convince your friend that this purchase would be a mistake?

b. List the various electrical appliances that you use on a regular basis. How many of these appliances do you feel are really necessary? How many of these appliances could you do without? Your essay could also be a response to someone who suggests that you do not need any electrical appliances at all in your daily life.

2. In his essay, Garrett De Bell argues that ''the quality of our lives would be higher with far less use of energy in this country.'' Choose an area of our lives where you feel that less of something would lead to positive results. For example, how would fewer plastic wrappers and containers lead to a better environment? How would less junk food lead to a healthier diet for everybody? How would less federal control of local government lead to more effective local management of civic affairs?

3. At the end of his essay, the writer gives a list of suggestions that he argues would help improve our environment. What is your judgment of each of the writer's suggestions? Choose one item from the author's list that you feel represents the most imporant step we could take to improve our environment. What are your strongest arguments in favor of that one step you have chosen?

✍ *Joseph Wood Krutch* ✍

Joseph Wood Krutch (1893–1970) was one of America's outstanding essayists. He was a sensitive observer of our world and in the words of one critic, he was well suited to be "a spectator and commentator on nature and man."

Krutch was a teacher, a scholar, and a writer. He was born in Knoxville, Tennessee, and was educated at the University of Tennessee and at Columbia University. He began his teaching career in New York City where he also worked as an associate editor of *The Nation*.

When he retired from teaching in 1952, Krutch moved to Tucson, Arizona, where he became deeply involved in the cause of conservation. While in Arizona, the writer served as a trustee of the Arizona Sonora Desert Museum at Tuscon. Another result of his stay in the Southwest was *The Desert Year*, a book that recorded his observations of the American desert with an unusual freshness and sense of curiosity. In 1954 he published *The Measure of Man*, a book in which the writer took pains to point out that modern culture has led us to abandon our responsibility to ourselves. We have to exercise this responsibility, Krutch points out, in order to be able to make the important decisions of our modern life.

In the following essay, Krutch shows his concern with nature and his concern with the responsibility we have toward our world. In "Lightning Water" the writer combines his observation of a natural phenomenon with some very pertinent comments on how we are using our resources and what we can expect for the future of our society.

PREVIEWING THE WRITER

• Note the writer's description of a phenomenon that seems to be destructive but actually has a purpose in the world of nature.

• What is the loss to the desert if people prevent flash floods from happening?

• What other destruction of the environment does the writer point out? Who is responsible for this other destruction?

LIGHTNING WATER

FLASH FLOODS, those wildly beautiful desert hallmarks, serve as a healthy reminder that nature on the rampage can quickly reduce to utter helplessness the careless individual or the person who naïvely assumes that the whole of the natural world has been "conquered." Strangers to the desert cannot believe that a sandy gully, which looks like a good place to camp, may become, without warning, a raging flood—a wall of water several feet high plunging forward with enormous speed and force.

Reclamation engineers, operating under a variety of names, are making a concerted effort to tame or conquer these floods—along with everything else that is free and natural. Their rationale often alludes to the fact that people have sometimes been drowned in them, but people have been killed rather more often in highway accidents, and no one talks about the necessity of eliminating automobiles. Perhaps the real reason for the often intemperate enthusiasm of the reclaimers is that the projects they dream up will provide them with jobs.

Like the road builders, the reclaimers are inclined to see needs where no one else can, and their consequent boondoggling threatens to destroy a large portion of the remaining natural environment. When every stream has been dammed and all the countryside has become a mere network of roads, their triumph will be complete—America the Beautiful will have become America the Conquered.

If we would only begin to question our naïve faith that road and dam builders "must know best because they are experts"; if, instead, we would only realize that the first concern of all of them is their vested interest in their own jobs, rather than in the public good, then their pointless vandalism of our countryside might be stopped. But this realization is likely to be too late in coming.

It doesn't rain often in the desert and the total annual rainfall is small. But when it does rain, the water often comes down in torrent proportions. This is one reason why the flash flood is primarily a desert phenomenon. Death Valley in California furnishes an extreme example. It is the driest spot in the United States. Average rainfall is about 1.5 inches and more than a year has been known to pass without a measurable trace. Yet in July, 1950, a cloudburst (a convenient but not very meaningful term) produced a flood which cut a 6-foot-deep gully across the main road and rolled along boulders 5 feet in diameter. In Arizona more than 5 inches of rain has fallen in a twenty-four-hour period; as much as 11 inches in the course of one storm. These are exceptional figures, but very heavy downpours within a short time are usual.

The other principal reason why the flash flood is almost 6 exclusively a feature of the desert is that nearly all the water that falls in a torrential rain runs off. Vegetation ground cover is sparse or nonexistent. The surface of the ground is often baked to an almost bricklike consistency. Very little water is absorbed. Most of it runs off into the dry riverbeds cut by previous floods. These gullies are among the most characteristic features of arid lands and are called by a variety of names—dry wash or draw in Arizona, arroyo in California, wadi in the Near East. Some of the floodwaters that periodically rage through an arroyo sink into its usually sandy or rocky bottom. A few feet below the surface, the soil may be damp, while that of the surrounding desert floor is completely dry. The difference in moisture creates a special environment for plant life. Near the borders of the dry wash there may be cottonwoods that cannot survive the desert and a special species of palo verde trees, which needs just a bit more water than the easily distinguishable species that grows in more arid situations.

Another geomorphic feature created by the flash floods is 7 the alluvial fan—characteristic of desert regions bordered by mountains. These are delta-shaped accumulations of sand and rock, deposited at the point where mountain ravines open onto the desert floor. Torrents arising from storms in the mountains plunge down these ravines, finally dumping their debris when their speed is reduced by emergence onto the flatness of the desert. Especially striking specimens can be seen in Death Valley. They look rather more like glaciers than like the flood deltas of moister regions, and they are among the most graceful of land forms.

Most paved roads in the desert are crossed at frequent 8 intervals by dips that conduct the water across the roadbeds. These dips, too, may be dangerous in flood season. Neither the pedestrian nor the motorist can quite believe the force of the water that occasionally rushes through these dry beds. But the presence of automobile-sized boulders in the arroyos attests to the carrying force of the water which increases enormously with an increase in speed.

It is said that the carrying power of a stream varies as the 9 sixth power of its velocity. But whether or not this figure is entirely accurate, all the lay traveler needs to remember is that an increased speed of flow increases manyfold the stream's power to sweep heavy objects along with it. He must not assume that because the flood doesn't look much swifter than it did when he crossed it safely a short time before, it is probably still safe. If he makes that assumption, he may be in for trouble. Flash floods are dangerous only if you don't take the trouble to know what they are and why they exist. But to some of us it seems that it would be better to teach people how to travel or live in the few remaining natural areas than to destroy their unique characteristics.

The ultimate endeavor of the reclaimers is to homogenize   10
the American earth, which today presents an infinite variety. The more it is crossed by freeways and the more its streams and lakes are regularized by engineers, the more every part of it will look like every other part. It will no longer be worth taking the journeys from one region to another that the superhighways are supposed to make so easy and so quick.

The Southwest without the flash floods would be no longer   11
recognizable, no longer unique, no longer beautiful in its own way. We have begun to hear some talk about preserving a few wild rivers, and the flash flood is the wildest of all wild rivers. On the other hand, the reclaimers seem determined to tame everything capable of inspiring awe and to put everywhere in its place the tame, the uniform, and the convenient. They are making this a far less interesting world.

THE WRITER'S THEMES

1. According to the writer, what are the effects of the flash floods on the natural life of the desert?
2. How does the writer's use of specific facts make his argument more convincing? To what extent does the writer depend upon scientific fact to make his case stronger?
3. What is Joseph Wood Krutch's view of the future of America? According to the writer, what can we look forward to if the present trend of "development" continues? In your view, are his predictions accurate?

THE WRITER'S TECHNIQUE

In paragraph eight of his essay, Joseph Wood Krutch describes the roads that are found in the desert. Here is that paragraph:

Most paved roads in the desert are crossed at frequent intervals by dips that conduct the water across the roadbeds. These dips, too, may be dangerous in flood season. Neither the pedestrian nor the motorist can quite believe the force of the water that occasionally rushes through these dry beds. But the presence of automobile-sized boulders in the arroyos attests to the carrying force of the water which increases enormously with an increase in speed.

The writer begins by describing both the roads and the dips in the roads. He also notes that these dips "conduct the water across the roadbeds" and that the dips may themselves become dangerous in the flood season. The author then indicates the surprising force of the water that sometimes "rushes through these dry beds." The evidence of this great force is the presence of "automobile-sized boulders," proof of the enormous "carrying force of the water" that washes through the arroyo when there is a flood.

PARAGRAPH PRACTICE

Write a paragraph of your own, using Joseph Wood Krutch's paragraph as your model. The main point of your paragraph might be that we should never underestimate the power of nature. For example, you could write about people who like to go to the beach but forget about the dangers of too much exposure to the sun. You could also take boating or swimming as your example, and discuss people's lack of awareness of how easily a normal situation can become dangerous. Begin your paragraph by describing people in a normal situation, and what they would ordinarily expect in that situation. For example, what kind of a tan would a person normally expect to get at the beach, using ordinary precautions? How would people normally prepare for a day of boating or an afternoon of swimming? What precautions would they normally take?

Develop your paragraph by describing some unexpected events that could take place in the situation you have chosen. What could happen to a sunbather that would result in a bad sunburn? What could suddenly happen to boaters or swimmers that would place their lives in danger?

Conclude your paragraph by giving an example, either from your own experience or the experience of others, that illustrates the kind of situation you have developed in your paragraph.

ESSAY PRACTICE

The following outline will help you plan a complete essay of at least five paragraphs. The theme of your essay will be closely related to the theme of the Joseph Wood Krutch essay.

The following sentence may serve as your thesis sentence, and will also be the main idea of your introductory paragraph:

¶ 1. Since experts are people who pay attention to their own interests, we cannot totally rely on their judgments.

Each of the sentences below is the topic sentence for one of the paragraphs that you will write to develop your thesis. You may use the suggested details to develop each paragraph, or you may supply details of your own.

¶ 2. We must try to recognize when an expert in some area is only being selfish.

[DETAILS: When have you encountered an expert and discovered that this person was being more selfish than professional? What did this person say or do that led you to this realization? What was your reaction?]

¶ 3. It is important that we protect ourselves against the self-interest of various experts.

[DETAILS: Is there a point at which we have to admit that we cannot compete with the experts? To what extent are we able to protect ourselves against the experts? Do the various institutions of society help us judge the advice or opinions of experts, or do these institutions use experts to strengthen their own points of view?]

¶ 4. Each of us must decide the extent to which we can afford to trust experts.

[DETAILS: Based on your own experience, or the experience of others, how much trust do you place in experts? What does an expert have to do in order to gain and hold your confidence?]

Be certain that you use transitions between paragraphs to make your writing flow smoothly. In addition, be sure that your conclusion gives your reader a clear signal that you have come to the end of your essay.

ESSAY TOPICS

1. What we think is destructive in nature really has its place in the order of things, but the real destruction that we see taking place in our environment is done by people.

    Agree or disagree with this statement. Use as many specific examples as you can to prove your point.
2. One of the ways people are currently trying to control nature is by building nuclear power plants. Write an argument for or against the construction of nuclear power plants as a solution to our energy problems.
3. a. What control should a country try to exercise over its rate of population growth? Argue for or against some type of population control, either sponsored by the government or approved by it, that would limit the number of children born in a country. Should the government supply birth control information to people who want it? Should the government pay for abortions? Should the government set up a program of incentives so that people will want to have smaller families?
    b. Argue for or against having a large family. What are the various factors in our society today that support your argument?

🐾 Rachel Carson 🐾

Rachel Carson (1907–1964) was born in Springdale, Pennsylvania. Beginning in her earliest childhood, she and her mother explored the woods, lakes, and ponds near their home, and this led to her deep and lasting interest in the world of nature.

Rachel Carson went to college determined to become a writer, but she soon decided on a different career and changed her major from English to biology. After college she went to Johns Hopkins University in Baltimore for graduate work in biology, supplementing this with studies at the Marine Biological Laboratory in Woods Hole, Massachusetts. It was in Massachusetts that Rachel Carson began her intensive study of the sea. During this period of her life she also taught biology at Johns Hopkins and at the University of Maryland.

She then joined the Federal Fish and Wildlife Service as a marine biologist. During this part of her career she began to share her observations and perceptions of her work, thus combining her interest in science and writing. In 1951 she published *The Sea Around Us*, a book that has been described as a "masterpiece of lyrical scientific writing." It was translated into thirty languages and became a best seller. Her next book was another highly praised study, *The Edge of the Sea*.

During World War II, Rachel Carson was engaged in research for the government. It was this investigation of new toxic substances that led her to reconsider her whole approach to science. Her attitude became less poetic and more critical, and when a friend in New England told her that area spraying programs had destroyed birds in a local wildlife sanctuary, Rachel Carson decided to write a book-length study of the effects of chemicals on our environment.

For six years the writer gathered materials, interviewed scientists, and worked on her manuscript. The result was her most famous work, *Silent Spring*, a book that many people believe started the modern environmental movement. One writer has noted that *Silent Spring* "has often been cited as perhaps the most influential single factor in creating public concern about the future of the world's ecology." In the following chapter from the book, the writer examines our use of chemicals and describes the implications of those chemicals on our lives and the lives of those who will follow us.

PREVIEWING THE WRITER

• What, specifically, does the writer point out as the central problem of our time?

- According to the writer, to what extent have chemicals already damaged the natural balance of our environment? How much of this damage is reversible?
- According to the writer, who is winning "the chemical war"?

THE OBLIGATION TO ENDURE

THE HISTORY OF LIFE on earth has been a history of   1
interaction between living things and their surroundings. To a large extent, the physical form and the habits of the earth's vegetation and its animal life have been molded by the environment. Considering the whole span of earthly time, the opposite effect, in which life actually modifies its surroundings, has been relatively slight. Only within the moment of time represented by the present century has one species—man—acquired significant power to alter the nature of his world.

During the past quarter century this power has not only   2
increased to one of disturbing magnitude but it has changed in character. The most alarming of all man's assaults upon the environment is the contamination of air, earth, rivers, and sea with dangerous and even lethal materials. This pollution is for the most part irrecoverable; the chain of evil it initiates not only in the world that must support life but in living tissues is for the most part irreversible. In this now universal contamination of the environment, chemicals are the sinister and little-recognized partners of radiation in changing the very nature of the world—the very nature of its life. Strontium 90, released through nuclear explosions into the air, comes to earth in rain or drifts down as fallout, lodges in soil, enters into the grass or corn or wheat grown there, and in time takes up its abode in the bones of a human being, there to remain until his death. Similarly, chemicals sprayed on croplands or forests or gardens lie long in soil, entering into living organisms, passing from one to another in a chain of poisoning and death. Or they pass mysteriously by underground streams until they emerge and, through the alchemy of air and sunlight, combine into new forms that kill vegetation, sicken cattle, and work unknown harm on those who drink from once pure wells. As Albert Schweitzer has said, "Man can hardly even recognize the devils of his own creation."

It took hundreds of millions of years to produce the life   3
that now inhabits the earth—eons of time in which that developing and evolving and diversifying life reached a state of adjustment and balance with its surroundings. The environment,
rigorously shaping and directing the life it supported, contained
elements that were hostile as well as supporting. Certain rocks
gave out dangerous radiation; even within the light of the sun,
from which all life draws its energy, there were short-wave ra-
diations with power to injure. Given time—time not in years
but in millennia—life adjusts, and a balance has been reached.
For time is the essential ingredient; but in the modern world
there is no time.

The rapidity of change and the speed with which new   4
situations are created follow the impetuous and heedless pace
of man rather than the deliberate pace of nature. Radiation is
no longer merely the background radiation of rocks, the bom-
bardment of cosmic rays, the ultraviolet of the sun that have
existed before there was any life on earth; radiation is now the
unnatural creation of man's tampering with the atom. The
chemicals to which life is asked to make its adjustment are no
longer merely the calcium and silica and copper and all the rest
of the minerals washed out of the rocks and carried in rivers to
the sea; they are the synthetic creations of man's inventive mind,
brewed in his laboratories, and having no counterparts in nature.

To adjust to these chemicals would require time on the   5
scale that is nature's; it would require not merely the years of
a man's life but the life of generations. And even this, were it
by some miracle possible, would be futile, for the new chemicals
come from our laboratories in an endless stream; almost five
hundred annually find their way into actual use in the United
States alone. The figure is staggering and its implicatons are not
easily grasped—500 new chemicals to which the bodies of men
and animals are required somehow to adapt each year, chemicals totally outside the limits of biologic experience.

Among them are many that are used in man's war against   6
nature. Since the mid-1940's over 200 basic chemicals have been
created for use in killing insects, weeds, rodents, and other
organisms described in the modern vernacular as "pests"; and
they are sold under several thousand different brand names.

These sprays, dusts, and aerosols are now applied almost   7
universally to farms, gardens, forests, and homes—nonselective

chemicals that have the power to kill every insect, the "good" and the "bad," to still the song of birds and the leaping of fish in the streams, to coat the leaves with a deadly film, and to linger on in soil—all this though the intended target may be only a few weeds or insects. Can anyone believe it is possible to lay down such a barrage of poisons on the surface of the earth without making it unfit for all life? They should not be called "insecticides," but "biocides."

The whole process of spraying seems caught up in an end- 8 less spiral. Since DDT was released for civilian use, a process of escalation has been going on in which ever more toxic materials must be found. This has happened because insects, in a triumphant vindication of Darwin's principle of the survival of the fittest, have evolved super races immune to the particular insecticide used, hence a deadlier one has always to be developed—and then a deadlier one than that. It has happened also because, for reasons to be described later, destructive insects often undergo a "flareback," or resurgence, after spraying in numbers greater than before. Thus the chemical war is never won, and all life is caught in its violent crossfire.

Along with the possibility of the extinction of mankind by 9 nuclear war, the central problem of our age has therefore become the contamination of man's total environment with such substances of incredible potential for harm—substances that accumulate in the tissues of plants and animals and even penetrate the germ cells to shatter or alter the very material of heredity upon which the shape of the future depends.

Some would-be architects of our future look toward a time 10 when it will be possible to alter the human germ plasm by design. But we may easily be doing so now by inadvertence, for many chemicals, like radiation, bring about gene mutations. It is ironic to think that man might determine his own future by something so seemingly trivial as the choice of an insect spray.

All this has been risked—for what? Future historians may 11 well be amazed by our distorted sense of proportion. How could intelligent beings seek to control a few unwanted species by a method that contaminated the entire environment and brought the threat of disease and death even to their own kind? Yet this is precisely what we have done. We have done it, moreover, for reasons that collapse the moment we examine them. We are told that the enormous and expanding use of pesticides is necessary to maintain farm production. Yet is our real problem not one of *overproduction?* Our farms, despite measures to remove acreages from production and to pay farmers *not* to produce, have yielded such a staggering excess of crops that the American taxpayer in 1962 is paying out more than one billion dollars a year as the total carrying cost of the surplus-food storage program. And is the situation helped when one branch of the Agriculture Department tries to reduce production while another states, as it did in 1958, "It is believed generally that reduction of crop acreages under provisions of the Soil Bank will stimulate interest in use of chemicals to obtain maximum production on the land retained in crops."

All this is not to say there is no insect problem and no   12
need of control. I am saying, rather, that control must be geared to realities, not to mythical situations, and that the methods employed must be such that they do not destroy us along with the insects.

The problem whose attempted solution has brought such   13
a train of disaster in its wake is an accompaniment of our modern way of life. Long before the age of man, insects inhabited the earth—a group of extraordinarily varied and adaptable beings. Over the course of time since man's advent, a small percentage of the more than half a million species of insects have come into conflict with human welfare in two principal ways: as competitors for the food supply and as carriers of human disease.

Disease-carrying insects become important where human   14
beings are crowded together, especially under conditions where sanitation is poor, as in time of natural disaster or war or in situations of extreme poverty and deprivation. Then control of some sort becomes necessary. It is a sobering fact, however, as we shall presently see, that the method of massive chemical control has had only limited success, and also threatens to worsen the very conditions it is intended to curb.

Under primitive agricultural conditions the farmer had few   15
insect problems. These arose with the intensification of agriculture—the devotion of immense acreages to a single crop. Such a system set the stage for explosive increases in specific insect populations. Single-crop farming does not take advantage of the principles by which nature works; it is agriculture as an engineer might conceive it to be. Nature has introduced great variety into the landscape, but man has displayed a passion for simplifying it. Thus he undoes the built-in checks and balances by

which nature holds the species within bounds. One important natural check is a limit on the amount of suitable habitat for each species. Obviously then, an insect that lives on wheat can build up its population to much higher levels on a farm devoted to wheat than on one in which wheat is intermingled with other crops to which the insect is not adapted.

The same thing happens in other situations. A generation or more ago, the towns of large areas of the United States lined their streets with the noble elm tree. Now the beauty they hopefully created is threatened with complete destruction as disease sweeps through the elms, carried by a beetle that would have only limited chance to build up large populations and to spread from tree to tree if the elms were only occasional trees in a richly diversified planting.

Another factor in the modern insect problem is one that must be viewed against a background of geologic and human history: the spreading of thousands of different kinds of organisms from their native homes to invade new territories. This worldwide migration has been studied and graphically described by the British ecologist Charles Elton in his recent book *The Ecology of Invasions.* During the Cretaceous Period, some hundred million years ago, flooding seas cut many land bridges between continents and living things found themselves confined in what Elton calls "colossal separate nature reserves." There, isolated from others of their kind, they developed many new species. When some of the land masses were joined again, about 15 million years ago, these species began to move out into new territories—a movement that is not only still in progress but is now receiving considerable assistance from man.

The importation of plants is the primary agent in the modern spread of species, for animals have almost invariably gone along with the plants, quarantine being a comparatively recent and not completely effective innovation. The United States Office of Plant Introduction alone has introduced almost 200,000 species and varieties of plants from all over the world. Nearly half of the 180 or so major insect enemies of plants in the United States are accidental imports from abroad, and most of them have come as hitchhikers on plants.

In new territory, out of reach of the restraining hand of the natural enemies that kept down its numbers in its native land, an invading plant or animal is able to become enormously abundant. Thus it is no accident that our most troublesome insects are introduced species.

These invasions, both the naturally occurring and those [20] dependent on human assistance, are likely to continue indefinitely. Quarantine and massive chemical campaigns are only extremely expensive ways of buying time. We are faced, according to Dr. Elton, "with a life-and-death need not just to find new technological means of suppressing this plant or that animal"; instead we need the basic knowledge of animal populations and their relations to their surroundings that will "promote an even balance and damp down the explosive power of outbreaks and new invasions."

Much of the necessary knowledge is now available but we [21] do not use it. We train ecologists in our universities and even employ them in our governmental agencies but we seldom take their advice. We allow the chemical death rain to fall as though there were no alternative, whereas in fact there are many, and our ingenuity could soon discover many more if given opportunity.

Have we fallen into a mesmerized state that makes us ac- [22] cept as inevitable that which is inferior or detrimental, as though having lost the will or the vision to demand that which is good? Such thinking, in the words of the ecologist Paul Shepard, "idealizes life with only its head out of water, inches above the limits of toleration of the corruption of its own environment . . . Why should we tolerate a diet of weak poisons, a home in insipid surroundings, a circle of acquaintances who are not quite our enemies, the noise of motors with just enough relief to prevent insanity? Who would want to live in a world which is just not quite fatal?"

Yet such a world is pressed upon us. The crusade to create [23] a chemically sterile, insect-free world seems to have engendered a fanatic zeal on the part of many specialists and most of the so-called control agencies. On every hand there is evidence that those engaged in spraying operations exercise a ruthless power. "The regulatory entomologists . . . function as prosecutor, judge and jury, tax assessor and collector and sheriff to enforce their own orders," said Connecticut entomologist Neely Turner. The most flagrant abuses go unchecked in both state and federal agencies.

It is not my contention that chemical insecticides must [24] never be used. I do contend that we have put poisonous and biologically potent chemicals indiscriminately into the hands of persons largely or wholly ignorant of their potentials for harm. We have subjected enormous numbers of people to contact with these poisons, without their consent and often without their knowledge. If the Bill of Rights contains no guarantee that a citizen shall be secure against lethal poisons distributed either by private individuals or by public officials, it is surely only because our forefathers, despite their considerable wisdom and foresight, could conceive of no such problem.

I contend, furthermore, that we have allowed these chemicals to be used with little or no advance investigation of their effect on soil, water, wildlife, and man himself. Future generations are unlikely to condone our lack of prudent concern for the integrity of the natural world that supports all life.

There is still very limited awareness of the nature of the threat. This is an era of specialists, each of whom sees his own problem and is unaware of or intolerant of the larger frame into which it fits. It is also an era dominated by industry, in which the right to make a dollar at whatever cost is seldom challenged. When the public protests, confronted with some obvious evidence of damaging results of pesticide applications, it is fed little tranquilizing pills of half truth. We urgently need an end to these false assurances, to the sugar coating of unpalatable facts. It is the public that is being asked to assume the risks that the insect controllers calculate. The public must decide whether it wishes to continue on the present road, and it can do so only when in full possession of the facts. In the words of Jean Rostand, "The obligation to endure gives us the right to know."

THE WRITER'S THEMES

1. In how many ways are people engaged in a "war against Nature"? Why is this war really an "endless spiral"?
2. In what ways are the lives of insects related to our own lives? To what extent is their fate connected to our own?
3. How many different arguments does the writer use against insecticides? Which of these arguments is the most convincing?

THE WRITER'S TECHNIQUE

In the concluding paragraph of her essay, Rachel Carson alludes to the threat to our environment, a threat she has described throughout the essay. Here is that concluding paragraph:

There is still very limited awareness of the nature of the threat. This is an era of specialists, each of whom sees his own problem and is unaware of or intolerant of the larger frame into which it fits. It is also an era dominated by industry, in which the right to make a dollar at whatever cost is seldom challenged. When the public protests, confronted with some obvious evidence of damaging results of pesticide applications, it is fed little tranquilizing pills of half truth. We urgently need an end to these false assurances, to the sugar coating of unpalatable facts. It is the public that is being asked to assume the risks that the insect controllers calculate. The public must decide whether it wishes to continue on the present road, and it can do so only when in full possession of the facts. In the words of Jean Rostand, "The obligation to endure gives us the right to know."

The writer begins by noting that people are still unaware of "the nature of the threat." She then describes our era, which she calls "an era of specialists," and "an era dominated by industry." One problem that results from this combination of narrow-minded specialization and greedy industrialism is that public protests result in only "little tranquilizing pills of half truth."

At this point in the paragraph the writer finishes her description of the situation and begins to prescribe some remedies. We "urgently need" an end to these "false assurances," and the public "must decide" if it wants matters to continue in the present way. The writer ends the paragraph by quoting the French biologist Jean Rostand, whose words provided Rachel Carson with the title for her chapter.

The writer has constructed her paragraph in two parts. First, she has described a situation that is in need of correction and she has indicated the source of the problem. Next, she has made some suggestions as to how the situation might be changed, and she has ended by including an appropriate quotation, one that summarizes not only the heart of this final paragraph but the spirit of her entire essay.

PARAGRAPH PRACTICE

Write a paragraph of your own, using Rachel Carson's paragraph as your model. You could write about a problem that you or a group of people are having, or you could describe a situation that is facing our society in general. For example, you could describe what is being done to our environment as a result of our enormous use of paper products. You could also write about the growing problem of our water supply, a situation that is becoming serious in many parts of our country.

Imitate Rachel Carson's technique by dividing your paragraph into two sections. In the first part of your paragraph indicate the problem and describe what you believe to be the main source(s) of that problem. How did this situation begin? Why has it been allowed to develop? In the second part of your paragraph, make some very specific suggestions that you believe would help to change the situation. What do you feel could be done?

You could, if you wish, end your paragraph by providing an appropriate quotation, one that would support what you have been writing about in your paragraph. For example, if you have written about either the waste of paper or the growing scarcity of water, you could end your paragraph by indicating that the old saying "There's more where that came from" is no longer true in our society.

ESSAY PRACTICE

The following outline will help you plan a complete essay of at least five paragraphs. The theme of your essay will be closely related to the theme of the Rachel Carson essay.

The following sentence may serve as your thesis sentence, and will also be the main idea of your introductory paragraph:

¶ 1. The problem of procrastination, which communities as well as individuals indulge in, must be overcome if we are to avoid disastrous results.

Each of the sentences below is the topic sentence for one of the paragraphs that you will write to develop your thesis. You may use the suggested details to develop each paragraph, or you may supply details of your own.

¶ 2. If communities delay in solving a problem, they often create a larger problem that will have to be taken care of at some point in the future.

[DETAILS: Here, use the example of a particular city or town that neglected some necessary maintenance or repair and later faced an even more costly problem.]

¶ 3. I remember a time when I neglected to take care of something when it was time to do so. I will never forget the results.

[DETAILS: Describe a situation you were faced with but which you did not deal with right away. Why did you put off doing something about it? What was the result of your procrastination? When you finally did act, how much more did you have to do in order to correct the situation?]

¶ 4. Now if I am faced with a problem that needs my attention, I . . .

[DETAILS: Do you no longer procrastinate, or do you still put off certain decisions or actions?]

Be certain that you use transitions between paragraphs to make your writing flow smoothly. In addition, be sure that your conclusion gives your reader a clear signal that you have come to the end of your essay.

ESSAY TOPICS

1. Toward the end of her essay, Rachel Carson observes that if our Bill of Rights contains no guarantee that we should be protected against poisons in our environment, "it is only because our forefathers . . . could conceive of no such problem."

   Write, in essay form, an environmental Bill of Rights for this generation and future generations. What rights should every generation be able to expect, in terms of its environment? Be specific, using as a guide for your essay the problems Rachel Carson raises in "The Obligation to Endure."

2. Rachel Carson states that in today's society "the right to make a dollar is seldom challenged." Under what circumstances should a company or an individual not be allowed to make money? When should a greater good be the major issue? For example, should a company be allowed to sell arms and ammunition to any country, regardless of that country's political philosophy? How much testing should be necessary before a product can be marketed? At what point should a company be allowed to sell a product, such as a new drug, that may have serious side effects? How

could society make it possible for an individual or an organization to work for the common good and not resent losing a profit?

3. Rachel Carson notes that we are living in "an era of specialists, each of whom sees his own problem and is unaware or intolerant of the larger frame into which it fits."

    Write an essay in which you argue for or against the training of specialists in our society. Do we depend too much on specialists? Do specialists in such areas as medicine or science contribute as much to society as individuals with more general backgrounds?

Focus on Terms: Connotation and Denotation

Connotation and *denotation* are twin terms that refer to the two kinds of meanings that a word may have. *Denotation* is the strict dictionary definition of a word, while *connotation* refers to other, associated meanings that may also be given to a word.

For example, in the selection from *Cross Creek*, Marjorie Kinnan Rawlings states that the earth "will survive bankers and any system of government, capitalistic, fascist or bolshevist." The dictionary definition of the term *fascist* is "a philosophy or system of government that advocates . . . a dictatorship of the extreme right," but there are also several connotations of the word *fascist* that may refer to a rigid, authoritarian personality, or any inflexible method of doings things.

On the other hand, when Rachel Carson is discussing radiation in her essay "The Obligation to Endure," she provides two definitions of the term:

> Radiation is no longer merely the background radiation of rocks, the bombardment of cosmic rays, the ultraviolet of the sun that have existed before there was any life on earth; radiation is now the unnatural creation of man's tampering with the atom.

Both of these definitions are examples of denotation because in each case the writer is concerned with the strict (in this case scientific) meaning of the word.

Every writer should keep in mind that, beyond its strict denotation, a word may have more than one connotation for a reader. It is therefore advisable to keep your audience in mind when you use particular words. For example, the word *dog* has a strict dictionary definition, but for many people the word may also have positive or negative connotations. For most people, a dog is associated with warmth and friendliness, but if a person has been attacked by a dog the association may be a negative one. The word *Christmas* also has generally positive connotations, but people who are alone at that time of year, or who see the holiday only as a time when there is more work than usual, may have negative connotations of Christmas.

In most of your writing, you will be making your word choices based on the clearest and most straightforward meanings of the words you use. Connotation is most obvious in such areas as politics and advertising, where success often depends on the different shades of meaning a single word can possess. Your own writing will be more successful if you are sensitive to the many connotations words can have.

Student Essay ᴕ ᴥ *Ray Flesch*

Many people today believe that a new emphasis on public transportation is the long-overdue solution to a problem that has been draining us of our energy and other resources.

In the following essay, the writer argues for what some people might see as a radical solution to our transportation problems. As you read the argument, try to imagine what our world would be like if the writer's proposal were to become reality.

• In the essay, the writer presents an objective argument, but several of his word choices show the use of connotation. For example, in the second paragraph the writer uses the word "streetcar," the denotation of which is "a means of public transportation." However, the word may also have certain connotations. For example, a person who has visited San Francisco may read the word and be reminded of the famous trolleys that are one of the romantic attractions of that city. Another person could think of a "streetcar" as an old-fashioned and outdated means of transportation.

As you read the essay, look for other words that could have more than one connotation.

THE NEED FOR TOTAL PUBLIC TRANSPORTATION

1 "HE WHO TURNS HALFWAY is only half in error." This piece of wisdom is often denied when it concerns money already spent on an ill-planned endeavor. And perhaps nowhere is this resistance to logic more fiercely preached and practiced than in the field of passenger transportation.

2 When the private automobile began to arrive on the scene early in this century, most urban and rural areas enjoyed rather adequate public transit systems. In fact, the electric tram—here

in this country called the streetcar or trolley or interurban—was conquering the world. It was clearly a time to recognize and appreciate and perpetuate a good thing when one saw it. And good they were, those electric street railways.

We could deliberate forever as to whether the authorities 3 stopped to think hard enough about the implications of the private car, which was initially intended only for the elite (and who were they?). If they had, their correct conclusion could hardly have been anything else but severe curtailment if not a total ban. Nothing of the sort did happen, and the disastrous consequences have been with us ever since—and they are getting worse all the time.

While lamenting this development, most commentators 4 take for granted that it is too late to reverse this course of events: the costs would be prohibitive, too many people would resist, and we would be left with a permanent feeling of regret and shame for all the wasted resources, human, monetary and natural, if we should have to start all over.

Nevertheless, an opposite view presents itself. Though it 5 would have been vastly preferable if governments always heeded the old saying, ''To rule is to foresee,'' the trend in this century has been, ''Seeing is believing.'' If the private car had been stopped in its (non) tracks, people would have continued to crave it, refusing to believe that traveling by car simply could not work on any large scale. So the lesson, however costly it has become, may be seen as historically unavoidable among people who are less than perfect.

Having come to this mitigating conclusion, we ought to 6 begin immediately with a gradual phasing out of private autos in favor of public transit vehicles. One particular obstacle must be overcome in this effort: the myth that we need mass transit only during rush hours, and that cars are no problem in the quiet of the day.

Logic and fairness are close relatives. If we concede, as we 7 must under the burden of the evidence, that our society cannot function without mass transit during peak traffic hours, then we should squarely face the need to create an environment for it where it can thrive, rather than have it be an unacceptable drain on our shrinking public funds, as is now the case.

For public transportation to be efficient, it must operate with the least possible fluctuation in its schedules. From this point of view, the policies of the last few decades, such as raising auto tolls during rush hours and building roads for comfortable off-peak travel which become saturated during rush hours (all of which encourages mass transit during peak hours only), are totally detrimental to the development of effective mass transit. On the contrary, we should temporarily condone and even facilitate the use of private cars during rush hours, until such time as mass transit will be expanded enough to do the whole job.

This also means that if mass transportation becomes important soon, people will not be asked to scrap their cars. But mass transit should be built up as rapidly as possible to become so attractive that more and more people will decide against replacing their cars when the time is up. For, as has been stressed in much of the literature on the subject, today's population has not really opted for the car. Instead, for lack of an alternative, the auto was forced on us.   9

There is no danger whatsoever that, once it has become as attractive as possible, people would reject mass transit. Enough research and opinion polls have established that the main reason a great majority does not favor mass transit at present is the fact that there is so little of it that is attractive.   10

Ultimately, the use of mass transit exclusively will become inevitable; all signs point to that. Why not cut short the agony that will continue to plague us until relief arrives, in the form of public transporation?   11

Strategies for Writing

1. Each of the following quotations is from the student essay, and each contains an italicized word. Two words that contain similar denotations (dictionary meanings) but different connotations are under each word. Review each quotation and discuss the effect you believe the writer intended by the use of that word. In each case, how would the use of the other word(s) have changed the writer's meaning?

   a. . . . the *myth* that we need mass transit only during rush
       (fabrication; idea)
       hours . . .

b. . . . our *shrinking* public funds . . .
(decreasing; shriveling)

c. . . . people will not be asked *to scrap* their cars.
(to abandon; to discard)

2. Each of the following excerpts has been taken from the student essay. In each case, provide another word for the word that has been italicized. By choosing another word that is similar in meaning, you will be changing the connotation of the sentence, therefore changing its impact.

a. . . . initially intended only for the *elite* . . .

b. . . . people would have continued *to crave* it . . .

c. Why not cut short the agony that will continue *to plague* us . . .

3. Write an essay in which you discuss the old saying quoted in the essay: "To rule is to foresee." To what extent is it important for our government to look ahead to our future needs, in the area of public transportation and in other areas?

4. Many students are faced with transportation problems because of the high cost of private cars, college policies that restrict the use of cars on campus, or poor public transportation. Write an argument that would provide a solution to the transportation problems students face today. Your answer to the problem could range from a free college bus service to privately organized car pools.

12

FURTHER READINGS

◆ *Leighton Brewer* ◆

Leighton Brewer (1896–1969) was an educator, a soldier, and a writer. During World War I he served in Europe as a volunteer ambulance driver and later as a fighter pilot. After the war he received his B.A. from Yale, and in 1928 he received his M.A. in English literature from Harvard.

During the 1920s and 1930s he taught at Harvard and Radcliffe, but when World War II began he became chief of the Psychological Warfare Service in London. In 1943 he returned to the United States to head the same service with the Army General Staff.

Leighton Brewer wrote several books, among them a war poem, *Riders of the Sky,* and a literary study of Shakespeare, *Shakespeare and the Dark Lady.* The following selection is taken from his book *Virgin Water* (1941), an account of his trout fishing experiences in Canada. The area Brewer describes is on the St. Anne river, north of Quebec, a wilderness of lakes, swamps, and smaller streams inhabited by a variety of wildlife. This area stretches a thousand miles to the north, until it reaches the Arctic Ocean.

One critic has noted that, in *Virgin Water,* Leighton Brewer "combines information with a sensitive feeling for the outdoor life." The following selection shows the writer's abilities as a reporter and as a sensitive observer, while he tells an unusual fishing story.

THE LAKE OF THE BEAUTIFUL TROUT

SOME YEARS AGO, on visiting the Lake of the Beautiful Trout for the third time without seeing any sign of life, I had come to the conclusion that it was all a myth—the tales of the 4- and 5- and 6-pounders—and that in reality it contained no fish at all. So one afternoon my fishing companion and I went over to the next lake and filled a couple of pails with a dozen fat trout ranging from one quarter to three quarters of a pound and, carrying them back, dumped them into the lake supposed to contain the fine fish. Of the dozen unfortunately eleven were females and only one a male, and thinking that should anything happen to the lone gentleman—should a mink or an otter way-lay him, or should he perish from our rough handling or some other cause—the lake would become, in effect, a nunnery, I decided another male would be desirable, and for that purpose set my companion fishing again while I waited, pail in hand, to convey the first he-victim that should be captured into the se-raglio. At last my friend hooked a fine 1¼-pound fish with red belly and big undershot jaw, an unmistakable male, and playing him with great care, we succeeded in getting him into the half-filled pail, whereupon I dashed off to cover the third of a mile that separated the two lakes in as short a time as possible, for large fish do not live long in cramped quarters and very quickly use up all the available oxygen. I had traversed perhaps two thirds of the distance when, in my haste, I stumbled over a projecting root and sprawled headlong onto my face in the dirt. Out shot the fish into the bushes, and all the water from the pail except an inch at the very bottom. With great self-control and presence of mind, however, my first thought was to pre-serve the life of the trout at all costs. Quickly discovering him flopping about among the ferns, I dexterously replaced him in the pail with his nose in the remnants of the water and his tail sticking out at the rim, and then sprinted over the remaining hundred yards in record time to toss him, gasping for air, into the Lake of the Beautiful Trout. He was pretty weary after his long fight and the harsh treatment to which I had subjected him, but he was young and tough, and as soon as he felt his familiar element, he righted himself and then lay motionless, breathing hard, like a runner after a race, for fully fifteen min-utes. Then, as I was watching him, he slowly wiggled out into the deeper water and was lost from view. Now, at any rate, I was certain that there were fish in the Lake of the Beautiful Trout.

....

From the Grand Lake Tourilli it is only six hours' traveling   2
time to the last known water, the Lake of the Beautiful Trout. It was more than eleven years now since I had been there, but I had not forgotten the legend which is handed down to each new generation of fishermen in these parts. Some of them smile and, winking knowingly at each other, speak of Ananias and people who like to be fooled; but there are others whose eyes grow big with delight and wonder to hear the stories old Potvin tells of the trout he has seen and weighed that have come from this far-away lake.

"I have seen six trout weighing 36 pounds; I weighed them   3
myself," old Potvin always begins. "But there are bigger trout there even than that!" And then someone, an unbeliever, who has heard it all many many times before, interrupts and suggests another highball.

The sixteenth of September dawned clear and cool. A con-   4
clave of loons made a mighty hullaballoo about half past six when a bull moose splashed into the lake at the northern end, and mist lay along the hillsides when I took my morning plunge in the icy water.

"Joe," I said as soon as breakfast was over, "today we go   5
to the Lake of the Beautiful Trout, you and I alone; we'll leave the others here."

Bob was content, after his haul of ninety, to remain where   6
he knew there was plenty of good fishing; and I was loath to take him through the big swamp and then back again the following day with less than one chance in a thousand of his catching anything.

The Grand Lake Tourilli was calm and silvery in the early   7
morning light as Joe and I dipped our paddles with our faces turned northward, where the pale blue sky of autumn lay above the irregular horizon line of spruce tops, here and there a giant among them rising far above his fellows on these unlumbered hillsides of the great forest. At the head of the lake we disembarked for a short carry; then on across another lake, named Bear Pond, upon whose northern shore we removed our coats prior to the tough four-mile portage across the Caribou Marsh, that lies on the height of land between the headwaters of the

St. Anne and Metabatchouan rivers. Looking back to the south across Bear Pond, I saw a giant circle around the sun, its lower rim partly hidden in thin gray clouds, and I thought then that a sundog was a bad sign; but after an hour or so it disappeared, and I felt less apprehensive for our adventure.

Five miles of very bad going through the swamps, across six lakes and down a lonely stretch of river and then a final short carry through a balsam wood—and there at last, before me once again, stretched the gray water of that lake of legend, that lake which all who live in these parts say hides the beautiful trout in its deep, dark water. 8

No inlet flows into this lake of mystery, but in its depths are hidden springs instead. Perhaps a mile in length and half as broad in the widest place, it is a fine body of water, shaped like a heart, with a long narrow stretch leading down to the outlet. I tried to sound it once to determine its depth in the middle. I had eighty-four feet of line, but I didn't find bottom 9

We were weary after our journey through the swamps with heavy packs, for we had to take our canoe, and it wasn't until 4:30 P.M. or thereabouts that I made my first cast on the ruffled waters. I recalled my earliest visit here with my father. That was nearly twenty-seven years ago. It was Joe's first visit also. I remember how eager I was to get out and fish. I couldn't even wait until after lunch. I had been back a number of times in the years between and had stocked the lake once, but I'd never yet seen a trout rise. I wondered what the Fates had in store for me this time. The sundog bothered me, and the wind was wrong; it seemed to be coming from the northeast. But the day was still fair, although thin, hazy clouds lay in long streaks across the middle of the sky. 10

I fished for about an hour and a half, I suppose, without any result; and as the wind was still blowing strong, I decided to have an early supper and then try it again. It must have been about eight o'clock when I kneeled down a second time in the bow of the canoe and Joe shoved off from the landing. The wind had diminished, although it still made a light ripple, and the sky was about the same. 11

Of all the nights in the year this was the one I'd have chosen above all others. It was exactly the proper time according to the legend, mid-September, and the moon was full; I could see its silvery light on the western hill, creeping lower and lower gradually toward the lake level. Joe silently dipped his paddle, 12 and we glided along, almost imperceptibly, down toward the long narrow outlet. There is a place, below a sort of narrows, where the lake widens out again just a little bit, and although mostly shallow and full of weeds and lily pads, there lies a round hole somewhat deeper than the rest, bordered on one side by a sandy bank and on the other by a thick patch of grass. As we approached this spot, the moon, coming out from behind the tall spruce tops, shone full on the water, and the wind at last had died, leaving the surface now completely calm.

Joe spoke quietly.   13

"This is the place." He pointed with his paddle to the   14 dark patch just beyond the grass. "Old Potvin told me."

I had refrained from casting while we passed through the   15 lily pads and was just about to raise my rod again when I saw something that arrested my attention. At the edge of the lily pads the surface broke ever so slightly, like a dead leaf submerging. It was very close; so I peered down into the water. I saw what looked like three big blades of grass, each separated from the next by about a foot, all pointing in the same direction, as if in a stream. Then in a flash I knew. They were white-edged fins, the fins of a monster trout. Now I saw his outline against the sand. The break on the top of the water was his dorsal. Then I saw other shapes and other fins.

"*Mon Dieu, monsieur, regardez!*"[1] Joe said before I was able   16 to speak. He, too, had seen.

There lay the trout of the legend, the beautiful trout.   17

All these years I had wanted to see them, and now here   18 they were. How many they numbered it would have been foolish to estimate. Probably there were not over twenty or thirty of them, but they all seemed immense. They lay like a school of salmon in a great river, clearly visible in the light of the full moon. Wherever I looked I could see their great white-edged fins waving gently in the shallow water, scarcely five feet away. At last one great male trout made a sudden turn, and I saw his side. It looked not red but rose-colored in the moonlight.

Stealthily Joe drew back into the grass, so quietly that not   19 a single fish was disturbed. I stripped off a few yards of line from the reel and, making a couple of false casts to get it out, dropped my fly almost imperceptibly right in the center of the group. Instantly the water curled back in a gigantic swirl. I

---

[1] "My God, sir, look!" (French).

struck, and what happened for the next twenty or thirty seconds I wasn't quite sure until afterwards. The fish rose into the air at once like a tarpon and shook himself, throwing water all over Joe. Then followed a series of mighty leaps and plunges that startled me so that I felt as if I had a moose on the end of my line. Each time he leaped his great speckled side flashed like a broken fragment of a moon rainbow. I could feel by the action of the rod and the fact that the reel did not scream that the line must be fouled somewhere, and frantically I tried to pull it loose. But the great trout gave me no opportunity. He just kept on crashing around on top of the water until, after six or seven of the most powerful plunges, the leader snapped and the monarch of fishes was free.

The world's largest trout may live in the Nipigon River; 20 the experts say so, but Joe and I have our own opinions. We don't agree—not after seeing what we saw in the moonlight.

I didn't even try to fish any more. Such a commotion as 21 had gone on in that pool would have frightened every trout for a quarter of a mile. The next morning a gale of wind was blowing, and we couldn't see into the water. But no amount of casting produced a rise. I have not told anyone about the beautiful trout I saw in the moonlight; no one would believe me. Perhaps I may tell old Potvin some day. But Joe and I have seen them, and we know.

◆ *Hermann Hesse* ◆

Hermann Hesse (1877–1962) was a German-born Swiss poet, novelist, and essay writer. He spent his childhood and adolescence in Switzerland and Germany and in 1904 published his first publicly acclaimed novel, *Peter Camenzind*. That same year he began a career as a novelist and freelance journalist.

In 1911, Hesse and a friend journeyed to India, a trip that greatly influenced the writer's thinking. Among the most famous novels Hesse produced are *Siddhartha* (1922), *Steppenwolf* (1927), and *Narcissus and Goldmund* (1930). In 1946 Hesse was awarded the Nobel Prize for Literature.

In the following essay, written in 1926, Hesse remembers his early experiences as a student in Germany. The first part of his recollections deals with his experiences in Calw, where he was born, while the second part of the essay describes his later education in the town of Göppingen.

FROM MY SCHOOLDAYS

TWICE DURING MY YEARS at school I had a teacher whom I could honor and love, in whom I could freely recognize the highest authority and who could direct me by a wink. The first was called Schmid, a teacher at the Calw Latin School, a man much disliked by all the other pupils as being severe and bitter, evil-tempered and terrifying. He became important to me because in his class (we students were twelve years old) instruction in Greek began. In this little half-rural Latin school we had grown accustomed to teachers whom we either feared and hated, avoided and deceived, or laughed at and despised. They possessed power, that was unalterably true, an overwhelming power completely undeserved, often frightfully and inhumanly exercised—it frequently happened in those days that the paddling of hands or the pinching of ears was carried to the point of drawing blood—but this pedagogic power was simply a hostile force, dreaded, hated. That a teacher might possess power because he stood high above us, because he represented intellect and humanity, because he instilled into us inklings of a higher world, this was something we had not yet experienced with any of our teachers in the lower classes of the Latin school. We had encountered a few good-natured teachers who lightened the boredom of school for themselves and for us by indifference and by gazing out the window or reading novels while we busily copied one another's written exercises. We had also encountered evil, dark, raging, maniacal teachers and had had our hair pulled by them and been hit over the head (one of them, a particularly ruthless tyrant, used to accompany his lectures to bad students by rhythmically thumping them on the head with his heavy latchkey). That there might also be teachers whom a student would follow gladly and with enthusiasm, for whom he would exert himself and even overlook injustice and bad temper, to whom he would be grateful for the revelation of a higher world and eager to render thanks—this possibility had remained hitherto beyond our ken.

And now I came to Professor Schmid in the fourth form. 2 Of the approximately twenty-five students in this form, five had decided upon humanistic studies and were called "humanists" or "Grecians," and while the rest of the class were engaged in profane subjects such as drawing, natural history, and the like, we five were initiated into Greek by Professor Schmid. The professor was by no means beloved; he was a sickly, pale, careworn, morose-looking man, smooth-shaven, dark-haired, usually solemn and severe in mood, and if on occasion he was witty it was in a sarcastic tone. What really won me over against the unanimous judgment of the class I do not know. Perhaps it was a response to his unhappiness. He was frail and looked as if he were suffering, had a delicate, sickly wife who was almost never visible, and he lived like all our teachers in shabby poverty. Some circumstance, very likely his wife's health, prevented him from increasing his small income as the other teachers did, by taking in boarders, and this fact gave him a certain air of distinction in contrast to our other teachers. To this was now added Greek. We five chosen ones always seemed to ourselves like an intellectual aristocracy in the midst of our fellow students. Our goal was the higher studies, while the others were destined to be hand workers or tradesmen—and now we began to learn this mysterious, ancient language, much older, more mysterious, and more distinguished than Latin, this language that one did not learn for the purpose of earning money or to be able to travel about in the world but simply to become acquainted with Socrates, Plato, and Homer. Certain features of that world were already known to me, for Greek scholarship had been familiar to my parents and grandparents, and in Schwab's *Myths of the*

Classical World I had long since made the acquaintance of Odysseus and Polyphemus, of Phaëthon, Icarus, the Argonauts, and Tantalus. And in the reader which we had recently been using in school there was amid a crowd of most prosaic pieces, lonesome as a bird of paradise, a marvelous poem by Hölderlin[1] which, to be sure, I only half understood, but which sounded infinitely sweet and seductive and whose secret connection with the world of Greece I dimly perceived.

This Herr Schmid did nothing to make our school year easy. Indeed, he made it extra hard, often unnecessarily hard. He demanded a great deal, at least from us "humanists," and was not only severe but often harsh and frequently ill-tempered as well; he would have attacks of sudden anger and was then feared, with reason, by all of us, including me, very likely as the young fish fry in a weir fear the pursuing pike. Now I had become acquainted with this under other teachers. With Schmid I experienced something new. I experienced, besides fear, respect, I discovered that you can love and honor a man even when he happens to be your enemy. Sometimes in his dark hours, when his haggard face beneath the black hair looked so tragic, oppressed, and malicious, I was forced to think of King Saul in his periods of gloom. But then he would recover, his face would grow smooth, he would draw Greek letters on the blackboard and say things about Greek grammar and language that I felt were more than pedagogic rigmarole. I fell deeply in love with Greek, although I was terrified of the Greek class, and I would draw in my schoolbook certain Greek letters such as upsilon, psi, omega, quite entranced and obsessed, as though they were magic signs.

During this first year of the humanities, I suddenly fell ill. It was a sickness that so far as I know is unknown and unregarded today, but that the doctors at that time called "growing pains." I was given cod-liver oil and salicylic acid, and for a while my knees were massaged with ichthyol. I enjoyed my sickness thoroughly, for despite my humanistic idealism I was far too accustomed to hate and fear school not to regard a halfway bearable illness as a gift of grace and a release. For a long time I lay in bed, and since the wall beside my bed was of wood painted white I began to work on this convenient surface with water colors, and at the level of my head I painted a picture

3

4

[1] Johann Hölderlin (1770–1843), a German Romantic poet who wished to see the spirit of ancient Greek writers reflected in the literature of his own time.

that was supposed to represent the Seven Swabians and was heartily laughed at by my brothers and sisters. But when the second and third weeks had gone by and I was still sick abed, some concern was felt lest, if this were to last much longer, I might be left too far behind in Greek. One of my classmates was summoned to keep me in touch with what went on in class, and then it became apparent that Herr Schmid with his humanists had by that time got through a formidable number of chapters in the Greek grammar. These I must now make up, and under the eyes of the Seven Swabians I struggled through many lonesome hours against my own indolence and the problems of Greek conjugation. At times my father helped me, but when I was well again and allowed to be up and around I was still very far behind, and some private lessons from Professor Schmid were thought necessary. He was willing to give them, and so for a short period I went every other day to his dim and cheerless apartment where Schmid's pale, taciturn wife was fighting a mortal illness. I seldom got to see her, she died shortly thereafter. The hours in this oppressive apartment were as though bewitched; the moment I crossed the threshold I stepped into a different, unreal, terrifying world; I found the honored wise man, the feared tyrant whom I had known in school, strangely and uncannily changed. Intuitively I began to understand his tormented expression, I suffered for him, suffered under him, for his mood was usually very bad. But twice he took me out for walks, strolled about with me in the open air unburdened by grammar or Greek, and on these short walks he was gracious and friendly to me; without sarcasm, without attacks of temper, he asked about my hobbies and about my dreams for the future, and from then on I loved him, although, as soon as I was back in his classroom once more, he seemed to have forgotten the walks completely. After his wife was buried I remember that he made his characteristic gesture of pushing his long hair back from his forehead more often and more abruptly. As a teacher he was very difficult at that time, and I believe I was the only one of his pupils who loved him, despite his harshness and his unpredictability.

Not long after I finished Schmid's class I left my home town and its school for the first time. This happened for disciplinary reasons, for at that time I had become a very difficult and wayward son and my parents did not know what to do with me. In addition to that, however, I had to be as well pre- 5 pared as possible for the "district examination." This official examination, which was held every summer for the whole province of Württemberg, was very important, for whoever passed it was granted room and board in a theological "seminary" and could study there on a scholarship. This course had been decided upon for me. Now there were certain schools in the district in which preparation for this examination was a specialty, and so to one of these schools I was sent. It was the Latin school in Göppingen, where for years the old rector, Bauer, had been cramming students for the provincial exam; he was famous for it in the whole district, and year after year a throng of ambitious students flocked around him, sent there from all parts of the province.

In earlier years Rector Bauer had had the reputation of being a harsh pedagogue, fond of caning; an older relation of mine who years before had been his pupil had been severely beaten by him. Now an old man, Bauer was regarded as a marvelous eccentric and also as a teacher who demanded a great deal from his students but could be nice to them. Nevertheless, it was with no little dread that I, after the first painful farewell to my family's house, waited, holding my mother's hand, outside the famous rector's study. I believe my mother was not at first enchanted by him as he came toward us and invited us into his den, a bent, aged man with tangled gray hair, somewhat protuberant eyes marked with red veins, dressed in an indescribably old-fashioned garment stained with greenish discolorations, wearing spectacles low on his nose and holding in his right hand a long pipe with a porcelain bowl reaching almost to the floor, from which he continuously blew mighty clouds of smoke into the already smoke-filled room. Even in class he would not be parted from his pipe. This strange old man with his bent, careless posture, his untidy old clothes, his sad, moody expression, his shapeless slippers, his long fuming pipe, seemed to me like an aged magician into whose custody I was now to be given. It would perhaps be terrifying with this dusty, gray, otherworldly ancient; also conceivably it could be pleasant and enchanting—in any case, it would be something strange, an adventure, an experience. I was ready and willing to meet him halfway.

But first I had to endure the moment at the station when my mother kissed me and gave me her blessing and got into the train and the train moved off, and for the first time I stood

outside and alone in "the world," in which I must now find
my way and defend myself—I have not yet been able to do so
even up to the present moment when my hair is beginning to
grow gray. Before the parting, my mother had prayed with me,
and although at that time my piety was no longer anything to
boast about, nevertheless during her prayer and her blessing I
had solemnly resolved in my heart to behave myself here, away
from home, and not to disgrace my mother. In the long run I
did not succeed! My later school years brought her and me
severe storms, trials, and disillusionments, much sorrow, many
tears, much strife and misunderstanding. But at that time in
Göppingen I remained completely true to my resolve and behaved well. This, to be sure, was not discernible to the model
students or, for that matter, to the house mother with whom I
and four other boys lived, and ate, and by whom we were cared
for, but whom I could not respect and obey in the manner she
expected from her charges. No, I never stood very high in her
regard, and although there were many days when I could turn
charmer and divert her to smiles and good will, she was a judge
in whom I acknowledged neither power nor importance, and
when on a bitter day after some small boyish misdeed she once
summoned her big, powerfully muscled brother to inflict cor-
poral punishment on me, I rebelled most stubbornly and would
sooner have thrown myself out the window or sunk my teeth
into the man's throat than allow myself to be punished by someone who in my opinion did not have the right to do it. He did
not dare touch me and had to withdraw without accomplishing
his purpose.

I did not like Göppingen. The "world" into which I had
been thrust did not appeal to me, it was barren and bleak, coarse
and impoverished. At that time Göppingen had not yet become
the manufacturing city it is today, but there were already six or
seven tall factory chimneys there, and the little river, in comparison with the one at home, was a proletarian, creeping shab-
bily between piles of rubbish, and the fact that the outer surroundings of the city were very beautiful was hardly known to
us since we had only brief periods when we could be away,
and I got onto the Hohenstaufen only a single time. Oh no, this
Göppingen displeased me completely, this prosaic manufacturing city could not really compare with my home town, and if I
told my schoolmates, all of whom like me were languishing in
a strange land and in durance vile, about Calw and the life

there, then I laid the colors on thick and created romances out of yearning and love of boasting for which no one could call me to account, since I was the only one from Calw in our school. Almost all sections of the province and all the provincial cities were represented in the school, barely six or seven in the class being from Göppingen, all others having come from afar to make use of the approved springboard for the provincial examination.

And the springboard continued to be effective with our class as it had been with so many others. At the end of our Göppingen stay an impressive number of students had passed the examination, and I was among them. Göppingen was not to blame if nothing good ever came of me.

Now, although the dull, industrial city, the imprisonment under the supervision of a strict house mother, and the whole exterior side of my life in Göppingen were highly unpleasant for me, this period (it was almost a year and a half) was nevertheless extraordinarily fruitful and important in my life. That relationship between teacher and pupil of which I had had an inkling in Calw with Professor Schmid, that infinitely rewarding and yet so subtle relationship between an intellectual leader and a gifted child, came to full bloom in the case of Rector Bauer and me. That strange, almost frightening-looking old man with his countless eccentricities and whimsies, who stared out, watchful and moody, from behind his small, greenish eyeglasses, who constantly filled the crowded schoolroom with smoke from his long pipe, became for a time in my eyes leader, exemplar, judge, demigod. We had two other teachers too, but as far as I was concerned, they did not exist; they receded like shadows behind the beloved, feared, honored figure of the old man, as though they had one less dimension. And just so the unappealing life in Göppingen disappeared for me, and even my friendships with fellow students, they too dwindled to nothing beside this looming figure. At that time when my boyhood was in full flower and when even the first intimations and premonitions of sexual love began to stir, school, a generally so despised institution, was for more than a year the central point of my life around which everything else revolved, even my dreams, even my thoughts during vacation time. I, who had always been a sensitive and critical pupil used to defending myself tooth and nail against every form of dependence and subjugation, had been completely caught and enchanted by this mysterious old man, simply because he called upon my highest efforts and ideals, seemed not to see at all my immaturity, my awkwardness, my inferiority, assumed the best in me and regarded the highest accomplishment as natural. He did not need many words to express his praise. If he commented on a Latin or Greek exercise: "You have done that quite nicely, Hesse," then for days I was happy and filled with enthusiasm. And if just in passing he happened to whisper without looking at me: "I'm not entirely satisfied with you, you can do better," then I suffered and went to mad lengths to propitiate the demigod. He often talked to me in Latin, translating my name as Chattus.

Now there was no way for me to tell how far this experi- 10 ence of a completely special relationship was shared by my fellow students. Certain favored ones, to be sure, my closest friends and rivals, were obviously, just like me, under the spell of the old catcher of souls and, just as I had been handed the boon of vocation, felt themselves initiates on the bottom step of the sanctuary. If I attempt to understand my youthful psyche, I find that the best and most productive part of it, despite many rebellions and many negations, was the ability to feel reverence, and that my soul prospered most and blossomed most beautifully when it could revere, adore, strive for that highest goal. This happiness, the beginnings of which my father had earlier recognized and cultivated in me, and which under a series of mediocre, lackluster teachers had almost withered away, which had burgeoned a bit once more under the dyspeptic Professor Schmid, came into full flower, for the first and last time in my life, under Rector Bauer.

Had our rector been able to do nothing except cause some 11 of his better students to fall in love with Latin and Greek and inspire in them a belief in an intellectual vocation and its responsibilities, even that would have been a great and praiseworthy accomplishment. However, the unique, the extraordinary thing about our teacher was his ability not only to nose out the more intelligent of his pupils and to supply their idealism with nourishment and support but to give proper due to the age of his pupils, to their boyishness and passion for play. For Bauer, an honored Socrates, was also a clever, a highly original schoolmaster who again and again found ways to make school attractive to thirteen-year-old youngsters. This sage, able with such wit to teach us Latin syntax and the rules of Greek accent, had constant pedagogic inspirations too, and they delighted us boys. One must have some inkling of the severity, stiffness, and boredom of a Latin school at that time to be able to imagine how fresh, original, and inspired this man seemed in the midst of the usual crowd of dry bureaucrats. Even his exterior, the fantastic appearance which at first made you want to laugh, soon became the instrument of his authority and discipline. Out of his oddities and hobbies, which seemed by no means suited to support his authority, he made new aids for education. For example, his long pipe, which had so horrified my mother, in the shortest time was no longer for us pupils a laughable or annoying appanage but rather a kind of scepter and symbol of might. Whoever was allowed to hold his pipe for a moment, whomever he entrusted with the office of knocking it out and keeping it in working order, he was the envied favorite. There were other honorary posts for which we pupils competed eagerly. There was the office of "windbag," which for a time I proudly filled. The windbag had to dust off the teacher's desk every day and he had to do this with two rabbit's feet which lay on top of the desk. When this job was taken away from me one day and given to another student, I felt severely punished.

On a winter day, if we were sitting in the overheated, smoke-filled schoolroom and the sun was shining on the frost-covered windows, our rector might suddenly say: "Boys, it stinks hideously in here and outside the sun is shining. Have a race around the house. And before you do, open up the windows!" Or, at those times when we candidates for the provincial examination were much overloaded with extra work, he would invite us unexpectedly to come up to his apartment, and there we would find in a strange room a huge table and on it a quantity of cardboard boxes filled with toy soldiers which we would then arrange in armies and battle array, and when the conflict was joined, the rector would solemnly puff clouds of smoke from his pipe between the battalions.

Beautiful things are transitory and fine times never last long. If I think of those Göppingen days, of the single short period in my school years when I was a good scholar, when I honored and loved my teacher and was heart and soul absorbed in study, then I always have to think too of the summer vacation in the year 1890, which I spent at my parents' home in Calw. For that vacation we were not assigned any school work. However, Rector Bauer had called our attention to the "rules of life" of Isocrates,[2] which were included in our Greek chrestomathy,[3] and he told us that formerly some of his best students had learned these rules of life by heart. It was left to each one of us to take this hint or not.

Of that summer vacation, a few walks with my father linger in my memory. Sometimes we spent an afternoon in the woods above Calw; under the old white pines there were barberries and raspberries aplenty, and in the clearings loosestrife bloomed, and summer butterflies, the red admiral and the tortoise-shell, fluttered about. There was a strong smell of pine resin and mushrooms, and occasionally we came face to face with deer. My father and I would wander through the forest or race here and there in the heather at the forest's edge. And once in a while he would ask me how far I had got with Isocrates. For I sat for a while every day with the book, memorizing those "rules of life." And even today the first sentence of Isocrates is the single bit of Greek prose I know by heart. That sentence from Isocrates and a few verses of Homer are the sole remnant of my whole Greek education. Also, I never attained a mastery of all the "rules of life." Several dozen sentences which I did learn by heart, and for a time carried around with me and could produce at will, have crumbled away and been lost in the course of the years, like everything a man possesses and believes is really his own. 14

Today I no longer know any Greek, and most of my Latin has long since disappeared—I would have forgotten it completely were it not for one of my Göppingen classmates who is still alive and still my friend. From time to time he writes me a letter in Latin and when I read it, working my way through the beautifully constructed classic sentences, then there is a faint smell of the garden of my youth and the pipe smoke of old Rector Bauer. 15

---

[2] Isocrates (436–338 B.C.), Greek orator and prose stylist. His work influenced many later writers and set a lasting standard for clear, rhythmic prose.

[3] A collection of literary passages used to study a language or its literature.

Maya Angelou

Maya Angelou is a writer and professional stage and screen performer. She was born in St. Louis, Missouri, in 1928 and went to school in Arkansas and California. Later she studied music privately and studied dance with Martha Graham. In 1954–1955, she went on a twenty-two nation tour with a production of *Porgy and Bess* under the auspices of the U.S. State Department. She also appeared in several off-Broadway plays and made her debut on Broadway in 1973. Maya Angelou has also worked in Africa as a teacher, writer, and theatrical performer.

Among the several volumes of autobiography she has written are *I Know Why the Caged Bird Sings* (1970), *Gather Together in My Name* (1974), and *The Heart of a Woman* (1981).

When Maya Angelou was a child, she and her brother were sent to live with their grandmother in Stamps, Arkansas. The following selection from *I Know Why the Caged Bird Sings* tells the story of a memorable incident that occurred during that stay. In the selection, the writer refers to her grandmother as "Momma." As Maya Angelou notes, soon after she and her brother arrived in Stamps, they "stopped calling her Grandmother."

MOMMA, THE DENTIST, AND ME[1]

THE ANGEL of the candy counter had found me out at last, and was exacting excruciating penance for all the stolen Milky Ways, Mounds, Mr. Goodbars and Hersheys with Almonds. I had two cavities that were rotten to the gums. The pain was beyond the bailiwick of crushed aspirins or oil of cloves. Only one thing could help me, so I prayed earnestly that I'd be allowed to sit under the house and have the building collapse on my left jaw. Since there was no Negro dentist in Stamps, nor doctor either, for that matter, Momma had dealt with previous toothaches by pulling them out (a string tied to the tooth with the other end looped over her fist), pain killers and prayer. In this particular instance the medicine had proved ineffective; there wasn't enough enamel left to hook a string on, and the prayers were being ignored because the Balancing Angel was blocking their passage.

[1] Editors' title.

I lived a few days and nights in blinding pain, not so much toying with as seriously considering the idea of jumping in the well, and Momma decided I had to be taken to a dentist. The nearest Negro dentist was in Texarkana, twenty-five miles away, and I was certain that I'd be dead long before we reached half the distance. Momma said we'd go to Dr. Lincoln, right in Stamps, and he'd take care of me. She said he owed her a favor.

I knew there were a number of whitefolks in town that owed her favors. Bailey and I had seen the books which showed how she had lent money to Blacks and whites alike during the Depression, and most still owed her. But I couldn't aptly remember seeing Dr. Lincoln's name, nor had I ever heard of a Negro's going to him as a patient. However, Momma said we were going, and put water on the stove for our baths. I had never been to a doctor, so she told me that after the bath (which would make my mouth feel better) I had to put on freshly starched and ironed underclothes from inside out. The ache failed to respond to the bath, and I knew then that the pain was more serious than that which anyone had ever suffered.

Before we left the Store, she ordered me to brush my teeth and then wash my mouth with Listerine. The idea of even opening my clamped jaws increased the pain, but upon her explanation that when you go to a doctor you have to clean yourself all over, but most especially the part that's to be examined, I screwed up my courage and unlocked my teeth. The cool air in my mouth and the jarring of my molars dislodged what little remained of my reason. I had frozen to the pain, my family nearly had to tie me down to take the toothbrush away. It was no small effort to get me started on the road to the dentist. Momma spoke to all the passers-by, but didn't stop to chat. She explained over her shoulder that we were going to the doctor and she'd "pass the time of day" on our way home.

Until we reached the pond the pain was my world, an aura that haloed me for three feet around. Crossing the bridge into whitefolks' country, pieces of sanity pushed themselves forward. I had to stop moaning and start walking straight. The white towel, which was drawn under my chin and tied over my head, had to be arranged. If one was dying, it had to be done in style if the dying took place in whitefolks' part of town.

On the other side of the bridge the ache seemed to lessen as if a whitebreeze blew off the whitefolks and cushioned everything in their neighborhood—including my jaw. The gravel road was smoother, the stones smaller and the tree branches hung down around the path and nearly covered us. If the pain didn't diminish then, the familiar yet strange sights hypnotized me into believing that it had.

But my head continued to throb with the measured insistence of a bass drum, and how could a toothache pass the calaboose, hear the songs of the prisoners, their blues and laughter, and not be changed? How could one or two or even a mouthful of angry tooth roots meet a wagonload of powhite-trash children, endure their idiotic snobbery and not feel less important? 7

Behind the building which housed the dentist's office ran a small path used by servants and those tradespeople who catered to the butcher and Stamps' one restaurant. Momma and I followed that lane to the backstairs of Dentist Lincoln's office. The sun was bright and gave the day a hard reality as we climbed up the steps to the second floor. 8

Momma knocked on the back door and a young white girl opened it to show surprise at seeing us there. Momma said she wanted to see Dentist Lincoln and to tell him Annie was there. The girl closed the door firmly. Now the humiliation of hearing Momma describe herself as if she had no last name to the young white girl was equal to the physical pain. It seemed terribly unfair to have a toothache and a headache and have to bear at the same time the heavy burden of Blackness. 9

It was always possible that the teeth would quiet down and maybe drop out of their own accord. Momma said we would wait. We leaned in the harsh sunlight on the shaky railings of the dentist's back porch for over an hour. 10

He opened the door and looked at Momma. "Well, Annie, what can I do for you?" 11

He didn't see the towel around my jaw or notice my swollen face. 12

Momma said, "Dentist Lincoln. It's my grandbaby here. She got two rotten teeth that's giving her a fit." 13

She waited for him to acknowledge the truth of her statement. He made no comment, orally or facially. 14

"She had this toothache purt' near four days now, and today I said, 'Young lady, you going to the Dentist.' " 15

"Annie?" 16

"Yes, sir, Dentist Lincoln." 17

He was choosing words the way people hunt for shells. "Annie, you know I don't treat nigra, colored people." 18

"I know, Dentist Lincoln. But this here is just my little   19
grandbaby, and she ain't gone be no trouble to you . . ."

"Annie, everybody has a policy. In this world you have   20
to have a policy. Now, my policy is I don't treat colored people."

The sun had baked the oil out of Momma's skin and melted   21
the Vaseline in her hair. She shone greasily as she leaned out
of the dentist's shadow.

"Seem like to me, Dentist Lincoln, you might look after   22
her, she ain't nothing but a little mite. And seems like maybe
you owe me a favor or two."

He reddened slightly. "Favor or no favor. The money has   23
all been repaid to you and that's the end of it. Sorry, Annie."
He had his hand on the doorknob. "Sorry." His voice was a
bit kinder on the second "Sorry," as if he really was.

Momma said, "I wouldn't press on you like this for myself   24
but I can't take No. Not for my grandbaby. When you come to
borrow my money you didn't have to beg. You asked me, and
I lent it. Now, it wasn't my policy. I ain't no moneylender, but
you stood to lose this building and I tried to help you out."

"It's been paid, and raising your voice won't make me   25
change my mind. My policy . . ." He let go of the door and
stepped nearer Momma. The three of us were crowded on the
small landing. "Annie, my policy is I'd rather stick my hand in
a dog's mouth than in a nigger's."

He had never once looked at me. He turned his back and   26
went through the door into the cool beyond. Momma backed
up inside herself for a few minutes. I forgot everything except
her face which was almost a new one to me. She leaned over
and took the doorknob, and in her everyday soft voice she said,
"Sister, go on downstairs. Wait for me. I'll be there directly."

Under the most common of circumstances I knew it did   27
no good to argue with Momma. So I walked down the steep
stairs, afraid to look back and afraid not to do so. I turned as
the door slammed, and she was gone.

Momma walked in that room as if she owned it. She shoved that   28
silly nurse aside with one hand and strode into the dentist's office. He
was sitting in his chair, sharpening his mean instruments and putting
extra sting into his medicines. Her eyes were blazing like live coals and
her arms had doubled themselves in length. He looked up at her just
before she caught him by the collar of his white jacket.

"Stand up when you see a lady, you contemptuous scoundrel."   29

Her tongue had thinned and the words rolled off well enunciated. Enunciated and sharp like little claps of thunder.

 The dentist had no choice but to stand at R.O.T.C. attention. 30
His head dropped after a minute and his voice was humble. "Yes, ma'am, Mrs. Henderson."

 "You knave, do you think you acted like a gentleman, speaking 31
to me like that in front of my granddaughter?" She didn't shake him, although she had the power. She simply held him upright.

 "No, ma'am, Mrs. Henderson." 32

 "No, ma'am, Mrs. Henderson, what?" Then she did give him 33
the tiniest of shakes, but because of her strength the action set his head and arms to shaking loose on the ends of his body. He stuttered much worse than Uncle Willie. "No, ma'am, Mrs. Henderson, I'm sorry."

 With just an edge of her disgust showing, Momma slung him 34
back in his dentist's chair. "Sorry is as sorry does, and you're about the sorriest dentist I ever laid my eyes on." (She could afford to slip into the vernacular because she had such eloquent command of English.)

 "I didn't ask you to apologize in front of Marguerite, because I 35
don't want her to know my power, but I order you, now and herewith. Leave Stamps by sundown."

 "Mrs. Henderson, I can't get my equipment . . ." He was shak- 36
ing terribly now.

 "Now, that brings me to my second order. You will never again 37
practice dentistry. Never! When you get settled in your next place, you will be a vegetarian caring for dogs with the mange, cats with the cholera and cows with the epizootic. Is that clear?"

 The saliva ran down his chin and his eyes filled with tears. "Yes, 38
ma'am. Thank you for not killing me. Thank you, Mrs. Henderson."

 Momma pulled herself back from being ten feet tall with eight- 39
foot arms and said, "You're welcome for nothing, you varlet, I wouldn't waste a killing on the likes of you."

 On her way out she waved her handkerchief at the nurse and 40
turned her into a crocus sack of chicken feed.

 Momma looked tired when she came down the stairs, but 41
who wouldn't be tired if they had gone through what she had.
She came close to me and adjusted the towel under my jaw (I
had forgotten the toothache; I only knew that she made her
hands gentle in order not to awaken the pain). She took my
hand. Her voice never changed. "Come on, Sister."

 I reckoned we were going home where she would concoct 42
a brew to eliminate the pain and maybe give me new teeth too.

New teeth that would grow overnight out of my gums. She led me toward the drugstore, which was in the opposite direction from the Store. "I'm taking you to Dentist Baker in Texarkana."

I was glad after all that that I had bathed and put on Mum and Cashmere Bouquet talcum powder. It was a wonderful surprise. My toothache had quieted to solemn pain, Momma had obliterated the evil white man, and we were going on a trip to Texarkana, just the two of us.   43

On the Greyhound she took an inside seat in the back, and I sat beside her. I was so proud of being her granddaughter and sure that some of her magic must have come down to me. She asked if I was scared. I only shook my head and leaned over on her cool brown upper arm. There was no chance that a dentist, especially a Negro dentist, would dare hurt me then. Not with Momma there. The trip was uneventful, except that she put her arm around me, which was very unusual for Momma to do.   44

The dentist showed me the medicine and the needle before he deadened my gums, but if he hadn't I wouldn't have worried. Momma stood right behind him. Her arms were folded and she checked on everything he did. The teeth were extracted and she bought me an ice cream cone from the side window of a drug counter. The trip back to Stamps was quiet, except that I had to spit into a very small empty snuff can which she had gotten for me and it was difficult with the bus humping and jerking on our country roads.   45

At home, I was given a warm salt solution, and when I washed out my mouth I showed Bailey the empty holes, where the clotted blood sat like filling in a pie crust. He said I was quite brave, and that was my cue to reveal our confrontation with the peckerwood dentist and Momma's incredible powers.   46

I had to admit that I didn't hear the conversation, but what else could she have said than what I said she said? What else done? He agreed with my analysis in a lukewarm way, and I happily (after all, I'd been sick) flounced into the Store. Momma was preparing our evening meal and Uncle Willie leaned on the door sill. She gave her version.   47

"Dentist Lincoln got right uppity. Said he'd rather put his hand in a dog's mouth. And when I reminded him of the favor, he brushed it off like a piece of lint. Well, I sent Sister downstairs and went inside. I hadn't never been in his office before, but I found the door to where he takes out teeth, and him and   48 the nurse was in there thick as thieves. I just stood there till he caught sight of me.'' Crash bang the pots on the stove. ''He jumped just like he was sitting on a pin. He said, 'Annie, I done tole you, I ain't gonna mess around in no niggah's mouth.' I said, 'Somebody's got to do it then,' and he said, 'Take her to Texarkana to the colored dentist' and that's when I said, 'If you paid me my money I could afford to take her.' He said, 'It's all been paid.' I tole him everything but the interest been paid. He said ' 'Twasn't no interest.' I said ' 'Tis now. I'll take ten dollars as payment in full.' You know, Willie, it wasn't no right thing to do, 'cause I lent that money without thinking about it.

''He tole that little snippity nurse of his'n to give me ten dollars and make me sign a 'paid in full' receipt. She gave it to me and I signed the papers. Even though by rights he was paid up before, I figger, he gonna be that kind of nasty, he gonna have to pay for it.''

Momma and her son laughed and laughed over the white man's evilness and her retributive sin.

I preferred, much preferred, my version.

⊷ *Hugh Garner* ⊷

Hugh Garner (1913–1979) was born in Yorkshire, England, but grew up in Toronto, Canada. During the 1930s he held a number of laboring jobs, and his experiences during this time gave him a deep understanding of the situation many people face in our modern industrial society.

Among his novels are *Storm Below* (1949), *Waste No Tears* (1950), and *Cabbagetown* (1950), a famous study of the depths to which poor people can be reduced.

"A Trip for Mrs. Taylor" is taken from *The Yellow Sweater and Other Stories*. The story is not only a penetrating anaysis of the loneliness of old age but also a moving portrait of a woman who refuses to live a passive life.

A TRIP FOR MRS. TAYLOR

MRS. TAYLOR got out of bed at five o'clock that morning, an hour ahead of her usual time for getting up. She moved around her attic room with the stealth of a burglar, making herself her morning cup of tea on the hot plate, and dressing quietly so as not to disturb her landlady, Mrs. Connell, on the floor below.

She dressed her tiny self carefully, donning a clean white camisole and her black Sunday frock. After she had drunk her tea and eaten a slice of thinly margarined toast she washed her cup and saucer in some water she had drawn from the bathroom the evening before, and put them away on her "kitchen" shelf in the clothes closet. Then she tiptoed down the steep stairs to the bathroom and washed her face and hands—"a lick and a spit" as she called it.

When she returned to her room her seventy-six-year-old face shone with wrinkled cleanliness and the excitement of the day. She combed her thinning gray hair and did it up with pins into an unsevere bun at the back of her head. Then, half guiltily, she powdered her face and touched her cheeks with a rouge-tipped finger. Going over to her old trunk in the corner she extracted from its depths two pieces of jewelry wrapped in tissue paper. One of the pieces was a gold locket holding a faded photograph of her dead husband Bert, while the other was an old-fashioned gold chain bangle with a small lock shaped like a heart. She had lost the key to the bangle long ago, but it did not matter; her hands were now so thin that it slipped easily over her wrist.

When she had adjusted the jewelry she took her old black   4
straw hat from its paper bag and put it on, primping a bit before the Woolworth mirror on the wall, smiling at herself and wishing that her false teeth were a little whiter.

All through her preparations she had been taking hurried   5
glances at the alarm clock on the dresser, but now, when she was ready to go, she saw that she still had nearly two hours before train time. The train left at seven o'clock Standard Time, which was eight o'clock Daylight Saving, and here it was only a quarter to six. Still, it would take a half-hour to get downtown to the station, and she couldn't afford to be late on this day of days.

She unclasped her small cardboard suitcase and carefully   6
checked its contents once again. There was a clean change of underwear, a towel and soap, some handkerchiefs, two pairs of black lisle stockings, Bert's picture in its frame, and one of the two boys in uniform, her blouse and blue serge skirt, and the red velvet dress that Mrs. Eisen had given her the year before. The dress didn't fit her, but she liked its rich color and the feeling of opulence it gave, just to possess it.

Picking up her heavy Bible from the top of the dresser,   7
she said to herself, "I really should take it along, I guess. It'll weigh me down, but I couldn't go anywhere without it." Quickly making up her mind she placed the Bible in the suitcase and fastened the lid. Then she sat down on the edge of the bed and let the wonderful coming events of the day take over her thoughts.

The idea for the trip had come to her about a week before,   8
on the day she had received her July old-age pension check. She had been down to the main post office, mailing a set of hand-crocheted runners to her daughter-in-law, Ruth, in Montreal when the idea struck her. Seeing all the holiday crowds hurrying into the maw of the station had prompted her to go in and inquire about train times.

The hurry and excitement of the place had brought back   9
the nostalgic memories of those happier times when she and Bert and young Johnnie—yes, and young Bert, too, who was killed in Italy—had gone away sometimes in the summer. Their trips hadn't been long ones, and their destination was usually

the home of her dead cousin Flora in Jamesville, but they had been filled with all the hustle and bustle of getting ready, packing salmon and peanut-butter sandwiches for their lunches, and making sure Bert had the tickets. There had been the warm picnicky feeling going to the station on the streetcar, trying to keep young Bert from kneeling on the seat and brushing his feet on the man beside him (she wiped away a vagrant tear at the memory) and the awareness that she *belonged* to the crowds around her.

That was the thing she had missed most during the past few years, the feeling of being one with those about her. The knowledge that she was old and ignored by younger people sometimes caused her to wish she were dead, but then appalled by the irreverence of such thoughts she would take refuge in her Bible, which was now her only solace.   10

Her loneliness and the striving to live on her old-age pension made mere existence a hardship. Mrs. Connell, her landlady, was a kindly soul, not much younger than herself, but she had no conception of what it was like to be cooped up month after month in a dreary little room, without even a radio to keep you company, without even a cat or a dog or a canary—nothing but the four walls, an electric plate, a bed, and a dresser.   11

Of course, she told herself, she could have gone to live with Johnnie and Ruth in Montreal, but she'd seen too much of that sort of thing in the past. When Johnnie had married down there after the war she had felt a sinking in the stomach at the thought that he, too, was leaving her. "Come on down there with me, Ma," he had said, but she had sensed the reluctance behind his words. "I'm not going to be a built-in baby sitter for my grandchildren," she had answered, trying to cover her sense of loss and disappointment under her bantering words. She was independent, a woman who had run her own home for years, and brought up her two boys on the skimpy and unreliable wages of a laborer husband. But sometimes her independence melted under her silent tears, and she wished that once, just once, somebody would need her again.   12

But today was not the time for such gloomy thoughts. She glanced at the clock and saw that it was after seven. She stood up, straightened her hat once more, and picking up the heavy suitcase, made her way from the room, closing the door silently behind her. She had no wish to waken Mrs. Connell and have to answer the surprised questions of that lady; this trip was going to be a secret one, known only to herself.   13

She hurried down the street through the cloying warmth 14
of the summer morning as fast as the heavy bag would allow
her. When she reached the streetcar stop she put the suitcase
down on the sidewalk and searched in her purse for a car ticket.
There was very little money left from her pension check, but by
doing without a few things to eat over the past week she had
managed to save the expenses for the trip.

When the streetcar came along she climbed aboard and sat 15
down near the front of the car. She was aware of the stares from
the men and girls who were going to work, and she felt important for the first time in months. There was something
friendly in the glances they gave her, and perhaps even a slight
envy that she should be going away while they could only look
forward to another stifling day in their offices and factories.

The downtown streets at this hour of the day were strange 16
to her, but there was a tired camaraderie among the people
getting on and off the car which brought back memories she
had almost forgotten; once again she saw herself as a young
woman going to work as they were, stepping down from the
open-sided cars they had in those days, proud of her narrow
waist and new high-buttoned boots. She felt almost young again
and smiled apologetically as a thin girl in slacks nearly tripped
over her suitcase.

As they neared the station several people carrying pieces 17
of luggage boarded the car, and Mrs. Taylor smiled at them as
if they were partners in a conspiracy. Most of them smiled back
at her, and she felt that the anticipation and preparation for a
journey was only exceeded by its actual beginning.

When she alighted from the streetcar a young man in army 18
uniform took her suitcase from her, and holding her by the arm,
led her across the street.

"This is a heavy bag for you to be carrying," he said in a 19
conversational tone.

"It is a little heavy," she answered, "but I haven't far to 20
go."

"Everybody seems to be going away today," he said. "I 21
guess I won't get a seat on the northbound train."

"That's a shame," Mrs. Taylor answered, trying to keep 22
up with the soldier's long strides. "Are you on leave?"

"Sort of. I was down here on a forty-eight hour pass from 23
camp. I should have been back last night."

"I hope you don't get into trouble," she said. She felt 24
suddenly sorry for the young man—only a boy really. She

wanted to tell him that both her sons had been overseas during the war, and that young Bert had been killed. But then she thought he might think she was bragging, or trying to make him feel bad because he'd been too young to go.

As they entered the cathedrallike station concourse, she 25
said to the young soldier, "I can manage now, thank you," and he stopped and placed the bag on the floor.

"If you're taking the northbound train I'll carry the suit- 26
case to the gates for you," he offered.

"No. No, thank you. I'm taking the Montreal train," she 27
answered.

"Well then, I'll have to leave you. Good-bye. Have a nice 28
holiday," he said.

"Yes," she whispered, her voice cracking with emotion. 29
As he walked away she shouted after him, "Good luck, son!" She watched him disappear into the crowd and felt a nameless dread for what might be before him. He was such a nice, polite young boy, but what was more he was the first person outside Mrs. Connell and the man at the grocery store that she had spoken to all week.

The man at the ticket window seemed surprised as she 30
bought her ticket, but he stamped it on the back and handed it to her without a word. When she asked him where to get the Montreal train he pointed across the station to a queue of people lined up before a pair of gates, and she picked up her suitcase and made her way toward it.

The crowd was a good-natured one, as she had known it 31
would be, and she spent several minutes taking stock of the other travelers. It was unbelievable that so many people had awakened this morning as she had done, with the idea of catching the same train. All night as she had tossed and turned in anticipation of the morning these other people had probably been doing the same thing, unknown to her. The knowledge that they all shared the same sense of immediacy seemed to bring them closer together, and they were united in their impatience to be going.

But Mrs. Taylor was not impatient. She knew the value of 32
time—she who had so little of it left—and this waiting with the others in the crowded station was as exciting to her as reaching the end of her trip—more so in fact.

She looked about her at the young people with their over- 33
night bags and their tennis rackets; at the older men carrying

haversacks and fishing rods, each looking a little sheepish like boys caught playing hookey; the three girls in the brand-new clothes whispering together ahead of her in line; the young couple with the baby in the go-cart standing outside the queue, smiling at one another and talking together in French; the two priests in white panama hats who nodded solemnly and looked hot and cool at the same time in their black alpaca jackets.

This was what she had looked forward to all week! It was just as she had expected it to be, and she didn't care if the gates never opened; the best part of any journey was the waiting for the train. 34

There was the sound of a small scuffle behind her, and a young woman's tired voice said, "Garry, stop that right now!" 35

Mrs. Taylor turned and saw a slight dark girl wearing a shabby suit trying to hold a young baby in her arms while she tugged at a little boy who was swinging on the end of a harness. The boy was trying desperately to break away. 36

"Here, young man, where do you think you're going!" Mrs. Taylor said sternly, bending down and catching him around the waist. The child stopped struggling and looked at her in surprise. 37

"He's been a little devil all morning," his mother said. "He knows I can't do much with him while I've got the baby in my arms." 38

"Now you just stand still!" Mrs. Taylor warned, letting him go and smiling at the young woman to show that she did not mean to override her authority. 39

"He'll stop for you," the girl said. "At home he'll do anything for his grandma, but when he knows I've got the baby to look after, he takes advantage of it." 40

Mrs. Taylor nodded. "I know; I had two boys myself," she said. "Is the baby a boy, too?" 41

"Yes. Four months." 42

Mrs. Taylor reached over and pulled the light blanket from the baby's face. "He's a big boy for four months, isn't he?" she asked. 43

She learned that the young woman's name was Rawlinson, and that she was on her way to New Brunswick to join her husband, who was in the Air Force. The girl's mother had wanted to come down to the station with her, but her arthritis had kept her at home. She also learned that the baby's name was Ian, and that his mother was twenty-two years old. 44

She in turn told the girl she had lived alone since her oldest ₄₅ boy's marriage, and that Johnnie now lived with his wife and a young daughter in Montreal. In answer to the other's questions she also told the young woman that her husband and youngest son were dead, that she received the old-age pension, and that it wasn't enough in these days of high prices.

Mrs. Rawlinson said that a friend of her mother's went to ₄₆ the same church as Mrs. Taylor. Mrs. Taylor didn't recognize the woman's name, although she thought she knew who the girl meant: a stout woman with short-bobbed bluish hair who wore a Persian lamb coat in the winter.

She realized now that she had been starved for conver- ₄₇ sation, and she was so grateful for having met the young woman with the children.

"They should be opening the gates pretty soon," said the ₄₈ girl, looking at her wristwatch. "The train is due to leave in twenty minutes."

From the loudspeaker came the voice of the stationmaster ₄₉ announcing that the northbound train was due to leave. Mrs. Taylor thought about the nice young soldier who had over- stayed his pass.

The little boy, Garry, indicated that he wanted to go to the ₅₀ toilet.

"Wait till we get on the train, dear," his mother pleaded ₅₁ desperately.

Mrs. Taylor said eagerly, "I'll hold the baby while you ₅₂ take him, if you like."

"Will you? Gee, that's swell!" the young woman ex- ₅₃ claimed. She handed the baby over, and Mrs. Taylor cradled him in her arms, while the young mother and the little boy hurried away.

She pulled back the blanket once again from the baby's ₅₄ face and saw that he was awake. She placed her finger on his chin and smiled at him, and he smiled back at her. The moment took her back more years than she cared to remember, back to a time when young Bert was the same age. She was filled with the remembered happiness of those days, and she thought, "I'd give up every minute more I have to live just to be young again and have my boys as babies for one more day." Then to hide the quick tears that were starting from her eyes she began talk- ing to the baby in her arms, rocking back and forth on her heels in a gesture not practiced for years.

When the woman and the little boy returned she gave up ₅₅

the baby reluctantly. She and the young woman stood talking together like old friends, or like a mother and daughter-in-law. They discussed teething troubles, the housing shortage, and how hard it was to raise a family these days. They were so engrossed in their new-found friendship that they failed to notice when the man opened the gates.

The crowd began pushing them from behind, and Mrs. Taylor picked up her suitcase in one hand and grasped Garry's harness with the other. Then, followed by Mrs. Rawlinson and the baby, they climbed the set of iron stairs to the platform. 56

Mrs. Taylor's feet were aching after the long wait at the gates, but her face shone with happiness as she steered the small boy alongside the train. The boy's mother drew up to her, and they walked together to the day-coach steps where a trainman waited to help them aboard. 57

"You've got your hands full there, Granny," he said, picking up the little boy and depositing him in the vestibule of the car. 58

She was pleased that he mistook her for the children's grandmother, and she beamed at him, not attempting to correct his mistake. 59

Inside the coach she led the way to a pair of seats that faced each other at the end of the car, and dropped into one with a tired sigh. Then she held the baby while its mother took the harness off Garry and placed her small case and shopping bags on the luggage rack. 60

"Am I ever glad to get aboard!" Mrs. Rawlinson exclaimed. "I'd been dreading the wait at the station. Now I've only got to change trains in Montreal and I'll be all set." 61

"It's quite a job traveling with children," Mrs. Taylor sympathized. "Don't worry, I know. I've done enough of it in my day," she said with slight exaggeration. 62

Mrs. Rawlinson laid the baby on the seat beside her, before sitting back and relaxing against the cushions. The coach soon filled up, and several people eyed their double seat enviously. Mrs. Taylor was glad she had been able to get well up in the queue at the gates. 63

When the train started she moved over close to the window and pointed out to the little boy the buildings and streets they passed, and the tiny inconsequential people they were leaving behind them. Young Garry shouted excitedly, "Choo-choo!" at every engine they passed in the yards. 64

The city looked hot and uncomfortable in the morning sun, 65 and Mrs. Taylor was surprised that all the antlike people didn't simply jump on a train and get away from it. It was remarkable that the ones she could see walking the streets were strangers to her now, as if there was no connection between them and the people on the train. They were a race apart; an earth-bound race separated from herself by movement and time, and the sense of adventure of her and her fellows.

She picked out landmarks as the train gathered speed; the streets she had lived on as a girl, now turned into industrial sites; the spinning mill where she had once worked; the soot-blackened park where she and Bert walked so many years ago. . . . 66

"We won't be getting into Montreal until suppertime," Mrs. Rawlinson said from the opposite seat, intruding upon her memories. 67

"No." 68

"I'll bet you'll be glad to get there and see your grand-daughter." 69

Mrs. Taylor shook her head. "I'm not going to Montreal today," she said sadly. "I can't afford to go that far." 70

"But—but couldn't your son send you the fare?" asked the girl. 71

She had to protect Johnnie, who wasn't really mean, just forgetful. "Oh, he could, but I've never really cared to go that far," she lied. 72

"Well—well, where are you going then?" the young woman asked, her curiosity getting the best of her. 73

"Not very far. Just up the line a piece," Mrs. Taylor answered, smiling. "It's just a short trip." 74

The train seemed to flow across the underpasses marking the streets. Soon the industrial areas were left behind, and they began rushing through the residential districts. 75

Mrs. Taylor was enthralled with the sight of the rows of houses as seen from the rear; yards waving with drying clothes, and every house having an individuality of its own. She only recognized some of the familiar streets after the train had passed them, they looked so different when seen from her hurtling point of vantage. 76

In a few minutes the train began to slow down for an outlying station, and the conductor came along the car collecting tickets. When Mrs. Taylor handed him her small bit of pasteboard, he asked, "Are you getting off here, madam?" 77

"Yes, I am," Mrs. Taylor replied, coloring with embar- 78
rassment.

"Have you any luggage?" 79

She pointed to the suitcase at her feet, ashamed to face 80
the stares of those who were watching her.

"Fine. I'll carry it off for you," the conductor said calmly, 81
as if old ladies took ten-cent train rides every day of the week.

She stood up then and said good-bye to the little boy, 82
letting her hand rest for a long minute on his tousled head. She
warned him to be a good boy and do what his mother told him.

"You must think I'm crazy just coming this far," she said 83
to Mrs. Rawlinson. "You see, I've wanted to take a trip for so
long, and this was sort of—pretending."

The young woman shook the surprised look from her face. 84
"No, I don't, Mrs. Taylor," she said. "I wish you were coming
all the way. I don't know what I'd have ever done without you
to help me with Garry."

"It was nice being able to help. You'll never know how 85
much I enjoyed it," Mrs. Taylor answered, her face breaking
into a shy smile. "Good-bye, dear, and God bless you. Have a
nice journey."

"Good-bye," the young woman said. "Thanks! Thanks a 86
lot!"

Mrs. Taylor stood on the station platform and waved at 87
the young woman and her son, who waved back at her as the
train began to move again. Then she picked up her bag and
walked along the platform to the street.

When she boarded a streetcar the motorman looked down 88
at her and said, "You look happy; you must have had a swell
vacation."

She smiled at him. "I had a wonderful trip," she an- 89
swered.

And it had been wonderful! While all the others in the 90
train would get bored and tired after a few hours of travel, she
could go back to her room and lie down on the bed, remembering only the excitement and thrill of going away, and the
new friends she had made. It was wonderful, just wonderful,
she said to herself. Perhaps next month, if she could afford it,
she would take a trip to the suburbs on the Winnipeg train!

INDEX

Copyright Acknowledgments

To the Student:

Now that you have used *The Holt Reader*, could you take a few moments to share your reactions with us? Your answers to the following questionnaire will help us plan future editions of the book. After you have filled in your answers, please detach these pages and mail them to: The English Editor, Holt, Rinehart and Winston, 383 Madison Avenue, New York, N.Y. 10017.

Please rate each selection according to the following categories:

	Enjoyed	Did Not Like	Did Not Read
FRANK, *The Diary of a Young Girl*	_____	_____	_____
DE BEAUVOIR, *The Prime of Life*	_____	_____	_____
GALARZA, *Barrio Boy*	_____	_____	_____
LINDBERGH, *Autobiography of Values*	_____	_____	_____
SCHANEL, "Privacy"	_____	_____	_____
SONNETT, "Dreamy"	_____	_____	_____
SYNGE, *The Aran Islands*	_____	_____	_____
ORWELL, " 'The Moon Under Water' "	_____	_____	_____
LORENZ, "On Feline Play"	_____	_____	_____
LEHMANN, "Some Are Alone"	_____	_____	_____
JOYCE, "Eveline"	_____	_____	_____
MUÑIZ, "Back, But Not Home"	_____	_____	_____
WHITE, "Once More to the Lake"	_____	_____	_____
O'REILLY, "The Girl I Left Behind"	_____	_____	_____

CASTALDO, ''Memory of a Stranger''   _____ _____ _____

DE MILLE, *Dance to the Piper*   _____ _____ _____

SUYIN, *A Mortal Flower*   _____ _____ _____

LAYE, *The Dark Child*   _____ _____ _____

SCHANEL, ''The Pests Have Pests''   _____ _____ _____

DIDION, ''On Going Home''   _____ _____ _____

BALDWIN, ''Sweet Lorraine''   _____ _____ _____

EISELEY, ''The Hidden Teacher''   _____ _____ _____

BROWN and OWEN, ''The Soul of a Tree''   _____ _____ _____

KASMIRE, ''For the Family Album''   _____ _____ _____

SHEEHY, *Passages*   _____ _____ _____

VIORST, ''Friends, Good Friends—and Such Good Friends''   _____ _____ _____

UPDIKE, ''Three Boys''   _____ _____ _____

KENT, ''Those Who Govern, Those Who Guide''   _____ _____ _____

HERODOTUS, ''The Amazons''   _____ _____ _____

THURBER, ''Courtship Through the Ages''   _____ _____ _____

MEAD, ''From Popping the Question to Popping the Pill''   _____ _____ _____

PORTER, ''The Necessary Enemy''   _____ _____ _____

ALLCROFT, ''Romantic Love or Self-Discovery''   _____ _____ _____

LESSING, "Being Prohibited" ___ ___ ___

JACOBS, *The Death and Life of Great American Cities* ___ ___ ___

MEAD and METRAUX, "The Nudist Idea" ___ ___ ___

ZINSSER, "Whatever Happened to Privacy?" ___ ___ ___

PALOMBI, "The Unbreakable Chain" ___ ___ ___

DINESEN, "The Oxen" ___ ___ ___

CLARKE, "The Electronic Revolution" ___ ___ ___

WOOLF, "Thoughts on Peace in an Air Raid" ___ ___ ___

WATT, "Man's Efficient Rush Toward Deadly Dullness" ___ ___ ___

BROSNAN, "Goodbye, Mom's Apple Pie" ___ ___ ___

GOODMAN and GOODMAN, "Banning Cars from Manhattan" ___ ___ ___

MANNES, "The Child Before the Set" ___ ___ ___

FROMM, "Our Way of Life Makes Us Miserable" ___ ___ ___

HUXLEY, "The Scientist's Role" ___ ___ ___

PALOMBI, "A World of Sports" ___ ___ ___

RAWLINGS, "Who Owns Cross Creek?" ___ ___ ___

DE BELL, "Energy" ___ ___ ___

KRUTCH, "Lightning Water" ___ ___ ___

CARSON, "The Obligation to Endure" ___ ___ ___

FLESCH, "The Need for *Total Public Transportation*"   _____ _____ _____

BREWER, "The Lake of the Beautiful Trout"   _____ _____ _____

HESSE, "From My Schooldays"   _____ _____ _____

ANGELOU, "Momma, the Dentist, and Me"   _____ _____ _____

GARNER, "A Trip for Mrs. Taylor"   _____ _____ _____

Please comment briefly on the reading and writing exercises you found most useful:

Previewing the Writer   _____

The Writer's Themes   _____

The Writer's Technique   _____

Paragraph Practice   _____

Essay Practice   _____

Essay Topics   _____

Focus on Terms   _____

Student Essays   _____

Additional Comments or Suggestions _____

_____

_____

_____

_____

Name _____

Address _____

Name of College _____